Behavioural Sports Economics

Economists have entered into the realm of sports to provide what they believe to be more cogent explanations for sport-related behaviour and to suggest ways in which incentives can improve sports outcomes. But prices and income, the traditional workhorses of conventional economics, can only provide partial explanations and understandings. Drawing on a bounded rationality approach to behavioural economics, this book demonstrates the analytical insights to be gained by supplementing the conventional economics toolbox with psychological, cognitive, sociological, and institutional factors.

The international cast list of contributors cover a wide range of sports topics on which a behavioural approach can reveal new insights. These include preferences, managerial, efficiency, choking, doping, favouritism, athlete well-being, and spectator behaviour. Throughout the book, there is an emphasis on the cognitive limits to smart decision-making as well as the critical role played by the decision-making environment. This volume demonstrates that adopting a bounded rationality approach, complimented with other behaviouralist approaches, helps to better explain sport-related behavioural, sub-optimal behavioural, and market failures. It also provides insights that could be used to improve sports outcomes and the well-being of those involved in sports and to better configure policy to enhance sports performance.

This groundbreaking book will be an indispensable reference to students and scholars of sports economics, sports management, and sports science.

Hannah Josepha Rachel Altman is in the final stages of her PhD in *Behavioural Sports Economics* at the Queensland University of Technology Business School (QUT) in Brisbane, Australia.

Morris Altman is Chair Professor of Behavioural and Institutional Economics, and Co-operatives, and Dean at the University of Dundee School of Business, Scotland, UK. He is also an Emeritus Professor at the University of Saskatchewan, Canada.

Benno Torgler is Professor of Economics at the Queensland University of Technology (QUT) and also at the Centre for Behavioural Economics, Society and Technology (BEST), leading the programme "Behavioural Economics of Non-Market Interactions" that covers the sub-programmes Sportometrics, Sociometrics, Scientometrics, and Cliometrics.

Routledge Advances in Behavioural Economics and Finance
Edited by **Roger Frantz**

Traditionally, economists have based their analysis of financial markets and corporate finance on the assumption that agents are fully rational, emotionless, self-interested maximizers of expected utility. However, behavioural economists are increasingly recognizing that financial decision-makers may be subject to psychological biases and the effects of emotions. Examples of this include the effects on investors' and managers' decision-making of such biases as excessive optimism, overconfidence, confirmation bias, and illusion of control. At a practical level, the current state of the financial markets suggests that trust between investors and managers is of paramount importance.

Routledge Advances in Behavioural Economics and Finance presents innovative and cutting-edge research in this fast-paced and rapidly growing area and will be of great interest to academics, practitioners, and policy-makers alike.

All *proposals* for new books in the series can be sent to the series editor, Roger Frantz, at *rabeandf@gmail.com*.

Social Neuroeconomics
Mechanistic Integration of the Neurosciences and the Social Sciences
Edited by Jens Harbecke and Carsten Herrmann-Pillath

The Art of Experimental Economics
Twenty Top Papers Reviewed
Edited by Gary Charness and Mark Pingle

Behavioural Sports Economics
A Research Companion
Edited by Hannah Josepha Rachel Altman, Morris Altman and Benno Torgler

For more information about this series, please visit www.routledge.com/Routledge-Advances-in-Behavioural-Economics-and-Finance/book-series/RABEF

Behavioural Sports Economics
A Research Companion

Edited by
Hannah Josepha Rachel Altman,
Morris Altman and
Benno Torgler

LONDON AND NEW YORK

First published 2022
by Routledge
2 Park Square, Milton Park, Abingdon, Oxon OX14 4RN

and by Routledge
605 Third Avenue, New York, NY 10158

Routledge is an imprint of the Taylor & Francis Group, an informa business

© 2022 selection and editorial matter, Hannah Josepha Rachel Altman, Morris Altman and Benno Torgler; individual chapters, the contributors

The right of Hannah Josepha Rachel Altman, Morris Altman and Benno Torgler to be identified as the authors of the editorial material, and of the authors for their individual chapters, has been asserted in accordance with sections 77 and 78 of the Copyright, Designs and Patents Act 1988.

All rights reserved. No part of this book may be reprinted or reproduced or utilised in any form or by any electronic, mechanical, or other means, now known or hereafter invented, including photocopying and recording, or in any information storage or retrieval system, without permission in writing from the publishers.

Trademark notice: Product or corporate names may be trademarks or registered trademarks, and are used only for identification and explanation without intent to infringe.

British Library Cataloguing-in-Publication Data
A catalogue record for this book is available from the British Library

Library of Congress Cataloging-in-Publication Data
Names: Altman, Hannah Josepha Rachel, editor. | Altman, Morris, editor. | Torgler, Benno, 1972– editor.
Title: Behavioural sports economics : a research companion / edited by Hannah Josepha Rachel Altman, Morris Altman and Benno Torgler.
Other titles: Routledge advances in behavioural economics and finance
Description: Abingdon, Oxon ; New York, NY : Routledge, 2022. | Series: Routledge advances in behavioural economics and finance | Includes bibliographical references and index.
Identifiers: LCCN 2021036913 (print) | LCCN 2021036914 (ebook)
Subjects: MESH: Sports | Economics, Behavioral
Classification: LCC RA781 (print) | LCC RA781 (ebook) | NLM QT 260 | DDC 613.7/1—dc23
LC record available at https://lccn.loc.gov/2021036913
LC ebook record available at https://lccn.loc.gov/2021036914

ISBN: 978-0-367-53184-3 (hbk)
ISBN: 978-0-367-53187-4 (pbk)
ISBN: 978-1-003-08082-4 (ebk)

DOI: 10.4324/9781003080824

Typeset in Bembo
by codeMantra

This book is dedicated to the memory of David Savage, one of the contributors to this book. A friend, a student, and a colleague, Dave passed away suddenly on 8 May 2021, just after delivering one of his co-authored chapters. He'll be sorely missed.

Contents

List of figures xi
List of tables xiii
List of contributors xv

1 Introduction: behavioural sports economics 1
   HANNAH JOSEPHA RACHEL ALTMAN, MORRIS ALTMAN AND
   BENNO TORGLER

PART 1
The big picture 9

2 Sport as a behavioural economics lab 11
   HO FAI CHAN, DAVID A. SAVAGE AND BENNO TORGLER

3 Sports performance, procedural rationality, and
   organizational inefficiency 52
   HANNAH JOSEPHA RACHEL ALTMAN AND MORRIS ALTMAN

4 Institutional dynamics in sports – how governance, rules
   and technology interact 78
   STUART THOMAS AND KIERAN TIERNEY

PART 2
Incentives, governance and sports behaviour 97

5 Wrong behaviour due to wrong incentives: how to
   transform doping into a self-defeating game 99
   WLADIMIR ANDREFF

6 Discrimination, disequilibrium and disincentives: behavioural economics in women's sport 119
STEPHANIE MANNING, HO FAI CHAN AND DAVID A. SAVAGE

7 Winner alright? New evidence on high-stakes bidding and returns to ownership in the thoroughbred horseracing industry 139
DAVID BUTLER AND ROBERT BUTLER

PART 3
Momentum and reference points in sports behaviour 157

8 Does psychological momentum differ for home and away teams? Evidence from penalty shoot-outs in European cups 159
ALEX KRUMER

9 Reference point behavior and sports 172
TIM PAWLOWSKI

10 The importance of the serve in winning points in tennis: a Bayesian analysis using data for the two winners of the 2019 French Open singles 186
VANI K. BOROOAH

PART 4
Heuristics, sports, behaviour and outcomes 199

11 Beauty, preferences and choice exemplified in the sports market 201
HANNAH JOSEPHA RACHEL ALTMAN, MORRIS ALTMAN, BENNO TORGLER AND STEPHEN WHYTE

12 Moneyball and decision-making heuristics: an intersection of statistics and practical expertise 222
HANNAH JOSEPHA RACHEL ALTMAN AND MORRIS ALTMAN

PART 5
Fans, fan behaviour, and sports outcomes 241

13 Reference-dependent preferences, outcome uncertainty, and sports fan behavior – a review of the literature 243
CLAY COLLINS AND BRAD R. HUMPHREYS

14 Moving toward behavioral stadium attendance demand research: first lessons learned from exploring football spectator no-show behavior in Europe 264
DOMINIK SCHREYER

PART 6
Happiness, and socioeconomics determinants of sports participation 287

15 The relationship of happiness and sport 289
BRUNO S. FREY AND ANTHONY GULLO

16 Using behavioral economics to improve health through sports participation and physical activity 302
MONICA M. MOSES AND JANE E. RUSESKI

17 Socioeconomic and demographic correlates of sports participation in Canada 328
NAZMI SARI

Index 345

Figures

3.1	Levels of Organizational Efficiency and Target Rates of Return	63
3.2	Determinants of Sports X-Efficiency	72
5.1	The No-Over-Doping Successful Game	113
6.1	Distribution of Male and Female Players at All Levels of Sport	129
7.1	Returns by Lots in Ascending Order	148
7.2	Average Net Returns for Alternative Bidding Ranges	149
11.1	Bad and Good Heuristics and Multiple Equilibria	209
12.1	Levels of Organizational Efficiency and Target Rates of Return	226
12.2	Improvements to Decision-Making Outcomes through Decision-Making Technical Change	230
12.3	Determinants of Optimal Decision-Making	232
14.1	Potential Strategies to Mitigate the Negative Consequences Arising from Frequent No-Show Behavior	274

Tables

2.1	Penalty Jump and Kick Direction and Stopping	27
5.1	The Ratio of Adverse Analytical Findings to Total Analysed Samples, 2008–2018	105
5.2	The Doping Game: A Prisoner's Dilemma	109
6.1	Proportion of Female Coaches in Female Competitions	127
6.2	Career Incentives for Women	131
6.3	Career Incentives for Men	132
7.1	Auction Details	145
7.2	Productivity Details	146
7.3	Ex Post Analysis	147
7.4	Pairwise Correlations of Bidding Categories	150
7.5	Alternative Behavioural Explanations – Returns to Diversification	152
8.1	Description of the Dataset	162
8.2	Descriptive Statistics	163
8.3	Comparison of Teams' Pre-treatment Characteristics	164
8.4	Logit Average Marginal Effect of Momentum on the Probability of Winning a Penalty Shoot-Out	165
8.5	Logit Average Marginal Effect of Momentum on the Probability of Winning a Penalty Shoot-Out at Home and Away	167
10.1	The Reliability of the Service in Winning a Point	189
10.2	Performance Statistics of Ashleigh Barty vis-à-vis Successive Opponents: Women's Singles French Open 2019	191
10.3	Performance Statistics of Rafael Nadal vis-à-vis Successive Opponents: Men's Singles French Open 2019	192
10.4	Bayesian Calculations for Barty and Nadal in the 2019 French Open Singles Championship	195
14.1	Determinants of Football Spectator No-Show Behavior in Germany	270
15.1	Descriptive Statistics of Sports Participation and Average Life Satisfaction	293
15.2	Relationship between Sports Participation and Happiness	295

xiv *Tables*

15.3	Causal Link between Sports Participation and Happiness	297
16.1	Demographic and Biological Factors	311
16.2	Determinants of Physical Activity, Theories Associated with Variables, and Summary of Evidence	313
16.3	Determinants of Physical Activity, Theories Associated with Variables, and Summary of Evidence	314
16.4	Determinants of Physical Activity, Theories Associated with Variables, and Summary of Evidence	315
16.5	Determinants of Physical Activity, Theories Associated with Variables, and Summary of Evidence	317
17.1	Reported Benefits from Participation in Sports Activities (percentage)	334
17.2	Reasons for Not Participating Regularly in Sports (percentage)	334
17.3	Reported Health Behavior by Participation in Sports (percentage)	335
17.4	Marginal Effects from Probit Regressions: Socioeconomic and Demographic Characteristics	336
17.5	Marginal Effects from Probit Regressions: Individuals' Health Behaviors	337
17A.1	List of Variables and Their Definitions	339
17A.2	Regression Results for Sports Participation	340
17A.3	Regression Results for Sports Participation (Married Subsample)	341

Contributors

Hannah Josepha Rachel Altman holds a BCOM BHS MPhil and is in the final stages of her PhD in *Behavioural Sports Economics* at the Queensland University of Technology Business School (QUT) in Brisbane, Australia, under the supervision of Benno Torgler and Rob Roberts. She prides herself with real-world motivated research that stems from 10 years of international fitness industry experience.

Morris Altman is Chair Professor of Behavioural and Institutional Economics, and Co-operatives, and Dean, University of Dundee School of Business, Dundee, Scotland, UK. He is also an Emeritus Professor at the University of Saskatchewan, Canada. He is former President of the Society for the Advancement of Behavioral Economics and former editor of the Journal of Socio-Economics. He has published more than 15 books and over 120 refereed papers in behavioural and institutional economics, theories of the firm, and economic history.

Wladimir Andreff is Honorary Professor at the University Paris 1 Panthéon-Sorbonne, received the 2019 Chelladurai Award of the European Association of Sport Management, and is the President of the Scientific Council at the Observatory of the Sports Economy (French Ministry of Sports), as well as the Honorary President of the International Association of Sports Economists and of the European Sports Economics Association. He has published 441 articles and 16 books, and edited 17 books in economics. His latest book was *An Economic Roadmap to the Dark Side of Sport*, Palgrave Macmillan 2019.

Vani K. Borooah is Emeritus Professor of Applied Economics at the University of Ulster, Northern Ireland, and a member of the Royal Irish Academy. He is a past President of the European Public Choice Society and of the Irish Economic Association.

David Butler is a lecturer in the Department of Economics at Cork University Business School, University College Cork, Ireland, and co-founder of the Centre for Sports Economics & Law. Dr Butler graduated from

Warwick University (PhD) in 2019, and his research interests focus on sports economics and behavioural economics.

Robert Butler is a lecturer in the Department of Economics at Cork University Business School, University College Cork, Ireland, and co-founder of the Centre for Sports Economics & Law. He has published in a variety of leading economics journals on sports such as boxing, football, horse racing, and rugby.

Ho Fai Chan is a Postdoctoral Research Fellow at the Queensland University of Technology and Deputy Program Lead at the Centre for Behavioural Economics, Society and Technology (BEST) of the Behavioural Economics and Non-Market Interactions programme. His research focuses primarily on Science of Science (SciSci) and Scientometrics, but he also takes interest in behavioural economic research in sport. His work has been published in journals such as Nature, PNAS, Scientific Reports, JAMA Network Open, Journal of Economic Behavior & Organization, Psychological Science, Scientometrics, Labour Economics, Journal of Business Research, and Journal of Economic Psychology.

Clay Collins is a PhD student in the Department of Economics at West Virginia University, USA. He holds a BS in economics from Berry College and a master's degree in economics from the University of North Carolina at Charlotte. His research interests include behavioural economics, sports economics, and urban economics.

Bruno S. Frey is a Distinguished Professor at the University of Warwick and also Permanent Visiting Professor at University Basel, and additionally Research Director at CREMA – Center for Research in Economics, Management and the Arts, Zurich. He holds five honorary doctorates and is the author of 30 books.

Anthony Gullo holds a Bachelor of Arts, and is a scientific collaborator at CREMA – Center for Research in Economics, Management and the Arts, Zurich, and at the University of Basel.

Brad R. Humphreys is Professor of Economics in the Department of Economics at West Virginia University, USA. His research focuses on urban economics, sports economics, and the economics of gambling. He has published more than 125 articles in peer-reviewed journals in economics, sports management, and public policy.

Alex Krumer is Professor of Sports Economics at the Faculty of Business Administration and Social Sciences at Molde University College in Norway. He received his PhD in Economics at Ben-Gurion University in Israel. His main fields of interest are behavioural economics and sports economics.

Stephanie Manning is a graduate student in Economics at the University of Newcastle, Australia.

Monica M. Moses is a fourth-year doctoral student at West Virginia University, USA. She completed her BS in statistics and economics at St. John Fisher College. Her current research lies within the fields of health education, broadly focusing on child outcomes.

Tim Pawlowski is Full Professor of Sports Economics and Associate Member at the LEAD Graduate School and Research Network at the University of Tübingen. His research was funded, for instance, by the German Research Foundation and the Swiss National Science Foundation.

Jane E. Ruseski is Professor of Economics at West Virginia University, USA. Her research interests lie within health and sports economics and health policy. She is the editor of International Journal of Sport Finance and a co-editor of Contemporary Economic Policy.

Nazmi Sari earned his PhD in Economics at Boston University. Currently, he is a professor of economics at the University of Saskatchewan, Canada. His research programmes include provider reimbursements, economics of health behaviour, and the quality and efficiency in hospital markets.

David A. Savage was Associate Professor of Economics at the University of Newcastle and a member of the Centre for Behavioural Economics, Society and Technology, Queensland University of Technology, Brisbane, Australia. He was well published, especially on the economics of disasters, and had a keen interest in behavioural economics and behavioural sports economics in particular. Sadly, Dave passed away suddenly on 8 May 2021 just after completing his contributions to this book.

Dominik Schreyer is a director of the Center for Sports and Management (CSM) at WHU – Otto Beisheim School of Management in Düsseldorf, Germany. In his research, he takes a keen interest in analysing stadium attendance demand (e.g. spectator no-show behaviour).

Stuart Thomas, B.Bus (RMIT), M.Comm. (UNSW), PhD (RMIT), is Associate Professor in the School of Economics, Finance and Marketing at RMIT. Prior to his academic career, he worked in business advice and consulting for a "Big 5" accounting and business advisory firm, and before that in the IT industry. He has a diverse portfolio of research interests including student performance, innovation economics, and industrial dynamics in the finance sector and in the sports industry and more recently in private retirement funding through alternatives to superannuation.

Kieran Tierney is Program Manager for Undergraduate Marketing at RMIT University in Melbourne. His research interests are at the intersection of service branding and consumer engagement. He is a founding member of the eSports Research Network and a member of the Market-Shaping special interest group of the Australia and New Zealand Marketing Academy. His research has won international awards and been published in internationally renowned academic journals.

Benno Torgler is Professor of Economics at the Queensland University of Technology and the Centre for Behavioural Economics, Society and Technology (BEST), leading the programme "Behavioural Economics of Non-Market Interactions" that covers the sub-programmes Sportometrics, Sociometrics, Scientometrics, and Cliometrics. He has a strong passion for doing research in the areas of sportometrics and behavioural sports economics.

Dr Stephen Whyte is a Behavioural Economist and Deputy Director at the Centre for Behavioural Economics, Society and Technology (BEST), Queensland University of Technology. His primary research interests focus on gender differences in large-scale decision-making in applied health and mate choice settings.

1 Introduction

Behavioural sports economics

Hannah Josepha Rachel Altman, Morris Altman and Benno Torgler

This book attempts to fill an important gap in the existing literature on sports economics, particularly as it pertains to behavioural approaches to the economics of sports.[1] To that end, we've adopted a pluralistic approach as our organizing framework, one well situated in the initial methodological advances of Herbert Simon. Simon always argued for a more holistic approach to economic analysis, one that not only incorporated price theory (Becker 1996, Stigler and Becker 1977) but also included important psychological, sociological, neurological, and institutional variables into the modelling of individuals and organizations engaged in sports.

We hope, therefore, that our contributions here will further enrich the existing behavioural sports economics literature as exemplified in the works of Downward, Dawson, and Dejonghe (2009), Kahane and Shmanske (2012), and Rodríguez, Kesenne, and Humphreys (2020). This book also takes as its starting point the well-known fact that naturally generated data from sports activities can facilitate the testing of a variety of economic hypotheses in both a rigorous and robust manner (Kahn 2000). Therefore, this book actively immerses itself into the world of sports to test our hypotheses and further enrich our understanding of human behaviour through the lens of behavioural economics.

Modelling realism and methodological pluralism

The realism of one's modelling assumptions is fundamentally important to behavioural economics, rooted as it is in its points of origin. For Simon, a hardwired fault of conventional economics is its lack of concern and attention to the realism of its behavioural and institutional (decision-making environment) simplifying assumptions, which underlie the models being specified. Unrealistic assumptions yield models that fail to adequately predict—and, just as importantly, fail to explain and fail to establish a proper causal relationship between dependent and independent variables. As such, one can often end up with models that omit variables that are actually the most analytically significant independent variables.[2]

Taking a pluralistic approach to behavioural economics as we have in this book opens the door to modelling sports in terms of a more recent focus on heuristics and biases and nudging, following upon the work of Kahneman and Tversky (2000; see also Kahneman 2003); and Thaler and Sunstein (2008), as well as the fast and frugal heuristics approach pioneered by Gigerenzer (2007; see also Gigerenzer and Todd 1999). As well, we try to incorporate approaches that focus on the decision-making environment and the decision-making capabilities of the decision-makers themselves as having a significant impact on their decisions and outcomes. This is very much in line with Simon's point of focus which is partially incorporated in the concepts of bounded rationality, procedural rationality, and satisficing (1959, 1978, 1987; see also March 1978 and Cyert and March 1963). These relate to the importance of institutional and related legal determinants of decision-making as underlined by institutional economists such as North (1990) as well as by Commons (1936), the latter being the pioneer of American institutionalism, celebrated by Simon in his work.

The importance of asymmetric information

Moreover, by going beyond the contemporary behavioural economics' focus on heuristics and biases, this book is a port of entry to the significance of asymmetric, imperfect, and costly information as key determinants of decision-making and decision-making protocols, ideas very much central to the work of Akerlof (1970) and earlier work by Stigler (1961). Finally, this book also addresses itself to the question of the persistence of systemic economic inefficiency in sports performance, also referred to more generally as x-inefficiency. This builds on the research of Leibenstein (1966, 1979) and Altman (1996, 2002). Together, these various tools in the expanded economics toolbox facilitate a more nuanced approach to an analysis of sports performance, incorporating in it the behaviour of larger organizations, teams, team members, athletes and fans.

Contributions to this volume

In "Sport as a Behavioural Economics Lab," Ho Fai Chan, David Savage, and Benno Torgler make the case that sporting events mimic the controlled, real-world, miniature laboratory environments, approaching the ceteris paribus assumption embedded in much economic theory. This also allows one to test a variety of hypotheses in a controlled environment by exploiting naturally generated data, as well as the implications of decisions, different incentives, and constraints on outcomes. They find that a growing number of studies use sports data to test decision-making related hypotheses which are critical to the behavioural economics enterprise. This economics laboratory remains fertile ground for future research. In "Sports Performance and Organizational Inefficiency," Hannah Altman and Morris Altman model how the persistence of inefficiency in sports performance is possible even in the realm of professional sports and why market forces can't easily correct this inefficiency. Specific organizational forms, the preferences of decision-makers, and specific mental models are critical determinants of the extent of efficiency. Furthermore, certain imperfect markets and asymmetric information inefficiency can be a product of errors in decision-making, which are correctable. But, inefficiency can prevail when fans support 'inefficient' (not very successful) sports teams due to the utility provided by their own teams, when owners' profits remain acceptable even in the face of organizational inefficiency, and when sports teams are vanity goods yielding erstwhile utility to owners. More generally, in their chapter, "Institutional dynamics in sports – how governance, rules and technology interact," Stuart Thomas and Kieran Tierney examine key institutional characteristics of technology-driven sports; i.e., sport that uses reasonably sophisticated equipment. They investigate the hypothesis that sports represent the intersection and interaction of institutions and technology, exemplified by bicycle, sailboard, motor car, and in e-sports, whilst the sustainability of a sport is largely determined by its institutional environment. The manner in which sports evolve is analysed through the prism of what they refer to as 'evolutionary sports dynamics'.

Wladimir Andreff, in "Wrong Behaviour due to Wrong Incentives: How Transform Doping into a Self-defeating Game?", discusses the evolution of doping from cheating to an economic crime, where the latter has been facilitated by an inappropriate incentive environment. This includes the rules to ban doping in sports events, which are not properly enforced and where the benefits of cheating outweigh the costs. Athletes' behaviour must be transforming through a dramatic change in the incentive environment, where the dominant strategy is not to 'over'-dope and over-doping becomes a self-defeating strategy. In "Disincentives, Disequilibrium's and Discrimination: Behavioural Economics in Women's Sport", Stephanie Manning, Ho Fai Chan, and David Savage make the fundamentally important point that incentives matter to gender equity in sport. This chapter provides a theoretical and empirical analysis of gender discrimination as it pertains to sports. One reason that women are not being better represented in professional sports and even in coaching and administrative roles is because there are inadequate pathways for women in sports, a product of discrimination that feeds back into gender differences in wages and human capital formation, for example.

In "Winner Alright? New Evidence on High-Stakes Bidding and Returns to Ownership in the Thoroughbred Horseracing Industry", Robert Butler analyses competitive bedding behaviour using a unique data set from Great Britain and Ireland. His results confirm the widespread belief that a large percentage of thoroughbreds incur losses or negative returns. These losses are consistent with the winner's curse hypothesis, but it is argued that one should also look to the motivation of owners (their preferences) for owning thoroughbreds to best explain the persistence of the large losses incurred in this sport.

Alex Krumer's "Does psychological momentum differ for home and away teams? Evidence from penalty shoot-outs in European Cups", an empirical analysis of penalty shootouts during two-leg ties of European Cup football (soccer) tournaments, suggests that scoring more goals than one's opponent in the second leg increases the probability of winning the shoot-out. But this is true only for the away team. This supports the view that there is a positive effect of psychological momentum, but only for the away team. Playing in front of one's fans has a negative effect on performance in this scenario. Tim Pawlowski, in "Reference Point Behavior and Sports", reviews and provides structure to the literature, empirically testing reference point behaviour in sports. This chapter reviews two strands of the literature, one referring to the behaviour and decisions of athletes and coaches and the other to the behaviour and decisions of fans. Data from sports settings are found to be highly relevant to analysing the importance of reference point behaviour more generally. In "The Importance of the Serve in Winning Points in Tennis: A Bayesian Analysis Using Data for the Two Winners of the 2019 French Open Singles", Vani Borooah adds empirical substance to Bayes' theorem in the context of professional tennis. Borooah examines the performance of Rafael Nadal and Ashleigh Barty, the winners of the men's and women's singles titles, respectively, at the 2019 French Open. A key finding of this chapter is that given the prior likelihood of their winning a point on their service game, this had to be revised upward if the data showed that their first serve was 'good' and had to be revised downward if the point required that they serve again. This application of Bayes' Theorem to tennis is an example of how evidence can be turned into insight.

In "Beauty and Preferences Formation Exemplified in the Sports Market", Hannah Altman, Morris Altman, Benno Torgler, and Stephen Whyte discuss and model the use of beauty and, relatedly, sexiness as a fast and frugal heuristic and therefore an important determinant of choice. Given asymmetric information, beauty represents a proxy for objective characteristics or an object of desire, according to an individual's preferences and can serve as a mechanism through which choices and payments (beauty premiums) are made with regards to athletes, trainers, and other members of sports organizations. The authors argue that beauty can be a good or bad heuristic, depending on the objective relationship between beauty and what it proxies. Conditions under which the beauty heuristic generates sub-optimal and optimal outcomes are discussed and modelled. The beauty premium is also discussed and modelled in the context of Becker's economic theory of discrimination. Hannah Altman and Morris Altman also elaborate on heuristics through their contribution: "Moneyball and Decision-Making Heuristics: An Intersection of Statistics and Practical Expertise", in the context of the issues and debates raised in the book *Moneyball* and the film, *Trouble with the Curve*. They build upon Herbert Simon's assumption of the brain as a scarce computational resource and heuristics as a decision-making shortcut given this decision-making constraint. They examine the intersection and complementarity between sports data and related statistical analysis (one type of heuristic) and the more traditional experiential (human capital) means of sports decision-making. They argue that both types of decision-making tools are critically important for optimal decision-making in sports, with sports statistics adding considerably to the sports decision-making toolbox. But, sub-optimal outcomes will result if one dominates the other.

Clay Collins and Brad Humphreys examine sports fan behaviour in their chapter, "Reference Dependent Preferences, Outcome Uncertainty, and Sports Fan Behavior: A Review of the Literature." Through their study of the pertinent literature, they examine a key concept in sports economics: namely, the uncertainty of outcome hypothesis (UOH), which suggests that fans are more likely to attend games with less certain outcomes than games with more certain outcomes. This hypothesis models fans in a world of uncertainty with reference dependent preferences (RDP). But the authors find that even with these types of preferences and loss aversion, the UOH does not hold. Reviewing the literature, they find limited support for the UOH and relatively strong support for loss aversion with regards to fan attendance. In "Moving Toward Behavioral Stadium Attendance Demand Research: First Lessons Learned from Exploring Football Spectator No-Show Behavior in Europe", Dominik Schreyer examines stadium attendance demand research, building upon Rottenberg's original 1956 contribution, which itself has been extended and elaborated upon over the decades. He attempts to address some of the methodological issues arising from the quasi-standard use of aggregated attendance data by developing behavioural stadium attendance research, analysing distinct football spectator no-show behaviour in Europe. In this context, he reviews the stadium attendance demand research literature for lessons learnt and to reflect on what needs to be addressed in future research.

In "The Relationship of Happiness and Sport", Bruno Frey and Anthony Gullo contribute to the happiness literature by extending this literature to sports. They analyse the causal relationship between happiness and sports by using longitudinal data from the German Socio-Economic Panel (GSOEP), finding a positive correlation between sports participation and reported life satisfaction. This correlation is stronger for individuals in bad health, compared to those of average health. More specifically, they find that individuals who engage in sport are happier, and those who are increasingly happy become more willing to participate in sport. But the correlation between sports participation and subjective well-being is strongest by far. Monica M. Moses and Jane E. Ruseski, in "Using Behavioral Economics to Improve Health Through Sports Participation and Physical Activity", argue that the evidence demonstrates the importance of sports participation and physical activity as determinants of health and wellbeing, inclusive of feeling and sleeping better to reduced risk for many chronic diseases. In spite of this evidence, most people worldwide do not sufficiently participate in sports and physical activity more generally to improve their health and wellbeing. This chapter reviews the literature on such participation through the lens of behavioural economics to better understand why individuals participate at such low levels. Such a treatment is critical if one is to develop a policy to change this behaviour towards greater participation in sports and physical activity. Nazmi Sari, in "Socioeconomic and demographic correlates of sports participation in Canada", addresses the gap in the literature of the determination of sports participation by using the Canadian General Social Survey. This study is important since it is widely recognized that participation in sports and related physical activity has positive effects on an individual's health and labour market outcomes.

Notes

1 This book is Hannah's brainchild. It was she who first approached Routledge with her idea of a book on behavioural sports economics during a meeting of the Western Economics Association International.
2 This assumptions matter approach to behavioural economics, adopted by Simon, is in contrast to the approach advocated by Friedman (1953) that what counts to the strength of the model's prediction, irrespective the realism of its underlying assumptions.

References

Akerlof, George A. (1970). The Market for 'Lemons': Quality Uncertainty and the Market Mechanism. *Quarterly Journal of Economics*, 84: 488–500.
Altman, Morris (1996). *Human Agency and Material Welfare: Revisions in Microeconomics and their Implications for Public Policy*. Boston, Dordrecht, London: Kluwer Academic Publishers.
Altman, Morris (2002). Economic Theory, Public Policy and the Challenge of Innovative Work Practices. *Economic and Industrial Democracy: An International Journal*, 23: 271–290.
Altman, Morris, ed. (2006). *Handbook of Contemporary Behavioral Economics: Foundations and Developments*. Armonk, NY: M. E. Sharpe.
Baddeley, Michelle (2017). *Behavioural Economics: A Very Short Introduction*. Oxford, New York: Oxford University Press.
Becker, Gary (1996). *Accounting for Tastes*. Cambridge, MA, London: Harvard University Press.
Commons, John R. (1934). *Institutional Economics*. New York: Macmillan.
Cyert, Richard M. & James C. March (1963). *A Behavioral Theory of the Firm*. Englewood Cliffs, NJ: Prentice-Hall.
Downward, Paul, Alistair Dawson & Trudo Dejonghe (2009). *Sports Economics: Theory, Evidence and Policy*. New York: Routledge.
Friedman, Milton (1953). The Methodology of Positive Economics. In Milton Friedman, ed., *Essays in Positive Economics*, 3–43. Chicago, IL: University of Chicago Press.
Gigerenzer, Gerd (2007). *Gut Feelings: The Intelligence of the Unconscious*. New York: Viking.
Gigerenzer, Gerd & Peter M. Todd (1999). *Simple Heuristics that Make Us Smart*. New York: Oxford University Press.

Kahane, Leo H. & Stephen Shmanske, eds. (2012). *The Oxford Handbook of Sports Economics: The Economics of Sports*, Volumes 1 and 2. Oxford: Oxford University Press.

Kahn, Lawrence M. (2000). The Sports Business as a Labor Market Laboratory. *Journal of Economic Perspectives*, 14: 75–94.

Kahneman, Daniel (2003). Maps of Bounded Rationality: Psychology for Behavioral Economics. *American Economic Review*, 93: 1449–1475.

Kahneman, Daniel & Amos Tversky, eds. (2000). *Choices, Values and Frames*. New York: Cambridge University Press & Russell Sage Foundation.

Leibenstein, Harvey (1966). Allocative Efficiency vs. 'X-Efficiency'. *American Economic Review*, 56: 392–415.

Leibenstein, Harvey (1979). A Branch of Economics Is Missing: Micro-Micro Theory. *Journal of Economic Literature*, 17: 477–502.

March, James G. (1978). Bounded Rationality, Ambiguity, and the Engineering of Choice. *Bell Journal of Economics*, 9: 587–608.

North, Douglass C. (1990). *Institutions, Institutional Change and Economic Performance*. New York: Cambridge University Press.

Rodríguez, Plácido, Stefan Kesenne & Brad R. Humphreys, eds. (2020). *Outcome Uncertainty in Sporting Events: Winning, Losing and Competitive Balance*. Cheltenham: Edward Elgar.

Simon, Herbert A. (1959). Theories of Decision Making in Economics and Behavioral Science. *American Economic Review*, 49: 252–283.

Simon, Herbert A. (1978). Rationality as a Process and as a Product of Thought. *American Economic Review*, 70: 1–16.

Simon, Herbert A. (1987). Behavioral Economics. In J. Eatwell, M. Millgate, & P. Newman, eds., *The New Palgrave: A Dictionary of Economics*, 221–225. London: Macmillan.

Stigler, George J. (1961). The Economics of Information. *Journal of Political Economy*, 69: 213–225.

Stigler, George J. & Gary S. Becker (1977). De Gustibus Non Est Disputandum. *American Economic Review*, 67: 76–90.

Thaler, Richard H. & Cass R. Sunstein (2008). *Nudge: Improving Decisions about Health, Wealth, and Happiness*. New York: Penguin Books.

Part 1
The big picture

2 Sport as a behavioural economics lab

Ho Fai Chan, David A. Savage and Benno Torgler

Introduction

Sports economics, or the study of sport using economic theory, has been with us for some time and has generated interesting insights into several different topics. Of course, one principle that sits behind all this analysis is the methodology or approach through which we try and apply our thinking to sports data. The behavioural economics revolution of recent years has given economists an additional lens through which they can examine the world around them – this is no different for the analysis of sports data. We have seen an increase in the number of papers that have utilized sports data to gain insight or understanding into individual, group, or other types of behaviour. We have used economics to explore sports data and aspects of the real world that are often very difficult to access or observe, such as performance and incentives. These aspects are much easier to study in the world of sports, as sports data is all-encompassing and available in almost every type of sport. To discuss how behavioural economics influenced research with sports data, we will first discuss setting conditions that provide insights into the advantage of sports data. Next, we will discuss a set of concepts that have been explored or are worth exploring in more detail. These concepts were chosen ad hoc and therefore are not a complete list of valuable concepts. Moreover, as the list is relatively substantial, we do not provide a full list of available studies but rather a set of studies that clarify the area of exploration and those where we see further possibilities and avenues. We, therefore, apologize in advance if some scholars feel that their work should have been mentioned under these concepts. This process was like wandering through a field of gems with only a small bag in which to collect them – you obviously cannot collect them all nor could you even be sure of the total gems available in the field. We cherry-picked the gems that we felt best represented the discussion we were trying to build. We finish the article by discussing some areas that have influenced or were influenced by behavioural economics, focusing specifically on biases and linking behavioural economics with AI, which will become a more dominant area in the future (Schmidt 2020, Torgler 2020). Looking at chess, for example, provides insights into the mechanism and machinery of decision-making and how such mechanisms can be programmed to derive more realistic cognitive architectures (Torgler 2021a). We will clarify why past insights are valuable from a behavioural economics perspective and what we can expect in terms of future perspectives.

Settings

In this section, we will identify interesting settings that allow us to understand how sports can be seen as a "real-world laboratory" (Goff and Tollison 1990, Kahn 2000, Torgler 2009) where we can test behavioural questions in a relatively controlled high-stakes environment and where information is transparently available for outsiders to explore (rather than hidden as is often the case in the labour market). However, as controllability is influenced by and subject to various elements and aspects, we try to provide a set of examples.

Rule changes

With game rule changes, we are approaching conditions of a natural experiment (Chan, Savage, and Torgler 2019); accordingly, scholars have focused on those rule changes since almost the beginning of sports economics. A frequent example that appears in the literature examines how changes in the number of referees (change in enforcement ability) affect players' behaviour in environments such as basketball (McCormick and Tollison 1984), ice hockey (Levitt 2002), or soccer (Witt 2005). There are historically fascinating examples in which randomization of referees was introduced, such as in the 1998–1999 National Hockey League (NHL) season when the assignment of one or two referees to a match was done randomly (Levitt 2002). Chan et al. (2019) also explored not just the one rule change but repeated changes that led to a return to the original condition. This allowed readers to see not just a first adaption process, but also re-adaption. Rule changes are particularly interesting from a behavioural economics perspective because a key intention of the sports rule change is to change the behaviour within the game (Elias and Dunning 1966, Chan et al. 2019). Such changes can affect aspects such as emotionality, predictability, uncertainty, cooperation, or the psychology of an athlete in general. The beauty is not only in the uncertainty created but also in understanding the implications of observing behaviour in a relatively close micro-environment that has only limited spill-over effects from other areas. Uncertainty in other natural environments beyond sports is usually more complex and less controlled.

Those empirical explorations are important as behavioural economics needs to get the psychology as well as the economics right, and therefore, how humans respond to incentive changes and changes in their constraints and opportunities. Thus, linking economics and psychology together is the way behavioural economics can help to gain insights into the mechanisms of behavioural change using data beyond experimentation. If we are keen to understand how a billiard player adapts to changes, it is not enough to just assume she/he is familiar with the physics and mathematics of producing perfect shots. We need to understand how those players act, learn, and adapt. Herbert Simon has clearly won that debate against Milton Friedman: training them requires answering "why" questions. Think about heuristics (and potential biases) and decision-making with a mindset that tries to understand how the actual world of sports works and evolves with all its underlying mechanisms. This means that rule changes can be seen as some sort of a resilience test that helps us to understand those mechanisms better.

Institutional factors

There are interesting links between the way that institutions are set up and how they influence human behaviour that is often overlooked, which borders on ironic, given that most are little more than social norms that are sufficiently long-lived, becoming an institution by formalizing a set of rules to govern how people should act and behave. The process of becoming an institution describes a feedback mechanism between individuals and groups on shared social norms and the mores of acceptable behaviour (Savage 2019). However, it also signifies that it takes a significant length of time and stability for a norm to become institutionalized, implying that they do not change quickly and are likely well out of step with the norms of a quickly evolving society. This is no different for sporting institutions, especially those that have been functional for centuries, as the values and norms of the society that built the institution may have moved on, leaving the institution struggling to remain relevant or effective.

Institutions define incentives and, therefore, behaviours. A good example is a study provided by Duggan and Levitt (2002). The ancient and noble sport of Sumo Wrestling was considered to be above the cheating and corruption that plagued nearly all others. However, the authors revealed that is not the case when looking at how the structure of the competition was examined through a more behavioural lens. The analysis focused on how the sport's unique competition structure incentivized collusive behaviours between opponents at a kink point in the tournament structure (when moving from seven to eight wins) where the payoff – a promotion of rank – significantly increased for one competitor if they were successful (eight wins). The eighth win has four times the value of a typical win. The analysis showed that on any other bout when there was no such increased incentive to win, the outcomes were within the expected win/loss ratios, but on the rounds where one player would receive the promotion, the probability of their winning escalated dramatically. Effectively they demonstrated that the opposing player was willing to collude by throwing the bout in order to ensure the promotion (moving up a single spot would be worth $3000), but they also found that when these competitors next faced each other the "favour" was returned as the promoted player would most likely lose the match. Such collusion shows that this cannot be explained purely by an athlete effort story. Match rigging also increased as the tournament ended. The results show that wrestlers on the bubble on day 15 are victorious 25% more often than would be expected. On the other hand, excess winning likelihoods disappeared in tournaments with a high level of media scrutiny. Their findings are interesting for several reasons. It shows that corruption was present in even a sport thought to be above such activities, but more importantly, it demonstrated that the incentive structure put in place by the sporting institution had a significant impact on the attitudes and behaviours of players i.e., it inadvertently created a focal point for player collusion at a specific point in every tournament. In addition, their results show that the cost of detection also matters. Increasing media scrutiny can help to reduce collusive behaviour, while an interesting avenue for further investigation would be whether, and to what extent, sports disciplines have barriers to entry in the market that affect corruption or innovation by lacking competitive pressure.

Institutions have been developed to help codify and regulate international sport with the creation of professional associations and the presence of referees as the on-field arbiter of the rules. These institutions ensure that the negative aspects of competitive sports, i.e., aggression, conflict, and violence do not degenerate into a free-for-all and that they mirror the acceptable behaviours we observe within our modern societies (Howell 1975, Cooper 1989, Riordan 1993). In line with this, Caruso et al. (2017) explored the relationship between international football competitions and conflict across several international football tournaments including the FIFA World Cups, Olympic Games, Champions Cups, and Under 20s World Cups between 1994 and 2014 to analyse the impact that national differences (identity) had on match aggression and conflict. They conclude that while the impact of any one referee on enforcing the institution's position is not clear, the analysis of several decades of competitions across numerous international tournaments enabled them to ascertain the true impact of the referees controlling conflict during those matches. Furthermore, they demonstrate that FIFA, the institution governing football, was able to have a positive impact on behaviour by limiting or directing social violence through the control of referees. By examining aggression and violence through the awarding of red or yellow cards and in-game fouls for minor indiscretions, they demonstrated that match referees had a significant institutional impact on the on-field transgressions that negated the significance of virtually all the national identity variables. This result demonstrates that when an institution's rules and expectations are well aligned and are consistently applied and updated, they can have a significant positive impact on behavioural outcomes. The authors also warn "that if an institutional approach is adopted the evidence suggests that it needs a certain degree of flexibility and prescience, rather than a rule based reactive rigidity" (Caruso et al. 2017, p. 538).

Disruptions

The sports environment, team sports in particular, provide an interesting environment to explore organizational disruptions. In-season changes, such as dismissing head-coaches, offers a natural avenue of investigation, allowing us to understand the implications of major management changes. Such head coach changes are frequent enough to allow detailed exploration. Van Ours and van Tuijl (2016) report mean in-season head-coach changes between 4.2 (Netherlands Eredivisie) and 8.4% (Italy Serie A) for seven European football leagues, covering 14 seasons, starting with the 2000/2001 season. Their results indicate that a replacement improves performance.

Another interesting aspect is understanding what happens if a team recruits a highly talented athlete; a star. Sports allows us to explore and track what happens individually and teamwise over time. It can therefore provide better insights into dynamics that are difficult to observe in the normal labour force. Evidence regarding CEOs indicates that top performers achieve success only for a while, fading out quickly and leading to a sharp decline in teams' functioning (Groysberg, Nanda and Nohria 2004). Those insights indicate that companies cannot gain from a competitive advantage by hiring stars, considering that they do not stay with organizations for a long time (Groysberg, Nanda and Nohria 2004). Having detailed data on how players interact with each other on the field (e.g., who interacts with whom throughout the game or even during training sessions) allows us to observe and understand better how stars are integrated into the team, how that integration evolves over time, and whether and to what extent an integration is affected by the actual structure of the team itself (e.g., level of heterogeneity across a number of factors such as age, experience, loyalty to the team, salary, etc.). Future studies can also explore in more detail how technological disruptions such as Big Data, AI, or quantum computing affect the game itself (Torgler 2020).

Pressure

Experiments involving pressure and stress have been directly linked to the breakdown in judgment, rational decision making, and the generation of mistakes via an individual's inability to correctly weigh options (Wright 1974). This can result in inefficient or poor outcomes as individuals fail to correctly scan alternative options (Keinan 1987). As pressure increases, individuals are less able to make rational choices, resulting in a greater number of irrational choices (Meichenbaum 2007). However, it remains unclear exactly how much additional pressure is required to detrimentally affect decisions (Jamal 1984), and part of this problem derives from differences in the underlying model being used in the stress function. For example, Sullivan and Bhagat (1992) outline four of the most common models, which included: (1) higher levels of performance require at least some moderate level of stress; (2) a positively correlated relationship such that only through high stress could high performance be achieved; (3) a negatively correlated relationship where high stress results in low performance levels; (4) and finally that stress and performance are totally unrelated. Additional issues arise when non-linear models like an inverted "U" shape function (Yerkes and Dodson 1908, Meglino 1977, Allen et al. 1982) are adopted over linear ones – where lower levels of stress may actually aid in performance, but once the turning point (threshold) has been reached any additional stress is detrimental to performance (see e.g., Baumeister 1984, Baumeister and Showers 1986).

Sports allow us to pinpoint the actual pressure experienced (magnitude and direction of stress) relatively precisely. Savage and Torgler (2012) explored the impact of different stress factors on elite athletes during penalty shoot-outs at the FIFA World Cup and the UEFA Euro Cup competitions between 1978 and 2008. They found that predicable, anticipated, and experienced stress factors (routinely experienced stress determinants), such as crowd size (noise) or game level, have no impact on performance. However, the less-anticipated stressors such as final shots to win/lose appeared to have significant impacts on the likelihood of success. A large positive difference promotes performance (positive stress) and improves the probability of a successful shot by about 17%, while a negative difference reduces performance (negative stress) and decreases the probability of a successful shot by about 45%. This indicates a substantial and asymmetric effect for top athletes, which means that they also respond differently to detrimental incentive effects (high rewards or the threat of severe failure). Krumer (2020) shows that penalty kicks are not just a "lottery". Exploring the probability of winning a shoot-out by looking at teams from different divisions indicates that higher-ranked soccer teams perform better in penalty kicks.

The penalty kick environment has also been used to understand the effect of a supportive audience on performance. Dohmen (2008) found that players in the German Bundesliga (seasons between 1963 and 2004) were more likely to "choke" when playing in front of their home audience. Thus, empirical evidence using sports data is useful as such data can help to discriminate between theories. For example, in this case, one can discriminate between a social facilitation or social support hypothesis that suggests that performance is boosted by a friendly environment and a social pressure hypothesis that argues that it can impair performance (Dohmen 2008) via a higher psychological pressure due to higher expectations. As Butler and Baumeister (1998) stress "it may be more painful to have friends and family see one fall flat on one's face. A supportive audience could conceivably increase pressure, concern, and self-consciousness, which in principle could have a detrimental effect on performance" (p. 1213). Applying an experimental approach, they observe that choking under pressure around a supportive audience is found in skill-based tasks but not in easy tasks, despite finding supportive audiences to be more helpful and less stressful. This led the authors to conclude that people were not aware of the debilitating effect of supportive audiences.

Beyond such experiments, sports data provides a controlled setting in the real world to explore whether or not – and in what conditions – choking under pressure matters. Dohmen (2008, p. 652) stresses that penalty kicks are not free of problems. Only a selected group of players is explored; therefore, a selection effect may lead to a lower bound estimate, as those who are better able to cope with stress are more likely to be selected for such penalty kicks. Using penalty kicks in World Cups after a draw would help to reduce such a problem as it may increase the distributions of ability to choke (or not) under pressure (despite some ex-ante training). Dohmen also stresses that for Bundesliga data, the stakes might not be high enough to observe significant choking, which also means that such results would be lower-bound estimates (compared to other settings). Using World Cup or UEFA European Cup data would mean exploring players in a higher stress environment:

> On 17 July 1994, at the Los Angeles Rose Bowl, Brazil attempted to secure its fourth Federation Internationale de Football Association (FIFA) World Cup trophy, in probably one of the most memorable shootouts in World Cup history. One of Italy's greatest ever players and a shining light of the tournament, Robert Baggio, took what was to be the final shot of the US World Cup. Baggio placed the ball on the spot, while Taffarel, the Brazilian goal keeper, took his position on the line in front of 94 000 spectators. The fascinating aspect of such a 'high pressure' situation is the fact that after 4 years of preparation, several matches before this final, 120 min of game time, and eight prior penalty attempts, one single shot held the match outcome in the balance. If Baggio misses then Italy loses the greatest prize of all in football, namely the World Cup; if he is successful Italy still can retain a glimmer of hope of being world champions. As many readers may know, Baggio's shot not only missed but it soared metres over the crossbar, which meant that Italy lost the tournament and Brazil became the 1994 World Cup champions.
>
> (Savage and Torgler 2012, pp. 2423–2424)

Beyond soccer, one can explore other environments that require a high level of precision. Harb-Wu and Krumer (2019) looked at professional biathlon athletes, as a biathlete has to perform the exact same non-interactive task of shooting the exact same number of times. As the authors point out, this allows exploration of within-biathlete variation (e.g., with and without being in front of a supportive audience). Moreover, as all biathletes need to perform the precision task, a selection effect as discussed in Dohmen (2008) is less of a problem (although individuals may select themselves into that sports field). Their large data set covers 16 seasons including 144 World Cup events, 12 World Championships and 4 Winter Olympic Games – and the results indicate for both genders that biathletes from the top quartile struggle more in their home turf compared to competitions abroad.

Basketball is another environment that allows exploration of performance under pressure in a more controlled way, especially when looking at free throw percentages as a measure of performance (for a discussion see Cao et al. 2011). Each free throw attempt is taken from the same location, which means that the physical difficulty is constant. In addition, contrary to a penalty kick, the performance is not confounded by a response of another player (e.g., goalkeeper in a penalty kick). Contrary to penalty kicks, free throws occur very frequently and for most players. This makes it possible to explore the heterogeneity in shooting skills and stress resistance and means that results are less driven by a selection effect. Moreover, psychological factors may still matter because, as Cao et al. (2011) stress, free throws are still a non-trivial task with failure rates for most NBA players. Their results indicate that there is some choking but the effects (e.g., playing at home) are small. However, choking becomes more dominant at the end of the game (decline in success by around four percentage points when the shooter's team is down by one or two points in the final minute). The negative effects increase to 6.3 and 8.8 percentage points for the last 15 seconds when down by two or one point, respectively. The choking effect is also stronger for players who are worse free-throw shooters. Toma (2017) followed up on basketball free throws looking at both females and males at the college and professional levels. Interestingly, male college players who eventually play at the professional level choke more in the final seconds of a close game. Toma's argument is that they feel more pressure to perform due to their career expectations. He also finds no evidence of a gender difference in choking behaviour.

Cohen-Zada, Krumer, Rosenboim and Shapir (2017) explored tennis to understand human behaviour under pressure. They looked at the effect of competitive pressure on the likelihood of winning the game, instead of focusing on the number of unforced errors or winning shots. The strength of their measure is its objectivity:

> While two observers can debate whether or not a certain shot should be considered as a forced or unforced error, and whether or not the previous shot led to the forced error, in our case winning a game is an undeniable fact.
>
> (p. 178)

Interestingly, they find that increasing the level of stakes reduces performance for men. They seemed to choke under competitive pressure, while women choke less. Thus, women show superiority in this setting regarding competitive pressure. They argue that those results are "consistent with evidence in the biological literature that levels of cortisol, which is known to impede the performance of both men and women, commonly escalate more substantially among men than women in response to achievement-related challenges" (p. 188).

Hickman and Metz (2015) take advantage of the ability to look at performance on the last hole of the golf tournament on PGA tours, allowing them to observe a substantial variation in key pressure situations. Obviously, making or missing a putt can have a considerable influence on the finishing position and the monetary reward. Their innovation is to have this direct link to a monetary reward, which is less in the case if you fail in your free throw performance in the NBA. An interesting addition is that they have data on the exact location of players' golf balls before and after each shot (down to an inch). Their results indicate that increasing the value of a putt by around $50,000 decreases the likelihood of a player making the putt by one percentage point. However, that magnitude is greater for specific shots such as those taken from five to ten feet away. Not surprisingly, less experienced players are more negatively affected by pressure.

One of the major issues limiting the empirical analysis of the stress/performance relationship beyond the sports environment is measurement (measuring an individual's performance and then comparing it to another). Performance is not fully comparable in most workplaces, even between two individuals doing the same job, because regardless of the metric used to measure performance it needs to be analysed using the same underlying characteristic or the statistical inference erodes (Allison 1999). For example, the environmental conditions, incentive structures, support systems, or any number of other exogenous factors may not be identical for both individuals. Given the broad availability of information on athletes and the relatively controlled conditions under which they compete, the use of the sporting environment has been fruitful. However, the modern era of Big Data may make this an even better experimental laboratory – many players now wear IoT (internet of things) devices that track heart rates, blood pressure, speed, distance, and a range of other geotagged data that could be coupled to the on-field behaviour and choices made by players during competition. This combination of new data could combine biological and physiological aspects with decision sciences (for a discussion, see Torgler 2020).

Beyond physical: esports

When it comes to the human body's non-sympathetic responses to stress, our brains cannot tell the difference between reality and imagination. Our bodies release stimulants like adrenalin and cortisol when we are stressed or when we imagine being stressed (Hamilton 2018). This psychological effect also works in a number of other situations, e.g., the placebo. Under the placebo effect, we believe we have received a drug that will have a certain effect. Since our mind is unable to distinguish between reality and imagination, it will often supply the required sensation or, where possible, the stimulation to replicate what was expected – such as the diminishing of pain. Studies have also shown that we can imagine our bodies fighting cancer (Eremin et al. 2009) or recovering body function after a stroke (Kho et al. 2014) and our mind rewires itself to make it happen. Many of the aspects of sports explored by behavioural economists in the past have more than likely been confounded with physical aspects or skill of the athletes being studied – one such example is sporting momentum (see e.g., Cohen-Zada, Krumer and Shtudiner 2017, Gauriot and Page 2018). Thus, eSports offers the opportunity to disentangle such mental and physical aspects. Psychological momentum (which will be discussed in more detail later) can work as positive and negative momentum and alters behaviour and performance by the perception of an individual (Iso-Ahola and Dotson 2016). It has been argued that positive psychological momentum improves the individual's confidence, and by extension their competence which allows them to successfully complete the task at hand in a better and faster manner – this then increases the individual's expectations of success on the next task. The problem with this argument is that it is directly related to the physical attributes of the individual, i.e., the assumption is that if the individual can complete a task faster (or better), they were either not exerting maximum effort or doing so inefficiently. The physicality issue poses a problem when trying to compare momentum between athletes as it is unclear if individuals were actively conserving energy for future effort (or if they were already at maximum effort), and how we can determine the comparative differences in effort and energy between players. Again, we could turn to eSports where physical aspects are less important in comparison to the mental (or psychological) ones – removing one of the confounds and making it clearer to analyse momentum.

Concepts

Prospect theory

There are many contentious or unclear theoretical concepts that are difficult to empirically prove, and several experiments and behavioural concepts are traditionally explored in laboratory settings that may be better served if we can utilize the quasi-natural field aspect of sports. For example, Prospect Theory has only occasionally been tested in the real world with real-world losses (Page et al. 2014), but it may be much easier to test in an environment with clear incentives, strategic actions, and real-world gains and losses. Prospect Theory relies on a lack of adaption (habituation) of losses in terms of the individuals' (or perhaps the groups') reference point (Kahneman and Tversky 1979). This point is supported anecdotally by gamblers who often "chase their losses" or take on additional risk when they are behind but may also take on more risk due to an endowment (house money) effect where a newly acquired gain has not been habituated and can be gambled without fear of loss (Thaler and Johnson 1990). However, it may be possible to explore this effect within the sporting context with variations in risk behaviour in game (during) and out of game (after) – where post game we would expect the players to now be in a "cold" state and able to habituate the losses, but during a game, the players in a "hot" state are likely to chase losses (see Loewenstein 2005). There may also be many potential avenues from which to approach this topic, from both the individual and team levels. Individual sports could be used to provide insight into how players habituate losses during highly incentivized tournament matches and may be compared to choices made during non-competitive or low incentive matches. Alternatively, this could be explored in conjunction with the group assessment of risk (see below) with team sports – where individuals and teams could be examined for changes in risk attitudes (behaviour) during matches. Additionally, it might be possible to explore differences between one-shot, repeated, and knock-out games – to see if strategic elements make a difference in choices being made.

Goal setting

The concept of goal setting, where a fixed goal provides an aspirational point of reference, is an extension to Prospect Theory, where the reference point moves after gains or losses have been habituated (see Locke 1968, Locke et al. 1990). If the theory holds, then individuals are more likely to work harder to achieve a difficult goal than they would if no goal or an easily achieved one was set. An extension of this theory could be that during sports competitions or tournaments (rather than single matches), losses could inspire players to strive harder or take on more risky options to achieve the stated goal. For example, as the probability of success wanes (decreases), the players may be willing to adopt riskier and riskier gambles in an attempt to overcome the lower probability. This often occurs in tournaments where teams or individuals hold an expectation of where they should finish (regardless of whether that is the first place, fifth, or merely making it out of the first stages).

Interdependent preferences

Another theory that has proven difficult to empirically explore has been that of interdependent preferences (Pollak 1976), where the preferences of an individual are co-dependent on the preferences of others. While this is fundamentally at odds with the rational choice self-interested homo-economicus model of a utility maximizer, behavioural economics has repeatedly shown that individuals regularly deviate from the behaviour expected from this model. However, the sporting environment may provide us with an interesting environment to explore what happens when both self and collective interests are present – such as wanting to maximize their own payoff, but where others are required to reach this goal. For example, player contracts or wages in individual sports are purely dependent on the players own performances and skills. However, in team sports, we observe that an individual's ability to excel in their own position is directly dependent on those around them, as such every player's success depends on that of another (Frank 1984). Sports data provides an unusually large amount of interconnected data on performance and earnings that can be exploited to explore how the contract negotiations of similar players are linked to the performance of teammates and other players of similar skills. As such, even superstars with the highest ranking may be concerned about the ranking and incentives of those around them (Postlewaite 1998), and not just their absolute position or earnings. A great example of this relationship could be seen between Michael Jordan arguably the greatest basketball player of all time and his long-time teammate Scottie Pippen:

> He helped me so much in the way I approached the game, in the way I played the game. Whenever they speak Michael Jordan, they should speak Scottie Pippen. Everybody says I won all these championships. But I didn't win without Scottie Pippen. That's why I consider him my greatest teammate of all-time.
> (Michael Jordan 2020: The Last Dance)

Strategic interactions

The analysis of sports in the sports economics methodology has been doubly focused on many traditional and mainstream sports but there may be some significant advantages to exploring more strategic games such as chess, go, or poker to analyse strategic and k-level thinking. Strategic thinking may also open the door to explore free riding, minimax, or maximin as sporting strategies.

(Group) risk

Early experiments in social psychology (Stoner 1961, Bem et al. 1965) show that groups are more likely to take on more risk than the individuals that make up those groups. Termed as a "risky shift", the analysed groups almost always took on more risk. It may be that individuals feel more comfortable adopting more risk if they can share the responsibility (blame) for a failure amongst the group, but if that responsibility falls on the individual, they are more risk-averse. This may also be related to the concept of "group think" (Janis 1972), where the individual may be more concerned about what others think as opposed to their own self-assessment. Rather than question those in charge or above them on the hierarchical chain, individuals will suppress their own views if they do not align and converge on a risk assessment based on a focal point rather than a distribution of the group (see, e.g., Bénabou 2013). We have observed the disasters that can occur when group think is allowed to flourish in the financial markets. The Global Financial Crisis (GFC) was rooted in the belief that the US housing market could not fail – until it did. This is not the first time the finance industry came close to collapse caused by a group-think situation, this problem was described as data-think, where everyone is relying on the same data: the fact that "everyone will be wrong about the same thing at the same time brought hedge fund Long-Term Capital Management close to collapse in 1998" (Hill 2018).[1] Thus far economics (especially behavioural) has predominately focused on individual decision makers and how risk preference, risk type, risk seeking/aversion has impacted their choices. Obviously, this becomes more complicated if we wish to explore group behaviour and attitudes, however, this may be where the sporting arena may be helpful. Goff and Tollison (1990, pp. 6–7) define it thus: "Sports events take place in a controlled environment and generate outcomes that come very close to holding 'other things equal'". Thus, sporting events can be seen as "quasi-natural field experiments" where subjects are acting in the natural environment instead of an artificial laboratory environment (natural incentives to perform) and players compete in an actual high-stakes contest with real incentives to be successful (Goff and Tollison 1990). In such an environment it may be possible to explore whether group assessments of risk differ from that of the individual. For example, an individual may be personally risk seeking, but they play in a team that has a demonstrable risk-averse attitude.

(Mismatched) incentives

We know that there have been mismatched incentives in sports due to the winner take all market (Frank and Cook 1995), where a small variation in performance or skill results in very large changes in payoffs. To quote Ricky Bobby[2] "if you're not first, you're last". Effectively summing up the problem: you are either the winner or you are nothing, and in such an environment any advantage can make the difference. This becomes especially apparent in the use of performance enhancing drugs , extreme training regimes, and the adverse health outcomes athletes may be willing to accept (Humphreys and Ruseski 2011). The short-term payoffs for cheating or abusing their health must outweigh any potential long-term damage or health concerns. The question for us to consider is: is there a behavioural approach on how we could realign incentives and payoffs? This seems to fit within a temporal discounting problem as current (or short term) rewards are valued much higher than future (long term) losses, where current consumption (utility) is overweighting the future negatives.

Biases

We will next discuss a set of biases and how sports have helped to explore such biases empirically. The list is far from complete; however, a nice overview of biases, in general, is provided by Dobelli (2013). Future studies could map them in more detail with available evidence in sports or how those biases can be analysed in detail in the sports setting. We focus on an interesting set that shows the power of sports data in exploring commonly discussed biases in behavioural economics. That also means that we do not intend to provide a detailed literature overview of papers within the area that we are discussing. Such an attempt would go beyond the aim and scope of this book chapter.

Sunk cost fallacy or escalation effects

One can only assume that sports clubs are subject to sunk cost fallacy when investing in players. This means that they deviate from the classical economics approach, which would assume that club decision-makers would only consider incremental costs in their decision making. The empirical design of using sports data has the advantage of holding the industry and competitive conditions constant, and of observing the actual reactions of the decision-makers (Pedace and Smith 2013). One of the first studies to explore sunk costs in the sports environment was conducted by Staw and Hoang (1995). They were inspired by experimental studies that explored sunk-cost effects focusing on resource utilization (see Arkes and Blumer 1985). When analysing the psychology of sunk costs, Arkes and Blumer (1985) find strong support that sunk costs are robust judgement errors (e.g., psychological justification of such a maladaptive behaviour is due to the desire to not appear wasteful (p. 125)). The innovation from Staw and Hoang (1995) was exploring the sunk-cost effect in a natural organizational setting using sports data (NBA data). They focused on the idea that people may perceive an association between draft order and the prospect of future performance (strong expectation of performance that persists long after the decline in court skills):

> In our view, the presence of cognitive bias, commitment, wastefulness, and justification may all be interwoven in natural situations. In the case of the NBA, taking a player high in the draft usually involves some extremely high, often biased, estimates of the person's skills. The draft also involves a very visible public commitment, one that symbolizes the linkage of a team's future with the fortunes of a particular player. Moreover, the selection of a player high in the draft signals to others that a major investment is being made, one that is not to be wasted. If the draft choice fails to perform as expected, team management can expect a barrage of criticism. Having to face hostile sports commentators as well as a doubting public may easily lead to efforts to defend or justify the choice. In the end, team management may convince itself that the highly drafted player just needs additional time to become successful, making increased investments of playing time to avoid wasting the draft choice.
>
> (p. 492)

The argument is that once the actual performance data in the NBA are available such a signal should not provide any further information about a player's ability (Borland, Lee, and Macdonald 2011). Focusing on playing time, survival in the league, and the likelihood of being traded, they found evidence for such a sunk-cost effect. For those better drafted players, they observed more playing time, a longer NBA career, and a lower probability to be traded (controlling for other important predictors such as performance, injury, or trade status). Camerer and Weber (1999) extended on that study by collecting a new sample and testing alternative rational explanations. They found an effect that was around half as strong in magnitude and statistical strength but that supported Staw and Hoang (1995)s basic conclusions while improving the methodological approach via accounting for alternative explanations. Such results are additionally supported by Coates and Oguntimein (2010) and Groothuis and Hill (2004), who found that the draft number affects NBA career duration even after controlling for performance measures. Leeds, Leeds, and Motomura (2015) further extend on those studies by focusing on the transition between states (lottery versus nonlottery or first- versus second-round picks) and allowing them to apply a regression discontinuity approach in the hope of handling omitted variable biases or causality issues. Their regression discontinuity results indicate that a lottery pick or first-round draft choices receive no more playing time for their draft status (over those drafted later).

On the other hand, further evidence for a sunk costs effect has been found when looking at Major League Baseball managers (Predace and Smith 2013) and the Australian Football League (AFL) (Borland et al. 2011), although the AFL study only found limited evidence that was largely concentrated around players' initial seasons at a club. Predace and Smith (2013) were motivated to understand whether new manager retention decisions were affected by whether or not the poor choice was made by a previous manager. Their results indeed indicate that poor performing players were significantly more likely to be divested by new managers than they were by continuing managers. Keefer (2015) criticized previous studies by stressing that players' draft numbers are a measure of expected productivity. Keefer (2017) also criticizes that the first-round players are not always the first player chosen by their team. Keefer (2017) uses the NFL draft as a natural experiment, using fuzzy RD as first-round players selected near the round cut-off receive a very large wage premium (first round wage premium of around 36–38%). Players selected near the round cut-offs are therefore essentially randomized and can be used to identify a sunk cost effect via the effect of compensation on, for example, the number of games started. One may also argue the superstars are easier to see as their overall level of skill stands out, but as you proceed back into the general draft pool, athletes become more clustered and the skill levels between players become smaller which means that it becomes much more difficult to observe skill differences. At this point the decision becomes much more random – this may not actually be a reflection of players' actual overall potential but just on what is observably different at this early point in their career. The results indicate sunk cost effect (a 10% increase in compensation was linked with 2.7 additional games started). However, Keefer (2015) criticized that such a result may just represent heuristic thinking and therefore the question emerges whether or not the sunk-cost fallacy persists when teams receive performance feedback. He, therefore, explored the exogeneous variation in compensation when players become eligible for free agency or change teams. Here, he also finds a substantial sunk cost effect.

It is interesting to look beyond these results to other sports fields, such as soccer. Soccer is fascinating, due to having fewer restrictions in maintaining a competitive balance between teams in the form of salary caps or a draft system. However, using German Bundesliga data, Hackinger (2019) finds that playing time is mainly driven by previous or predicted performance, which means that coaches and managers ignore high transfer fees in that decision process. Alternatively, the Oakland Athletics (A's) baseball club fiscal and statistical strategy was made famous by the 2011 movie Moneyball starring Brad Pitt as club manager Billie Beane (see also Lewis 2004). The A's have built a highly competitive and successful team, able to compete with baseball heavyweights like the New York Yankees or the Boston Red Sox by going against the mainstream by embracing sunk cost thinking. In recent years they have been trading away "superstars" to build a better team – in a statement to the Wall Street Journal[3] Oakland GM David Forst said:

> We've always had to operate a little differently than everybody else. We're never afraid to be wrong, and if that involves trading away good players, then we're OK with that, because, ultimately, we have a lot of conviction in the players we're getting in our half of the deal.

Action bias

Behavioural economics has challenged the classical assumption that how an outcome comes about should not matter. We often feel the emotion of regret when looking back on what turned out to be bad decisions. There is substantial available evidence that indicates people regret actions more if the outcome is reached by action rather than inaction (for an overview see Zeelenberg et al. 2002). But Zeelenberg et al. (2002, p. 314) also stress the importance of accounting for decisions made in response to things that happened earlier. This means that if the prior outcomes were negative, you are more likely to be inclined to improve future outcomes and therefore regret inactions more. Using scenarios from the sports domain (soccer coach decisions), they confront subjects in an experiment with a situation in which soccer coaches either won or lost a match prior to the current one. Their findings indicate that previous negative outcomes provide a reason to act and that decisions not to act, which are followed by a negative outcome, trigger regret. Thus, when a prior game was lost, a coach who acted would feel less regret than one who did not act. At least the active coach tried to prevent (further) losses.

In general, experiments are useful in that context as you can explore what happens if two individuals arrive at the same negative outcome with and without acting. Such laboratory experiments can be extended by applying physiological measures such as heart rate variability monitors, that have been used as physiological markers of emotions (see, Dulleck et al. 2011, 2014, 2016, Torgler 2019, Macintyre et al. 2021). Sports data is also useful as it allows going beyond using hypothetical questions which was the core methodological approach to explore action biases (Bar-Eli et al. 2007). Bar-Eli et al. (2007) therefore looked at elite goalkeepers during penalty kicks to explore whether an action bias existed in the real world. Goalkeepers are experienced in their decision-making domain and highly motivated to perform well. Penalty kicks are also interesting in that context; due to the almost simultaneous-move game characteristic, goalkeepers cannot de facto afford to wait to see how the player kicks the penalty (Bar-Eli et al. 2007). The authors stress that the norm for goalkeepers in penalty kicks is to act, which means jumping to the right or the left. Data from 286 penalty kicks shows that goalkeepers chose to jump to their right or left in 93.7% of cases, while the utility-maximizing behaviour would have been to stay in the goal's centre if the decision were based on the probability of stopping the ball. The authors show that if a goalkeeper behaves according to the probability matching principle, they should stay in the centre for around 28.7% of the kicks but they only choose to stay in 6.3% of the time (see Table 2.1). They, therefore, conclude that action bias could explain such a behaviour: "[I]f the goalkeeper stays in the centre and a goal is scored, it looks as if he did not do anything to stop the ball" (p. 614).

Future studies could explore whether the level of action bias is influenced by specific contextual factors (e.g., importance of the game) or individual characteristics (e.g., experience, gender, age, etc.). Bar-Eli et al. (2007) also note issues around the dynamics: "If goalkeepers will always choose to stay in the center, however, kickers will start aiming all balls to the sides, and it will no longer be optimal for the goalkeeper to stay in the center" (p. 616). This may also be linked to the general question of whether biases attenuate, fully disappear, or even reverse once they are reported to a broader audience (see, e.g., Schwert 2003).

Outcome bias

A commonly discussed bias in behavioural economics is outcome bias, which means that we evaluate decisions based on the results rather than the actual

Table 2.1 Penalty Jump and Kick Direction and Stopping

		Jump direction			
		Left	Centre	Right	Total
Kick direction	Left	18.90% 29.6%	0.30% 0.0%	12.90% 0.0%	32.20% 17.4%
	Centre	14.30% 9.8%	**3.50%** **60%**	10.80% 3.2%	**28.70%** **13.4%**
	Right	16.10% 0.0%	2.40% 0.0%	20.60% 25.4%	39.20% 13.4%
	Total	49.30% 14.2%	**6.30%** **33.3%**	44.40% 12.6%	39.20% 14.7%

Source: Derived from Bar-Eli et al. (2007, pp. 612–613).

decision process itself. Sports are an interesting setting to explore outcome biases because of the importance of performance appraisal. Sports data allows going beyond the lab, which has been the dominant method to explore outcome biases and performance appraisal. Kausel et al. (2019) focused on penalty shoot-outs as the outcome of a penalty shoot-out (who wins or loses), which seemed to be unrelated to actual in-game performance beforehand (performance at the individual player level as well as the team level). The ability to work with these data is a significant improvement over working with field data, as in the latter we are faced with the problem that actual performance is correlated with outcomes, which makes it hard to explore an outcome bias. Such independence between performance and outcome can then be linked to football players' subjective performance ratings. Kausel et al. (2019) therefore tested whether players on the winning team received better ratings than those on a losing team. Their data (which were derived from major soccer tournaments such as FIFA World Cup, UEF European Championship, and UEFA Champions League) indicate that winning the penalty had a positive effect on reporters' performance ratings, even after excluding players who participated in the penalty shoot-out. Beyond that, they found such an effect remains when using fixed effects (within-players' design).

Expert and judge's biases

Merkel et al. (2021) explored performance appraisal by looking for signs of optimism and/or positivity bias in rating semi-annual performance appraisals in the youth academy of a German Bundesliga. The interesting thing is that this allowed exploration of three types of evaluations: a rating of predicted future performance, a rating of remembered performance during the last half-year, and a record of instantly reported ratings of the actual performance in individual matches. Those ratings are important as they affect athletes' possibility to progress to the next age group. Their results indicate that predicted and remembered performance ratings significantly exceeded actual ratings. Such a deviation is more pronounced for the predicted performance, which indicates some asymmetry between looking forward and backward. Such biases may be unintentional, while other biases can be more intentional.

Nationalistic biases have offered an interesting avenue for past explorations. In general, events such as the Olympics provide a rich data source to explore such biases; as various fields such as ski jumping, figure skating, diving, etc. rely on judges' scores. As Zitzewitz (2006, p. 68) points out:

> [I]n most settings, attempts to study favoritism empirically would be frustrated by the difficulty of observing where one should expect favoritism.
> (e.g., who is "friends" with whom)

The sports environment, on the other hand, allows us to explore whether judges are nationalistically biased. Beyond that, Zitzewitz (2006) explored whether such a bias varies with strategic considerations, which would indicate *intentionality*. The sports setting also provides the opportunity to explore incentives based on different institutional conditions. Zitzewitz (2006, p. 69) discusses the differences between ski jumping and figure skating. In ski jumping, judges are chosen by the Federation International du Ski (FIS), while national federations choose the judges to be represented at Olympics in figure skating. Zitzewitz (2006) even observes that in figure skating, bloc judging or vote trading is found. One would therefore expect more nationalistic biases in figure skating. In addition, as FIS selects judges based on pre-Olympic events, one may expect to observe more nationalistic biases in the Olympics compared to the pre-Olympic events (which he finds to be true). In general, Zitzewitz (2006) finds a relatively large effect. For example, a nationalistic bias in figure skating translates to an average of 0.7 higher ranking position placement. He stresses that some of his findings make it difficult to rationalize with tastes (e.g., for a particular national style of skating) or unconscious biases:

> Examples include the fact that the national identity and past judging bias record of the other panel members appears to affect scores or the fact that biases vary in a way that accords with judges' career concerns.
>
> (p. 70)

Emerson, Seltzer and Lin (2009) looked at diving competitions from the 2000 Summer Olympic Games to see whether judges have preferences for individual divers due to, for example, style. They stress that a residual from their model represents the difference between judges' scores and the predicted score of judges for a diver given the nationalities of the judge and the diver. They conduct an analysis of variance predicting the residuals using individual divers as an explanatory factor, which means that the coefficient would indicate a judge's preference for individual divers due to unobserved reasons after controlling for nationalistic preferences (p. 130). Their results indicate that only one judge reported differences that are of statistical significance. Overall, they observe strong evidence of nationalistic favouritism.

Further studies judges' or referees' biases looked at gymnastic judges (Flessas et al. 2015, Heiniger and Mercier 2019), combat sports (Myers et al. 2006), soccer (Torgler 2004, Pope and Pope 2015). Ansorge and Scheer (1988) looked at the gymnastic competition at the 1984 Olympic Games and found judges not only overscore gymnasts from their own countries but also underscore gymnasts from countries who are in close competition with their own country. Campbell and Galbraith (1996) find some evidence that the bias against Olympic figure-skaters is stronger for medal contenders than for competitors who are less strong.

Zitzewitz (2014) also explored the interesting policy adjustment of reducing transparency among the International Skating Union (ISU) via no longer reporting which judge gave which score after the vote-trading scandals in the

1998 and 2002 Olympics. ISU hoped to reduce outside pressure on judges in order to reduce favouritism and corruption, but Zitzewitz (2014) was able to show that nationalistic bias and vote trading actually increased slightly without being statistically significant after the reforms. He points out that "[i]f nationalistic bias has increased in importance relative to vote trading, we might expect to see a single positive outlier score when a compatriot is on the panel" (p. 23).

The literature on referees' home court biases is closely connected to this literature, particularly in the area of soccer. The paper by Garicano, Palacios-Huerta, and Prendergast (2005) on extra allowance time when the home team is behind by one goal (compared to when being ahead by one goal) influenced many studies. Dohmen and Sauermann (2016) provide an excellent overview of that area of research. When looking at the extra time, they conclude that there is evidence for systematic referee bias in the second half of the game. The effect is strongest when the home team is one goal behind before the stoppage time begins. In addition, the bias is larger in Spain compared to Germany, possibly due to the higher travel distance (longer than 700 kilometres, compared to 400 in Germany). Dohmen and Sauermann (2016) also review other decisions such as awarding goals or penalty kicks, as they have a more immediate impact on the outcome of a game. The overview indicates that home-biases are visible for penalty kicks. Home teams benefit from a larger fraction of awarded penalty kicks that are wrongly given or disputable when being behind by one goal (see Dohmen 2008b). Similarly, various studies (but not all) found a bias regarding the award of yellow and red cards, controlling for players' behaviour, noting that bias is triggered by the crowd density (Dohmen and Sauermann 2016). Overall, Dohmen and Sauermann (2016) summarize the biases into two categories: those driven by social and those by material payoffs. Social payoffs are linked to the size and composition of the supporting crowd or distance to the crowd. However, they stress that social forces can be partly offset by material payoffs, such as increasing the referees' wages, or by better monitoring their decisions.

The question of what happens with referee bias once the stadium is empty is an interesting avenue to consider. After a serious act of hooligan violence between supporters from Calcio Catania and Palermo Calcio in 2007, the Italian government forced teams to play their home games without spectators if they had stadiums with deficient safety standards. Pettersson-Lidbom and Priks (2010) took advantage of the situation to study the difference in an empty stadium. Using data from Serie A and Serie B for the season 2006/2007 up to the point when all teams (apart from Catania) played in front of spectators again (842 games), they find that referees significantly change their behaviour in games played without spectators. Home teams are punished less harshly than the away teams with spectators, but more harshly without spectators. Similarly, Bryson et al. (2021) take advantage of the COVID-19 pandemic as a natural experiment that induced a near-complete absence of fans in sporting arenas. Using a large data set from 6481 football games and 17 leagues played before and after the mid-season shutdown, they find that the absence of crowds reduces home advantages. Significantly fewer yellow cards were awarded to the away team without a crowd, narrowing down the gap between the home and away teams by around a third.

Hot hand fallacy and momentum effect

A natural avenue in the history of behavioural economics was the exploration of whether we see patterns where there is actual randomness. Our brains are usually well-equipped to see patterns, as such a skill increases survival chances. However, one cannot exclude the possibility that we are subject to cognitive illusions. In one of the most famous sports papers, Gilovich, Vallone, and Tversky (1985) investigated whether or not there is a hot hand in basketball by looking at the Philadelphia 76ers in the 1980–1981 season, as a large number of individuals (including sports experts) believe that a player has a better chance of making a successful shot after having made the last two or three. The innovative approach looked at conditional probabilities for nine players (shooting percentage of having missed or hit the last shot, last two, and last three). Their study could not find a hot hand. In fact, eight of the nine players' probability of a hit was actually lower following a hit than a miss.

That result inspired a very large set of different studies, which are too numerous to properly discuss. One goal of the studies was to achieve more controllability. The problem is that the game itself is subject to a rich context where other effects may take place. For example, a "hot shooter" may believe they are on fire and may therefore take more difficult shots, which may reduce the success rate. Or the opposing team may start guarding a "hot shooter" more closely, reducing future success rates (Koehler and Conley 2003). Consequently, studies focused on measuring and analysing free-throw successes. However, this focus is not free of problems. First, there is a high probability of success in free throws (around 75%) and this brings the problem of potential time lags (Koehler and Conley 2003). New free throw opportunities are often too far apart. Thus, researchers started looking at long-distance shootout contests such as the annual NBA competition where eight of the best three-point shooters compete against each other, taking five uncontested shots for five pre-determined sports around the three-point arc, allowing for 60 seconds to finalize all the shots. A hot hand hypothesis would suggest that a shooter would have fewer runs (e.g., HHHHH (one run) versus HMHMH (five runs) but that does not seem to be the case (Koehler and Conley 2003)). When comparing expected and actual runs, Koehler and Conley (2003) indicate a lack of a hot hand effect on NBA Long Distance Shootouts. However, Burns (2004) emphasizes that the hot hand phenomenon has two separate components: the hot hand belief regarding dependence and a hot hand behaviour following streaks. In other words, invalidating a belief does not necessarily invalidate the behaviour that is based on that belief (p. 300):

> There is no doubt that the beliefs people hold play an important role in their decision making and thus identifying those beliefs is useful. However, unless one thinks it is better to score less in basketball than would

be possible if a simple cue was given some weight, then it appears that a research focus on belief without regard to behavior has led to the misanalysis of an important decision-making phenomenon.

(p. 327)

Stressing the advantage of analysing reason in Gigerenzer's (2000) framework of adaptiveness, Burns (2004) uses simulations to show that streaks are valid allocation cues for deciding who should be given a shot, allowing the team to score more.

Studies around the hot hand fallacy or a momentum effect have explored beyond basketball (namely in baseball, tennis, golf (including golf putting), soccer, volleyball, darts, tenpin bowling, or horseshoe tossing), but a key problem remains that such studies fail to understand the actual cognitive processes around it in more detail (Alter and Oppenheimer 2006). Focusing on neuroscientific insights or identifying settings are interesting avenues that have a biological background. Burns (2004), for example, cites neuroscientific evidence that:

demonstrated that different areas of the brain are more activated by streaks than by nonstreaks. Not only do specific areas of the brain react to streaks, but the strength of the signal is related to the length of the streak. If the brain is wired to notice streaks, then it is unsurprising if it is also found that people utilize streaks in making choices. Furthermore it also implies that doing so is probably useful in some way.

(p. 299)

Page and Coates (2017) used professional tennis matches to understand the importance of a winner effect that could be driven by testosterone changes, arguing that the winner effect might be mediated by a physiological feedback loop: "winning leads to higher levels of, or increased sensitivity to, testosterone, which in turn raises the likelihood of further victories" (p. 531). However, testosterone should not drive the results for female tennis players (females have 10–20% of the testosterone levels of males, Coates 2012). Their results indeed indicate sex differences. Men who won a closely fought tie-break had around 60% chance of winning the following set, while this winner effect did not exist among women. The importance of focusing on the biology has been advocated by Coates (2012), looking in detail at traders. He stresses that:

economics needs to put the body back into the economy. Rather than assuming rationality and an efficient market – the unfortunate upshot of which has been a trading community gone feral – we should study the behavior of actual traders and investors, much as the behavioural economists do, only we should include in that study the influence of their biology.

(p. 36)

In general, behavioural economics has failed to fully explore the possibilities of biology (Torgler 2016). Several recent contributions have shown that we can learn a lot by studying humans from an evolutionary perspective (see, e.g., Wilson 2019). Surprisingly, several behavioural economists have been very critical regarding evolutionary psychology. Thaler (2015), for example, stresses in his book *Misbehaving* that "accepting the theory of evolution as true does not mean that it needs to feature prominently in an economic analysis. We know people are loss averse; we don't need to know whether it has an evolutionary explanation" (p. 261). Tversky is also said to have pointed out: "Listen to evolutionary psychologists long enough and you'll stop believing in evolution" (Lewis 2017, p. 336). This somehow goes back to the academic fight or intellectual battle between Gigerenzer and Tversky and Kahneman (see in detail Lewis 2017). Gigerenzer emphasized the importance of adaptive theories and the relation between the mind and the environment rather than the mind alone (for a discussion see also Torgler 2021b). In his *Psychology Review* article Gigerenzer (1996) stressed that "the issue is not whether or not, or how often, cognitive illusions disappear. For him, the focus should be rather the construction of detailed models of cognitive processes that explain when and why they disappear" (p. 592). Gigerenzer (2004) also recollects the following discussions with Herb Simon:

> Herb applauded the demonstrations of systematic deviations from expected utility by Kahneman, Tversky, and others. But what did he think when the followers of Kahneman and Tversky labeled these demonstrations the study of "bounded rationality?" I asked him once, and his response was "That's rhetoric. But Kahneman and Tversky have decisively disproved economists' rationality model." Herb was surprised to hear that I held their notion of cognitive illusions and biases to be inconsistent with his concept of bounded rationality. I think he liked their results so much that he tended to overlook that these experimenters accepted as normative the very optimization theories that Herb so fought against, at least when the results were interpreted as cognitive illusions. A true theory of bounded rationality does not rely on optimization theories, neither as descriptions nor as norms of behavior ... A systematic deviation from an "insane" standard should not automatically be called a judgmental error, should it? "I hadn't thought about it in this way".
>
> Herb replied (pp. 396–397)

(Limited) attention or hyper attention

Players and fans alike are always looking for a win, and anything that might help that outcome is warmly embraced, however, anything that "might" impinge upon success quickly becomes anathema, even if it is completely illogical. For example, the colour green is seen as a major problem for equestrian riders and NASCAR drivers – even a hint of green being worn in the audience spells bad luck for a horse and its rider,[4] because green was linked back to major NASCAR accidents in the 1920s.[5] While some of the superstitions held by players when it comes to certain colours may seem odd, there is a good amount of research to back some of it up. While it sounds like a myth, being in the red corner for Olympic combat sports such as boxing, taekwondo, Greco–Roman wrestling, and freestyle wrestling, does statistically improve the chances of winning (Hill and Barton 2005). This colour effect has been shown to carry over to eSports with "death matches" in 2004s First-Person Shooter (FPS) game Unreal Tournament. Ilie et al. (2008) found that over a three-month period (1347 observations) the red teams won 54.9% of the matches – even though players were anonymous, and the player avatars were visually identical except for the team colours. Piatti et al. (2012) undertook an analysis of the red effect on professional Rugby League (Australia) teams over 30 years (1979–2008), which covered 5604 individual matches. They found that wearing some amount of red resulted in teams winning more often than teams without any red in their jersey stripes – specifically, that by shifting from no-red to a little increased the probability of winning by 4.3 percentage points and by shifting from a little red to red being a major colour in the strip increased the probability of winning by 7.5 percentage points. While the effect has been shown to be present across several sports, the underlying cause of the effect is still not clear, i.e., is it as simple as just the increased visibility of the colour, or is it biologically encoded in our DNA from a millennium of evolution? It would be interesting to extend this research to understand the role of colour in all aspects of sport.

One of the oldest sports training tips across the world is probably "keep your eyes on the ball," it does not matter which sport was being talked about – but one would assume it is relevant for non-ball sports as well i.e., watch the puck (clay pigeon), focus on the target (bullseye), etc. But what happens when athletes become stressed and take that maxim to extremes? As discussed above, high levels of stress and pressure can lead to individuals making sub-optimal decisions – one of the reasons for this is hyper-vigilance (Schultz 1966, Janis and Mann 1977). Essentially, this is when athletes begin to second-guess their choices and switch from the usual automatic and instinctual behavioural responses into a more laborious and time-consuming step-by-step thought process (Lehner et al. 1997, Beilock and Carr 2001, Bourne and Yaroush 2003). The hyper attention focus on every detail, rather than natural processes, results in slowed reaction times and degraded performance, reverting to maladaptive overthinking (Epstein and Katz 1992) or obsessive focus on singular aspects or tasks to the neglect of all else. This can lead to an inability to respond to or quickly react to changes outside the focal point – a possible example of this is Biaggio's 1994 FIFA World Cup finals penalty shot miss, where he was so focused on correctly striking the ball, he may have not given enough attention to aiming where he was kicking the ball (which went flying well above the cross bar).

Challenging topics: some examples

In this section, we will discuss how sports data can provide a tool for the exploration of challenging topics, particularly if we try to go outside the laboratory or observe human behaviour in the labour force. We will briefly discuss three examples.

Cooperation

Team sports data allow us to explore in detail how players cooperate and interact, as one is able to see how athletes interact together and under what circumstances (e.g., decisiveness of the game situation). While the cooperation literature is quite extensive (for an overview, see, e.g., Christakis 2019), the dynamics of cooperation are still not well enough understood beyond a lab or simulation setting. In repeated interactions, a higher payoff can be achieved through conditional cooperation or reciprocity. In other words, following rules of good behaviour can be a good strategy. Game theorists have explored this question in detail. Through repeated interaction, you can achieve peaceful cooperation; for example, as exemplified by the Folk theorem. Future expected punishment can enforce cooperation, despite a strong short-term conflicting interest (incentive to cheat). In other words, "prospect of vengeful retaliation paves the way for amicable cooperation" (Nowak and Highfield 2011, p. 29). Various punishment strategies can then be discussed, as by Axelrod (1984), via a tournament or competition that resulted in identifying the winning strategy. Tit-for-tat, developed by Anatol Rapoport, performed best in this setting. Nowak and Highfield (2011) report fascinating simulations conducted by Martin Nowak. His innovation was introducing chance (cooperation with a certain probability). The most powerful strategy in the dynamic interplay of cooperation and selfishness in a world that started with primordial chaos (random strategy) was a generous tit-for-tat strategy. Always meet cooperation with cooperation; but when faced with defection, cooperate for one in every three encounters. In other words, the recipe for forgiveness was probabilistic. In another simulation the winning strategy was:

> If we have both cooperated in the last round, then I will cooperate once again. If we have both defected, then I will cooperate (with a certain probability). If you have cooperated and I defected, then I will defect again. If you have defected and I have cooperated, then I will defect.
>
> (p. 43)

We argue that the sports environment can also provide an interesting environment in which to understand cooperation and free-riding behaviour. Accordingly, we discuss an interesting study by Brouwer and Potters (2019) that focused on cyclists' breakaways. During such a breakaway, riders are required to cooperate if they are keen to build a lead over the chasing peloton that has more manpower. But there is a social dilemma in this situation. As air resistance can fatigue a rider, anyone in this newly formed "team" may try to minimize being in the leading position to have more energy for a final sprint (effort-saving strategy). A rotation formation would be a highly cooperative formation to deal with free-riding incentives. Free-riding would mean refusing to lead the group, or underperforming by exerting less effort when at the front.[6] Such shirking is, as Brouwer and Potters (2019) found, harder to detect. The authors find a positive effect of group size and group strength on breakaway success, but the effect is concave (reaching the optimal level at 26 riders, meaning that adding another rider reduces the chances of success). In those situations where the benefits of free-riding are smaller, such as during mountain stages, breakaways are more likely to be successful.

Furthermore, we have previously stressed that interactions can be clearly measured in the sports context. This means we can explore how individual characteristics (e.g., dominance, beauty, experience, being new in a team, etc.) are connected to collaboration.

Emotions

Understanding emotions is important for behavioural economics as it contributes to a better understanding of human nature. As Simon (1983) emphasized, a general theory of thinking and problem solving requires incorporating the influence of emotion. We have substantial evidence in cognitive psychology or neuroscience that emotions influence memory, judgment, or decision-making. They have important functionalities that helped humans survive in meeting threats, challenges, and opportunities. They provide guidance in providing rapid and reliable information, acting as communication mechanisms in our social interactions and therefore acting as a coordination tool (Keltner and Lerner 2010). Elster (1998) classified emotions into social emotions (e.g., anger, hatred, guilt, shame, pride, admiration, or like), counterfactual emotions (unrealized possibilities such as regret, rejoicing, disappointment, or elation), anticipatory emotions (e.g., fear or hope), realized emotions (e.g., grief or joy), and material emotions (e.g., envy, malice, indignation, or jealousy). Material emotions are a particularly interesting area when exploring emotions with sports data. There is substantial evidence that your relative income situation is connected to positional concerns and can affect your happiness or wellbeing or can trigger envy and jealousy (for a discussion, see Frey et al. 2013). One empirical challenge is identifying the proper reference group, another is the ease with which one can explore behavioural responses in the work environment due to positional concerns. The sports environment provides a unique opportunity to explore whether an increase in income differences, which is transparently available for some disciplines such as basketball, leads to a performance increase or decrease in a competitive environment that often encourages social comparisons (Frey et al. 2013). Looking at basketball (NBA) and soccer (German Bundesliga) Frey et al. (2013) find support that relative income disadvantage is correlated with a decrease in individual performance. Such results are interesting from a policy perspective if those consequences are also found in other work environments (e.g., how to design pay-for-performance mechanisms to encourage performance and cooperation within teams). Schaffner and Torgler (2008) show that closeness affects positional concerns when comparing different reference groups using NBA data. The strongest effects of positional concerns on performance are found among players with similar work profiles (playing the same position and being a teammate) compared to other characteristics such as geographical closeness, age, and experience closeness.

Social capital

Social capital has widely explored how social capital creates human capital (Coleman 1998, Paldam 2000), lubricates economic exchange (Putnam 1983), builds networks, and creates trust (Coleman 1988, Portes 1998, Woolcock and Narayan 2000, Fukuyama 2003). While sport has been examined through the lens of social capital theory, for the most part it has been outward looking. Specifically, researchers have explored how sport is used to engage with society to better the lives of players or the community, e.g., community development (Walseth 2007, Skinner et al. 2008), health and wellbeing (Kawachi, et al. 2008, Kim et al. 2020), participation rates (Kumar et al. 2018), or volunteerism (Kay and Bradbury 2009, Darcy et al. 2014). However, there seems to be very little research that looks inward to the effect of social capital on the way that players interact with each other or use their social capital to be more successful. Even though little research has looked internally, discussions have pointed to areas that would be of great interest, for example, if social capital leads to more efficient transactions through access to more information, it should result in coordinated activities for mutual benefit and a reduction in the likelihood of opportunistic behaviour (Dasgupta 1999). The question remains: if this would be relevant in competitive interactions as well as those of mutual benefit?

Social capital theory has been explored in many real-world environments but is always difficult to truly capture what is occurring, due to the amount of noise and other observable events. However, it may be possible to explore such theories in sport, specifically in strategic games where we could observe changes in player behaviour based on increased levels of social capital. The additional advantage here is that the sporting environment enables all other factors to be held constant. Poker tournament is one sport in which we could observe players' strategies and styles as they play against differing opponents where they have greater or fewer interactions over time (interaction being a proxy for social capital or at least social experience). Some of this could be explained with information theory, where players with more information on the competitors should result in more even or close competitions, and by extension, it should be less likely that players directly engage each other and pick hands on which to compete. However, social capital would explain why these players engage in a form of competition where rather than compete directly with each other, they collaborate with each other to remove other players from the table – increasing the probability of winning overall.

One of the benefits of social capital in a strategic competitive environment like poker could be that players who have built up capital between them may be able to compete at a lower cost with each other than we would expect otherwise. For example, in multiplayer hands, players with social capital would not "push" as hard at each other and may engage in a type of strategic interaction known as coopetition or cooperative competition (Nalebuff and Brandenburger 1997). Rather than a zero-sum outcome, players may be willing to engage in this type of activity to lower losses even whilst competing. This theory has been very difficult to explore in the real world as data where companies are engaged in competition are difficult to obtain and few laboratory experimentations in economics have been published (see management study by Kraus et al. 2018).

Back to the future

From chess to alphago and beyond

The miniaturization of electronics was led by the invention of the transistor in 1947 by Bell Labs, replacing the large vacuum tubes used up until that point. One of the unexpected side effects of this process was enabling computer technology to be used beyond its intended goals. This included the creation of the first "home" computers, and computers being used in games like chess (Los Alamos chess in 1957). For the most part, these initial offerings were clunky and relatively easy to beat by human players, mostly due to the lack of a single winning strategy and the near-infinite number of move options available to players. This began to change in the late 1970s with the Bell Labs offering (Belle) regularly beating Master level players. Over time the games have become better, mostly through brute force processing, i.e., memorizing countless winning games and the pruning of irrelevant outcomes as moves are made. More recent systems have deviated from this blunt approach in lieu of more nuanced systems using artificial intelligence (AI) to play more like a human and anticipate moves. The first generation of these systems began with Deep Blue (IBM), which lost to world champion Garry Kasparov (4–2) in 1996, but after major upgrades beat Kasparov in 1997. Interestingly, the attempt to use AI to play chess was the easier option (and possibly based on the Western bias of chess being the difficult game): Go is the much harder game for computers to solve. Go originated in China sometime around 1000BC and is still widely popular today in eastern Asia. It is played on a larger board (generally 17×17 or 19×19) with a greater number of possible moves. Estimates of the number of legal moves[7] available on a 19 $\times$ 19 board are approximately 2.08×10^{170}. This is vastly more than chess and has the additional problem that a player can move to any open space on the board and is not restricted to the moves available to the remaining pieces. Given the massive numbers of potential moves it is not possible to follow the same strategies used by early Chess programs, thus Go requires a significant degree of intuition to pre-empt the opponent's strategy.

Historically, chess offered an ideal lab setting to test and explore cognitive processes (for a detailed discussion see Rasskin-Gutman 2009). In his autobiography *Models of My Life*, Herb Simon (1996) stresses that:

> For most of us those of us who have not won million-dollar lotteries, or suffered sudden crippling accidents life is much like the chess game. We make hundreds of choices among the alternative paths that lie before us and, as the result of those choices, find ourselves pursuing particular, perhaps highly specialized, careers, married to particular spouses, and living in particular towns. Even if we point to a single event as the "cause" of one of these outcomes, closer scrutiny of the path we have trod would reveal prefatory or preparatory events and choices that made the occurrence of the critical event possible.
>
> (p. 113)

Pioneers of AI such as Allen Newell, Herbert Simon, and others realized that chess could be used as a vehicle to try simulating thought processes via computer programming.[8] A good example is Allen Newell's (1954) paper *The Chess Machine: An Example of Dealing with Complex Task by Adaptation*. He was interested in the problem of playing good chess as an ultra-complicated problem that requires thinking about mechanisms and programs necessary to handle such problems. His approach was to use a broad collection of rules of thumb (e.g., chess principles to follow, measurements to make, what to do next, how to interpret those rules of thumb etc.) and focus on describing how such a set of rules is defined and organized to achieve solutions: "the intent to see if *in fact* an organized collection of rules of thumb can pull itself up by its bootstraps and learn to play good chess" (p. 23). Newell and Simon (1972) also derived insights from how individuals played chess, using a protocol in which persons were asked to talk aloud, mentioning moves considered and aspects of the situation. Out of that problem-behaviour, they generated graphs that show the person's searches in a space of chess positions. They were fascinated to discover what an experienced chess player was able to see or perceive when looking at a chess position. Chase and Simon (1973) concluded in their analysis that superior performance is achieved from the ability to encode positions into larger perceptual chunks, which consisted of familiar sub-configuration of pieces. Thus, selective search guided by heuristics can compensate for being subjected to bounded rationality (Simon 1996).

Adriaan de Groot's (1965) *Thought and Choice in Chess*[9] was a pioneering book on the cognitive processes of chess; outlining an attempt to understand the thought processes underlying skilled chess playing by also using thinking aloud protocols with experimental sessions already held between 1938 and 1943:

> [A] subject was presented with an unfamiliar position taken from an actual tournament or match game and asked to find and play a move as though he were engaged in a tournament game of his own. The verbal report was to be as full and explicit a rendering of the subject's thoughts as possible, to include his plans, calculations, and other considerations leading to the move decision.
>
> (p. v)

Rasskin-Gutman (2009) acknowledges that de Groot's research helped us understand that grandmasters have a larger amount of chess knowledge that helped them to focus better on general patterns of the position and identify particular characteristics.

Herb Simon (1996) also stresses in his autobiography that he always celebrated December 15, 1955 as the birthday of heuristic problem solving by computer, because it was

> the moment when we knew how to demonstrate that a computer could use heuristic search methods to find solutions to difficult problems. According to Ed Feigenbaum, who was a graduate student in a course I was then teaching in GSIA, I reacted to this achievement by walking into class and announcing, "Over the Christmas holiday, Al Newell and I invented a thinking machine." We were not slow in broadcasting our success. In a letter to Adriaan de Groot, on January 3, 1956, I reported: You will be interested to learn, I think, that Allen Newell and I have made substantial progress on the chess-playing machine except that at the moment it is not a chess-playing machine but a machine that searches out and discovers proofs for theorems in symbolic logic. The reason for the temporary shift in subject matter is that we found the human eye and the portions of the central nervous system most closely connected with it to be doing too much of the work at the subconscious level in chess-playing, and we found this aspect of human mental process (the perceptual) the most difficult to simulate. Hence, we turned to a problem-solving field that is less "visual" in its content. Two weeks ago, we hit upon a procedure that seems to do the trick, and although the details of the machine coding are not yet worked out, there seem to be no more difficulties of a conceptual nature to be overcome. By using a human (myself) to simulate the machine operating by rule and without discretion this simulated machine has now discovered and worked out proofs for the first twenty five or so theorems in Principia Mathematica. The processes it goes through would look very human to you, and corroborate in many respects the data you obtained in your chess studies.
>
> (p. 2006)

Deepmind's[10] solution was to adopt an AI strategy with the development of AlphaGo, and its ability to beat the best human player in the world was not programmed – AlphaGo learned how to play and win by itself. This is machine learning AI at its best: the system was not programmed in any way to play Go. Instead, it started by watching thousands of games and learnt the game through observation. Thus, AlphaGo is classified as a General AI. It was not programmed or taught to do a task; it used its own ability to learn in order to gain information about the game. This AI revolution demonstrated that not only can machines learn to imitate human behaviours but can also anticipate them, and because it is a General AI it can potentially learn to do anything that it is presented with.

What happens next should also be very interesting for behaviouralists. If General AI can learn to play any game (once we provide it with some framework) then the scope for its interaction with humans and our response may be astounding. One of the general issues we have had running experimental economics was the absence of realism (the abstractness) and our inability to create realistic experimental conditions where we could elicit real human responses and behaviours. The use of computing in experiments (over pen and paper) means that we can observe every aspect of an experiment. By adopting General AI, we could start to run experiments that might be otherwise impossible with real people. For example, high-cost, high-risk, or life-and-death situations experiments that would be too dangerous or stressful for humans to undertake could be replaced with AI participants. Additionally, we could observe the impact of any number of changes to how sports are played using AI players (e.g., rules changes) or learn human behaviours that are difficult for most of us to understand.

Poker AI

Poker is often thought of as simply a game of probabilities or risk, and as such it should be easy to generate unbeatable computer players. However, much like the game of Go, it is the human elements of the game that make it so hard to emulate human players. One of the central skills of the game is bluffing (misleading opponents), which is not only about the players' ability to control tells (ticks that give away the bluff) but also the correct betting sequences. As early as 1998, Billings et al. (1998) flagged poker as a potential testbed for AI describing it as:

> a game of imperfect knowledge, where multiple competing agents must deal with risk management, agent modelling, unreliable information and deception, much like decision-making applications in the real world.
>
> (p. 228)

This prediction become a reality when the poker program dubbed "Pluribus" learned to play six-player no-limit Texas Hold'em and performed significantly better than humans over the course of 10,000 hands of poker (Brown and Sandholm 2019). This demonstrated that a General AI is able to learn just about everything we can think of throwing at it; thus, the question for us is, what do we want to do with it in the future?

AI and eSport

While the idea of eSport is relatively new to most people, it has been around in some form since at least 1972, through a Space Invaders tournament with over 10,000 contestants (Picknell 2019).[11] eSports are one of the few sports not based on physical attributes such as strength but on reflex speed and mental acuity. This means that size and strength are no longer factors, and everyone, regardless of age or gender, can compete on an even playing field. Even so, there still is some inherent bias as computer games have long been seen as something that boys do rather than girls, resulting in a much higher pool of male players versus females on a competitive level. There also appears to be a fundamental difference in the type of games preferred by male and female players. While the economics of the business (prize money, sponsorships, viewership, etc.) have been explored, the players and their decision making have remained relatively untouched. eSport represents an untapped field for analysis and potentially the running of experiments – as these computer-based environments lend themselves to the development of specific types of choices and behaviours made by players. That is, modules and game designs could be specifically set up to test decision-making, collaboration, altruism, and a broad range of other human insights.

Another major advantage of eSport tournaments is that they are played live or live streamed players are seen, while the online version of the games is played anonymously. This results in a comparable environmental difference; because in one the player is an anonymous avatar, and in the other, the player is an identifiable person. This poses some interesting questions about how decision-making and behaviour could be impacted by information and identity, i.e., do players change behaviour if all they know is an avatar? Some previous research has indicated that players endow their avatars with their own beliefs and social norms, but there is also a likelihood that some players use their avatar as an aspirational representation of themselves (Wiederhold 2013, Praetorius and Görlich 2020, Ratan 2020). This could include choosing avatars of a different gender or race or choosing to behave in a matter that they would like to in the real world but feel for whatever reason they are unable. Running experiments in such an environment would enable participants to be much more invested in the outcomes and may elicit a more realistic response than we would observe in purely laboratory experiments.

Another advantage of eSports is what Slovic (2010) describes as the "feeling of risk". These digital environments are able to manipulate and measure sensory input and alter the perceived and actual levels of risk faced by players. Just like experimentalists do in a laboratory setting, programmers would be able to test the perceptions of risk versus actual risk by control or set the probability of certain events occurring and explore player reactions and decision-making.

Conclusion

Throughout this book chapter, we have tried to show how powerful sports data can be in understanding questions that are at the core of behavioural economics. We sought to show how scholars have advanced knowledge by finding new avenues through which they might improve on previous papers that used sports data, by finding other areas of exploration within the sports environment. We have also tried, without searching for completeness, to discuss throughout the paper what else can be explored in the future in more detail. When exploring biases Camerer and Weber (1999) raise an important point:

> First, establishing systematic mistakes using naturally occurring data is very difficult. Of course, this does not mean we should avoid such hard work and exploit the superior control of the lab; it just means that the standard of proof for mistakes outside the lab is high, and should be. It is also likely that important field anomalies will not be established by a single study, but by a series of studies which build on earlier results. Behavioral economists have learned that the best way to win an argument about the existence of systematic mistakes is to take complicated rationalizations offered by critics seriously (no matter how cockamamie they are), and collect more data to test them.
>
> (p. 81)

Using sports data is a strategy to move towards that direction when working with naturally occurring data. Sports data allow us to use a variety of different datasets and look at different sport disciplines when exploring aspects in the area of behavioural economics. Our aim was to show that sports data are a valuable tool of thought and exploration in the interplay between speaking to theorists and searching for facts, which is particularly important when challenging the status quo in a particular scientific field.

Acknowledgements

For helpful comments and suggestions, thanks are due to Jillian Cortese and Alison Macintyre.

Notes

1 Hill, A. (2018). Why groupthink never went away. Financial Times, May 7th, 2018. Available from https://www.ft.com/content/297ffe7c-4ee4-11e8-9471-a083af05aea7.

2 Talladega Nights: The Ballad of Ricky Bobby – starring Will Ferrell and Sacha Baron Cohen, directed by Adam McKay is a parody on NASCAR Racing (2006).
3 Story sourced from the Wall Street Journal at https://www.wsj.com/articles/the-moneyball-as-find-a-new-inefficiency-other-teams-players-11566322019.
4 Sourced from Eclipse magazine https://eclipsemagazine.co.uk/5-horse-racing-superstitions-explained/.
5 Sourced from https://jalopnik.com/how-the-color-green-became-a-deadly-bad-luck-superstiti-1763008917.
6 There is also the strategic issue where rider from leading teams try to join breakaways with the intention of slowing the overall pace to allow the peloton to catch up within a certain distance to the finish or to burn out the breakaway. Alternatively, they may also seek to ensure the peloton does success if the breakaway does not contain any GC contenders.
7 See Tromp and Farnebäck (2016) Combinatorics of Go. Working Paper p. 22 (Table 4). Accessed from https://tromp.github.io/go/gostate.pdf.
8 For a discussion on pioneering work on computer chess by Claude Shannon, Alan Turing, Alex Bernstein, and his authors, see Newborn (1975).
9 For follow up books see, e.g., Avni (2004) or Aagard (2004).
10 Deepmind is a London based AI lab that is a subsidiary of internet juggernaut Google.
11 Accessed from https://learn.g2.com/esports.

References

Aagaard, J. (2004). *Inside the chess mind: How players of all levels think about the game.* Gloucester Publishers plc.

Allen, R. D., Hitt, A. M., and Greer, C. R. (1982). Occupational stress and perceived organizational effectiveness in formal groups: An examination of stress level and stress type. *Personal Psychology*, 35, 359–370.

Allison, P. D. (1999). *Multiple regression: A primer.* Pine Forge Press.

Alter, A. L., and Oppenheimer, D. M. (2006). From a fixation on sports to an exploration of mechanism: The past, present, and future of hot hand research. *Thinking & Reasoning*, 12(4), 431–444.

Arkes, H. R., and Blumer, C. (1985). The psychology of sunk cost. *Organizational Behavior and Human Decision Processes*, 35(1), 124–140.

Avni, A. (2004). *The grandmaster's mind: A look inside the chess thinking-process.* Gambit Publications Ltd.

Bar-Eli, M., Azar, O. H., Ritov, I., Keidar-Levin, Y., and Schein, G. (2007). Action bias among elite soccer goalkeepers: The case of penalty kicks. *Journal of Economic Psychology*, 28(5), 606–621.

Baumeister, R. F. (1984). Choking under pressure: Self-consciousness and paradoxical effects of incentives on skill performance. *Journal of Personality and Social Psychology*, 46, 610–620.

Baumeister, R. F., and Showers, C. J. (1986). A review of paradoxical performance effects: Choking under pressure in sports and mental tests. *European Journal of Social Psychology*, 16, 361–383.

Beilock, S. L., and Carr, T. H. (2001). On the fragility of skilled performance: What governs choking under pressure? *Journal of Experimental Psychology: General*, 130, 701–725.

Bem, D. J., Wallach, M. A., and Kogan, N. (1965). Group decision making under risk of aversive consequences. *Journal of Personality and Social Psychology*, 1(5), 453–460.

Bénabou, R. (2013). Groupthink: Collective delusions in organizations and markets. *The Review of Economic Studies*, 80(2), 429–462.

Billings, D., Papp, D., Schaeffer, J., and Szafron, D. (1998). Poker as a testbed for AI research. In: Mercer, R. E., and Neufeld, E. (Eds.), *Advances in Artificial Intelligence. Canadian AI 1998.* Lecture Notes in Computer Science (Lecture Notes in Artificial Intelligence), vol 1418. Springer, Berlin, Heidelberg.

Borland, J., Lee, L., and Macdonald, R. D. (2011). Escalation effects and the player draft in the AFL. *Labour Economics*, 18(3), 371–380.

Bourne, L. E., and Yaroush, R. A. (2003). Stress and cognition: A cognitive psychological perspective. Technical Report. Washington, D.C.: National Aeronautics and Space Administration (N.A.S.A.).

Brouwer, T., and Potters, J. (2019). Friends for (almost) a day: Studying breakaways in cycling races. *Journal of Economic Psychology*, 75, 102092.

Brown, N., and Sandholm, T. (2019). Superhuman AI for multiplayer poker. *Science*, 365(6456), 885–890.

Bryson, A., Dolton, P., Reade, J. J., Schreyer, D., and Singleton, C. (2021). Causal effects of an absent crowd on performances and refereeing decisions during Covid-19. *Economics Letters*, 198, 109664.

Burns, B. D. (2004). Heuristics as beliefs and as behaviors: The adaptiveness of the "hot hand". *Cognitive Psychology*, 48(3), 295–331.

Butler, J. L., and Baumeister, R. F. (1998). The trouble with friendly faces: Skilled performance with a supportive audience. *Journal of Personality and Social Psychology*, 75(5), 1213–1230.

Camerer, C. F., and Weber, R. A. (1999). The econometrics and behavioral economics of escalation of commitment: A re-examination of Staw and Hoang's NBA data. *Journal of Economic Behavior & Organization*, 39(1), 59–82.

Cao, Z., Price, J., and Stone, D. F. (2011). Performance under pressure in the NBA. *Journal of Sports Economics*, 12(3), 231–252.

Caruso, R., Di Domizio, M., and Savage, D. A. (2017). Differences in national identity, violence and conflict in international sport tournaments: Hic Sunt Leones! *Kyklos*, 70(4), 511–545.

Chan, H. F., Savage, D. A., and Torgler, B. (2019). There and back again: Adaptation after repeated rule changes of the game. *Journal of Economic Psychology*, 75, 102129.

Chase, W. G., and Simon, H. A. (1973). Perception in chess. *Cognitive Psychology*, 4(1), 55–81.

Christakis, N. A. (2019). *Blueprint: Evolutionary origins of a good society.* Little, Brown Spark.

Coates, J. (2012). *The hour between dog and wolf: Risk-taking, gut feelings and the biology of boom and bust.* Penguin Books.

Coates, D., and Oguntimein, B. (2010). The length and success of NBA careers: Does college production predict professional outcomes. *International Journal of Sport Finance*, 5(1), 4–26.

Cohen-Zada, D., Krumer, A., and Shtudiner, Z. (2017). Psychological momentum and gender. *Journal of Economic Behavior & Organization*, 135, 66–81. https://doi.org/10.1016/j.jebo.2017.01.009

Cohen-Zada, D., Krumer, A., Rosenboim, M., and Shapir, O. M. (2017). Choking under pressure and gender: Evidence from professional tennis. *Journal of Economic Psychology*, 61, 176–190.

Coleman, J. S. (1998). Social capital in the creation of human capital. *American Journal of Sociology*, 94, S95–S120.

Cooper, J. (1989). The military and higher education in the USSR. *The ANNALS of the American Academy of Political and Social Science*, 502, 108–119.

Darcy, S., Maxwell, H., Edwards, M., Onyx, J., and Sherker, S. (2014). More than a sport and volunteer organisation: Investigating social capital development in a sporting organisation. *Sport Management Review*, 17(4), 395–406.

Dasgupta, P. (1999). Economic progress and the idea of social capital. In: Dasgupta, P. and Serageldin, I. (Eds.), *Social capital: A multifaceted perspective*. Washington, D.C.: World Bank, pp. 325–424.

de Groot, A. (1965). *Thought and choice in chess*. Mouton Publishers.

Diamond, J. (2019). The 'moneyball' A's find a new inefficiency: Other Teams' Players. In the *Wall Street Journal*, August 20, 2019. Available at https://www.wsj.com/articles/the-moneyball-as-find-a-new-inefficiency-other-teams-players-11566322019.

Dobelli, R. (2013). *The art of thinking clearly: Better thinking, better decisions*. Hachette, UK.

Dohmen, T. J. (2008a). Do professionals choke under pressure? *Journal of Economic Behavior & Organization*, 65(3–4), 636–653.

Dohmen, T. J. (2008b). The influence of social forces: Evidence from the behavior of football referees. *Economic Inquiry*, 46(3), 411–424.

Dohmen, T., and Sauermann, J. (2016). Referee bias. *Journal of Economic Surveys*, 30(4), 679–695.

Duggan, M., and Levitt, S. D. (2002). Winning isn't everything: Corruption in sumo wrestling. *American Economic Review*, 92(5):1594–1605.

Dulleck, U., Fooken, J., Newton, C., Ristl, A., Schaffner, M., and Torgler, B. (2016). Tax compliance and psychic costs: Behavioral experimental evidence using a physiological marker. *Journal of Public Economics*, 134, 9–18.

Dulleck, U., Ristl, A., Schaffner, M., and Torgler, B. (2011). Heart rate variability, the autonomic nervous system, and neuroeconomic experiments. *Journal of Neuroscience, Psychology, and Economics*, 4(2), 117–124.

Dulleck, U., Schaffner, M., and Torgler, B. (2014). Heartbeat and economic decisions: Observing mental stress among proposers and responders in the ultimatum bargaining game. *PLoS One*, 9(9), e108218.

Elias, N., and Dunning, E. (1966). Dynamics of sports groups with special reference to football. *British Journal of Sociology*, 17(4), 388–402.

Elster, J. (1998). Emotions and economic theory. *Journal of Economic Literature*, 36(1), 47–74.

Emerson, J. W., Seltzer, M., and Lin, D. (2009). Assessing judging bias: An example from the 2000 Olympic Games. *The American Statistician*, 63(2), 124–131.

Eremin, O., Walker, M. B., Simpson, E., Heys, S. D., Ah-See, A. K., Hutcheon, A. W., Ogston, K. N., Sarkar, T. K., Segar, A., and Walker, L. G. (2009). Immuno-modulatory effects of relaxation training and guided imagery in women with locally advanced breast cancer undergoing multimodality therapy: A randomised controlled trial. *Breast*, 18(1), 17–25.

Flessas, K., Mylonas, D., Panagiotaropoulou, G., Tsopani, D., Korda, A., Siettos, C., Di Cagno, A., Evdokimidis, I., and Smyrnis, N. (2015). Judging the judges' performance in rhythmic gymnastics. *Medicine & Science in Sports & Exercise*, 47(3), 640–648.

Frank, R. H. (1984). Interdependent preferences and the competitive wage structure. *RAND Journal of Economics*, 15(4), 510–520.

Frank, R. H., and Cook, P. J. (1995). *The winner-take-all society*. The Free Press.

Frey, B. S., Schaffner, M., Schmidt, S. L., and Torgler, B. (2013). Do employees care about their relative income position? Behavioral evidence focusing on performance in professional team sport. *Social Science Quarterly*, 94(4), 912–932.

Fukuyama, F. (2003). Social capital and civil society. In: Ostrom, E. and Ahn, T. K. (Eds.), *Foundations of Social Capital*. Edward Elgar, pp. 291–308.

Garicano, L., Palacios-Huerta, I., and Prendergast, C. (2005). Favoritism under social pressure. *Review of Economics and Statistics*, 87(2), 208–216.

Gauriot, R., and Page, L. (2018). Psychological momentum in contests: The case of scoring before half-time in football. *Journal of Economic Behavior & Organization*, 149, 137–168.

Gigerenzer, G. (1996). On narrow norms and vague heuristics: A reply to Kahneman and Tversky. *Psychological Review*, 100, 592–596.

Gigerenzer, G. (2000). *Adaptive thinking: Rationality in the real world*. Oxford University Press.

Gigerenzer, G. (2004). Striking a blow for sanity in theories of rationality. In: Augier, M., and March, J. G. (Eds.), *Models of a man: Essays in memory of Herbert A. Simon*. MIT Press, pp. 389–409.

Gilovich, T., Vallone, R., and Tversky, A. (1985). The hot hand in basketball: On the misperception of random sequences. *Cognitive Psychology*, 17(3), 295–314.

Goff, B. L., and Tollison, R. D. (Eds.). (1990). *Sportometrics*. Texas A&M University Press.

Groothuis, P. A., and Hill, J. R. (2004). Exit discrimination in the NBA: A duration analysis of career length. *Economic Inquiry*, 42(2), 341–349.

Groysberg, B., Nanda, A., and Nohria, N. (2004). The risky business of hiring stars. *Harvard Business Review*, 82(5), 92–101.

Hackinger, J. (2019). Ignoring millions of euros: Transfer fees and sunk costs in professional football. *Journal of Economic Psychology*, 75, 102114.

Hamilton, D. R. (2018). *How your mind can heal your body*. Carlsbad, California: Hay House.

Harb-Wu, K., and Krumer, A. (2019). Choking under pressure in front of a supportive audience: Evidence from professional biathlon. *Journal of Economic Behavior & Organization*, 166, 246–262.

Heiniger, S., and Mercier, H. (2019). Judging the judges: A general framework for evaluating the performance of international sports judges. arXiv preprint arXiv:1807.10055.

Hickman, D. C., and Metz, N. E. (2015). The impact of pressure on performance: Evidence from the PGA TOUR. *Journal of Economic Behavior & Organization*, 116, 319–330.

Hill, A. (2018). Why groupthink never went away. *Financial Times*, May 7, 2018. Available at https://www.ft.com/content/297ffe7c-4ee4-11e8-9471-a083af05aea7

Hill, R. A., and Barton, R. A. (2005). Red enhances human performance in contents. *Nature*, 435, 293–293.

Howell, R. (1975). The USSR: Sport and politics intertwined. *Comparative Education*, 11(2), 137–145.

Humphreys, B., and Ruseski, J. (2011). Socio-economic determinants of adolescent use of performance enhancing drugs: Evidence from the YRBSS. *The Journal of Socioeconomics*, 40(2), 208–216.

Ilie, A., Ioan, S., Zagrean, L., and Moldovan, M. (2008). Better to be red than blue in virtual competition. *Cyber Psychology and Behaviour*, 11(3), 375–377.

Iso-Ahola, S. E., and Dotson, C. O. (2016). Psychological momentum-a key to continued success. *Frontiers in Psychology*, 7, 1328.

Jamal, M. (1984). Job stress and job performance controversy: An empirical assessment. *Organizational Behavior and Human Performance*, 33, 1–21.

Janis, I. L. (1972). *Victims of groupthink: A psychological study of foreign-policy decisions and fiascos*. Houghton Mifflin.

Janis, I. L., and Mann, L. (1977). *Decision making*. The Free Press.

Kahn, L. M. (2000). The sports business as a labor market laboratory. *Journal of Economic Perspectives*, 14(3), 75–94.

Kahneman, D., and Tversky, A. (1979). Prospect theory: An analysis of decision under risk. *Econometrica*, 47(2), 263–291.

Kausel, E. E., Ventura, S., and Rodríguez, A. (2019). Outcome bias in subjective ratings of performance: Evidence from the (football) field. *Journal of Economic Psychology*, 75, 102132.

Kawachi, I., Subramanian, S., and Kim, D. (2008). Social capital and health. In: Kawachi, I., Subramanian, S., and Kim, D. (Eds.), *Social Capital and Health*. Springer, New York.

Kay, T., and Bradbury, S. (2009). Youth sport volunteering: Developing social capital? *Sport, Education and Society*, 14(1), 121–140.

Keefer, Q. A. (2015a). Performance feedback does not eliminate the sunk-cost fallacy: Evidence from professional football. *Journal of Labor Research*, 36(4), 409–426.

Keefer, Q. A. (2017). The sunk-cost fallacy in the national football league: Salary cap value and playing time. *Journal of Sports Economics*, 18(3), 282–297.

Keltner, Da., and Lerner, J. S. (2010). Emotion. In: Gilbert, D., Fiske, S., and Lindsey, G. (Eds.), *The handbook of social science*, Vol. 1., Wiley, pp. 317–352.

Keinan, G. (1987). Decision making under stress: Scanning of alternatives under controllable and uncontrollable threats. *Journal of Personality and Social Psychology*, 52, 639–644.

Kho, A. Y., Liu, K. P., and Chung, R. C. (2014). Meta-analysis on the effect of mental imagery on motor recovery of the hemiplegic upper extremity function. *Australian Occupational Therapy Journal*, 61(2), 38–48.

Kim, A. C. H., Ryu, J., Lee, C. et al. (2021). Sport participation and happiness among older adults: A mediating role of social capital. *Journal of Happiness Studies*, 22, 1623–1641.

Koehler, J. J., and Conley, C. A. (2003). The "hot hand" myth in professional basketball. *Journal of Sport and Exercise Psychology*, 25(2), 253–259.

Kraus, S., Meier, F., Niemand, T., Bouncken, R. B., and Ritala, P. (2018). In search for the ideal coopetition partner: An experimental study. *Review of Managerial Science*, 12, 1025–1053.

Krumer, A. (2020). Pressure versus ability: Evidence from penalty shoot-outs between teams from different divisions. *Journal of Behavioral and Experimental Economics*, 89, 101578.

Kumar, H., Manoli, A. E., Hodgkinson, I. R., and Downward, P. (2018). Sport participation: From policy, through facilities, to users' health, well-being, and social capital. *Sport Management Review*, 21(5), 549–562.

Leeds, D. M., Leeds, M. A., and Motomura, A. (2015). Are sunk costs irrelevant? Evidence from playing time in the National Basketball Association. *Economic Inquiry*, 53(2), 1305–1316.

Lehner, P., Seyed-Solorforough, M., O'Connor, M. F., Sak, S., and Mullin, T. (1997). Cognitive biases and time stress in team decision making. *Transactions on Systems, Man, and Cybernetics Part A: Systems and Humans*, 27, 698–703.

Levitt, S. D. (2002). Testing the economic model of crime: The national hockey league's two-referee experiment. *Contributions in Economic Analysis & Policy*, 1(1).

Lewis, M. (2004). *Moneyball: The art of winning an unfair game*. W. W. Norton & Company.

Lewis, M. (2017). *The undoing project: A friendship that changed our minds*. W. W. Norton & Company.

Locke, E. A. (1968). Toward a theory of task motivation and incentives. *Organizational Behavior and Human Performance*, 3(2), 157–189.

Locke, E. A., Latham, G. P., Smith, K. J., and Wood, R. E. (1990). *A theory of goal setting & task performance*. Prentice Hall.

Loewenstein, G. (2005). Hot-cold empathy gaps and medical decision making. *Health Psychology*, 24(4), S49–S56.

Macintyre, Alison, Ho Fai Chan, Markus Schaffner, and Benno Torgler (2021). National Pride and Tax Compliance: A Laboratory Experiment Using a Physiological Marker. CREMA Working Paper No. 2021–07. Center for Research in Economics, Management and the Arts (CREMA).

McCormick, R. E., and Tollison, R. D. (1984). Crime on the court. *Journal of Political Economy*, 92(2), 223–235.

Meglino, B. M. (1977). Stress and performance – are they always incompatible. *Supervisory Management*, 22, 2–13.

Meichenbaum, D. (2007). Stress inoculation training: A preventative and treatment approach. In: Lehrer, M., Woodfolk, R. L., and Slime, W. S. (Eds.), *Principles and practices of stress management*. Guilford Press.

Merkel, S., Chan, H. F., Schmidt, S. L., and Torgler, B. (2021). Optimism and positivity biases in performance appraisal ratings: Empirical evidence from professional soccer. *Applied Psychology*, 70, 1100–1127.

Myers, T. D., Balmer, N. J., Nevill, A. M., and Al Nakeeb, Y. (2006). Evidence of nationalistic bias in muaythai. *Journal of Sports Science & Medicine*, 5(CSSI), 21–27.

Nalebuff, B. J., and Brandenburger, A. M. (1997). Co-opetition: Competitive and cooperative business strategies for the digital economy. *Strategy & Leadership*, 25(6), 28–33.

Newborn, M. (1975). *Computer chess*. ACM Monograph Series. Academic Press.

Newell, A. (1954). The Chess Machine: An Example of Dealing With a Complex Task by Adaptation, P-620, Rand Corporation.

Newell, A., and Simon, H. A. (1972). *Human problem solving*. Prentice-Hall, Inc.

Nowak, M., and Highfield, R. (2011). *Supercooperators: Altruism, evolution, and why we need each other to succeed*. Simon and Schuster.

Paldam, M. (2000). Social capital: One or many? Definition and measurement. *Journal of Economic Surveys*, 14(5), 629–653.

Page, L., and Coates, J. (2017). Winner and loser effects in human competitions. Evidence from equally matched tennis players. *Evolution and Human Behavior*, 38(4), 530–535.

Pedace, R., and Smith, J. K. (2013). Loss aversion and managerial decisions: Evidence from major league baseball. *Economic Inquiry*, 51(2), 1475–1488.

Pettersson-Lidbom, P., and Priks, M. (2010). Behavior under social pressure: Empty Italian stadiums and referee bias. *Economics Letters*, 108(2), 212–214.

Piatti, M., Savage, D. A., and Torgler, B. (2012). The red mist? Red shirts, success and team sports. *Sport in Society*, 15(9), 1209–1227.

Picknell, D. (2019). What is esports and how did it become a $1 billion industry? Learning hub article August 20th, 2019. Accessed at https://learn.g2.com/esports

Pollak, R. A. (1976). Interdependent preferences. *The American Economic Review*, 66(3), 309–320.

Portes, A. (1998). Social capital: Its origins and applications in contemporary sociology. *Annual Review of Sociology*, 24, 1–24.

Postlewaite, A. (1998). Social status, norms and economic performances: The social basis of interdependent preferences. *European Economic Review*, 42, 779–800.

Praetorius, A. S., and Görlich, D. (2020). How Avatars Influence User Behavior: A Review on the Proteus Effect in Virtual Environments and Video Games, FDG '20: International Conference on the Foundations of Digital Games 49, 1–9.

Rasskin-Gutman, D. (2009). *Chess metaphors: Artificial intelligence and the human mind*. MIT Press.

Ratan, R., Beyea, D., Li, B. J., and Graciano, L. (2020). Avatar characteristics induce users' behavioral conformity with small-to-medium effect sizes: A meta-analysis of the proteus effect. *Media Psychology*, 23(5), 651–675.

Riordan, J. (1993). The rise and fall of soviet Olympic champions. *Olympika: The International Journal of Olympic Studies*, 2, 25–44.

Savage, D. A., and Torgler, B. (2012). Nerves of steel? Stress, work performance and elite athletes. *Applied Economics*, 44(19), 2423–2435.

Schaffner, M., and Torgler, B. (2008). Meet the Joneses: An Empirical Investigation of Reference Groups in Relative Income Position Comparisons. CREMA Working Paper No. 2008–13. Center for Research in Economics, Management and the Arts (CREMA).

Schmidt, S. L. (Ed.). (2020). *21st century sports: How technologies will change sports in the digital age*. Springer.

Schultz, D. P. (1966). *An experimental approach to panic behavior*. Group Psychology Branch.

Schwert, G. W. (2003). Anomalies and market efficiency (Chapter 15). In: Constantinides, G. M., Harris, M., and Stulz, R. M. (Eds.), *Handbook of economics of finance*. Elsevier, pp. 939–974.

Simon, H. (1983). *Reason in human affairs*. Stanford University Press.

Simon, H. A. (1996). *Models of my life*. MIT press.

Skinner, J., Zakus, D. H., and Cowell, J. (2008). Development through sport: Building social capital in disadvantaged communities. *Sport Management Review*, 11(3), 253–275.

Slovic, P. (2010). *The feeling of risk: New perspectives on risk perception*. Routledge.

Staw, B. M., and Hoang, H. (1995). Sunk costs in the NBA: Why draft order affects playing time and survival in professional basketball. *Administrative Science Quarterly*, 40, 474–494.

Stoner, J. A. (1959). A comparison of individual and group decisions involving risk, Master's Thesis, Antioch College, Available at https://dspace.mit.edu/bitstream/handle/1721.1/11330/33120544-MIT.pdf

Sullivan, S. E., and Bhagat, R. S. (1992). Organizational stress, job satisfaction and job performance: Where do we go from here? *Journal of Management*, 18, 353–374.

Thaler, R. H. (2015). *Misbehaving: The making of behavioral economics*. W. W. Norton & Company.

Thaler, R. H., and Johnson, E. J. (1990). Gambling with the house money and trying to break even: The effects of prior outcomes on risky choice. *Management Science*, 36(6), 643–660.
Toma, M. (2017). Missed shots at the free-throw line: Analyzing the determinants of choking under pressure. *Journal of Sports Economics*, 18(6), 539–559.
Torgler, B. (2004). The economics of the FIFA Football Worldcup. *Kyklos*, 57(2), 287–300.
Torgler, B. (2009). Economics of sports: A note to this special issue. *Economic Analysis and Policy*, 39(3), 333.
Torgler, B. (2016). Can tax compliance research profit from biology? *Review of Behavioral Economics*, 3, 113–144.
Torgler, B. (2019). Opportunities and challenges of portable biological, social, and behavioral sensing systems for the social sciences. In: G. Foster (Ed.), *Biophysical measurement in experimental social science research*. Academic Press, pp. 197–224.
Torgler, B. (2020). Big data, artificial intelligence, and quantum computing in sports. In: S. L. Schmidt (Ed.), *21st century sports: How technologies will change sports in the digital age*. Springer, pp. 153–173.
Torgler, B. (2021a). Symbiotics> Economics? CREMA Working Paper No. 2021-15. Center for Research in Economics, Management and the Arts (CREMA).
Torgler, B. (2021b). The Power of Public Choice in Law and Economics. CREMA Working Paper No. 2021–04. Center for Research in Economics, Management and the Arts (CREMA).
Van Ours, J. C., and Van Tuijl, M. A. (2016). In-season head-coach dismissals and the performance of professional football teams. *Economic Inquiry*, 54(1), 591–604.
Walseth, K. (2008). Bridging and bonding social capital in sport – experiences of young women with an immigrant background. *Sport, Education and Society*, 13(1), 1–17.
Wiederhold, B. K. (2013). Avatars: Changing behavior for better or for worse? *Cyberpsychology, Behavior, and Social Networking*, 16(5), 319–320.
Wilson, D. S. (2019). *This view of life: Completing the Darwinian revolution*. Pantheon Books.
Witt, R. (2005). Do players react to sanction changes? Evidence from the English Premier League. *Scottish Journal of Political Economy*, 52(4), 623–640.
Woolcock, M., and Narayan, D. (2000). Social capital: Implications for development theory, research and policy. *The World Bank Research Observer*, 2, 225–249.
Wright, P. (1974). The harassed decision maker: Time pressures, distractions and the use of evidence. *Journal of Applied Psychology*, 59, 555–561.
Yerkes, R., and Dodson, J. D. (1908). The relationship of stimuli to rapidity of habit formation. *Journal of Comparative Neurological Psychology*, 18, 459–482.
Zeelenberg, M., Van den Bos, K., Van Dijk, E., and Pieters, R. (2002). The inaction effect in the psychology of regret. *Journal of Personality and Social Psychology*, 82(3), 314–327.
Zitzewitz, E. (2006). Nationalism in winter sports judging and its lessons for organizational decision making. *Journal of Economics & Management Strategy*, 15(1), 67–99.
Zitzewitz, E. (2014). Does transparency reduce favoritism and corruption? Evidence from the reform of figure skating judging. *Journal of Sports Economics*, 15(1), 3–30.

3 Sports performance, procedural rationality, and organizational inefficiency

Hannah Josepha Rachel Altman and Morris Altman

Introduction

There is significant evidence that organizational inefficiencies often persist in professional sports teams. We refer to these as x-inefficiency following upon Harvey Leibenstein's seminal contribution (1966). In other words, sports teams do less well than they ought to given the resources available to them since they are not making the best use of these resources. It follows, therefore, that they also might not be securing the best resources or inputs given their budget constraints. Such inefficiencies tend to be assumed away in the conventional models of the firm of which a sports team is but one example. It is a type of firm producing sports-related outcomes. Moreover, many sports teams, such as soccer, American football, rugby, baseball, basketball, and ice hockey teams are often embedded within larger organizational structures. These larger organizations produce their own specific outcomes of which the sports team is only a partial contributor.

The conventional wisdom tends to assume that market forces and/or the preference function of decision-makers will yield efficient outcomes. Outcomes that are not deemed to be satisfactory, therefore, are attributed to a lack of traditional factor inputs and, relatedly, to an absence of scale economies. As well, the absence of sufficient competitive markets or sub-optimal government policies is viewed as contributing causes to sub-optimal or non-satisfactory outcomes.

From this perspective, if one wishes to improve sports team outcomes, it follows that one would need to increase inputs (such as purchasing more expensive players and managers) and search for or try to develop improved technology (of which, sports data analytics is a more recently acknowledged contributing factor). Ceteris paribus, spending more money will yield improvements in sports team outcomes. This is, of course, unrelated to improvements in organizational efficiency since the latter is assumed to be maximized, a popular working assumption. Thus, if one makes this efficiency assumption, one rules out managerial and related inefficiencies as a potential cause of poor sports outcomes. One also tends to rule out how the sports team and organization is structured as a potential cause of poor sports

DOI: 10.4324/9781003080824-4

outcomes. The default cause of sub-optimal performance must be, by assumption, the lack of resources.

We model why and how performance outcomes of sports teams can be sub-optimal or x-inefficient (therefore, how the sports team and the larger organization within which it is embedded is managed becomes significant in any analysis) and why market forces can't easily correct this type of inefficiency (Altman and Altman 2015a, 2015b). Our theoretical narrative builds on:

- X-efficiency theory
- The concept of procedural rationality
- Information complexity and asymmetric information (related to bounded rationality)
- Outcome uncertainty
- The importance of heuristics to decisions-making
- Errors in decision-making
- Mental models
- The notion that decision-makers (team managers and owners) are not simply guided by the desire to maximize their teams' performance (related to their preference function).[1] This is especially the case when their sports team is embedded within a larger organization and when the sports team's performance is not the only determinant of the larger organization's profitability.

Consistent with the evidence we argue that different organizational forms (how the sports team and the larger organization are managed) and different understandings or mental models of what constitutes excellence in sports performance by decision-makers can significantly affect sports outcomes and are critical determinants of the level of organizational efficiency. Also, decision-makers can be characterized by 'managerial slack,' information gaps, and various decision-making 'biases' that yield sub-optimal outcomes from the perspective of sports performance. These inefficient outcomes can be a product of errors in decision-making, but they can also be consistent with the preferences of a cohort of decision-makers (what we refer to as rational inefficiencies). Also, the ability of inefficient sports organizations to be protected from market forces is critically important. This can impede the realization of efficient outcomes. But we also argue that inefficient or sub-optimally performing sports teams can remain competitive and survive in the face of better performing sports teams. There is a form of multi-equilibrium that allows for an array of sustainable sports teams and organizations across a spectrum of levels of performance outcomes.

In this chapter, we also distinguish between a sports team and a sports organization within which the sports team is embedded, and also, between the latter two and the owner of the sports team and organization. A sports team does not necessarily equal a sports organization of which the sports team is but one component. And, additionally, a sports team can be owned by a non-sport corporation where the sports team is but one component of this organization. The sports team might serve as a vanity component of the larger corporation. Owning a sports team, even if it loses and is not a top-ranked team or champion team, generates utility to the owner (Andreff 2014a; Sloane 1971). The sports team, even if it is not a winner, can also add to the marketing capacity of the owner-corporation to the extent that supporting a community's sports teams provides social value and utility to the community.[2] This can translate into supporting the other products of the larger organization that owns the sports team, controlling for the price and quality of the product.

Bearing this in mind, to be a profitable sports team does not imply being organizational efficient or x-efficient as a sports team. This is especially true when profitability depends on the popularity of a sports team. Losers can be extremely popular if they are an integral part of their community generating significant demand for them as a product. This demand can be comprised of ticket sales, team products, television rights, and the like. The conventional economic model presumes that efficient outcomes will prevail, at least in a reasonable period of time, possibly even in the long run. Inefficient outcomes should not, in theory, be tolerated by the market. But this prediction is not consistent with the evidence. In this chapter, we model how the persistence of inefficiency is possible and how even inefficient teams can serve to enhance the utility or happiness of the community they serve and, in so doing, be protected from the wrath of the market.

Finally, it is important to recognize that sports team ownership is not all about maximizing material gain or profit. Owners can maximize their utility simply by owning a team, even if it is x-inefficient. We argue that rational individuals would be most concerned about 'utility maximization' not necessarily about profit maximization, albeit the latter can feed into the former—it can be an argument or element in the owner's preference function (Andreff 2014a; Sloane 1971). And, not all forms of organizational structure are oriented to profit maximization. There are critical differences between investor-owned sports teams and community-owned sports teams wherein the latter often borrows from the cooperative or member-owned model of organizational structure. Community-owned sports teams seek to maximize the benefits accruing to members of the community whereas the investor-owned teams are oriented towards the interests of its much narrower membership based. Moreover, x-inefficient sports teams can also serve to generate community benefits which outstrip their x-inefficient performance. But, being x-efficient in sports performance, on the other hand, does not necessarily coincide with maximizing social welfare.

The major contribution of this chapter is to develop a unique behavioral economics framework (more generally, see Coates and Humphreys 2018). This framework will help determine the extent and origins of organizational inefficiency rooted in the theoretical concepts of procedural rationality, bounded rationality, smart decision-making, and the mental models of decision-makers as well as other teams members and the fans who are the ultimate customers of the output produced by sports teams. Unlike other theoretical and descriptive narratives in behavioral economics (Kahneman 2003; Kahneman and Tversky 1979), putting us more in line with Herbert Simon's perspective, we don't rely on irrational or systematically biased behaviour to explain the sup-optimal behavior of sports teams. The analytical framework we develop can be generalized to other organizations. What's critical to our approach, consistent with behavioral theories of the firm, is appreciating the importance of what actually transpires within the black box of the firm. Optimal outcomes need to be assessed from the perspective of decision-makers as well as from their decision-making environment and capabilities.

Rational decision-makers

When modeling organizational efficiency, it is important to determine and define what one means. From the perspective of more conventional economic models, the assumption is made that one has rational agents and rational behavior yields organizational efficiency. Organizational efficiency is defined in relation to the assumptions being made on what rational members of the organization should achieve in terms of productivity or outcomes (especially important for sports teams) given the organization's endowment of traditional factor input. Rational agents, therefore, should yield optimal outcomes. This means that in more conventional models there should be no organizational inefficiency, or what Leibenstein refers to as x-efficiency (1966).

Realizing optimal outcomes assumes that firm members are working as smart and as hard as they can (or, at least 'optimally' wherein effort inputs into the production function are fixed). In this modeling scenario with rational agents there is no analytical space for sub-optimal performance. Organizations with rational agents can't be performing inefficiently or x-inefficiently. Only irrational agents (assumed away) can yield sub-optimal outcomes. This theme is developed in a more conventional behavioral economics version pioneered by Kahneman and Tversky (1979) (see also Thaler and Sunstein (2008)), where sub-optimal outcomes become possible given their assumption that agents behave irrationally as they are given to systematically error-prone and biased (non-neoclassical) behavior (the heuristics and biases approach to behavioral economics). This stands in marked opposition to Simon's bounded rationality approach to behavioral economics wherein economic agents are rational even though their behavior may yield sub-optimal outcomes.

This point is clearly articulated by James March (1978), a close colleague of Simon's. Rationality, he argues, can't be defined and modeled outside of the context of the decision-making environment and the decision-making capabilities of decision-makers. March writes (1978, p. 589):

> Engineers of artificial intelligence have modified their perceptions of efficient problem solving procedures by studying the actual behavior of

human problem solvers. Engineers of organizational decision making have modified their models of rationality on the basis of studies of actual organizational behavior ... Modern students of human choice behavior frequently assume, at least implicitly, that actual human choice behavior in some way or other is likely to make sense. It can be understood as being the behavior of an intelligent being or group of intelligent beings....

This argument sits well with the smart decision-making narrative (Altman 2006, 2017c). Agents are smart, intelligent, they think things through, even when some of their choices are intuitive, meaning they are experientially informed. Therefore, choices are rational even if they are not what one would predict for neoclassical rational decision-makers. Even if one concludes that the coaches and managers of a sports team are making sub-optimal decisions, this does not imply that these choices aren't smart given their decision-making environment and decision-making capabilities. From this perspective, it becomes imperative to determine why smart decisions can generate sub-optimal performance in a sports team. Rationality, for Simon as it is for March, is context-dependent, and for this reason, this particular behavioralist approach to rationality differs from that of conventional economics. Moreover, this behavioralist approach is consistent with what one finds in other social sciences. Simon (1986, S210) argues:

> In its treatment of rationality, neoclassical economics differs from the other social sciences in three main respects: (a) in its silence about the content of goals and values; (b) in its postulating global consistency of behavior; and (c) in its postulating 'one world' that behavior is objectively rational in relation to its total environment, including both present and future environment as the actor moves through time.

Once again, critical to March and Simon's behavioralist approach to rationality is that it is directly related to the decision-making context. If rational decision-making is a key determinant of optimal performance, then it is important to understand the context within which these decisions are being made. Simon clearly develops the point that context matters. He and March do not dispute that human beings acting in the economic sphere (economic agents) are rational. They do not challenge this important assumption of conventional economics. Rather they disagree on how conventional economics *defines* rationality. Simon writes (1986, S210):

> I emphasize this point of agreement at the outset-that people have reasons for what they do-because it appears that economics sometimes feels called on to defend the thesis that human beings are rational. Psychology has no quarrel at all with this thesis. If there are differences in viewpoint, they must lie in conceptions of what constitutes rationality, not in the fact of rationality itself. The judgment that certain behavior is 'rational'

or 'reasonable' can be reached only by viewing the behavior in the context of a set of premises or 'givens.' These givens include the situation in which the behavior takes place, the goals it is aimed at realizing, and the computational means available for determining how the goals can be attained.

Thus, a helpful analytical starting point to better understanding why organizations are or are not efficient and why their outcomes are optimal from this behavioralist perspective is to assume that decision-makers are rational. This forces us to carefully examine the context in which decisions, be they good or bad, are made.

Vernon Smith (1962), a pioneer of experimental economics, makes a related point, basing his understanding of rational behavior and on what type of actual behavior contributes to generating the preferred outcomes of decision-makers (this is a form of satisficing behavior). This behavior can very well be, and usually is, non-neoclassical. But when such behavior yields optimal results from the perspective of the decision-makers, this should form the basis for constructing general norms for best practice behavior or decision-making processes. Smith does not define best practice behavior in terms of esoteric and quite general neoclassical behavioral norms, but rather from the ground up— how do real decision-makers generate optimal-satisficing outcomes in a particular context. Actually, using neoclassical norms to inform decision-making might very well result in an organization performing sub-optimally. Smith (2005, pp. 149–150; see also Smith 2003) writes:

> It is shown that the investor who chooses to maximize expected profit (discounted total withdrawals) fails in finite time. Moreover, there exist a variety of nonprofit-maximizing behaviors that have a positive probability of never failing. In fact, it is shown that firms that maximize profits are the least likely to be the market survivors. My point is simple: when experimental results are contrary to standard concepts of rationality, assume not just that people are irrational, but that you may not have the right model of rational behavior. Listen to what your subjects may be trying to tell you. Think of it this way. If you could choose your ancestors, would you want them to be survivalists or to be expected wealth maximizers?

This behavioralist approach does not presume that economic agents in general and decision-makers specifically are error-producing machines because they don't behave according to neoclassical theory. Rather, we need to learn from actual organizational behavior about what works and what does not work so as to generate optimal behavior and outcomes. Smith uses experimental settings to inform his thinking.

Gigerenzer (2007) develops a related bottoms-up approach to rational or smart decision-making. He argues that what appears to be persistent errors in decision-making because decision-makers are making use of decision-making short-cuts or heuristics, especially of the fast and frugal variety, and which deviate from the neoclassical behavioral norms, are often relatively optimal outcomes. He finds that these heuristics-based outcomes can be expected to be superior to what can be achieved when applying neoclassical behavioral norms.

Gigerenzer and Todd argue (2003, pp. 147–148):

> ...bounded rationality can be seen as emerging from the joint effect of two interlocking components: the internal limitations of the (human) mind, and the structure of the external environments in which the mind operates. This fit between the internal cognitive structure and the external information structure underlies the perspective of bounded rationality as ecological rationality – making good (enough) decisions by exploiting the structure of the environment ... Heuristics that are matched to particular environments allow agents to be ecologically rational, making adaptive decisions that combine accuracy with speed and frugality. (We call the heuristics "fast and frugal" because they process information in a relatively simple way, and they search for little information.) The study of ecological rationality thus involves analyzing the structure of environments, the structure of heuristics, and the match between them.

In defining rationality relative to decision-making Simon (1986, S211) points out that:

> The rational person of neoclassical economics always reaches the decision that is objectively, or substantively, best in terms of the given utility function. The rational person of cognitive psychology goes about making his or her decisions in a way that is procedurally reasonable in the light of the available knowledge and means of computation.

Simon further elaborates on his concept of bounded rationality to make it more specific and nuanced. This brings him to a discussion of process rationality which refers to the process of and the procedures used in arriving at a decision given the decision-making environment, the capabilities of the decision-maker, and the objectives of the decision-maker. Moreover, process rationality takes into consideration the possibility that decision-makers' understanding of what's best practice or optimal might be misconstrued or flat out wrong, but they rationally act upon such a misperception. Simon (1986, p. S211) argues that:

> ...if we accept the proposition that knowledge and the computational power of the decision maker are severely limited, then we must distinguish between the real world and the actor's perception of it and reasoning about it ... we must construct a theory (and test it empirically) of the

processes of decision. Our theory must include not only the reasoning processes but also the processes that generate the actor's subjective representation of the decision problem, his or her frame ... The rational person of neoclassical economics always reaches the decision that is objectively, or substantively, best in terms of the given utility function. The rational person of cognitive psychology goes about making his or her decisions in a way that is procedurally reasonable in the light of the available knowledge and means of computation [it is context dependent].

Our approach to 'optimality' is similarly different from the conventional approach. It also differs from the heuristics and biases approaches developed through the work of Kahneman and Tversky (1979). We apply this approach to sports teams and focus on the objectives of decision-makers and the reality of their decision-making environment and their decision-making capabilities. This, in turn, relates to Simon's narrative on procedural rationality. From the modeling perspective that we introduce in this chapter, it is important to focus on how decision-making actually takes place inside the firm or organization—in our case the sports team and the organization within which it is embedded. It is critically important therefore to venture into the black box of the firm, something that conventional economics has tended to avoid as it tries to explain how, in theory, firms or organizations behave optimally. But understanding how the firm actually works is central to a behavioral theory of the firm with no-prior assumption of optimality being made (Cyert and March 1963; Leibenstein 1966; Williamson 1975).

We approach the concept of optimality, in part, as consisting of what decision-makers wish to achieve and whether or not, and the extent to which, they have realized these objectives given their decision-making environment and their decision-making capabilities. Again, this is fundamental to Simon's notion of procedural rationality. A firm or an organization is procedurally rational if it achieves this type of optimality in outcomes. For Simon, this procedural rationality is a form of behavior which he calls satisficing to distinguish it from neoclassical rationality. Satisficing is a form of *practical* rationality.

Neoclassical rationality results in the highest possible outcome levels (in sports, wins relative to losses, championships, ranking, etc) and is typically associated with highly calculating behavior, perfect knowledge of all pertinent information (and no information asymmetries), and perfect foresight. It is also associated with all members of the organization working as hard or as smart as possible (a more minimalist assumption would be effort inputs are fixed at some high level). Deviations from the neoclassical ideal, some would argue, represents a form of irrational (and certainly sub-optimal) behavior. We argue, consistent with March, that satisficing, herein referred to more generally as smart decision-making, is rational because it is a product of a cognitive, thought-out process.

Smart behavior that is procedurally rational yields optimal outcomes given the preferences of decision-makers. And, from the perspective of sports teams, this need not translate into maximizing wins or league standings or the profit of the sports organizations. This would be even more true of the organizations that own sports teams. Moreover, smart decision-making is consistent with errors in decision-making. Decision-makers might believe that they are doing the best they can, given their preferences, but their organizations can be underperforming from the perspective of procedural rationality given errors in decision-making. These errors result in rational inefficiencies—one can be rational and smart without operating along a procedurally rational 'production possibility frontier'. We explicitly incorporate errors in decision-making and, relatedly, Bayesian updating (where decision-makers update their behavior), into Simon's procedural rationality narrative.

But from an objective perspective, a satisficing type of outcome, consistent with the preferences of decision-makers, even if it is procedurally rational, need not be the best that the firm or broader organization can achieve if the preferences of decision-makers are not oriented towards optimizing outcomes. There are higher level outcomes that are achievable given the decision-making environment of decision-makers and their decision-making capabilities. These higher-level outcomes are achievable given the appropriate preferences of decision-makers and the appropriate incentive environment within the organization. This level of organizational efficiency would be the best that can be achieved given the decision-making environment and the decision-making capabilities of decision-makers. Therefore, this makes no reference to neoclassical efficiency which in turn makes no reference to the actual decision-making environment and the actual decision-making capabilities of decision-makers. If the environment and capabilities are improved upon, such as the introduction of data analytics in sports team decision-making (embedded as one component of the decision-making machine), this would improve the potential and realizable outcomes of the firm or organization. Simon's main point of focus is on how to achieve procedural rationality. We integrate Leibenstein's concept of x-efficiency, which incorporates aspects of procedural rationality, with his focus on the sub-optimal preferences of decision-makers as a source of organizational inefficiency. We refer to this as x-efficiency plus.

In this x-efficiency plus narrative, the sources of x-inefficiency or organizational inefficiency can be related to the preferences of decision-makers (this is distinct from errors in decision-making) and errors in decision-making. The latter can incorporate factors related to imperfect information, power relationships across decision-makers, and 'biases' such as focusing on the look of the athlete as opposed to looking at evidence of the athlete's performance or the dominance of sports data analytics versus the latter being part of a decision-making organizational matrix. This broad analytical framework addresses the issue of x-inefficiency from the perspective of how the firm is organized by smart decision-makers, where these decision-makers can make choices that result in sports teams and organizations performing sub-optimally from the perspective of our x-efficiency plus analytical framework. This also allows us to identify the factors that contribute to sports teams doing the best they can, given their constraints, where the best might require changes in the preferences of decision-makers. In sports teams, this could involve changes in the preferences of owners, managers, coaches, and scouts—the decision-making team.

Sports x-inefficiency or organizational inefficiency and multi-equilibria

Sports x-inefficiency or organizational inefficiency or their opposites can be situated in relation to the context within which decisions are made—the decision-making environment and decision-making capabilities of the decision-makers. But what is also critical here is to explain x-inefficiency with regards to sports performance and what the benchmarks of x-efficiency might be. One need also address the important question of how and why organizational inefficiency can persist amongst sports teams, especially given our assumption that decision-makers are rational. This takes us well beyond that conventional economics approach wherein organizational efficiency should be delivered either by the rational preferences of decision-makers or by market forces.

There are two types of outcomes that are typically evaluated with regard to sports teams. One relates to the profitability of the sports organization within which the sports team is embedded. It may be that the sports team is the same as the sports organization. In that case, the sports organization is built around the sports team. The second outcome relates to the performance of the sports team in terms of winning percentage, league standing, championship, and the ranking of the team's players, for example.

From a theoretical and practical perspective, it is important to explicitly model how x-inefficient sports teams and organizations can survive and persist over time. This modeling would apply to any organization, not only sports-related ones. Some of these points have been elaborated on in our *Moneyball* chapter included in this book. Building upon some of one of the authors previous research (Altman 2017a), we argue that a multi-equilibrium framework helps to explain a wide array of sports team related outcomes that persist over time, inclusive of sports teams that perform relatively poorly or persistently never make it to the top of their sport. In conventional economic modeling reducing the level or extent of x-efficiency should result in higher average cost. In a very simply model, reducing x-efficiency (increasing x-inefficiency) results in lower productivity and, therefore, in higher average cost. This is illustrated in Equation (1) below, a very simple model with one factor input, where w is the cost per unit of factor input and (Q/L) is productivity. With regards to sports teams, w would incorporate player salaries, that of managers, coaches, trainers, health professionals, scouts, and marketers, for example. Productivity is related to sales, inclusive of ticket sales, revenue from the media and sponsors, sales of sports paraphernalia, and the like.

$$AC = \frac{w}{\left(\frac{Q}{L}\right)} \quad (1)$$

In this chapter, our focus is on target rates of return as it relates to organizational efficiency. There are different ways of measuring rates of return, but for our purposes, we can focus on the net gain or loss from an investment as a percentage of the cost of the investment. This is a very simple definition. But it allows us to focus on the relationship between x-efficiency or organizational efficiency and the target rate of return. Revenue is directly related to productivity and thereby to the level of x-efficiency. An x-efficient organization should be maximizing revenue, ceteris paribus. The rate of return can be expressed as:

$$\frac{\left[\left(\frac{Q}{L} \star L\right) \star P\right] - IC}{IC} \quad (2)$$

Where, $((Q/L) \star L) \star P$ is total revenue (and P is price) and IC is the cost of investment, which incorporates w in Equation (1).

By maximizing total revenue and minimizing investment costs, the firm or organization maximizes its rate of return. Therefore, if the team's players' salary increases, the target rate of return will fall unless x-efficiency increases sufficiently or the sport's team can increase the price of its products and/or sell more products above total costs. Moreover, becoming more x-efficient will not generate a higher rate of return, it might generate an even lower rate of return if this increase in x-efficiency requires an increase in expenditure (proxied by w) that more than outweighs the increase in x-efficiency. An x-inefficient sports organization can also achieve its target rate of return if it can generate sufficient surplus generating products to compensate for its relatively low level of productivity. We argue that it is possible that there is an array of levels of organizational or x-efficiency consistent with a fixed rate of return and this rate of return can be the industry norm. In this case, being x-inefficient need not translate into being economically or financially unsustainable in terms of the organization's rate of return. This is consistent with the empirical literature that x-inefficiency persists in the economy (Frantz 1997; Shiller 2003) and with the argument, popularized in *Moneyball* (Lewis 2004) that there are inefficiencies latent in sports teams because of poor team management, especially with the underutilization of sports analytics (see our chapter on *Moneyball* in this book). If x-inefficiency is sustainable then it becomes more difficult to identify, especially through the lenses of conventional neoclassical theory, where it is assumed that x-inefficiency is eliminated by market forces or through efficiency-oriented preferences of decision-makers. This modeling scenario is illustrated in Figure 3.1 below.

0A is the rate of return that can be achieved with organizational efficiency. But it can be achieved with an array of levels of organizational efficiency or x-efficiency given by Ad. Along Ad, there is multi-equilibria of levels of organizational efficiency consistent with the rate of return 0A. Point c represents the x-efficient level of organizational efficiency, where the level of x-efficiency is maximized. In the conventional economics narrative, given by Ad, increasing organizational efficiency yields increases to the target rate of return to a maximum of 0A or cd, given by the maximum level of x-efficiency. But in the conventional narrative, organizational efficiency is achieved by assumption. There are no proverbial big bills lying on the sidewalk (organizational inefficiency) waiting to be pick-up by the more entrepreneurial decision-makers.

In this chapter, our specific interest is how sports team inefficiency and efficiency relate to the realization of the target rate of return. The sports team can be one sub-organization that is part of the larger organization that owns the sports team such as an owner of a conglomerate, a media concern, a brewery, an automobile manufacturer, or a financial firm(s).[3] We must bear in mind that inefficiency in a sports team is often measured by the performance of the team in terms of wins, losses, ties, league standing, championship wins, and qualifying for the finals in the sport or qualifying for the world cup, such as in football (soccer in North American jargon). These measures of success are sometimes directly related to the resources available to the sports teams in the conventional narrative given the assumption of organizational or x-efficiency. To the extent that organizational efficiency in sports teams does not have a one-to-one relationship with the target rate of return then it

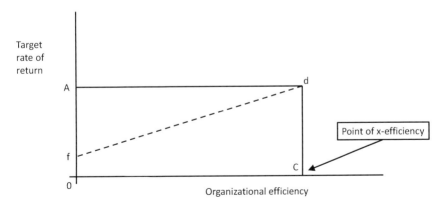

Figure 3.1 Levels of Organizational Efficiency and Target Rates of Return.

would be possible for sub-optimal, x-inefficient performance to be consistent with a target rate of return acceptable to investors.

Sports teams need not be consistent winners or champions to be successful in terms of being financially viable. What is critically important to the team's success is the viability of its brand and its fan base, the extent and depth of its fan loyalty. Winning helps, but so does the extent to which there exists a community of fans, of fan loyalists, where being part of this community generates increased levels of utility, satisfaction, happiness, or euphoria. Being part of the action, part of the team, part of 'your' community, even in the face of defeat, contributes to this sense of euphoria. Losers can be winners even in defeat. Simon (2013) clearly articulates this point with regard to fans. He had the experience of being a sports fan of the University of California (UC) Berkeley football (American football) team, an allegiance that he shared with his father. He was a fan even though his team was not a consistently winning team, but his fan loyalty held fast and remained true. Simon (2013) describes the end of one game experience on October 13, 2007, when UC had the opportunity to beat the unranked Oregon State whilst UC was ranked number 2 in 2007. Ten seconds remained in the game to determine the winner or loser with Berkeley controlling the ball. It looked like a sure win. Simon (2013, p. 10) describes his experience at this time:

> In those 10 seconds my hormone system blew up. My brain blew up. Neurons fired away like gangbusters in the centers for empathy, action, language, pride, identity, self, reward, relationships, love, addiction, perception, pain, and happiness. If you've seen those images at the end of heartbreaking games, where the fan is standing there with his hands on his head and his mouth yawning—or if you've been that fan—you know that it feels like all this stuff is frothing around on the inside trying to beat its way out of your body like an alien chest-burster.

By the way, Berkeley lost. A bad (sub-optimal) call made by the quarterback cost Berkeley the game.

Fan loyalty, we argue, shields a relatively poorly performing team from the 'wrath of the market'. It allows such teams to achieve acceptable rates of return in spite of not doing well. Sports fans' utility is no doubt enhanced by winning. But being a fan, being part of a community, often generates sufficient utility for teams' to sell tickets and team products and, in certain markets, broadcasting rights, sufficient for the team to be economically sustainable and to meet investor objectives.

What's critical to this chapter is that fan loyalty may mitigate the need for sports teams to perform more efficiently. We also note the importance of the preferences of sports teams where, for some, the utility gained in such ownership is not a direct function of profits, meeting a certain rate of return, but rather in the ownership of the team itself (Sloane 1971). As previously mentioned, sports team ownership can be a type of vanity good (Frank 2010; Veblen 1899). Such team owners can tolerate sub-optimal performance because of the utility generated from sports team ownership. This does not mean that owners would not prefer their team to do better. But a sports teams' survival, in this case, is not solely determined by it realizing a higher rate of return. Also, community-owned sports teams tend to maximize member benefits not financial rates of return, per se. This also provides room for inefficiencies in sports team performance.

Overall, we argue that the fan base, fan loyalty, is critically important to the financial sustainability of a sports team and this is not directly linked to the efficiency or organizational efficiency of sports teams. Relatedly, efficient sports team performance is not directly related to the realization of the target rate of return.

Measuring sports team x-efficiency

In the conventional economic framework, one assumes that economic agents, members of the firm (in our case the sports team), inclusive of decision-makers, behave in a manner consistent with x-efficiency or organizational efficiency, yielding optimal outcomes (maximizing productivity) given traditional factor inputs. Since x-efficiency is assumed, one assumes that agents behave as if they are x-efficient or optimal (Berg and Gigerenzer 2010). Hence any observed behavior should be expected or predicted to be optimal. Following from this logic there is little need for empirical examination of actual (as opposed to assumed) behavior within the 'traditional' black box of the firm. Given the assumption of organic x-efficiency within the organization or sports team in such a conventional scenario, to improve performance simply requires increasing factor inputs or technological change. Given this modeling narrative, relatively poor performance outcomes must be a function of a lack of financial resources. However, once one allows for the possibility of x-inefficiency, one then has to determine measures of sports team x-inefficiency.

When one discusses the performance of a traditional firm one can analyze the firm in terms of its ability to meet specific target rates of return and the extent to which it meets this target. From the perspective of x-efficiency, one can also then analyze the extent to which the firm is x-efficient: how many computers or cars or bikes is the firm producing per unit of traditional factor input, for example. Given the existence of multiple equilibria, there is no clear unequivocal positive relationship between average cost, the rate of return, and the level of x-efficiency. With regards to measuring the extent of x-efficiency, this task becomes more complex with respect to sports teams given that it is possible for x-efficiency to prevail even when a team is not a consistent winner. One way of highlighting this point is that if all teams were x-efficient, controlling for financial resources, all teams cannot all be winners at the same given point in time. Therefore, being a consistent winner is not a necessary measure of the level of sports team x-efficiency or organizational efficiency. Much depends on how relatively x-efficient other sports teams in your competitive set happen to be. In comparison, all x-efficient car firms can all be winners in terms of maximizing productivity with respect to being x-efficient.

Sports teams can only strive to maximize the probability of winning, of being the best. If this represents optimal performance and all teams are behaving optimally, ceteris paribus, it is impossible for all such teams to win. There can only be one champion, only one first-place team. There can only be a subset of teams qualifying for the playoffs. There can only be a subset of teams amongst the top teams in the league. However, ceteris paribus, one would expect that x-efficient sports teams would be competitive, to be amongst the top teams, at least on average. For the x-efficient sports teams, if these were all equally x-efficient, being the top team would be largely a random process controlling for exogenous variables such as luck, which one should then also expect to be a random process. This suggests that one possible indicator of sports team x-inefficiency is being a consistently poorly performing team, controlling for the team's available financial resources.

This latter point is critically important since we know that a highly x-inefficient sports team can meet with considerable success if it is afforded considerable financial resources. And this success can then positively impact on the team's revenue. For this very reason, the x-efficiency approach adopted in this chapter is of central importance as it allows for the existence of x-inefficiency. This then lends itself to an understanding of the core determinants of success going well beyond a simple focus on financial resources.

Procedural rationality and sports team x-efficiency

Stipulating a possible measure of sports team x-efficiency in terms of firm or team level outcomes is not the same thing as creating a narrative about how x-efficient outcomes can be achieved and why they are not. This type of question demands that we investigate the inner workings of the sports team and this relates, more generally, to what Leibenstein refers to as a micro-micro economic theory of the firm (Leibenstein 1979; see also Cyert and March 1963; Coase 1937, 1998). In terms of procedural rationality, one must determine if team decision-makers have been able to achieve the objectives they set for themselves. And, if these objectives are not met, then why not. From this perspective, the decision-makers are rational agents who have set targeted outcomes, but they might fail to achieve these outcomes given the resources that they have at hand. Failure to achieve these outcomes, such as being the top team in the league, qualifying for the playoffs, or winning the championship, would constitute important components of x-inefficiency. The reasons for this could relate to errors in decision-making that have rational foundations and can, therefore, be corrected. Another determinant relates to decision-makers setting relatively low achievement targets relating to their preferences. Leibenstein regards this to be, in part, a function of managerial slack. Here one has team decision-makers preferring not to work as smart and as hard as they can potentially. And, this decision can be rational in the sense of being a utility-maximizing choice, yielding x-inefficient, sub-optimal outcomes. In this case, it is the preferences of decision-makers that yield the x-inefficient, sub-optimal outcomes. But for the purposes of this chapter, we look to place our primary focus on errors in decision-making by rational agents as the primary determinant of x-inefficiency, although clearly, managerial slack can also be of some consequence.

To determine, at the micro-micro level, the extent of sports team x-inefficiency, one needs to determine the inputs needed for a team to become relatively successful with regards to their specific determinants of success. What's critical in a behavioral approach is the context-dependent factors that determine outcomes. These factors can be economic but also non-economic in nature. What is central to the productivity of a car manufacturer would not be identical to what's important to a sports team. And, of course, different sports teams would not require identical inputs, albeit some similar inputs can be expected. To understand the determinants of a sports team's x-efficiency one has to deconstruct the team's black box (and more generally, the black box of the firm), to better understand which variables are most important to their efficiency and, relatedly, to their relative success. One would then have to identify those success-related factors common across teams in the same sport and across sports. It is also important to determine the reasons for achieving x-efficiency or for persistently deviating from a specified efficiency frontier as some measure of success as a sports team (see, for example, Terrien and Andreff 2020). In this behavioral micro-micro economics approach to the determinants of x-efficiency, one cannot simply apply generalist concepts such as: decision-makers and other agents within the sports teams must maximize team performance or financial rates of return. These concepts are too vague to be of any operational or analytical use.

The x-efficiency sports team narrative must be framed in terms of how a sports team can best perform given the financial resources at hand. This also allows one to better identify the extent to which financial resources are the determining factor or variable with regards to sports team success. To recap. Our analytical framework first assumes (consistent with March and Simon) that agents are rational or smart decision-makers. This being said, we ask, if sports team success (or x-efficiency in sports performance) is the objective of the decision-makers, why has x-efficiency not been achieved and, if it has been achieved, how was this objective realized. This links directly to procedural rationality and the micro-micro-economics narrative. This type of analytical inquiry can be generalized to a behavioral model of the firm such as specified in Cyert and March (1963).

Given rational decision-makers, sub-optimal performance can be attributed to a number of variables.[4] At a very general level, this can be related to the mental model adopted by decision-makers at different levels in the organization (Altman 2014; Denzau and North 1994; Keynes 1936). Mental models are how individuals interpret the world and assess what is the most effective way to develop and operate a successful organization. False mental models can result in sub-optimal performance—x-inefficient choices being made by rational decision-makers and, thereby, x-inefficient performance outcomes. Therefore, the mental models adopted by team owners, managers, coaches, and trainers, for example, are critical determinants of the extent to which a sports team is relatively successful. Relative success can be achieved when an organization's or team's leaders adopt a more effective mental model as compared to what's in place in their competitors' teams. Determining whether or not decision-makers are using appropriate mental models is an important aspect of determining the existence of sub-optimal performance and one of its determinants. The difference between outcomes realized using an effective as compared to a false mental model is a measure of performance x-inefficiency.

Herding (Baddeley 2013; Keynes 1936) can also result in x-inefficient performance when rational or smart decision-makers flock to adopt mental models and heuristics that have been adopted by, in their mind, credible herd leaders. If these mental models and heuristics are inappropriate for the follower teams, such follow-the-leader or herding strategy (used to save on decision-making costs or, relatedly, transaction costs) can result in suboptimal team performance. What then becomes critically important is whether the team's decision-makers are willing to correct the errors of their ways and adopt more appropriate, fit-for-purpose mental models and heuristics. But herding based choices can be subject to confirmation bias where individuals refuse to modify their opinions or choices because changing one's opinion is regarded as a loss which carries with it a heavily weighted loss of utility (related to Prospect Theory). This loss can be related to a sense of embarrassment or a belief that changing one's mind would result in a loss of power and credibility within the organization. Confirmation bias can persist (be an equilibrium outcome) resulting in a suboptimal performance for sports teams when it is sustainable.

One can also have a team leader who believes that he or she is correct in his or her beliefs and choices irrespective of what the evidence might stipulate. This type of behavior has been classified as overconfidence bias and can be reinforced by confirmation bias. Such behavior can also be related to the illusion of control wherein an individual believes that she or he has more control over outcomes than is actually the case. Such behavior becomes problematic when the decision-makers refuse to revise their beliefs and related choices based on experience which previously resulted in persistent performance x-efficiency. As discussed above, such sub-optimal choices can persist if decision-makers can convincingly (but incorrectly) blame other factors for their failures, such as the lack of financial resources. Also, if the sports team's rates of return are acceptable in the face of sub-optimal, x-inefficient performance, this serves to protect the decision-makers' sub-optimal choices.

Using inappropriate mental models can cause errors in decision-making, ceteris paribus. But even if one adopts the correct mental model this does not mean that x-efficient performance will automatically result. Other factors now come into play. At a more general level, imperfect and costly information and the inability to understand the information at hand can be problematic. When information is imperfect it can be easily misleading and rational decision-makers can end up making choices which yield sub-optimal performance for their team. This directly follows from the fact that individuals rely on heuristics (a rational choice given imperfect information) to determine the quality of available information and what information to choose given the abundance of information and the costliness of sorting through this information (Akerlof 1970; Arrow 1963). For example, sports teams might engage the services of trainers, data analysts, and health professionals, using information about credentials which they believe to be true. But if the regulatory process on credentials is flawed then decision-makers will rationally choose human capital inputs that can yield sub-optimal outcomes (Altman 2020). These would be similar to errors made in financial markets where information is flawed and misleading. Correcting such potential errors in decision-making would require more expertise in distilling and understanding the information at hand—a type of *sports information literacy*, akin to financial literacy advocated for firm decision making (Sheffrin 2008). Related to this, better regulated and transparent standards that signal the quality of sports-related human capital inputs would be important (Altman 2020). Accurate signaling tends to reduce errors in decision-making in the real world of bounded rationality.

With respect to errors, some experts in sports analysis argue that in the recent past sports data analytics was a much-neglected tool in driving the decision-making process in sports teams (Lewis 2004; see also Moskowitz and Wertheim 2011). Too much of the decision-making process was left to what some believed to be non-objective factors, such as the intuition of managers, coaches, scouts, trainers, as opposed to hard data and the statistical analysis of these data. Choosing incorrect analytical and decision-making platforms resulted in errors in decisions. This could have been a function of decision-makers adopting incorrect mental models. This resulted and can result in sports teams performing sub-optimally, x-inefficiently. The details of this particular debate are elaborated upon and analyzed in our *Moneyball* chapter in this book. Currently, more and more teams are switching to sports data analytics as core to their decision-making process. We argue in the *Moneyball* chapter, following the preponderance of evidence, that both sports data analytics and the experienced-based decision-making process (sometimes referred to derogatorily as intuition-based) are important in driving optimal decision-making and contributing to more x-efficient sports performance. Making this more nuanced choice on the optimal combination of sports data analytics and experienced-based decision-making (where both interact synergistically) requires that a more objective mental model be applied to the decision-making process. And this requires an organizational team decision-making platform that facilitates modifying mental models—this is a form of Bayesian updating (see also, Carleton and Passan 2018). One should also note here that leading experienced-based decision-makers typically never ignored data. They just did not use the advanced statistical techniques and the large data sets used by sports data analysts. Moreover, sports statisticians who have little in-depth knowledge of their sports are prone to serious errors in decision-making.

At a more general level, x-efficiency in sports performance requires an appropriate management platform that coordinates all the components of the sports team into an effective and successful competitive team. What is important is not that each component (each athlete, for example), is performing optimally, but that each component is selected and organized in such a fashion that the team's overall performance is x-efficient. This argument is a subset of a general behavioral model of the firm. It bears repeating, that unlike in the conventional economic model of the firm, how the firm is actually managed is critically important. Therefore, the quality of management is significant and the preferences of decision-makers irrespective of their quality are also significant.

Some experts argue that more collaborative and less hierarchical forms of management yield better outcomes (Altman 1996, 2002; Kastelle 2013; Leibenstein 1982, 1987; Tomer 1999), or higher levels of x-efficiency. It yields better coordination with respect to all members of the firm and elicits better performance from each firm member overall, yielding higher levels of x-efficiency. This often involves facilitating alternative and diverse views on how the team should be managed and organized (Syed 2019). This also involves building on past successes of one's organization. With regards to football (or soccer), one of the greatest managers, Bob Paisley's many successes, rested on having (Herbert 2018, p. xi):

> ...an innate distrust of grandstanding and the grandiose ... [working] in the finer details and [building] a route to success through the accumulation of small improvements ... Equally integral to his success was the capacity ... the crucial component of the quiet man's armoury, to empower others and embrace their input.
> (see also Rapaport (1993), on similar points made by coach Bill Walsh from American football)

This type of management, we argue, facilitates the adoption and development of more objective mental models and reduces errors in decision-making thereby increasing the level of performance x-efficiency in the sports team. This narrative also fits into the voice/exit paradigm introduced by Hirschman (1970), wherein providing an organizations' members with effective voice tends to improve the organization's performance. Effective voice is a key component of democratic governance providing for the unique, personalized, and experienced-based, human capital inputs that contribute to the organization's performance. Otherwise, these critical human assets exit the organization or if they remain in the organization their potential positive contribution to firm performance can flip from positive to negative in an adverse incentive environment. This requires team decision-makers and leaders to embrace this more inclusive and holistic approach to management and firm governance. But not all firm leaders are so inclined to adopt this more inclusive managerial approach.

A sub-optimal outcome need not be a persistent or stable equilibrium, especially when an immediate sub-optimal outcome is the product of one or two (or a few) individuals dominating the decision-making process. This is not consistent with effective input from other members of the organization. Errors in decision-making that can be a product of overconfidence and confirmation biases and illusions of control, for example, can be mitigated and reversed if decision-making takes place in a more democratic platform, in particular, if structured efforts are in place to de-bias decision-making. This point has been made, for example, by Sheffrin (2008), wherein he argues that Board decisions should not be the monopoly of a narrow group of individuals or only of one individual. This is particularly important when a leader suffers from sociopathic tendencies (weak on empathetic, sympathetic, and moral/ethical traits combined with highly focused self-interested preferences). Allowing decision-making to be more transparent and inviting a difference of opinion can also contribute to de-biasing decision-making and can serve to override sub-optimal decision-making tendencies by specific individuals. This is not unlike Bob Paisley's approach to coaching for example.

These arguments/hypotheses with regards to governance are generalizations but they apply to sports teams as much as to the ubiquitous firm. A micro-micro-economics approach to the firm suggests that the conditions needed to achieve efficiency in sports performance can be expected to differ somewhat across sports teams, especially across sports teams in different sports. Nevertheless, a more effective and efficient governance structure within a sports organization or within sports team serves to restrain overconfidence and confirmation biases and illusion of control, all of which are highly correlated and is crucial in providing a mechanism for changing preferences amongst decision-makers and reducing errors in decision-making (see, for example, Andreff 2011; Molan, Kelly, Arnold, and Matthews 2019; O'Boyle 2017; Ruta, Lorenzon, and Sironi 2019; Scully 1994; Wolsey, Minten, and Abrams 2012).

Some of the above points are illustrated in Figure 3.2, below, which serves to highlight some of the key determinants of the level of x-inefficiency.

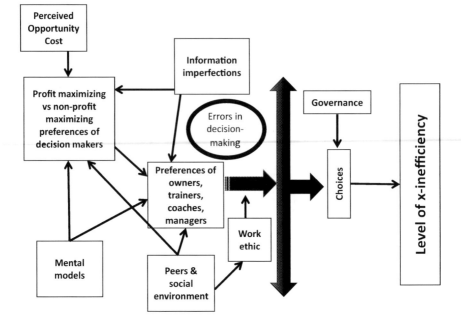

Figure 3.2 Determinants of Sports X-Efficiency.

Conclusion

We develop a modeling framework and narrative built around the realistic assumption that organizational inefficiency and, therefore, x-inefficiency, can exist and persist amongst sports teams and organizations. By allowing for the existence of x-inefficiency, which is assumed away in the conventional economic model of the firm, we open the door to explaining the sub-optimal performance of sports teams or sports outcomes that are below what a sports team can achieve given their traditional inputs, which include financial resources. Ultimately, what is critically important in our approach to analyzing sports performance inefficiencies is introducing more realistic and nuanced modeling assumptions. Such assumptions form the core building block of the behavioral economics approach first articulated by Herbert Simon.

We focus and further develop Simon's concept of procedural rationality, which, unlike conventional economics, addresses the question of the extent to which an organization has achieved the objectives set forth by its leadership (which typically is related to doing the best that it can) given its real-world decision-making environment and the capabilities it has at hand. Our initial point of focus is smart or rational decision-makers who may or may not realize sports performance efficiency. We identify the significance of errors in decision-making and the preferences of decision-makers (inclusive of correctable biases) as key determinants of sports performance x-inefficiencies. One need not resort to notions of irrational decision-makers (and biases are not necessarily or typically a sign of being irrational) to explain sub-optimal sports performance outcomes. Sport performance efficiencies can be achieved given the appropriate decision-making environment and capabilities.

But we also argue that there is no market or preference-based imperative for sports teams and organizations to become x-efficient in performance outcomes. Inefficient sports teams can be highly profitable given the importance of their fan base as a revenue-generating machine, so that losers or sub-optimal performers can be winners in terms of revenue generation and profitability. One can explain the persistence of sports performance x-inefficiency by modeling multiple equilibria in target rates of return for relatively x-inefficient and x-efficient sports teams. This being said, we argue that a sports team's success can be built by identifying the degree of organizational x-inefficiency and its determinants specific to that particular team. Doing so helps pave the path to procedural rationality. This is particularly important given that all so many fans, team members, and team leaders actually prefer to be x-efficient (as we define it) and reap its benefits, including the enhanced pride that comes with being a winning organization.

Acknowledgments

The authors thank Wladimir Andreff and Louise Lamontagne for their helpful comments and suggestions.

Notes

1. This is a critical assumption in Leibenstein's (1966) x-efficiency theory, wherein manager's preferences are not focused on profit maximization per se. They are utility maximizers and self-interested agents, but they are concerned with the survival of their firm and their firm meeting certain thresholds. This is not the same thing as being a neoclassical profit maximizer.
2. There are a large number of sports teams that are community owned. And, these teams yield utility to their community and command significant fan and broader community loyalty which is enhanced by its community-based ownership structure. Such teams might better sustain economic losses through broad-based community support as compared to privately owned sports teams.
3. The sports team is also part of a league which is a larger corporation which typically serves to regulate the teams in the league and often cross-subsidizes low revenue generating teams. One might ask if this serves to facilitate x-inefficiency or organizational inefficiency.
4. Econometrically this measurement issue can be addressed through the DEA (data envelope analysis) methodology (Barros, Assaf and Sá-Earp (2010); Barros and Leach (2006); García-Sánchez (2007); Haas (2003); Kashian and Pagel 2014; and Terrien and Andreff 2020).

References

Akerlof, George A. (1970). The Market for 'Lemons': Quality Uncertainty and the Market Mechanism. *Quarterly Journal of Economics*, 84: 488–500.

Alaminos, David, and Manuel Ángel Fernández (2019). Why Do Football Clubs Fail Financially? A Financial Distress Prediction Model for European Professional

Football Industry. *PloS*, 14. Accessed November 10, 2020. Available at: https://www.ncbi.nlm.nih.gov/pmc/articles/PMC6932787/pdf/pone.0225989.pdf.

Altman, Hannah (2020). *The Behavioural Economics of Organisational Inefficiency: The Example of the New Zealand Fitness Industry*. Master of Philosophy Thesis, Queensland University of Technology. Brisbane: Australia.

Altman, Hannah, and Morris Altman (2015a). Sport Economics and Performance Inefficiencies, in Morris Altman, ed., *Real World Decision Making: An Encyclopedia of Behavioral Economics*. New York: Praeger, ABC-CLIO: 410–412.

Altman, Hannah, and Morris Altman (2015b). Sports Economics and Economic Psychology, in Morris Altman, ed., *Real World Decision Making: An Encyclopedia of Behavioral Economics*. New York: Praeger, ABC-CLIO: 412–415.

Altman, Morris (1996). *Human Agency and Material Welfare: Revisions in Microeconomics and their Implications for Public Policy*. Boston: Kluwer Academic.

Altman, Morris (2002). Economic Theory, Public Policy and the Challenge of Innovative Work Practices. *Economic and Industrial Democracy: An International Journal*, 23: 271–290.

Altman, Morris (2006). What a Difference an Assumption Makes: Effort Discretion, Economic Theory, and Public Policy, in Morris Altman, ed., *Handbook of Contemporary Behavioral Economics: Foundations and Developments*. New York: Armonk: 125–164.

Altman, Morris (2014). Mental Models, Bargaining Power, and Institutional Change. World Interdisciplinary Network for Institutional Research, Old Royal Naval College, Greenwich University. London, UK, September 11–14.

Altman, Morris (2017a). Policy Consequences of Multiple Equilibria and the Indeterminacy of Economic Outcomes in a Boundedly Rational World: Closing the System with Non-Economic Variables. *Forum for Social Economics*, 64: 234–251.

Altman, Morris (2017b). A Bounded Rationality Assessment of the New Behavioral Economics, in Roger Frantz, Shu-Heng Chen, Kurt Dopfer, Floris Heukelom, and Shabnam Mousavi, eds., *Routledge Handbook of Behavioral Economics*. London and New York: Routledge: 179–193.

Altman, Morris, editor (2017c). *Handbook of Behavioural Economics and Smart Decision-Making: Rational Decision-Making within the Bounds of Reason*. Cheltenham, England: Edward Elgar.

Andreff, Wladimir (2007). French Football: A Financial Crisis Rooted in Weak Governance. *Journal of Sports Economics*, 8: 652–661.

Andreff, Wladimir (2011). *Contemporary Issues in Sports Economics: Participation and Professional Team Sports*. Cheltenham: Edward Elgar, Cheltenham.

Andreff, Wladimir (2014a). Building Blocks for a Disequilibrium Model of a European Team Sports League. *International Journal of Sport Finance*, 9: 20–38.

Andreff, Wladimir (2014b). French Professional Football: How much Different? in J. Goddard and P. Sloane, eds., *Handbook on the Economics of Professional Football*. Cheltenham: Edward Elgar, 298–321.

Arrow, Kenneth J. (1963). Uncertainty and the Welfare Economics of Medical Care. *American Economic Review*, 53: 941–973.

Baddeley, Michelle (2013). Herding, Social Influence and Expert Opinion. *Journal of Economic Methodology*, 20(1): 35–44.

Barros, Carlos Pestana, and Stephanie Leach (2006). Performance Evaluation of the English Premier Football League with Data Envelopment Analysis. *Applied Economics*, 38: 1449–1458.

Barros, Carlos Pestana, Albert Assaf, and Fabio Sá-Earp (2010). Brazilian Football League Technical Efficiency: A Simar and Wilson approach. *Journal of Sports Economics*, 11: 641–651.

Berg, Nathan, and Gerd Gigerenzer (2010). As-If Behavioral Economics: Neoclassical Economics in Disguise? *History of Economic Ideas*, 18: 133–166.

Carleton, Russell A., and Jeff Passan (2018). *The Shift: The Next Evolution in Baseball Thinking*. Chicago: Triumph Book.

Coase, Ronald H. (1937). The Nature of the Firm. *Economica*, 4: 386–405.

Coase, Ronald H. (1998). The New Institutional Economics. *American Economic Review*, 88: 72–74.

Coates, Dennis, and Brad R. Humphreys (2018). Behavioral and Sports Economics, in: Victor J. Tremblay, Elizabeth Schroeder, and Carol Horton Tremblay, eds., *Handbook of Behavioral Industrial Organization*. Cheltenham, England: Edward Elgar, 307–342.

Cyert, Richard M., and James C. March (1963). *A Behavioral Theory of the Firm*. Englewood Cliffs, NJ: Prentice-Hall.

Denzau, Arthur, and Douglass C. North (1994). Shared Mental Models: Ideologies and Institutions. *Kyklos Fasc*, 1: 3–31.

Drewes, Michael (2003). Competition and Efficiency in Professional Sports Leagues. *European Sport Management Quarterly*, 3(4): 240–252.

Frank, Robert H. (2010). *Luxury Fever Weighing the Cost of Excess*. Princeton, NJ: Princeton University Press.

Frantz, Roger S. (1997). *X-Efficiency Theory, Evidence and Applications*. Topics in Regulatory Economics and Policy 23. Boston, Dordrecht, and London: Kluwer Academic.

García-Sánchez, Isabel María (2007). Efficiency and Effectiveness of Spanish Football Teams: A Three-Stage-DEA Approach. *Central European Journal of Operations Research*, 15: 21–45.

Gigerenzer, Gerd (2007). *Gut Feelings: The Intelligence of the Unconscious*. New York: Viking.

Haas, Dieter J. (2003). Technical Efficiency in the Major League Soccer. *Journal of Sports Economics*, 4: 203–215.

Herbert, Ian (2017). *Quiet Genius: Bob Paisley, British Football's Greatest Manager*. London: Bloomsbury Sport.

Hirschman, Albert O. (1970). *Exit, Voice, and Loyalty: Responses to Decline in Firms, Organizations, and States*. Cambridge, MA: Harvard University Press.

Kahneman, Daniel (2003). Maps of Bounded Rationality: Psychology for Behavioral Economics. *American Economic Review*, 93: 1449–1475.

Kahneman, Daniel, and Amos Tversky (1979). Prospect Theory: An Analysis of Decisions Under Risk. *Econometrica*, 47: 313–327.

Kashian, Russell D., and Jeff Pagel (2014). Measuring X-Efficiency in NCAA Division III Athletics. *Journal of Sports Economics*, 17: 558–577.

Kastelle, Tim (2013). Hierarchy Is Overrated. *Harvard Business Review*. Accessed March 15, 2021, Available at: https://hbr.org/2013/11/hierarchy-is-overrated.

Keynes, John Maynard (1936) [2007]. *The General Theory of Employment, Interest and Money*. London: Macmillan.

Leibenstein, Harvey (1966). Allocative Efficiency vs. 'x-Efficiency'. *American Economic Review*, 56: 392–415.

Leibenstein, Harvey (1979). A Branch of Economics Is Missing: Micro-Micro Theory. *Journal of Economic Literature*, 17: 477–502.

Leibenstein, Harvey (1982). The Prisoner's Dilemma in the Invisible Hand: An Analysis of Intrafirm Productivity. *American Economic Review*, 72: 92–97.

Leibenstein, Harvey (1987). *Inside the Firm: The Inefficiencies of Hierarchy*. Cambridge, MA: Harvard University Press.

Lewis, Michael (2004). *Moneyball: The Art of Winning an Unfair Game*. New York: W. W. Norton.

March, James G. (1978). Bounded Rationality, Ambiguity, and the Engineering of Choice. *Bell Journal of Economics*, 9: 587–608.

Molan, Conor, Seamus Kelly, Rachel Arnold, and James Matthews (2019). Performance Management: A Systematic Review of Processes in Elite Sport and Other Performance Domains. *Journal of Applied Sport Psychology*, 31: 87–104.

Moskowitz, Tobias, and L. Jon Wertheim (2011). *Scorecasting: The Hidden Influences behind How Sports are Played and Games are Won*. New York: Crown Archetype.

O'Boyle, Ian (2017). *Organisational Performance Management in Sport*. New York: Routledge.

Olson, Mancur (1996). Big Bills Left on the Sidewalk: Why Some Nations are Rich, and Others Poor. *Journal of Economic Perspectives*, 10: 3–24.

Rapaport, Richard (1993). To Build a Winning Team: An Interview with Head Coach Bill Walsh. *Harvard Business Review*, January-February. Assessed December 3, 2020. Available at: https://hbr.org/1993/01/to-build-a-winning-team-an-interview-with-head-coach-bill-walsh.

Ruta, Dina, Luca Lorenzon, and Emiliano Sironi (2019). The Relationship between Governance Structure and Football Club Performance in Italy and England. *Sport, Business and Management*, 10: 17–37.

Scully, Gerald W. (1994). Managerial Efficiency and Survivability in Professional Team Sports. *Managerial and Decision Economics*, 15: 403–411.

Sheffrin, Hirsh (2008). *Ending the Management Illusion: How to Drive Business Results Using the Principles of Behavioral Finance*. New York: McGraw-Hill.

Shiller, Robert J. (2003). From Efficient Markets to Behavioral Finance. *Journal of Economic Perspectives*, 17: 83–104.

Simon, Herbert A. (1978). Rationality as a Process and as a Product of Thought. *American Economic Review*, 70: 1–16.

Simon, Herbert A. (1979). Rational Decision Making in Business Organizations. *American Economic Review*, 69: 493–513.

Simon, Herbert A. (1987). Behavioral Economics, in: J. Eatwell, M. Millgate, and P. Newman, eds., *The New Palgrave: A Dictionary of Economics*. London: Macmillan: 266–267.

Simon, Herbert A. (1997). *Models of Bounded Rationality. Empirical Grounded Economic Reasons*, Vol. III, Cambridge, MA: MIT Press.

Simons, Eric (2013). *The Secret Lives of Sports Fans: The Science of Sport Obsession*. London: Overlook Ducklook.

Sloane, Peter (1971). The Economics of Professional Football: The Football Club as a Utility Maximiser. *Scottish Journal of Political Economy*, 18: 121–146.

Smith, Vernon L. (1962). An Experimental Study of Competitive Market Behavior. *Journal of Political Economy*, 70: 111–137.

Smith, Vernon L. (2003). Constructivist and Ecological Rationality in Economics. *American Economic Review*, 93: 465–508.

Smith, Vernon L. (2005). Behavioral Economics Research and the Foundations of Economics. *Journal of Socio-Economics*, 34: 135–150.

Syed, Matthew (2010). *Bounce: Bounce: Mozart, Federer, Picasso, Beckham, and the Science of Success.* New York: Harper.
Terrien, Mickael, Nicolas Scelles, Stephen Morrow, Lionel Maltese, and Christophe Durand (2017). The Win/Profit Maximization Debate: Strategic Adaptation as the Answer? *Sport, Business and Management,* 7: 121–140.
Terrien, Mickaël, and Wladimir Andreff (2020). Organisational Efficiency of National Football Leagues in Europe. *European Sport Management Quarterly,* 20: 205–224.
Thaler, Richard H., and Cass R. Sustein (2008). *Nudge: Improving Decisions about Health, Wealth, and Happiness.* New York: Penguin Books.
Tomer, John F. (1999). *The Human Firm: A Socio-Economic Analysis of Its Behavior and Potential in a New Economic Age.* London/New York: Routledge.
Vamplew Wray (2018). Products, Promotion, and (Possibly) Profits: Sports Entrepreneurship Revisited. *Journal of Sport History,* 45: 183–201.
Veblen, Thorstein (1899). *The Theory of Leisure Class.* New York: MacMillan.
Williamson, Oliver E. (1975). *Markets and Hierarchies: Analysis and Antitrust Implications.* New York: Free Press.
Wolsey, Chris, Sue Minten, and Jeffrey Abrams (2012). *Human Resource Management in the Sport and Leisure Industry.* New York: Routledge.

4 Institutional dynamics in sports – how governance, rules and technology interact

Stuart Thomas and Kieran Tierney

Introduction

In this chapter, we examine institutional characteristics of technology in sports – in particular how the development and adoption of technology in sports is either managed or not by a governing body. We contrast technology-driven sports, sports that require some reasonably sophisticated equipment in order to participate, to 'rules-based' sports, when the sustainability or the very nature of the sport in question is threatened by the march of technology. In this context, it is useful to think of a sport through the lens of an intersection between a set of rules and a technology. Our thesis is that the longevity of such sports will be influenced in large part by the presence or absence of governing institutions with effective capacity to control the core components of the sport.

How such sports form and spread will be contingent on the strength or weakness, and global cohesion of the rules governing that sport and the strength of the governing bodies that emerge to enforce them. This view is somewhat different from the 'conventional' paradigms of sports economics and sports management that are, for the most part, concerned with efficient resource allocation and valuation in mature (i.e. professional, team) sports, viewed as competitive entertainment industries. We explore a different way to understand how sports evolve in culture, society and the economy through 'evolutionary sports dynamics'.

In order to make sense of the dynamics at work, we posit a model of 'technology-first sports', that is sports that (generally) start as a recreational activity based on a novel item of equipment, such as sailboard, motor car or even a computer system or network as we find in eSports, that evolves into a competitive pursuit with the development of rules and the emergence of some coordinating body to facilitate competition, enforce rules, manage media rights and so on. We explore, through short case studies, the trajectory by which a sport originates, grows and may then stabilise or collapse depending on the drivers of development in the sport and the efficacy (or lack of it) in governing institutions and their ability to manage those evolutionary dynamics.

DOI: 10.4324/9781003080824-5

A taxonomy of sports

As noted earlier, we are interested in the evolutionary trajectories of what we describe as technology-driven sports, but in order to understand that, we need first to define our terms. A useful way to do this is to draw a distinction between 'technology-driven' sports and those we might otherwise describe as 'rules-driven', as defined and explored by Potts and Thomas (2018). In general, newer sports such as x-games, surfing and drone-racing, to name a few, tend to fall into the category of technology-driven sports, whereas the more 'traditional' forms of sport such as football, athletics and swimming fall into the rules-driven category.

Rules-driven sports

Examples of rules-driven sports include in the main those that have an origin in some manner of ritualistic or martial activity that then became successively codified. Most *incursion sports*, as modelled on battle – where one team attempts to achieve an arbitrary goal, such as moving an object, e.g. a ball, to an arbitrary point, e.g. into a fixed location net, in the territory of another team, who try to defend – are examples of rules-driven sports, the rules relating to what the particular objective is and the constraints on how it is achieved. These rules typically relate to dimensions of the sport such as the size of the field of play, the number of players, the permissible moves, the duration of the play, consequences for illegal play and the scoring system (Potts and Thomas 2018).

Most physical ability-related sports, or *martial sports*, can be thought of as stylised versions of natural activities that would be valued in some state of the world – running, jumping, throwing, fighting, etc. We regard these as rules-driven sports, in that the rules define a basic standardised form of competition, say over a fixed distance, or for a fixed time, or with a given weighted object. The ancient Olympic Games are the acme of this, as they are associated with the amateur ideals of a sport that involves timeless traditions and minimal ancillary equipment or technologies.

Rules may change over time – an illustrative comparison can be drawn between a historic form of football, '*Calcio Fiorentino*', that is still played in Italy today and modern soccer and rugby. Calcio Fiorentino (also known as calcio storico – 'historic football') is an early form of football originating in 16th-century Italy, somewhat akin to a blend of soccer and rugby. Once widely played, the sport is thought to have started in the Piazza Santa Croce in Florence. In some respects, it bears little resemblance to either of the modern sports in that physical conflict between players is effectively unfettered, clashes are often insanely violent and bloody, and the passage of play is seemingly unconstrained, but the fundamental elements of the game are the same. The players are organised into two opposing teams, the playing area is defined as a rectangle, the game time is strictly defined (50 minutes), and the aim is to transfer a ball into the opposing team's goal more times than they do into yours.

Rules-driven sports develop as new technologies are added to the sport, but under the condition of conforming to the extant rules. Technologies may thus improve gameplay by adding safety features (helmets, pads) or the speed of play, by making gear lighter or stronger, but usually within tightly prescribed limits (e.g. the size of a bat in baseball or cricket, or the materials they are made from). Technologies can be added to improve detection of rule violation (line-cameras in tennis), spectator immersion (e.g. video-assisted referees in soccer or rider telemetry in *Le Tour De France*) or the reach of spectators (satellite broadcasting of games).

While technologies of various sorts may enhance some dimensions of the gameplay or the player or audience experience, the underlying game and its objectives and patterns of play remain much the same. Importantly, for the purpose of our thesis it is the governing bodies controlling these sports, such as the International Olympic Committee (IOC), Federation Internationale De Natation Amateur (FINA) in swimming, FIFA in football and World Athletics, that determine the circumstances under which these technologies are adopted (or not), at least for the purposes of recognised or accredited competition. The sport may develop on its margins as technologies add to the characteristics of the game (e.g. the speed at which it is played, the scale at which it can be observed) but do not fundamentally change the game. The point is that the new technology fits to the given rules and the extent to which it is allowed is at the reasoned judgement of the governing bodies.

Technology-driven sports

By contrast, technology-driven sports, or as might otherwise be usefully described as 'technology-first' sports, begin with a new activity, typically a recreational activity, that invariably requires a 'new' device of some sort – a piece of equipment or 'kit', such as the horse, automobile, surfboard, rifle, skis, crampons and ropes, hang-glider and bicycle – that makes it possible to undertake a new activity – to do a new thing. This 'new thing' may have pre-existing functional utilitarian purposes (such as transport, or hunting), or it may just be an unexplored potential arising from the new materials technology – such as plastics or carbon fibre, changing what can be done for aero-sports or on-water sports.

A sport is created when the use of this new technology extends beyond its original, recreational or utilitarian purpose and into some form of competitive pursuit – going faster, jumping higher or exceeding over peers at some other dimension of performance. Rules are typically then framed to define its competitive application – in other words, to define 'who wins'. The clearest example of a technology-driven sport is motorsport, where first comes the technological capability, and then rules are added to organise (i.e. to bring competitive order to) the technology into a sport. The purpose of the rules is to organise competition about a given technology (or suite of technologies).

These rules may spontaneously self-organise, and then be codified, or they may be deliberately constructed by an entrepreneurial governing body and then selectively adopted by others. The point is that the sport develops by adding governance to bring order to the exploration of possibilities of a technology, or it starts with a new technology, and the purpose of the rules is to explore the potential within that technology. A rules-driven sport is the opposite, where it starts with an order of rules, and the purpose of new technology is to explore the potential within those rules.

Technology-driven sports tend to be younger and more recent; indeed, most new sports are technology-driven sports. A paradigmatic example is windsurfing (Thomas and Potts 2016), along with mountain biking (Buenstorf 2003), snowboarding and skateboarding (Shah 2000, Shah and Tripas 2007). These sports began when amateur enthusiasts who had some engineering capabilities, and wanting to extend the capabilities of the equipment and/or exceed the performance of their peers, experimentally built their own equipment and tried to do new things, usually in a community context (Franke and Shah 2003) but with entrepreneurial consequences (Shah and Tripas 2007).

The development of a technology-driven sport tends to have two phases: first, the formation of a community of users (early adopters) who pool and share information and knowledge about technological developments. In this way, the user community is much like an innovation common (von Hippel 2000); second, the development of rules for the governance of the new sport often emerges from the same group of users. This early adopter community is often the basis for new firms that emerge to commercialise the development of the sport. They have an obvious stake in the provision of order to the new market, including standards and rules.

Of course almost no sport conforms purely to this taxonomy, with rule changes to rules-driven sports (e.g. changing the points in a try from 4 to 5 in Rugby Union in 1992), and new technologies coming into technology-driven sports that radically change the sport, in effect creating a new sport. In an important sense, many exemplars of rules-first sports (football, or athletic throwing sports) had a technology at the point of origin (a ball, a javelin). These represent different characteristic modes by which a sport comes into existence and develops, with differing roles and opportunities for entrepreneurs in respect of technology and governance.

For all that, it is a plausible hypothesis that rules-driven and technology-driven sports display systematic differences that make them prone to different, characteristic dynamics and pathologies. Rules-driven sports will be prone to *rent-seeking* (Krueger 1973) and *capture* (in the sense of Stigler's (1971) model of regulatory capture) by insiders. Technology-driven sports will be prone to *overshooting* and collapse due to capture by elite performers and the rents associated with innovation–competition and subsequent neglect of entry-level markets. The phenomenon of 'overshooting' is observed in equipment-based sports (i.e. primarily 'lifestyle' sports, such as windsurfing, kitesurfing, paddle-boarding or yachting) that can get caught in technological 'arms races' where manufacturer-led competition at the elite high-performance-level results in technological developments that significantly drive up the skill level and cost of participation (Shah 2000). While this is not generally a problem at the elite end of the sport, where competitors are highly skilled and are sponsored by equipment manufacturers, the unintended consequence of this competition is to raise the cost of entry and ongoing participation of amateur and aspirational participants, both in money terms as exotic materials and design lead to more expensive equipment, and in skills acquisition. 'Overshooting' occurs when where the cost and effort of participation exceed the appetites of amateurs and aspirationals and they either leave the sport or choose not to start, thus harming, sometimes catastrophically, the long-run viability of the sport and its associated industries. Earl and Potts (2013, 2015), building on Christensen (1997) and Minsky (1986), describe this phenomenon in the creative industries, and in many aspects of consumer engineering. It is described more fully in the context of sports in Thomas and Potts (2016).

Technology-driven sports will also experience significant variety in the early stages of the industry through exploration that will be prone to *shakeouts* (Klepper and Graddy 1990, Klepper and Simons 2005) when rules are still forming and there are still high levels of uncertainty about the scale and scope of the sport as well as its technological possibilities. New institutional economics (North 1990, Williamson 2000) provides a natural analytic basis for the study of rule formation in new sports, and Schumpeterian or evolutionary economics is the natural analytic basis for the study of technological dynamics in sports driven by entrepreneurship and innovation.

On the origin of new sports

The generic form of the evolutionary economic approach is that the origin of a new sport – like the origin of a new market, or industry – is a consequence of entrepreneurial action: a sports entrepreneur. Stephen Hardy (1986) suggests that historians should see sports in terms of entrepreneurial founders and of the development of the sport as akin to a Schumpeterian technological trajectory (Chacar and Hesterly 2004, Fuller et al. 2007, Terjesen 2008).

We can observe entrepreneurship in a rules-driven sense – Naismith inventing the rules of basketball *de novo* (and then coaching the men's basketball programme at the University of Kansas), and Camp inventing the new game of American football by a series of adaptations and changes to the rules of rugby football. But we can also observe entrepreneurship in the technology-first sense, as when the sport of mountain biking, with the technology of 'clunkers', developed (Buenstorf 2003), or windsurfing (Shah 2000).

Goff et al. (2002) argue that racial integration of baseball teams was an act of entrepreneurial innovation in a competitive market that had the spillover consequence of lowering discrimination in sports. Coyne et al. (2007: 230) explain 'simply put, the entrepreneur's decision to integrate must be viewed in the context of his overall desire to maximize profits'. Wright and Zammuto (2013) show how entrepreneurship in sports relates strongly to institutional roles within sports organisation. Ratten (2011) argues that the entrepreneurial perspective can be integrated into the theory of sports management.

A sports trajectory

At the core of evolutionary economics is the notion of the *technological trajectory*, onto which are mapped concepts such as an industry lifecycle (Klepper and Graddy 1990), and an innovation diffusion process (Rogers 2003). New sports may also evolve from existing sports through a branching process. Consider motorsports. From the initial development of a technology – chassis-mounted engines – and the development of industries and markets for the manufacture and sale of cars, bikes, trucks, etc., we can also observe a corresponding development of organised sports associated with this technology and industries (such as Formula 1 and Formula 2). These are more than simply clubs, but governing bodies that create and enforce rules that enable the organisation of championship events in a motorsport class. What we observe is the development and differential replication and selection (the evolution) of both increasingly popular and increasingly specialised sporting niches by governance bodies that organise sporting competition about particular technological capabilities.

A further implication of a trajectory focus on sports industries is the application of models of diversity and shake-out in which the early periods of an evolutionary trajectory (into an open niche) are characterised by an explosion of variety, followed by a long period of subsequent winnowing of that variety (selection) to a smaller set of dominant species or technologies. Steve Klepper and colleagues (Klepper and Graddy 1990, Klepper and Simons 1997, 2005) have studied this industrial process in car and tyre manufacturing in the USA and noted the same dynamic pattern: hundreds of small diverse firms at the beginning of the industry (phase 1), followed by a consolidation to a few dominant designs through a process they call 'shake-out' (phase 2), resulting in an oligopolistic mature industry (phase 3).

A working hypothesis is that the evolution of a sport follows a similar pattern. We would expect this to apply differently to technology-first sports compared to rules-first sports in respect of the dimensions over which the initial explosion of variety and diversity applied to, and the focal point of the subsequent shake-out. The period of variety generation can be understood as an exploration phase in several dimensions.

An obvious one is *design* dimensions of the sports technology – shapes of bicycle frames, say, or rigging set-ups on sailing equipment, or the 'formula' for motorsports. Sports technology, like any technology, is largely experimentally developed, and the capabilities opened by any new technological innovation (in engine power, or materials) will lead to a period of exploration followed by subsequent differential selection (see Desbordes 2001 for a study of innovation in skis). Other dimensions may be in relation to the operational and governance rules, of the sport, such as tournament structure, business models, scale and frequency and other factors.

Again, the initial explosion of variety may reflect fundamental uncertainty about participant supply, sponsor requirements, spectator demand, media economics and so on, all of which may only be entrepreneurial conjectures and market tests. We would thus expect to observe a phase of learning and consolidation to follow the period of exploration in any sport. Furthermore, we would expect this period to correspond with the main growth phase of a sport, and with the creation of capital and wealth associated with the owners of that model and its key complementary assets (Teece 1986). Economic models of excess entry and winner-takes-all effects would be expected to apply through the trajectory of a new sport.

A further phenomenon we may see in the trajectory of any technology-first sport is overshooting (Earl and Potts 2013). Thomas and Potts (2016) explain how overshooting unfolds in the sport of windsurfing in consequence of technological (rather than price) competition between firms, driving a wedge between entry-level users and elite-level equipment. Overshooting can also be observed in many board sports and on-water sports (paddle-boarding, canoeing, kayaking), but is notably absent in some other sports such as cycling.

Overshooting in motorsports, which tend to have strong governance, usually results in the formation of new 'formulas' for competition, rather than the collapse of the sport. Overshooting is not an oversight by the producers, but a dynamic consequence of manufacturer-led technological competition with weak governance. The result is the risk of destroying the sport in the long run because of the harm to entry-level users. Unconstrained technological competition can destroy a sport through this 'overshooting' trajectory. Not all sports experience this dynamic pathology – indeed, it is characteristic only of technology-first sports and, furthermore, ones with governance that is too weak to effectively constrain competitive technological development. Examples of these will be explored later in this chapter. Control of competitive technological overshooting is thus one of the important functions of the development of sports governance and rules in technology-first sports.

User innovation is a further aspect of technological change in sports. In the standard model of technological competition, firms invest in research and consumers choose over the rival offerings. This model of the passive consumer began to be challenged by models of 'open innovation' (Chesbrough 2003) and 'user innovation' (von Hippel 1986).

It has been widely observed that the origination and technological development of new sports seems to disproportionately lie with the role of users and participants, particularly of technology-first sports (Boyce and Bischak 2010, Buenstorf 2003, Franke and Shah 2003, Lüthje 2004, Lüthje et al. 2005, Shah 2000, 2005). (Counterexamples are rules-first sports, such as cricket, which developed new game forms, such as the one-day match or the new 20–20 match, as a governing body- and corporate-led new rule form that was then imposed on the game.) The development of a new sporting technology is almost entirely an experimental endeavour that benefits from pooling and sharing of such knowledge, much of which is tacit, is difficult to acquire or maintain property rights over and is of limited external value. Reputational mechanisms (as in science; Kealey and Ricketts 2014) can function as economic incentives to investment and disclosure of innovations.

The rise and fall of windsurfing – a cautionary tale

The trajectory of windsurfing is usefully described in Almudi et al. (2018) in three stages: the emergence of the industry; the sectoral consolidation; and its decline or innovative reversion and lack of dynamism.

Stage 1: the emergence of the sector (1970–1980)

The windsurfing industry traces its origins to 1968 when Americans Hoyle Schweitzer and Jim Drake achieved a grant of US patent for the 'sailboard' – a contraption consisting of a surfboard-like board, with a sailing rig attached via a universal joint. With their patent secured, Hoyle and Schweitzer embarked on ambitious licensing programme, primarily in the USA and Europe, to encourage manufacturers to take up production. Windsurfing struggled initially to gain credibility in countries such as Australia and the USA that had strong surfing and water sports traditions, but in places like Germany, France and Holland that had no strong surfing culture, it very quickly became a 'cool' sport [19]. Boardsailing (as it was then known) became the world's fastest growing sport (Thomas and Potts 2016).

While the equipment and its application remained relatively static in Europe, from the mid-1970s users in other parts of the globe, including Hawaii and Australia, began to modify their equipment to exploit and explore local conditions (waves and wind). The pioneer manufacturing firms for windsurfing equipment emerged largely as a result of early user-innovators forming commercial concerns to manufacture and distribute their versions of equipment, in response to demand from aspirational users (e.g. Lüthje 2004, Shah 2006).

Stage 2: the consolidation of the sector (1980–1985)

As the popularity and participation of the sport grew, the innovation paths broke down clearly into two very different strands: one strand developed a high-performance-based sport equipment that was oriented to an elite of athletes (the Hawaiian user-innovators) and a growing cohort of aspirational participants willing to follow them; and the other strand focussed on the populist route, maintaining the equipment in the simple and low-cost traditional level (primarily in Europe).

It was finally the elite who led the rate and direction of the inventive activity in windsurfing equipment. In a relatively short span of time (three to five years), the equipment design became highly technical and, with the advent of new materials and manufacturing processes such as the incorporation of Kevlar and carbon-fibre sandwich construction methods, a more expensive, high-performance entry-level for newcomers. Innovation was being led by manufacturers, who, responding to the demands of their high profile, sponsored elite athletes seeking to sail faster, jump higher and otherwise push the performance boundaries of the sport.

Stage 3: the decline of the sector (1985–2000)

Together with the advance in the performance level, another significant change occurred in the sector by the end of the 1980s. An early feature of the 'industry' was the existence of windsurfing schools, borne of the fact that while the early equipment and use was *relatively* simple, there was still some investment in skills acquisition needed to enjoy the sport. A natural progression of these schools was to sell equipment to their clients, and as equipment became more expensive (and higher margin), many of these businesses became retailers and neglected their school operations and the windsurf schools progressively closed down.

Motivated by higher profits with less effort from selling more technical, more expensive products with higher retail margins, they left aside training activity that was crucial to developing an entry-level pipeline of new users. As equipment evolved further in sophistication, materials and expense, for aspirational participants and recreational and social users it became increasingly difficult to keep up with their peers, leading to technical overshooting where the pace of innovation exceeds the absorptive capacity of the user community (e.g. Earl and Potts 2013, Thomas and Potts 2016).

In the windsurfing case, a peripheral observation is that there were, at least in the early and consolidation phases of the sport's development, schools that facilitated skills acquisition and development for new and aspirational participants. Instruction was a useful way of introducing new participants into the sport and more quickly building their capacity to enjoy the sport and grow in capability (therefore leading them to demanding higher-performance equipment). When manufacturer-led competition subsequently drew firms' attention to the fact that it was more lucrative to sell high-margin equipment to existing users rather than selling lessons, the capacity of the 'industry' servicing the sport to meet the needs of new users subsequently declined. This short-term expediency on the part of the retail sector, under pressure from manufacturers and distributors to sell more and higher-end products, led to many recreational users and aspirational participants abandoning the sport. Without a pipeline of entry-level users to replace them, the capacity of the consumer side of the market began to taper off, and we observe with it a decline of the sector dynamism (mostly regarding new varieties of the sport), and ultimately, many firms went bankrupt (Thomas and Potts 2016).

Against this backdrop, the sport of windsurfing was not completely bereft of organisation or regulation. Windsurfing associations formed in many jurisdictions and disciplines within the sport, from wave sailing to flat-water racing and everything in between branches of the sport, and for many years, there were numerous carnivals and events around the globe. But there was no legitimate governing body that managed to effectively claim dominion over the sport and arrest or even manage the technical trajectory. We should also not ignore here that 'boardsailing' has become an Olympic sport, and for the purposes of Olympic and Olympics-focussed competition, it is governed by the International Sailing Association, but it should also be noted that the forms of equipment and competition in that setting bear much more resemblance to dinghy sailing than to the roots and traditional 'maverick' attractions of windsurfing as it is more widely known.

When sports technology meets rules

In recent years, 'conventional' or 'rules-driven' sports have not been immune from technological advances that, while designed to enhance human performance, challenge the 'rules' of the sport and at some perhaps philosophical level raise questions about how much human performance matters. Advances in materials technology and equipment design have even raised the notion of 'techno-doping', where technology is seen to unbalance the playing field and technology serves to afford one competitor an unfair advantage over another.

A fundamental debate follows around the intersection of rules and technology within the conduct of the sport – where rules try to keep sports relatively fair so the best person, rather than the best equipment, wins. As examples, let us consider the emergence of hydrodynamic full-body swimsuits in swimming competition, the emergence of fluid-dynamics-optimised javelins in field athletics and the emergence of aerodynamic aids in cycling, and the respective governing bodies' responses to these advances.

FINA and the hydrodynamic swimsuit

The FINA, based in Lucerne, Switzerland, is the international federation that governs competition in six aquatic sports, these being swimming, diving, high-diving, artistic swimming (formerly synchronised swimming), water polo and open-water swimming. FINA also oversees 'Masters' competition (for adults) in its disciplines.

In the 2007–2008 period, swimming became the (then) latest sport to embrace materials engineering, in the form of a variety of swimsuits that were designed to achieve two things – to help swimmers maintain their most streamlined shape possible and to reduce hydrodynamic drag as they move through the water. Suits based on similar design principles were produced by several manufacturers, but the most prominent example of the time was the 'LZR Racer' swimsuit by the company Speedo, reportedly developed in conjunction with scientists and engineers from NASA. By utilising advances in computational fluid dynamics, the Speedo company produced a full-body suit that was claimed to reduce the swimmer's drag through water by up to 5%. The suit featured a tight, corset-like midsection that was claimed to reduce muscle fatigue and streamline the swimmer's shape, and seamless construction from a polyurethane-based, hydrophobic (water repelling) material (Smith 2008). These design features were intended to address three limiting factors on a swimmer's performance:

- Pressure drag – reduced by compressing a swimmer's body into a more streamlined shape;
- Viscous drag – reduced by providing a textured surface (as in riblets for yachts and shark skin); and
- Buoyancy – aided by trapping air within the swimsuit, enabling the swimmer's body to sit higher in the water. The consequence of this is that less of the swimmer's energy is expended in maintaining flotation and more can be directed to propelling the swimmer forward through the water.

Initially, FINA sanctioned the use of the LZR Racer suit in official competition, but in the period from its release in February 2008 through the 2008 Beijing Olympics and the 2009 World Swimming championships, some 130 world records fell to swimmers using the LZR suits and their imitators (Krouse 2009). Records were not merely broken; they were shattered by large margins not at all consistent with the 'normal' relatively steady incremental progression through the history of the sport.

A further feature of concern in relation to these suits was their cost – in the order of $US500–700 each – making swimming, traditionally a simple, low-cost, low-equipment sport, an expensive pursuit, potentially prohibitively so for many new entrants and budding champions with the attendant risk that swimming could become a financial arms race with the rewards going to the better funded competitor, rather than the more able or better-trained one.

Prompted by growing concerns about the trajectory of the sport, and the moral question of whether the sport is about who is the best swimmer or who has the best equipment, in July 2009, at its general congress, FINA banned the use of the LZR racer and similar suits, specifying that with effect from 2010 only textile suits affording minimal body coverage would be permitted in sanctioned competition. In this way, swimming followed the path previously set by the (then) International Amateur Athletic Federation (IAAF) and Cycling's Union Cycliste Internationale (UCI) in addressing the issue of 'techno-doping' by adopting rules designed to constrain the use of performance-enhancing equipment technologies in their respective sports (Smith 2009).

Engineering in athletics: javelin throwing

By the early–mid-1980s, performance in the field athletics discipline of javelin had developed to the point where, due to the massive distances that were being thrown by men in competition, concerns arose among those governing the sport that there was a looming danger that a javelin would be thrown so far as to clear the designated throwing area, specified at a length of 100 m. Alongside this arose a concern that the (relatively flat) trajectory of long throws was resulting in flat landings of the javelin itself, making adjudication of distance difficult and presenting a potential safety risk to others on the field. These concerns had been raised about the progression of throws over a period of years, but the catalyst for change came with a throw by German athlete Uwe Hohn, who in July 1984 threw the javelin 104.80 metres, breaking the previous world record by more than 5 metres.

The solution to the 'problem' was found in engineering. To reduce the javelin's flight time and distance, the 'official' specification of the javelin for sanctioned competition was altered by the IAAF to put its centre of gravity in front of its centre of pressure, so its nose pitched downwards in flight. The new javelins succeeded in reducing distances by about 10%. Significantly, unlike the previous example of the LZR Racer swimsuit, this is an example of a sport's governing body using engineering to justify a rule change, in contrast to the more usual rule change in response to an engineering innovation by a competitor (Smith 2008b).

Not to be outdone, javelin manufacturers of the day were able to recoup some of the lost distance by increasing the javelin's tail drag by roughening the tail's surface, using holes or dimples similar to those on a golf ball, to reduce laminar flow over the tail section. This modification effectively shifted the centre of pressure back towards the centre of gravity, improving the javelin's flight characteristics. The IAAF responded in 1991 by banning tail roughening, and all records achieved with tail-modified javelins were nullified. Despite that effort, distances crept up again with the current record being 98.48 metres (Smith 2008b). That being noted, most contemporary throws in men's competition at the time of writing are in the order of 90 metres.

Cycling's one-hour world record

Cycling by its nature is a 'technology-driven' sport in our taxonomy, with a sophisticated piece of equipment, namely the bicycle, being required to participate. Cycling competition takes many forms, from road and track racing through mountain bike racing to BMX, but arguably the most prestigious and difficult achievement for a cyclist is the 'hour record'. Simply explained, 'The Hour', as it is reverentially known, is the record for the longest distance cycled in one hour on a bicycle from a stationary start. Cyclists typically attempt the record alone on an oval-shaped velodrome track with no other competitors present.

Cycling's governing body, UCI, has several times modified its rules with respect to the one-hour cycling world record in an attempt to keep the record as a measure of human performance rather than innovative bicycle design. The first challenge to the rules occurred in 1933 when Francis Faure set a new one-hour record of 45.055 km (27.996 miles) using an aerodynamic recumbent bicycle – a bicycle characterised by the rider seated recumbent or laying down, as opposed to seated upright. Riding in a typical recumbent position, sitting low to the ground with feet outstretched, yields a significant reduction in aerodynamic drag due to reduced frontal area and affords a greater application of leg strength to the pedalling effort compared to the traditional upright riding position. In 1934, the UCI banned recumbent bikes from competing for the one-hour record, which caused a splinter group to form, currently called International Human Powered Vehicle Association (IHPVA). IHPVA allows any human-powered vehicle to compete for its version of the one-hour record, whereas UCI allows only upright bicycles (Clemitson 2014).

The one-hour record had a long and fabled history among cyclists and pundits. The first hour record was set in 1876 by American rider Frank Dodds who completed 26.508 km on a penny farthing. The record has been attempted sporadically over the many decades since. One of the most distinguished holders of the UCI one-hour record was five-time Tour De France winner Eddy Merckx, who claimed the record in 1972 with a ride of 49.431 km (30.715 miles). Merckx travelled to Mexico City to perform the feat – the high altitude and thinner air of that location reducing the drag force acting on the rider. Merckx undertook his ride on a relatively standard (for the day) upright, drop-bar track bike. Merckx' record stood for 12 years until it was beaten by Francisco Moser in 1984, recording 51.51 km, but distinct from Merckx in that Moser employed an aerodynamic disc-wheel and wore a drag-reducing skinsuit.

The 1990s saw the most radical changes in equipment, and approaches to aerodynamics used to tackle 'The Hour'. In 1993 and 1994, Scotsman Graeme Obree, who built his own bikes, posted two records with his hands tucked under his chest. His 'praying mantis' position, although legal under UCI rules, was seen as controversial by purists, pundits and the UCI and was ultimately banned by the UCI in May 1994. Also in 1994, Moser beat his 1984 record, using bullhorn handlebars, a bicycle with sleek airfoil tubing, disc-wheels and skinsuit.

Innovation didn't stop there. Englishman Chris Boardman set a new record of 56.375 km (35.030 mi) in 1996, employing a highly aerodynamic monocoque bicycle frame constructed of moulded carbon fibre, and a controversial arms-forward 'superman' riding position (also pioneered by Graham Obree). The UCI took issue with both Boardman's bicycle design and his riding position, outlawing both although his record was allowed to stand. However, this too was considered controversial by the UCI, and the riding position was banned making Boardman's record set in 1996 effectively unbeatable using traditional bike position (Clemitson 2014).

In 1997, the UCI effected a rule change to 'reign in' the technological advances and defined two categories of Hour Record – *the UCI Hour Record* which restricts competitors to equipment roughly the same as Merckx rode in 1972, and *Best Human Effort*, also known as the UCI *'Absolute Record'*, which permits modern equipment.

In 2014, the UCI reunified the two classifications into a single classification in line with regulations for current track pursuit bikes. Records previously removed for Chris Boardman and Graeme Obree were reinstated; however, the official benchmark record would remain at 49.7 km (30.9 mi) set in 2005 by Ondrej Sosenka, even though that was not the farthest distance ever recorded. To allow some innovation in equipment, under the new regulations riders *may use any bike allowed by the UCI standards for endurance track events in place at the time of the attempt* (Outside Online 2014). Sosenka's record has since been surpassed several times, and at the time of writing, the record is held by Belgian rider Victor Campenaerts, who with a nod to his countryman Merckx travelled to Mexico where he set the record at 55.059 km in April 2019.

While for the purposes of this chapter we focus our 'technology-driven' sports more on 'newer' sports such as windsurfing, we would also regard bat-and-ball sports as 'technology-driven' even though most are not 'new' sports in the way we think of them (e.g. baseball, cricket, tennis), insofar as they are dependent on equipment to play them. And like cycling and swimming, their respective governing bodies have from time to time imposed controls over equipment – for example on the size and composition of tennis racquets, baseball bats and cricket bats.

A new dawn: the emerging trajectory of eSports

The phenomenon that is eSports is widely believed to be of relatively recent vintage. However, the first eSports event was organised by the Laboratory for Artificial Intelligence at Stanford University in 1972 (Larch 2019). Since then, through the advent and development of games console and PC technology in the early 1990s and the proliferation of domestic Internet that facilitated networked online gaming in the late 1990s and early 2000s, eSport has grown to become a multi-billion-dollar global phenomenon, slated as a formal event in the 2022 Asian Games, and recognised by the IOC (Graham 2017). Further, eSports, and the ecosystem of actors that has developed around it, currently generates annual revenues exceeding US$1.1bn with audiences of 443 m across the globe, predicted to reach 645 m by the end of 2020 (Ayles 2019). However, the rise from arcade hobby to global sport has not followed a standard linear trajectory. Its growth has been characterised by development of, and competition for, resources between networks of powerful actors within the ecosystem imposing their own agendas (Peng et al. 2020).

In the mid-1980s, for example, the games console industry failed to capitalise on content and hardware developments, leading to the collapse of the video-game industry and curtailing its influence in eSport (Mitew and Moore 2017). This allowed PC developers to change the rules of the game and reshape gaming hardware and modes of play, taking gaming from the arcade to the home and, arguably, laying the foundation for eSports (Mitew and Moore 2017). In more recent times, games publishers have emerged as the powerful actors in the eSports ecosystem.

As the owners of the intellectual property, publishers exert significant control under the guise of governance (e.g. through licensing, updates and game deletions) over teams, leagues, events and indeed the hobbyist consumer (Ashton 2019, Peng et al. 2020). These examples illustrate the influence of technology actors in the eSports ecosystem and their ability to shape the normative institutions on how the game is played and where it is played and indeed regulated. However, these examples also underscore how, as a technology-driven sport, the rules of engagement are being shaped by a few powerful actors essentially for their own entrepreneurial gain (Thomas and Potts 2016).

Taking this influence further, Mitew and Moore (2017) identify three pillars of influence that are shaping the normative institutions of eSport. The authors highlight the influence of modes of gameplay, technology and material space. To illustrate, technological developments (e.g. single player to multi-player, portable to mobile, home Internet to digital platforms) have shaped and evolved how players interact and compete. In turn, influence has been exerted on the design of gaming modes (e.g. first-person shooter, role-playing, multi-player online battle arenas) that further changed and fragmented the playing landscape and facilitated competitive gaming. The combined influence of these elements has evolved the material spaces where eSports can take place (e.g. bedrooms, Internet cafes, public transport, arenas) challenging spatial social norms and conventions by turning any space into a gaming venue, and cities into an epicentre for global eSports events (McCauley, Tierney and Tokbaeva 2020). These pillars of influence represent complex, interdependent interactions between networks of competing technology-developing actors within the gaming ecosystem, bringing new opportunities that influence social structures and conventions shaping the sport and its market (Potts and Thomas 2018).

In essence, the eSports ecosystem is characterised by a global network of interdependent actors from separate but related markets (e.g. game design, hardware, playing, watching and governing) who each bring their own agenda to the ongoing development and shaping of the sport (Scholz 2019). Within these conditions, a range of national, regional, league, player and gaming industry governance associations have sprung up (Ashton 2019). However, what is lacking is a legitimate, overarching regulative body to represent the interests of actors in the eSports ecosystem and oversee regulative and normative aspects of the sport and its market (Peng et al. 2020).

The upshot of this is a fragmented regulatory system lacking legitimacy, with a small number of influential actors setting the regulative and normative landscape to suit their aims, and as eSports continues to grow financially, the potential for legitimacy-eroding activities is ever present (Peng et al. 2020). In the absence of independent oversight that can establish legitimacy within the eSports ecosystem, it is viewed as unstable compared to other sports with the potential for further fragmentation or even collapse of the eSports ecosystem.

Conclusion

Sports industries offer some useful insights into how collective action by user groups or industry self-regulation might manage a potentially destructive dynamic – such as the case of swimming, which faced elite/manufacturer-led equipment development in the form of (expensive) hydrodynamic swimsuits. Recognising the potential of new and expensive swimsuit technology to increase the cost of competitive equipment, the world governing body for swimming, FINA, banned the use of the suits in competition. This was not so much an action to support or build the capacity of participants, rather a regulatory response designed to limit equipment development to maintain the perception of fairness and to preserve the accessibility of what has traditionally been a low-cost–low-equipment sport.

In a similar vein, the sport of cycling faced similar risk of technical overshooting in the late 1990s with the advent of new materials such as carbon fibre and Kevlar allowing more exotic, aerodynamic bicycle design. These new materials and exotic designs extended the performance of athletes but also led to competitive equipment becoming more specialised and expensive, potentially limiting users' access to competitive equipment, as well as seeming to blur the lines between human performance and equipment performance. The governing body for the sport, UCI, took steps to constrain the design parameters of bicycles for the purposes of sanctioned competition.

Again, equipment development was artificially constrained by regulation to preserve a dimension of 'fairness' and accessibility to match the perceived capacity of the user community. If a truly revolutionary performance innovation appears in a sport, there are two options for the sport's governing body to consider:

- Allow it either unchecked or within modified rules; or
- Ban it and risk creating a new branch of the sport

By contrast, and unlike swimming, cycling and athletics, the sport of windsurfing did not have a unifying, global governing body with power to impose similar constraints on equipment design and the sport and the mass participation the sport earlier enjoyed withered. The case of windsurfing presents a cautionary tale for the emerging domain of eSports, which, as has been observed, appears to be demonstrating a similar early trajectory, and while there is some degree of nascent regulation, it is fragmented and so far, lacking a widely accepted legitimacy.

Acknowledgement

The authors wish to thank Distinguished Professor Jason Potts for guidance and insightful comments in the development of this chapter.

References

Almudi, I., Fatas-Villafranca, F., Potts, J., and Thomas, S. (2018). 'Absorptive Capacity of Demand in Sports Innovation' *Economics of Innovation and New Technology* 27(4): 328–342.

Ashton, G. (2019). Governing the Wild West: An Introduction to Esports Federations and Associations. *The Esports Observer.* Accessed online 22 October 2020 https://esportsobserver.com/esports-federations-intro/

Ayles, J. (2019). Global eSports Revenue Reaches More Than $1 Billion As Audience Figures Exceed 433 Million. *Forbes Magazine.* Accessed online 22 October 2020 https://www.forbes.com/sites/jamesayles/2019/12/03/global-esports-revenue-reaches-more-than-1-billion-as-audience-figures-exceed-433-million/#63620d511329

Boyce, J., and Bischak, D. (2010). 'Learning by Doing, Knowledge Spillovers and Technological and Organizational Change in High-Altitude Mountaineering' *Journal of Sports Economics* 11(5): 496–532.

Buenstorf, G. (2003). 'Designing Clunkers: Demand-Side Innovation and the Early History of the Mountain-Bike' in J. S. Metcalfe and U. Cantner (eds) *Change, Transformation and Development.* Springer Verlag, Heidelberg. pp. 53–70.

Chacar, A., and Hesterly, W. (2004). 'Innovations and Value Creation in Major League Baseball, 1860–2000' *Business History* 46(3): 407–438.

Chesbrough, H. (2003). 'The Era of Open Innovation' *MIT Sloan Management Review* 44(3): 35–41.

Clemitson, S. (19 September 2014). 'Why Jens Voigt and a New Group of Cyclists Want to Break the Hour Record' *The Guardian.* Accessed 1 November 2020. https://www.theguardian.com/sport/100-tours-100-tales/2014/sep/19/why-jens-voigt-and-a-new-group-of-cyclists-want-to-break-the-hour-record.

Coyne, C., Isaacs, J., Schwartz, J., and Carilli, A. (2007). 'Put Me in Coach I'm Ready to Play' *Review of Austrian Economics* 20: 237–246.

Crouse, K. (2009). 'Swimming Bans High-Tech Suits, Ending an Era' Accessed 1 November 2020 https://www.nytimes.com/2009/07/25/sports/25swim.html

Desbordes, M. (2001). 'Innovation Management in the Sports Industry: Lessons from the Salomon Case' *European Sport Management Quarterly* 1(2): 124–149.

Earl, P., and Potts, J. (2013). 'The Creative Instability Hypothesis' *Journal of Cultural Economics* 37: 153–173.

Franke, N., and Shah, S. (2003). 'How Communities Support Innovative Activities: An Exploration of Assistance and Sharing Among End Users' *Research Policy* 32(1): 157–178.

Füller, J., Jawecki, G., and Mühlbacher, H. (2007). 'Innovation Creation by Online Basketball Communities' *Journal of Business Research* 60(1): 60–71.

Goff, B., McCormick, R., and Tollison, R. (2002). 'Racial Integration as an Innovation: Empirical Evidence from Sports Leagues' *American Economic Review* 92: 16–26.

Graham, B. A. (2017). 'eSports to be a Medal Event at 2022 Asian Games' *The Guardian.* Accessed online 22 October 2020 https://www.theguardian.com/sport/2017/apr/18/esports-to-be-medal-sport-at-2022-asian-games

Hardy, S. (1986). 'Entrepreneurs, Organizations and the Sports Marketplace' *Journal of Sports History* 13(1): 14–33.

Kealey, T., and Ricketts, M. (2014). 'Modelling Science as a Contribution Good' *Research Policy* 43(6): 1014–1024.

Klepper, S., and Graddy, E. (1990). 'The Evolution of New Industries and the Determinants of Market Structure' *RAND Journal of Economics* 21(1): 27–44.

Klepper, S., and Simons, H. (2005). 'Industry Shakeouts and Technological Change' *International Journal of Industrial Organization* 23(1–2): 23–43.

Krueger, A. (1974). 'The Political Economy of the Rent-Seeking Society' *American Economic Review* 64: 291–303.

Larch, F. (2019). 'The History of the Origin of eSports' Accessed online 20 October 2020 https://www.ispo.com/en/markets/history-origin-esports#:~:text=On%20October%2019%2C%201972%2C%20however, day%20to%20compete%20in%20%22Spacewar!

Lüthje, C. (2004). 'Characteristics of Innovating Users in a Consumer Goods Field: An Empirical Study of Sport-Related Product Consumers' *Technovation* 24: 683–695.

Lüthje, C., Herstatt, C., and von Hippel, E. (2005). 'User-Innovators and "Local" Information: The Case of Mountain Biking' *Research Policy* 34: 951–964.

McCauley, B., Tierney, K., and Tokbaeva, D. (2020). 'Shaping a Regional Offline eSports Market: Understanding How Jönköping, the "City of DreamHack", Takes URL to IRL' *International Journal on Media Management* 22(1): 30–48.

Mitew, T. E., and Moore, C. L. (2017). 'Histories of Internet Games and Play: Space, Technique, and Modality' in G. Goggin and M. J. McLelland (eds) *The Routledge Companion to Global Internet Histories*. London, UK: Routledge, pp. 448–460.

North, D. C. (1990). *Institutions, Institutional Change and Economic Performance*. Cambridge: Cambridge University Press.

Peng, Q., Dickson, G., Scelles, N., Grix, J., and Brannagan, P. M. (2020). 'Esports Governance: Exploring Stakeholder Dynamics' *Sustainability* 12(19): 8270–8285.

Potts, J., and Thomas, S. (2018). 'Toward a New (Evolutionary) Economics of Sports' *Sport, Business and Management: An International Journal* 8(1): 82–96.

Ratten, V. (2011). 'Sport-Based Entrepreneurship: Towards a New Theory of Entrepreneurship and Sport Management' *International Entrepreneurship and Management Journal* 7(1): 57–69.

Rogers, E. (2003). *Diffusion of Innovations* (5th ed). New York: Free Press.

Scholz, T. M. (2019). *eSports Is Business*. London, UK, Cham: Palgrave Pivot.

Shah, S. (2000). 'Sources and Patterns of Innovation in Consumer Products Field: Innovation in Sporting Equipment' Sloan Working Paper #4105.

Shah, S. (2005). 'From Innovation to Firm Formation in the Windsurfing, Skateboarding and Snowboarding Industries' University of Illinois working paper #05–0107.

Shah, S., and Tripas, M. (2007). 'The Accidental Entrepreneur: The Emergent and Collective Process of User Entrepreneurship' *Strategic Entrepreneurship Journal* 1: 123–140.

Smith, R. (2008(a)). 'Engineering in Sports: LZR Racer Swimsuit' Accessed 7 November 2020 https://www.symscape.com/blog/engineering-in-sports-lzr-racer-swimsuit

Smith, R. (2008(b)). 'Engineering in Sports: Javelin Throwing' Accessed 7 November 2020 https://www.symscape.com/blog/engineering-in-sports-lzr-racer-swimsuit

Smith, R. (2009). 'Swimsuits Banned as Technology Doping' Accessed 7 November 2020 https://www.symscape.com/blog/swimsuit-banned-as-technology-doping

Stigler, G. (1971). 'The Theory of Economic Regulation' *Bell Journal of Economics and Management Science* 2: 3–21.

Terjesen, S. (2008). 'Venturing Beyond the Marathon: The Entrepreneurship of Ultrarunning and the IAU World Cup in Korea' *Asian Business & Management* 7(2): 1–30.

Thomas, S., and Potts, J. (2016). 'How Industry Competition Ruined Windsurfing' *Sport, Business and Management: An International Journal* 6(5): 565–578.

von Hippel, E. (1986). 'Lead Users: A Source of Novel Product Concepts' *Management Science* 32(7): 791–805.

Williamson, O. E. (2000). 'The New Institutional Economics: Taking Stock, Looking Ahead' *Journal of Economic Literature* 38(3): 595–613.

Wright, A., and Zammuto, R. (2013). 'Creating Opportunities for Institutional Entrepreneurship: The Colonel and the Cup in English Country Cricket' *Journal of Business Venturing* 28: 51–68.

Part 2
Incentives, governance and sports behaviour

5 Wrong behaviour due to wrong incentives

How to transform doping into a self-defeating game

Wladimir Andreff

Introduction

Doping can be considered from either a health or a sporting standpoint, or from both. Here, the focus is more on the sporting aspect and the economic consequences of doping even though the health aspect is quite important since doping can drive an athlete down to his/her own death. This happened to British rider Tom Simpson who died when climbing Mont Ventoux in a Tour de France stage in 1967. Uncontrolled behaviour of a sporting doper – i.e. self-doping without medical control – may result in the paradoxical unwitting suicide of the athlete.

When it comes to sporting, doping is regarded as wrong because it results in unfair behaviour since it usually distorts the outcome of a sporting contest or delivers a non-credible sporting outcome. A natural experiment exhibited doping distortions in Russian medal totals at Sochi Winter Games (Andreff, 2019). Based on an economic forecasting model of medal totals (Andreff, 2013a), Russia was expected to win 24 medals and rank 4th in the medal count. However, the Russian Olympic winter sports team won as many as 33 medals and ranked 1st at 2014 Sochi Games. The author was not able to identify doping among the explanatory variables of teams' sporting performances because of the lack of data. However, by 2018, 11 Russian athletes lost their medals won in Sochi after doping disqualification. Then, Russia fell back to 22 medal wins, and 5th rank, much closer to the model's forecast. This supports the hypothesis of unfair distortions in sports outcomes that are a consequence of doping.

The second impact of doping on sporting outcomes is that a competition may simply be left without a winner for ever. In this respect, 1998–2010 was the darkest period ever for cycling Tour de France. The doping scandal started up in 1998 when the Festina team was expelled from the peloton; it followed with Armstrong, Landis, and Contador disqualifications, so that the Tour lost nine out of its 12 final yellow jersey winners between 1999 and 2010.

Winning or not winning a sporting contest boils down to earning more or less money (prizes, salaries, sponsorship contracts) in high-level and professional sports. Such economic consequences of doping behaviour provide strong incentives to dope. Doping dates back to the early times of competitive sports. But it has switched to a concealed strategy of performing against the law or the rules of the game as soon as it has happened to be definitely forbidden, sanctioned and even sentenced in justice courts.

The chapter reads as follows. The first section discusses how doping was transformed from simple cheating behaviour into a systematic hidden strategy when growing streams of money were poured into elite and professional sports. This occurred as major rewards for athletes' performances increased on the one hand and, on the other hand, when new rules were introduced that started prohibiting and sanctioning doping were unveiled. A second section tackles the issue of how current anti-doping policy turned out to be inefficient with the outcome that, instead of curbing the growth in the number of doped athletes, it practically resulted in ever more widespread doping behaviour. The last section suggests that athletes' behaviour has to be transformed if one wants the anti-doping policy to be more efficient in reducing the number of doped athletes. But transforming their behaviour can only result from changing incentives to dope into incentives not to dope, which requires a new set of rules targeting such behavioural transformation.

Doping: from cheating behaviour to economic crime

Long ago, 1,000 B.C., when physical exercise, usually associated with military training, started to be organised as a series of sporting contests, new manipulations emerged for winning by cheating, basically corruption and doping (Maennig, 2002). In the ancient Olympics, athletes consume large quantities of meat for increasing their strength despite this being a violation of the Olympics rules. In the third century B.C., opium was already taken occasionally to stimulate athletes (Bourg & Gouguet, 2017). Cocaine started being consumed as a sport performance-enhancing drug (PED) in 1863; alcoholic beverages in 1881; ammoniac in 1891; cannabis in 1898; and arsenic in 1899. From the 1890s on, professional cyclists took caffeine and cocaine to improve their performance, reduce pain and delay fatigue; in the 1930s, amphetamines replaced strychnine among doping substances whereas Soviet athletes started using male hormones in the 1950s (Riordan, 1993), and the Americans followed soon after with steroids. Thousands of Olympic medals have been won by doped athletes. Despite using well-known substances, only a small number of them have been caught and disqualified since 1896.

In more recent decades, outside sport, taking PEDs became widespread in a more liberal, competitive, self-centred society, coined as a winner-takes-all society (Frank & Cook, 1995). Doping can improve performance at work and labour productivity, and hence revenues. Therefore, it goes unheeded or is tolerated in various jobs and professions such as rock 'n roll bands, movie stars, various kinds of on-the-stage show performances, and security services. Making money by any means is felt to be more important than aligning to the rule of law in a greed-led economy (Andreff, 2013b). Consequently, monetary incentives to dope are much stronger than doping prohibition or regulation, if any. In such a context, where many are pressured by everyday economic competition and a daily race for earning more and more money, this increasingly stressed life increasingly requires drugs as life or lifestyle sustaining or for leisure time consumption. Now PEDs account for a noticeable share in the current basket of goods purchased by a growing number of consumers.

Why is a similar tolerance shown to PED consumption by competitive athletes? What is wrong with their doping behaviour? Increasing money streams flowing into sports have transformed sport into a commodity traded in globalised markets (Andreff, 2012) somewhat in contradiction to a supposedly initial pure sporting ethics (Andreff, 2000). Transgressions of sport rules, including doping behaviour, are nurtured by irrepressible athletes' willingness, or even eagerness, to win sporting contests in view to pocketing prizes, bonuses, higher salaries and more profitable sponsorship contracts and, at the end of the day, to upgrading the athletes' status, reputation and market value (i.e. transfer fee and salary).

A second consequence of increased monetary incentives to win in sporting contests is the widespread use of PEDs. While until the 1960s doping was not explicitly forbidden by sport rules and was not systematically tested, repressed and sanctioned as such (Bourg, 2016), its prohibition was triggered by some publicised doping scandals broadcast on TV and premature athlete deaths. An anti-doping law was enforced in the Tour de France through instant unexpectedly administered doping tests since 1966. The first reaction of riders was to oppose such tests, then cheat by delivering fake urine and blood samples or sometimes take strike action through work stoppages. The law did not prevent Tom Simpson's death, evidencing that anti-doping combat was based on wrong, below-discussed incentives.

The IOC Medical Commission established the first list of prohibited classes of substances and medical doping protocols in the 1960s. Since then, the IOC's current definition of doping has evolved up to the 'use or attempted use of a prohibited substance or a prohibited method', both being specified in a now-famous negative list. All major sports associations have established at national and international levels particular enforcement institutions that rely on one regulatory system where the negative list is used as a benchmark for detecting and sanctioning doping behaviour. This institutional change has, by the same token, modified the major reason why doping is wrong behaviour, transforming it from simply unfair cheating – which it still is to some extent – into explicitly violating a new fundamental sport rule, in other words into criminal behaviour. The latter can result in criminal charges.

When adopting inappropriate or wrong and now potentially sanctioned behaviour, athletes primarily follow the objective of drawing some net economic benefit from doping. And, this relates to the standard economic theory of doping treated as an economic crime. Thus, doping emerged as a major issue in modern sports even though it was prohibited for the sake of protecting athletes' health and with the rational of enforcing moral sporting ethics.

Moreover, soon assimilated into the realm of an economic crime and under threat of potential detection, doping behaviour was increasingly covered with secrecy and *omerta* (the law of silence). But with this doping became a most common practice among athletes.

The starting point for an economic analysis of doping cannot assume that so many top-level athletes make the decision to dope because they are bad people, thugs, professional cheaters, delinquents or naked criminals. Those first economists who attempted at explaining doping behaviour considered it as economic crime after its prohibition, but a crime which is worth being committed if it corresponds to athletes' deeply rooted economic and financial interests. They were able to rely on standard economics of crime due to Becker (1968) where criminal behaviour is supposed to result from an individual's cost–benefit analysis when the outcome of such economic calculation turns out to be a net benefit. If so, an individual develops a personal interest in crime and eventually invests in a targeted crime. For years, doping was analysed through the lenses of the economics of crime.

In a typical Beckerian standard model, the decision to dope (to commit a crime) depends on the value of $E(G_d)$ such as the following:

$$E(B_d) = E(R_d) - C_d - E(S_d) > 0 \qquad (1)$$

$$\text{or}: \quad E(B_d) = (1-p)(R_d) - C_d - p(S_d) > 0 \qquad (1')$$

$$E(G_d) > D \qquad (2)$$

where $E(B_d)$ stands for the expected value of net benefit derived from doping, $E(R_d)$ for the expected revenues earned thanks to doping, C_d for the actual cost of a doping programme, $E(S_d)$ for the expected cost of sanctions if the doped athlete is caught and tested positive, and p is the probability of being sanctioned ($0 \leq p \leq 1$); hence, $(1 - p)$ is the probability of not being caught and sanctioned. An athlete makes the decision to dope if the expected net benefit is positive – if doping pays. However, as assumed by Becker, anyone has some personal ethical values, including those athletes intending to dope, so that the latter transgress to a certain extent their own values when doping. Here, there is a non-monetary disutility D of doping to the athlete. Expected net economic benefit must exceed this disutility for a crime to be committed, for the athlete to decide to dope.

A clue for how to combat doping in sport can be found in the aforementioned model as well as legitimacy for the tools implemented to combat doping. One lever of anti-doping policy could consist of lowering the expected value of monetary gains made through doping *(1 – p) R_d*. A drastic solution would attempt to dry up the money flowing into competitive sports, shrinking the potential value of R_d. This is neither realistic nor feasible in the world of highly monetised 21st century's sport. A second option would be to try decreasing the probability *(1 – p)*, that is increasing the probability p of being detected. This calls into question the efficiency of current anti-doping tools.

Except for assigning a policeman to each individual athlete, there is no way to push p down to zero.

Increasing the monetary cost of a doping programme C_d is not really an option since it does not depend on either sport governing bodies' or other sports participants' decisions but on what happens on the market for PEDs and on innovations in the pharmaceutical and medical industry. Therefore, sticking to the Beckerian model of crime, we are left with two actually feasible options. One is to adjust or vary the level of sanctions S_d, while the other one is to augment and improve education (of moral values) provided to athletes in such a way as to increase their non-monetary disutility D of doping. At best it is a complementary weapon to the threat of sanction and increasing the probability of detection $(1-p)$ which, together, increase the price of doping. The maximum price is a life ban from competitive sports (a rather rare sentence so far).

Policy recommendations for restricting doping practices and the number of those addicted are straightforward: (1) upgrade and randomise athlete testing; and (2) lengthen the negative list, thus raising the cost of doping programmes.[1] A proxy for pushing up the disutility of doping should involve stronger athlete ethical education, completed with deterrence and prevention. Notice that aforementioned standard anti-doping tools are targeted at curbing the willingness to dope through creating disincentives, not at transforming current doping practices into different behaviour.

Testing for PEDs was introduced at the Mexico Olympic Games in 1968, but it took 20 years to make combatting anti-doping an urgent priority, namely with Ben Johnson having been tested positive for using steroids. Since then, the negative list is enforced by randomly testing athlete blood and/or urine samples. Testing for illegal substances has become a business with athletes trying to hide or mask their use from officials and fellow competitors, while laboratories are developing additional and more sensitive procedures enabling them to detect even small residues of illegal PEDs. Thus, detecting PED use and evading detection has become a specific form of arms race (Frick, 2008).

In the wake of Festina scandal, the World Anti-Doping Agency (WADA) was created in 2000.

The emergence of WADA has not changed the above-described anti-doping approach: an athlete is tested positive when a prohibited substance is found in his/her body beyond a pre-defined quantitative threshold; then, the sanction applies. The WADA list of prohibited products is based on three principles: the product has the potential to enhance performance, it represents a health risk, and it is contrary to sport ethics. For a PED to be part of this list, it is enough for just two out of three criteria to be met. WADA policy is rooted in using punitive measures to secure compliance through rigid penalties combining shaming with fines, disqualifications and, in extreme cases, lifetime exclusion from participation in sporting contests. For a first violation involving the use or possession of a prohibited PED, athletes may be disqualified for up to two years, while for a second violation players are disqualified for life.

In 2008, WADA introduced a biological passport, longitudinal follow-up and geo-location system (Anti-Doping Administration and Management

System) that requires each athlete to signal his/her residence location every day of the year. After three unsuccessful checks, an athlete is suspended for two years as if doping is proved. This more stringent anti-doping fight may explain the decline in doping sanctions in the 2010s with the optimistic assumption that WADA and national anti-doping agencies have become more efficient. An alternative assumption is that athletes have adjusted to the new regulation in finding new doping substances or some ways for circumventing doping tests and everyday surveillance.

In order to fulfil his/her first objective of drawing net benefits from doping, an athlete usually considers that he/she also has to achieve a second objective: holding a differential advantage over fellow competitors and, therefore, an increased probability to win sporting contests that will translate into improving economic gains owing to doping, or yielding a return on doping. Thus, doping is part of a search of a positive differential competitive advantage. If a regulatory device succeeds in convincing athletes that doping does not provide such a differential advantage, a very significant step forward would be reached in transforming doping behaviour into something else. But this is not what WADA is targeting.

Consequently, there are two reasons for *omerta* about doping. First, not even a criminal is happy to publicising his/her crime since a successful crime is an undetected one. Second, a doped athlete involved in competitive sport will never reveal to opponents the source of his/her differential advantage. Doping behaviour makes all doped athletes mute with regard to doping. Beyond health and unfairness, the fight against silence (*omerta*) must be a third pillar of anti-doping combat.

Now, if doping is widespread or even generalised to nearly all competitive athletes,[2] a positive differential advantage is assumed by any athlete to be related to a qualitatively better designed doping programme or an increased quantity of PEDs being absorbed. Or the individual athlete might benefit from the most recent product innovation achieved in the pharmaceutical industry until it spreads across all competitors. If there were a means to convince all athletes that they have access to adopting the best (therefore identical) doping programme, qualitatively and quantitatively, then the search of a positive differential would become a useless and inefficient empty shell, and the demand for doping for the purpose of enjoying a differential advantage would vanish.

The current combat against doping behaviour: inefficiency and wrong incentives

Nowadays, presumably most athletes in competitive sport would dope if no anti-doping measures were enforced. If policy to combat doping were 100% efficient, no one athlete would dope or, if he/she eventually doped, he/she would be detected and sanctioned at a 100% probability. The reality of anti-doping policy is far below the latter percentage, which raises the question of efficiency in combating doping behaviour in sport.

In 1998, about 1% of doping tests were positive out of 155,000 controls, but with WADA, the number of tests grew to over 300,000 every year. WADA statistics (Table 5.1) synthetise the results of over 300,000 tested samples with about 5,000 athletes testing positive. The ratio of positive to total tests remained between 1% and 1.6% from 2008 to 2018, as if doping had not expanded meanwhile – or only slightly. During the same period, the ratio doubled in non-Olympic sports that are under less anti-doping surveillance than Olympic sports.

In 2018, WADA analysed 344,177 samples, out of which 4,896 were positive (1.42% of total sample). Does this mean that only 4,896 athletes were doping in competitive sports in the world? Of course not, because 344,177 is only the sample drawn from the whole population of participants in sporting contests where it may be worth doping. Assume that there were 3.44 million participants[3] competing in sporting contests in the world in 2018 and that those 344,177 tested samples had been taken at random checking that it is a representative sample. Then, the 1.42 percentage would clearly mean that about 50,000 (48,960) athletes were doped overall. Thus, data published by WADA must not be misunderstood or misinterpreted. These data do not reveal but an insignificant part of the actual magnitude of doping. Doping is widespread, and WADA testing figures only unveil the tip of an iceberg (Andreff, 2019).

Moreover, WADA data are often thought to be dubious and the aforementioned ratio seems to be underestimated according professionals, in particular doctors involved in the sports business. Alain Garnier, who worked at WADA, guesstimates the proportion of actually doped high-level athletes to be between 15% and 25% (Bourg & Gouguet, 2017). More sophisticated empirical studies show far higher rates of doping, as high as 41.8% of questioned athletes declaring that they have used doping at least once in their entire

Table 5.1 The Ratio of Adverse Analytical Findings to Total Analysed Samples, 2008–2018

AAF^a/total	Olympic sports	Non-Olympic sports	Total
2008	0.98	1.35	1.08
2009	0.90	1.56	1.11
2010	0.90	1.50	1.08
2011	1.05	1.49	1.19
2012	0.99	1.64	1.19
2013	0.97	1.95	1.31
2014	0.77	1.77	1.11
2015	0.83	2.04	1.26
2016	1.00	2.70	1.60
2017	0.77	2.59	1.43
2018	0.75	2.62	1.42

Source: WADA (2019).
[a] Adverse analytical findings (positive tests).

career (from a German survey). In recreational and amateur sports, 49% of athletes have used PEDs during their career (Daumann, 2018). According to the testimony of athletes, coaches, doctors and managers, the percentage athletes taking PEDs exceeds 75% in a number of sport disciplines.

A major source of inefficiency in WADA testing is the anti-doping budget, and expenditures are not proportionate to the size of the doping problem. From 2007 to 2015, €2 billion has been spent on combating doping in the world with the outcome of detecting between 1 and 1.3% of cheaters. It has been estimated on official world-level data that with 12 tests a year, the probability of detection of continuous doping is 33%. To detect 100% of doping in one year, 16–50 tests per athlete must be conducted, costing $25,000 (Hermann & Henneberg, 2014). With its current budget, WADA could efficiently test only 1,200 athletes per year in the world!

WADA's low budget (€30 million in 2019) by itself speaks to a lack of willingness to combat doping more efficiently; it is smaller than the cycling Ineos Grenadiers team's budget or one single French Top 14 (1st division) rugby club. In 2014, AFLD (the French branch of WADA) has convicted 46 athletes of doping with a €8 million budget that is a cost of €174,000 per positive test. In 2014, FIFA has spent €30 million to detect ten positive cases, that is €3 million by detected cheater. This is inefficient and costly!

For athletes involved in competitive contests, the risk of being detected is extremely low (1–1.6%; Table 5.1) on average. In addition, very few athletes were sanctioned by national anti-doping agencies after testing positive for doping. In 2016, out of 7,445 tested athletes, AFLD found 1.9% positive tests, but only 61 out of 142 doped athletes were eventually sanctioned (0.8% of those tested, eight chances out of 1,000 to get a sanction). USADA (the US branch of WADA) publishes every year the list of athletes sanctioned after adverse analytical findings; they were 25 in 2015, i.e. 1.9% of those detected, and 70 in 2016 (4.1%) and 277 in 2017 (5%). If an athlete has about 1% probability of being detected and then a 2–5% probability of being sanctioned after detection, he/she has 2–5 chances out of 10,000 of not having to bear any punishment for doping. This is much too low of a threat for erecting a real disincentive against doping given the prospective gains accruing from doping.

The risk of being sanctioned after a positive control is extremely low, nearly nil given all the possible ways that can be used to nullify a disciplinary proceeding: therapeutic justification of using PEDs banned by the negative list, suing anti-doping authorities in the court, scientific uncertainty, incompatibilities between sport rules and the law enforced by the state, and the time lag between the emergence of a new doping substance and the date when it is introduced in the negative list. Finally, once detected for doping, the probability of being sanctioned is much too low to impact on most athletes' behaviour.

In many countries, the risk of being criminally sentenced for doping by a court is practically non-existent. At 2004 Athens Olympics, 600 athletes had the opportunity to legally use drugs under the cover of treating themselves. WADA, over its 20 years of existence, did not unveil any of the major doping scandals that occurred meanwhile (BALCO scandal in 2003, Puerto scandal in 2006, Armstrong scandal in 2012, state-organised doping in Russia in 2015) which illustrates its inefficiency.

Inefficiency of anti-doping measures also results from athletes' circumventing behaviour: they are used to take PEDs that pharmaceutical labs do not detect, and the anti-doping labs are searching PEDs that athletes do not take; and athletes circumvent the tests and controls each time they can or use substances that mask PED consumption in case of testing. Lax enforcement of anti-doping regulation has protected doped athletes for years. Some suggest that a non-official, though crucial, WADA function consists in indirectly providing credibility to the performances of doped athletes (Bourg & Gouguet, 2017).

As regards incentives, anti-doping inefficiency is deeply rooted in the negative list system for three reasons (Bird & Wagner, 1997):

1 The negative list indirectly advertises the PEDs that seem to work and, since any athlete under the quantitative threshold is considered as not violating the rule, competition incentivises athletes to use the drugs up to the threshold; the list tacitly encourages doping until the threshold is met, evading the list beyond the threshold, or consuming PEDs that are not included in the list. This is typically an inappropriate incentive that becomes ever more inappropriate the more effective the controls and the more severe the sanctions are.
2 If anything not yet prohibited is potentially legal, the negative list encourages the development of new PEDs and provides inappropriate incentives to both athletes and drug suppliers. Newly discovered doping products (innovations) are always unfair to competing against athletes who do not use them, and performance-enhancing for athletes who do use them, and often bad for the athlete's health. For a while, these new products remain either off the negative list or undetectable through testing until a parallel technical progress emerges in anti-doping testing techniques on the one hand. On the other hand, the very existence of the negative list creates incentives to invest and innovate in the area of new drugs, pharmaceutical products and blood treatment protocols in order to supply new unlisted products and doping techniques for athletes. Such incentive-triggered innovation process is double-faceted: it achieves technical progress in the pharmaceutical and medical industries while supplying new PEDs as well as products that are used to mask forbidden substances in case of blood or urine testing.

Consequently, using new PEDs without sanction will last up to the point when, with a substantial time lag, they will be included in the negative list. Forbidden since 1976, some anabolic steroids are not yet detectable; stanozolol, a steroid that triggered Ben Johnson disqualification in 1987, is controlled with certainty only since 2015. Banned since 1989, growth hormones are undetectable. Corticoids were on the negative list since 1978 but clearly detectable only since 1999. EPO, prohibited in 1990, became detectable in 2000. Forbidden since 1984, blood self-transfusion remains randomly undetectable, and so on and so forth.

3 Enforcement of the negative list implies that disputes are removed from the field of play and are resolved in profoundly unsporting ways such as in court cases.

It was suggested that WADA should be independent of sports federations and the IOC. Since it is not so, various critics of anti-doping strategies have argued that WADA's creation reflected more of a political commitment rather than a genuine attempt to rid sports of PED use.

New rules that turn doping upside down into a self-defeating strategy

In competitive sports, it has become increasingly evident that individual decisions to dope are not independent. They are influenced by coaches, managers and anti-doping control agencies, but first and foremost by the decisions of competing athletes. In this scenario, game theory provides tools for analysing strategic interaction, and this game theoretic approach has replaced the Beckerian economics of crime as applied to doping. Since the pioneering work of Breivik (1992), the interaction between competing athletes in a doping game is often modelled as a prisoner dilemma where doping is the dominant strategy.

Let us assume (Andreff, 2015) that:

- The use of PEDs enables any rider to enhance his/her performance;
- Under the simplifying assumption of a two-rider race, if both riders dope, the final ranking remains unchanged compared to a doping-free situation;
- If one of the two riders is tested positive for doping, he/she will never confess or denounce the other rider for doping (the *omerta* behaviour).

Such a prisoner dilemma game is represented by the below pay-off matrix in an assumed two-rider race with two riders of identical psychic (fighting spirit, willingness to win) and physical capacities, i.e. with perfect competitive balance (Table 5.2).

Table 5.2 reads as follows:

a if the two riders are not doping, then they both have 0.5 probability of winning the race; if they compete in a cycling season with several races, their economic expectation is to share 50%/50% the winner prizes;

b if rider A is doped and rider B is not doped, then A's probability of winning the race is 1; and over the season, A will take all prizes, i.e. 100% (and the reverse, if B is doping and A is not doping);

c   if the two riders are both doping, then again their probability of winning is 50% each, and they will share the prizes 50/50.
    Moreover, they will not denounce each other as being doped.

In such prisoner dilemma, the Nash equilibrium is (Doping, Doping) since doping is a dominant pure strategy and will be chosen by the two riders in any case because both riders' interest is to dope whatever the other rider's behaviour. If I dope and the other one dopes as well, we will share the gains 50/50; if the other one does not dope and I dope, I take it all and he/she will not denounce me. Consequently, *doping tends to spread throughout the whole peloton*. At least 75% of the Tour de France peloton doped after the Second World War (Mondenard & Garcia, 2009).

Now assume that favourite rider A is stronger with 0.6 probability of winning (therefore, B's probability of winning is 0.4) if no one dopes. Rider B's incentive to dope in an attempt to win is even higher than with a balanced competition. But if favourite rider A loses against a weaker, though doped, opponent, A will have an extremely strong incentive to dope. Doping is a dominant pure strategy with competitive imbalance as well.

The prisoner dilemma narrative has two main implications. First, the existence of a negative list in combination with random testing cannot be efficient, and second, the problem for each athlete is to convince his/her opponent that he/she will not cheat and dope. Such assurances are highly unlikely to be credible; thus, doping is a robust phenomenon that occurs even when all athletes would prefer not to dope.

The inappropriate outcome of the prisoner dilemma game – the whole peloton dopes – cannot vanish on its own since it is a non-cooperative game. It can only be alleviated by means of *ad hoc* regulation or avoided by changing (voluntarily or compulsorily) the riders' non-cooperative into cooperative behaviour. This boils down to transforming a non-cooperative into a co-operative game, and then finding the focal point of the cooperative game (Schelling, 1960). A specific Nash equilibrium can be found as the focal point through imposing or, better, favouring the emergence of a social norm of behaviour.

However, finding a social norm is a challenge when it comes to sporting contests where the objective of each participant is competition and not cooperation. Often cooperation between opponent athletes is forbidden by the very rules of competitive sports and one ends up with manipulation,

Table 5.2 The Doping Game: A Prisoner's Dilemma

		Rider B			
		No doping		Doping	
Rider A	No doping	0.5	0.5	0	1
	Doping	1	0	0.5	0.5

cheating, collusion, tanking, match fixing or corruption (Andreff, 2019). Consequently, game theory has been geared towards finding how to better regulate and deter athletes from using PEDs.

Indeed, a non-exhaustive literature review shows that game theory has been used to search for a recipe for combating the doping prisoner dilemma solution. A first option is to trade-off between strong tests and high-value prizes on the one hand and, on the other hand, inefficient testing and low-value prizes (Eber & Thépot, 1999). Ranking-based punishment schemes have been suggested since they are less costly to implement than are IOC regulations and require fewer tests to attain a no-doping equilibrium (Berentsen, 2002).

Haugen (2004) concluded that improved testing may not be the most efficient way to fight doping, and one should allow doping even though moral arguments are hard to fit into an economic framework. Savulescu *et al.* (2004) argued that, paradoxically, allowing PEDs in sport may protect athletes because it would allow switching from the current situation where the incentives are to develop undetectable drugs with little concern for safety to a new regime where the pressure would be to develop safe drugs.

Eber (2008) incorporated fair play norms in the doping game so as to modify the prisoner dilemma in such a way that it becomes a stag hunt game characterised by two pure-strategy equilibria: a risk-dominant doping equilibrium and a payoff-dominant no-doping one. But the main problem for athletes is then to coordinate their intentions and, hence, find a reliable coordinating device. Another kind of coordination mechanism is to recognise whistle-blowers as an important element in the fight against doping and educate athletes about whistle-blowing (Zhang, 2018). Buechel *et al.* (2016) introduced consumers as an additional player in the PED game and concluded that a crucial change is to establish transparency in the sense that consumers know whether there were positive tests or not, then conditioning their support on serious doping tests.

Most studies focused on developing incentives so that athletes comply with anti-doping rules or that makes sanctioning more efficient. All these solutions are based on the idea of reducing directly the economic incentives to dope, but they may be very difficult to implement and probably insufficient in deterring athletes from using PEDs (Eber, 2006). Few, like Haugen or Savulescu, advocate free allowance to use PEDs. In any case, this recipe is quite different from looking for incentives that would make athletes not willing to dope.

Bird & Wagner (1997) stressed that the development of social norms would be more efficient for controlling doping behaviour because such norms would change the athletes' system of preferences. They propose a drug diary system based on the principle that no drugs would be explicitly forbidden, but athletes would have to publish a drug diary in which they record all the drugs they take. Doping would be defined as hidden use of any undeclared drug. A peer monitoring system is suggested which is the basis for our own anti-doping scheme below.

The idea is to conceive and implement anti-doping rules where the riders (athletes)[4] themselves lose interest in doping or, better, have strong no-doping incentives when other competitors dope because they will obtain bigger gains (wins, prizes) without doping than with doping. Appropriately structured incentives must be designed to trigger such rider behaviour.

The suggested device for combating doping is as follows:

Rule 1: Compulsory doping diary

At the dawn of cycling season, all riders must compulsorily register the list of all pharmaceutical substances and medical techniques that aim at enhancing their sporting performances (PEDs) which they are going to use over the whole season. Registering the list is a precondition for obtaining a sporting license and participating in sporting contests (cycling races); it is also an absolutely binding commitment to stick to the declared list of PEDs, definitely no more (but possibly less). Such doping diary is kept secret to other riders.

Rule 2: Unveiling the diary on request

Any whistle-blowing riders (at least two of them)[5] are allowed to request a suspected rider unveiling his/her doping diary. The accused rider will be tested accordingly in order to control whether he/she complies with his/her diary.

Such requests will inevitably emerge if, say, rider A wins all – or too many – races over the season.

Rule 3: Doping-negative tests

In the course of the cycling season, if a rider tests positive as against the WADA negative list but, beyond the latter, the test finds only PEDs that are actually listed in his/her registered diary, then the test is considered negative and no sanction applies.

Rule 4: Doping-positive tests: life ban

If a rider is found having taken PEDs off (beyond) his/her own list, the sanction is a life ban from cycling.

Motivation of Rule 4: the sanction must be extremely severe because not only the rider has over-doped compared to his/her diary, but he/she has also hidden the information, cheated, lied, denied his/her initial commitment and blurred the transparency required for the new rules to function properly and efficiently; he/she is definitively excluded from cycling because he/she does not comply with the basic rules of the game.

Rule 5: Not unveiling the diary and doping test refusal: life ban

Rules 2–4 cannot be enforced if a rider refuses to make transparent his/her PED diary and refuses to submit himself/herself to the requested doping test.

Then, he/she is banned for life from competitive cycling. (This solution is equivalent to Bird & Wagner's rule stipulating that a suspected athlete should be able to avoid testing only by retiring definitively.)

Rule 6: Outcome of requested doping tests and potential sanction

If a suspected and then tested rider does not comply with his/her unveiled doping diary, he/she is banned for life from cycling (enforcing Rule 4). If the doping test confirms that he/she sticks to his/her diary, only using all (or less than) PEDs declared there, the accused rider is not sanctioned (enforcing Rule 3).

What would be the result of Rule 6 enforcement when a suspected rider A sticks to his/her diary? First, whistle-blowing riders would have to admit either that rider A is definitely stronger than they are and deserves all his/her wins or that his/her doping diary is more efficient or better designed and programmed than their own. Second, they would be incentivised, as would the whole peloton, to copy the transparent doping diary of the recurrent winner A given its revealed performance-enhancing efficiency. Third, if all of the peloton were to copy the winner's diary, this would trigger three beneficial effects:

1. The same doping norm (diary) would prevail throughout the whole peloton – a typical story of social norm formation.
2. With all riders using a same transparent most efficient or best conceived doping programme, it would not take long for them to become aware that doping is basically useless and inefficient as a means to achieve a differential competitive advantage. This would make a large change from the results that flow from the hidden doping that prevails nowadays in cycling.
3. The *omerta* system would vanish on its own since the best doping diary would be known to everyone and openly used by all riders once the doping diaries of the best-performing athletes are made public.

When such a point is reached, it would not be difficult to convince all riders that the optimal doping programme is not necessarily 'the more doped the better' one. Step by step, a socially optimal doping programme would probably prevail, which reduces the quantity of PEDs taken, namely in changing the social norm reflected in the diary from athletes taking a large amount of and the most threatening substances. In the long run, only the safest stimulating PEDs required by a hard stamina-demanding sport such as cycling would be maintained in the diary probably with unanimous riders' consent and willingness.

Furthermore, such an anti-doping regulatory environment features an incentive system where each rider is not interested in more and more doping for him/herself but is rather interested in benefiting from his/her competitors' decision to over-dope above what is registered in their diaries.

Wrong behaviour due to wrong incentives 113

The situation no longer takes the form of a prisoner dilemma but, to some extent, takes the form of a coordination game with regard to doping behaviour owing to the social norm that would emerge from stringent enforcement of Rules 2, 5 and 6. Beyond competitive behaviour required in any sporting contest, these three rules, step by step, would generate both a common transparent doping programme and a group of those riders eager to benefit (winning races and earning more money) from such rules in the long run, i.e. in repeated games. In a repeated game over the season, the non-over-doped athletes will take it all. Unknown at the beginning of the game, when all doping diaries are veiled, the best unveiled or transparent doping programme would emerge through the whistle-blowing and unveiling process, and finally become the focal point of the entire peloton, ending up as the prevailing social norm (Crawford & Haller, 1990).

Let us exemplify the suggested anti-doping device during an assumed five-rider cycling circuit (season) with evenly distributed strength across the riders that compete under Rules 1–6. Adopting a representation of the extensive form – or Kuhn tree (Kuhn, 1953) – of a game, Figure 5.1 shows that Rules 1–6 drive the riders to play a kind of Kreps (1990) game where riders will not adopt the most profitable strategy (over-doping) in the short term, because it is associated with a high risk of losing it all afterwards. They preferably will opt for the safest (no-over-doping) strategy, less profitable in the short term though securing the highest gain in the long run if other riders play the first

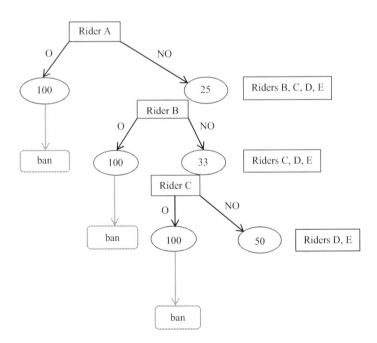

Figure 5.1 The No-Over-Doping Successful Game.

risky strategy. Those who would opt for the wrong over-doping strategy would be banned for life in the course of the season and would have to quit the repeated game.

At the beginning of season, each of the five riders has 0.2 probability of winning. Let us assume that rider A starts winning all the races; then, riders B, C, D and E will demand that A unveil his/her doping diary (Rule 2). If testing A shows that he/she complies with his/her diary, he/she will not be banned (Rule 3) and the other four riders will adopt a same doping programme. The five riders will share expected wins and prizes at 20% each.

Now if rider A, in order to keep or restore his/her initial advantage (100% wins), decides after a while to cheat and over-dope beyond his/her registered diary, then he/she will temporarily win 100% of the races again – instead of 20% – so that B, C, D and E will demand to see A's diary. Imagine that the anti-doping test will find that A does not comply with his/her registered diary any longer; this rider will be banned for life from cycling (Rules 4 and 6) and the four remaining riders will share all the wins at 25% each (Figure 5.1).

Having learned from rider A's poor experience, B, C, D and E probably would not cheat on their own diaries and would be satisfied with 25% of all wins each (instead of previous 0%, then 20%). If by chance one of them started cheating on his/her registered doping diary, the three others would demand the suspected cheat reveal her/his diary. This person would be banned for life, and the three remaining athletes would share all wins at 33% each. The three of them will be better off with no over-doping (sticking to their diaries) and waiting for a next life ban due to another rider succumbing to the temptation of over-doping behaviour. If, say, C succumbed, then D's and E's share would rise up to 50%.

With the suggested Rules 1–6, the more the other riders cheat with over-doping, the more a no-cheating rider increases his/her market share in total wins and prizes as long as he/she does not over-dope/cheat himself/herself. A rider cannot expect durably increasing his/her share in total wins when he/she over-dopes (a too risky strategy), but he/she can expect his/her share to increase when competitors over-dope beyond their diary because they will be banned for life and give up their shares. Adopting a safer no-over-doping strategy will have higher long-term return with certainty because it benefits from possible inappropriate doping behaviour and exclusion of fellow competitors. A rider is basically interested in not doping beyond his/her registered diary because such a strategy increases his/her gains (win percentage, market share in total prizes) each time another rider decides to cheat and over-dope. Sticking to one's own diary and not over-doping is a dominant strategy in the repeated game designed by Rules 1–6. Whatever the others do, a rider is better off when sticking to his/her diary.

A no-over-doping strategy by itself phases out any need for cheating or searching for a competitive differential advantage by means of using PEDs. It is also a dominant strategy in that it generates more benefits to a rider than searching for a differential competitive advantage through doping; this is due to non-cheaters capturing the cheaters' share in total wins. Therefore, over-doping behaviour shows up as a self-defeating strategy and should be rejected by all riders.

Finally, owing to Rules 3, 4 and 6, the WADA negative list would switch from being inefficient to being effective, and probably after some time, it might well be forgotten and possibly abolished. Furthermore, with an identical doping programme for all, cycling races (and other individual sporting contests) would benefit from a 'non-doping-distorted' competitive balance.

A crucial point is that athletes/riders must be taught the new anti-doping programme before implementing it because they must understand that they can never win by playing against Rules 1–6. If they are not definitely convinced (through teaching) that it will be so, tragic scenarios may occur and must be ex ante explained to the riders.

In the early times of the new regulation enforcement, some riders might feel or assume that the best-performing doping diary is the most overloaded in PEDs that are dangerous for their health or life longevity, but they might take the risk of adopting it anyway. As a result, they would win all races and be copied by other riders. There would be transition costs of moving from current WADA anti-doping rules to the ones suggested here. A transition crisis would be the price to pay for adopting the new rules and new no-over-doping behaviour with a dramatic though temporary increase in the number of sicknesses and deaths in the peloton. After some time, riders would comprehend that with the new rules, they would be better off with no over-doping and earning more money than with over-doping and dying or being affected with serious diseases, before a life ban. However, it would be cautious to straightforwardly teach riders rather than letting them discover by themselves the price to be paid for wrong over-doping behaviour at the expense of their health or life longevity.

Now imagine a cunning rider A who assumed that a countervailing strategy to circumvent Rules 1–6 would be to register all existing PEDs in his/her diary that is potentially the maximum and most dangerous doping programme for his/her health and life. He/she would successfully pass all and any existing doping tests since whatever the PEDs found in his body, they would be all registered in his/her diary. Then, he/she would be free, in a sense, to take whatever PEDs he/she wants, namely much less than the whole diary, but quite enough for winning most races. His/her diary would be unveiled on request of other riders. Obviously, they would adopt a same doping strategy, registering all existing PEDs in their own diaries.

Then, rider A would face a new kind of prisoner dilemma: would competitors having copied and registered the maximum doping programme use it or not? If they used it, they would win all races against rider A unless he/she also decided to use all the PEDs in the maximum doping diary. The ultimate outcome – maybe after a number of iterations (repeated games) – would be the death of the whole peloton after a sort of war of attrition killing all the riders. Such a war of attrition or overbidding doping process would also destroy the entire economy of cycling since sponsors, media and financiers would quit cycling with an increasing number of riders dying due to over-doping. This would happen except if, during this sort of 'collective suicide' of the peloton, riders would come up with an agreement that there is better way than committing suicide which is no-over-doping and registering a reasonably decent PED diary. Anyway, it would be a safety net to teach all the peloton in advance what would be the collective suicide outcome of circumventing Rules 1–6 with registering and eventually using the maximum doping diary, i.e. the one that would kill anyone and everyone.

Conclusion

In the face of deceivingly low efficiency of current anti-doping initiatives, a more efficient regulatory device must be tested, targeted at modifying incentives which induce no-over-doping behaviour – as opposed to sanctioning which tends to increase doping. The initiative and programme suggested here is likely to be more than a safety valve, rather a proper launching pad for revised anti-doping programmes that are effective and credible. It possibly may be adapted, after some research work, to all sports (team sports included), which opens an avenue for further research. However, a major hindrance to enforcing such new anti-doping rules probably would spring from sports governing bodies which might fear that transparency would highlight current doping practices in their sport. Why not attempt convincing them that experimenting with good incentives is always preferable to sticking with the current failed incentives that have not served to reduce doping in sports?

Notes

1 Forbidden PEDs cannot be found in free market and must be purchased in black markets for drugs where prices are several times higher than in free-market for (allowed) pharmaceutical products. Thus extending the negative list translates into higher cost of doping.
2 Actually, PEDs have more or less generalised in all professional and high-level non-professional sports during the past three decades or so. This is a major consequence of the below-presented prisoner dilemma.
3 World population as of December 2018 was 7,669 million people; assuming that 3.44 million were competitive sports participants (0.04% of world population) is a very conservative assumption, surely underestimated. Therefore the number of doped athletes is for sure much higher than 50,000 every year.
4 Cycling is taken as an example, but the same rules should be efficient in any individual sport.
5 The number of two whistle-blowers may be changed (increased). The basic idea is more than one whistle-blower so that the request of unveiling the diary can turn out to become a peer monitoring system. Bird & Wagner suggest, in order avoiding false accusations, that whistle-blowers be punished (suspended or banned) if the accused athlete is found not guilty.

References

Andreff, W. (2000). Financing modern sport in the face of a sporting ethic. *European Journal for Sport Management*, 7(1), 5–30.
Andreff, W. (2012). *Mondialisation économique du sport. Manuel de référence en Economie du sport*. Bruxelles: De Boeck.
Andreff, W. (2013a). Economic development as major determinant of Olympic medal wins: Predicting performances of Russian and Chinese teams at Sochi Games. *International Journal of Economic Policy in Emerging Economies*, 6(4), 314–340.
Andreff, W. (2013b). Crisis as unexpected transition … to a greed-based economic system. In: P. Zarembka (Ed.). *Contradictions: Finance, Greed, Labor Unequally Paid*. Research in Political Economy, Bingley: Emerald, 28, 1–48.
Andreff, W. (2015). The Tour de France: A success story in spite of competitive imbalance and doping. In: D. Van Reeth & D.J. Larson (Eds.). *The Economics of Professional Road Cycling*. Heidelberg: Springer, 233–255.
Andreff, W. (2019). *An Economic Roadmap to the Dark Side of Sport*. Cham: Palgrave Macmillan.
Becker, G. (1968). Crime and punishment: An economic approach. *Journal of Political Economy*, 76(2), 169–217.
Berentsen, A. (2002). The economics of doping. *European Journal of Political Economy*, 18(1), 109–127.
Bird, E.J. & Wagner, G. (1997). Sport as a common property resource: A solution to the dilemmas of doping. *Journal of Conflict Resolution*, 41(6), 749–766.
Bourg, J.-F. (2016). Dopage et mondialisation financière du sport: ce que nous apprend l'analyse économique. *Drogues, santé et société*, 15(1), 66–84.
Bourg, J.-F. & Gouguet, J.-J. (2017). *La société dopée: Peut-on lutter contre le dopage sportif dans une société de marché?* Paris: Editions du Seuil.
Breivik, G. (1992). Doping games: A game theoretical exploration of doping. *International Review for the Sociology of Sport*, 27(3), 235–253.
Buechel, B., Emrich, E. & Pohlkamp, S. (2016). Nobody's innocent: The role of customers in the doping dilemma. *Journal of Sports Economics*, 17(8), 767–789.
Crawford, V. & Haller, H. (1990). Learning how to cooperate: Optimal play in repeated coordination games. *Econometrica*, 58(3), 571–595.
Daumann, F. (2018). Doping in high-performance sport – The economic perspective. In: M. Breuer & D. Forrest (Eds.). *The Palgrave Handbook on the Economics of Manipulation in Professional Sports*. London: Palgrave Macmillan, 71–90.
Eber, N. (2006). Doping. In: W. Andreff & S. Szymanski (Eds.). *Handbook on the Economics of Sport*. Cheltenham: Edward Elgar, 773–783.
Eber, N. (2008). The performance-enhancing drug game reconsidered – A fair play approach. *Journal of Sports Economics*, 9(3), 318–327.
Eber, N. & Thépot, J. (1999). Doping in sport and competition design. *Recherches Economiques de Louvain*, 65(4), 435–445.
Frank, R.H. & Cook, P.J. (1995). *The Winner-Take-All Society: Why the Few at the Top Get So Much More than the Rest of US*. New York: Free Press.
Frick, B. (2008). The doping trap: Why negative lists and random testing don't work. In: P. Rodriguez, S. Késenne & J. Garcia (Eds.). *Threats to Sports and Sports Participation*. Oviedo: Universidad de Oviedo, 41–59.
Haugen, K. (2004). The performance-enhancing drug game. *Journal of Sports Economics*, 5(1), 67–86.

Hermann, A. & Henneberg, M. (2014). Anti-doping systems in sports are doomed to fail: A probability and cost analysis. *Journal of Medicine & Doping Studies*, 4, 148. doi: 10.4172/2161-0673.1000148

Kreps, D. M. (1990). *Game Theory and Economic Modelling*. Oxford: Oxford University Press.

Kuhn, H. (1953). Extensive games and the problem of information. In: H. Kuhn & A. Tucker (Eds.). *Contributions to the Theory of Games*. Princeton: Princeton University Press, vol. 2, 193–216.

Maennig, W. (2002). On the economics of doping and corruption in international sports. *Journal of Sports Economics*, 3(1), 61–89.

Mondenard, J.-P. & Garcia D. (2009). *La grande Imposture*. Paris: Hugo & Co.

Riordan, J. (1993). Soviet-style sport in Eastern Europe: The end of an era. In: I. Allison (Ed.). *The Changing Policies of Sport*. Manchester: Manchester University Press, 37–57.

Savulescu, J., Foddy, B. & Clayton, M. (2004). Why we should allow performance enhancing drugs in sport. *British Journal of Sports Medicine*, 38, 666–670.

Schelling, T.C. (1960). *The Strategy of Conflict*. Cambridge, MA: Harvard University Press.

WADA (2019). *2018 Anti-Doping Testing Figures*. Montreal: World Doping Agency.

Zhang, Z. (2018). Establishing an anti-doping internal whistleblower policy in China. *Journal of Sport and Health Science*, 7(3), 337–338.

6 Discrimination, disequilibrium and disincentives

Behavioural economics in women's sport

Stephanie Manning, Ho Fai Chan and David A. Savage

Introduction

As of 2020, women made up 49.58% of the world population (UN World Population data),[1] but have until recently only made up a small fraction of the world's professional athletes. For example, women's participation in the Olympic games has risen from 2.2% (1900) to 9.5% (1948) to 23% (1984) and then to close to 50% in the Tokyo games (2021).[2] But why do gender imbalances still exist in one of the most watched and celebrated of world sporting events if not for a constant stream of disincentives, disequilibriums and discrimination that women face across the entirety of the sporting playing field. Adding to this issue has been, that until recently, the vast majority of professional sports positions were held by men (coaching and administration roles) regardless of the gender playing the sport.

The lack of clear pathways and career options available to girls (women) when compared to boys (men) creates disincentives for women to join or stay in the sporting sector. These disincentives can be costly and can obviously affect the behaviour and choices of female athletes. We know that gender discrimination exists, but its existence also has a negative impact on economic growth and the efficient use of labour resources. The misallocation of workers results in women of high skill earning lower returns from sports. Furthermore discrimination against women in sports and female sports result in lower-skilled earning higher returns. This chapter explores and presents theoretical and empirical examples of gender discriminations and how they are impacting the behaviour of women (girls) in the sports marketplace. This will include exploring the lack of potential pathways, career prospects and promotion of female sports. It also explores the problems associated with winner-takes-all markets, status and positional concerns, human capital theory, the misallocation of talent and market inefficiencies.

DOI: 10.4324/9781003080824-8

Background

Unfortunately, this is not a new phenomenon as women in sport have been actively discriminated against throughout history stretching back as far as the 8th century B.C.E. with their exclusion from the original Olympic Games. Olympic athletes were seen as noble and if successful became wealthy with no need to do menial or manual labour, which was in general limited to men. However, this was not the case in Sparta as women were not only able to compete in foot races but encouraged to do so, as the societal norm was the pursuit of physical perfection. In Sparta, like in nature (Wilson, 2000), a woman's fitness was a good signal that her offspring would be stronger and healthier than her less athletic rivals – making her a more sought-after mate. However, over time "sport has developed in parallel with our social evolution, in so much that it has created an outlet for our violence and aggression becoming the socially acceptable form of violence – if not the weekend version of combat and war" (Caruso et al., 2017, p. 517). In line with this, we observed that as western societies became more civilised, sport became more and more codified to reflect the moral and social norms of the day.

Under the rule of the Roman Caesars, gladiatorial combat was the ultimate blood sport, but being a gladiator was only accessible to those of the lowest social classes such as criminals, slaves and the truly desperate. While this did not exclude female gladiators, they were often included to provide amusement for the spectators and not perceived as being serious competitors (much like the clowns at a rodeo). Starting in the 'Dark Ages' and extending throughout the Middle Ages, from the age of chivalry and the knight to 19th-century "gentleman." Central to the tenets of both was the strict adherence to a code of conduct which included deference and courtesy towards women at all times at any cost to self (see Braithwait, 1994). As a result, men were expressly forbidden from ever hurting (striking) a woman, and by extension, women were banned from participating in activities that would be deemed unladylike – this included physical or violent activities such as the sport of jousting where knights (men) could practise and perfect the art of war. This of course did not prevent women from attending or feigning disinterest in the sporting contests, but the social mores of the day dictated that they should neither participate nor enjoy such violent delights.[3]

It was a commonly accepted social norm in this period that females were weak and in constant need of protection and should not participate in sport for their own safety – a point of view that was carried into the modern age. Even the re-emergence of the Olympic Games in the late 19th century continued the 2500-year-old tradition of not allowing women to compete, and it was not until 1928 that women were included to compete in track and field events. This also held true for the world's most popular sport, football (soccer), which saw the first organised match played on 9 May 1881, but females did not have a FIFA World Cup tournament until 1991 (Jenkel, 2020). Unfortunately, modern society has not yet overturned the regressive views of women, whether it be women in combat, sport or the workplace. Furthermore, even when women were allowed to engage in sport, they have been viewed as women first and athletes second, needing to meet some impossible double standard of beauty, femininity, grace, strength and competitiveness (aggression) while their male counterparts are under no such constraints (Trolan, 2013).

Discrimination based on gender is mainly classified into the following two forms:

- *an unequal access* to work where equally qualified men and women have unequal access to labour markets; and/or
- *unequal pay for equal work* where equally productive men and women in identical positions are paid unequally.

Unfortunately, we must use the "and/or" term here as it is quite often the case that women suffer both of these two forms of discrimination at the same time. An additional corollary to gender discrimination is a misallocation of workers in that women of high skill are unfairly kept in lower-paid positions. In most modern societies, a new and much more insidious form of discrimination emerged and was widely adopted, that of benevolent sexism, which is an interconnected set of sexist stereotypes, directed towards women in order to limit or control their behaviour (Glick and Fiske, 1996). This is in stark contrast to the openly misogynistic hostile sexism that views women as hostile and feminism as an active attack on men and traditional values (this is also the most violent form of sexism and poses a real danger to women). Practitioners of benevolent sexism argue (mostly men) that it is actually in the best interest of women that they actively discriminate against them; i.e., it is for their own good (Rogers, 2020). Many industries have quietly adopted this form of sexism by limiting females into restricted or stereotypical roles. For example, benevolent sexism in sport has limited female athletes to less violent/low-contact sports (e.g. athletics and gymnastics) and to low-level jobs in related areas.[4]

We also observe benevolent sexism in many other industries where women are "protected" from their male counterparts, and female employees are often judged on their appearance rather than their ability to do their job, as might be seen as unfair to expect a woman to be held to the same performance metric as a man in the same role. This is a common problem in western politics where women are subjected to fashion critique rather than the same rigorous assessment as her male colleagues (Dupas et al., 2020). Some may argue that this is well intentioned in order to protect her from judgement, but such actions are rooted in the ideals of chivalry where women were seen as soft or weak and by extension not seen as an equal. Despite the fact that benevolent sexism is difficult to detect and easy to dismiss, the sports industry has embodied this ideal for thousands of years. However, it is not only the issue of benevolent sexism in modern sport that it creates disincentives, discrimination and disequilibrium for females if they chose to participate in this industry. The knock-on effect of women being seen as less able to do the same job as their male colleagues results in demand-side discrimination (Colander and Woos, 1997). Over time, this preference (taste) for discrimination becomes a norm, which would eventually impact the women's willingness to enter the industry (lower supply), and those that do enter are likely to conform to the norm of pay discrimination. The weight of historical discrimination has opened up large chasms in numerous aspects of the sporting industry resulting in ongoing disincentives for women to participate which reinforce the status quo disequilibrium. This limits the same encouragement and opportunities to participate/work in the sport industry to females that has always been on offer for males.

Media and sponsorship discrimination

The stereotypical image of modern sports is that of a masculine activity, with men watching men play sport and role of the sporting superstars being the sole purview male athletes and reinforced by the media (Messner, 1988; Rowe and Brown, 1994). While sport has generally become a much more inclusive environment for women athletes, this evolution within this industry has not completely carried over into sports media with their limited coverage of women's sport supporting the notion that sport is a male pursuit (Bernstein, 2002). This inadequate portrayal of female athletes reinforces the idea that only male sports are of interest to the sports audiences (Cooky et al., 2013; Trolan, 2013; Hull, 2017). This is in direct contradiction to the significant increase in the numbers of women playing sport and growth in professional sporting leagues as longitudinal studies have found that during this time media coverage has actually declined (Cooky et al., 2013). Figures reported in Sherry, Osborne, and Nicholson (2016) show that coverage of women in sport was only 9% in news sources and 7% in non-news (Lumby et al., 2010). Additionally, the little coverage women's sport received in Australia actually fell by 2% between 1997 and 2010 (Phillips, 1996; Australian Sports Commission, 2001; Hughson et al., 2001; Lumby et al., 2010).

This continued discrimination comes at a very high price, as the underrepresentation of women's sport on broadcast media severely limits their ability to survive or grow. This is predominately due to the fact that the vast majority of sports revenue is generated from broadcast rights and sponsorship deals – the latter being very much dependent on the former. Sponsors have a need to maximise investment returns that generally come from media coverage and brand recognition, specifically a large television (or other media) presence. When women's sports do not receive equal broadcast coverage (which in most cases is little to none), sponsors are forced to reconsider investing in a sport (or team) that would not promote their brand at the same level as a male sport (Bernstein, 2002). Ultimately, this deters many would-be sponsors from investing in women's sporting competitions as the lack of broadcast coverage reduces the ad buy-ins and the value of the broadcast right. Unfortunately, this creates a viscous feedback loop where sponsors won't invest without broadcast coverage and the media outlets won't broadcast these sports without being backed by sponsors – both of which disincentivise support and growth, ultimately leading to lower participation and slower growth rates for the sport.

One of the few examples of where women receive equal airtime as men is during internationally broadcast sports events consisting of both men's and women's sporting, e.g. the Olympic Games. However, even this coverage is limited to sports that are deemed to be socially acceptable for females to play, such as gymnastics, swimming and diving, as these are individual events seen as feminine (Jones et al., 1999) while team events are generally ignored or given very little attention (Tuggle and Owen, 1999). This is unfortunate as these mega-events are one of the few times that non-mainstream sports can receive coverage that they would not normally be able to receive for other tournaments (Jones, 2006). Even during the pinnacle of an international sporting event, broadcasters assume that there is a limited spectator interest in female team events (e.g. baseball, soccer and basketball). However, the number of fans physically attending only these events only highlights the ever-increasing interest in female sports and demonstrates that media outlets are lagging behind by not broadcasting them (Tuggle and Owen, 1999; Cooky et al., 2013) or are actively trying to limit the growth of women's sport. The 2019 FIFA Women's World Cup final was the most watched match to date with an average of 82.18 million live viewers (FIFA, 2019). This amount of coverage is not awarded to female sport outside of major international tournaments, with female sport receiving only 10% of sport broadcasts in the UK (Women in Sport, 2018). It is also important to note that just because a sport has female athletes does not mean that the fans are only women as estimates of the Women's World Cup placed the gender split of viewers at 53% male compared to 61% for the Men's World Cup.[5]

The sporting renaissance is not just limited to the visual broadcast media. Where newspapers once relegated sports to their last pages, they now recognise it as a vital tool for the continued success (survival) of print media and social media. Again, we observe a major area of gender disparity as sports journalism has retained its worldwide male dominance (Franks and O'Neill, 2016) and this disparity extends into sports commentary. It is a commonly believed myth held by the male-dominated industry either that female commentators deliver an inferior product or that it would not be accepted by the viewers. Such sentiments limit the legitimacy of female reporters, such that all broadcasts are subjected to additional scrutiny. This is especially valid in traditional male sports as females "cannot" play (excluded from) the sport, and they conclude that it makes women incapable of making an accurate call of the game (Rogers, 2020). Ironically, this sentiment does not appear to hold for male commentators who have neither played nor coached the sport at an elite level, but their divinely bestowed knowledge or commentary ability remains unquestioned. The decisions of what sports are covered and by which journalists (or commentators) across virtually all media platforms are made by male executives (Caple et al., 2011). In an effort to appear socially responsive and to reduce criticism, some networks started including token female commentators and journalists into their male-dominated rosters (Farh et al., 2020) often as eye candy and they were not taken seriously by their male counterparts.[6] One of the augments put forward was that the locker room was no place for a woman as she could be exposed to inappropriate male behaviours or scenes. This is textbook benevolent sexism, as the exclusion of women from this environment was in the best interest or protection of the women involved – which of course assumed that all dressing rooms were full of men (as only men were athletes) and all men acted inappropriately in locker rooms. More recently, we observe that as more female sports are added to mainstream media and the need for expert commentators has risen, the glaring omission of women from these roles became apparent – especially in sports that are the sole province of female athletes but were commentated by so-called male "experts." However, these issues appear to be less clear in the print media where advancement appears to be based on talent and ability, not gender (Miloch et al., 2005), but there is still a high amount of churn as employment has not resulted in the hoped-for empowerment (Hardin and Shain, 2007).

When combined, the media coverage and the lack of females leading (hosting) in sports media or journalism have created negative externalities in sponsorship of female sport. Research (Borland and MacDonald, 2003) has shown that the broadcast/sponsorship nexus is key to the successful growth (expansion) of any sports league. Furthermore, sponsorship can be the difference between a successful "high-profile" and an unsuccessful "low-profile" team or franchise. While this is evident when it comes to the sponsorship divide between male versus female leagues and across different sports, it becomes blatantly apparent when examining the value of sponsorship between genders of the same sporting code. Conversely, some companies have intentionally taken on the sponsorship of female athletes or teams to link their brands directly to anti-discrimination and female empowerment (Morgan, 2019) and to encourage women to be more active and engage in sports. The new-found growth in female athletes and sports leagues has attracted a range of new companies to enter into sport sponsorship for the first time, not only those who want to align themselves with female athletes (Morgan, 2019) but also those that may not have wanted to be seen supporting sexist or discriminatory sports. The counter-argument often posed by broadcasters and media outlets is that, while there may be growth in girls (women) playing sport and an increase in popularity, this does not necessitate an increase in viewers watching female sport – or even an increase in females watching female sport.

Such arguments are rarely empirically supported, but when direct comparisons are made, they do not allow for the vastly different sums of money spent on advertising nor the years of promotion that have gone into building up male sports. Even so, the small number of female sports that have successfully made it to mainstream media coverage (Whiteside and Hardin, 2011) has always done so with significantly lower amounts invested into the production cost for their televised events (this includes salaries). As such, direct comparisons usually result in female sporting events looking like a lower quality product when compared to their male counterparts. Additionally, female sports not only receive smaller promotion but are often aired in much less favourable timeslots or in direct competition with another highly popular male event that has received extensive promotion and much higher production budgets. In the end, this ongoing inequality and lack of promotion for female sports hinders their ability to gain and maintain an enthusiastic fan base (Eastman and Billings, 2001; Whiteside and Hardin, 2011). This in turn lowers the likelihood of major sponsorships at either the league or franchise level, which also lowers the prospect of high-value broadcast deals being offered. The absence of high-value broadcasting deals leads to much lower amounts of money feeding into the sport, resulting in lower salaries, smaller tournaments and less players being attracted to the sport which ultimately results in weaker competitions. It is likely that neither the athletic abilities nor the growing popularity among female spectators is taken into consideration when negotiating broadcasting deals – as media outlets have little interest in growing sports but only in ratings and revenue streams. Some of these choices may have been taken as a defensive position to intentionally limit the growth of female sports in order to maintain the dominance of established status quo in male sports (Caple et al., 2011; Morgan, 2019).

Pathways and disincentives

One possible explanation for the lack of female engagement in sport could be caused by the lack of career pathways that are available to girls (women) in comparison with boys (men), or the very limited visibility girls have of professional female sporting role models. This is not to suggest that women cannot be or have not been successful in sport, but if we consider the absolute numbers, there is a magnitude smaller in number when compared to male sports stars. Not only is there a lack of pathways to a viable professional sporting career for women, but there is also a significant number of social barriers limiting the acceptability of women competing in sports. With an estimated 30 million girls and women playing soccer globally (FIFA, 2014), one might assume that in highly successful soccer nations such as Brazil, female involvement in the sport would be a given. However, this is not always the case. The 1941 Decree (Law 3199) prohibited females from participating in sports in Brazil as this was concerned to be incompatible with their nature. This law was enforced until it was annulled in 1975 (Da Costa, 2014; Wood, 2018). While the women's team was finally given official recognition in the 1980s, very few clubs would openly support women's soccer, which resulted in very few opportunities for young females to become professional players within their own country. There is still a stigma attached with women playing soccer in Brazil, which is viewed as a male-only sport, and women who do play are often derided and assumed to be lesbian by the press. This type of discrimination is generally limited to women in soccer and not those playing basketball, volleyball and gymnastics (Da Costa, 2014). One can only assume that in Brazil, these sports are in some way accepted as being more feminine than soccer. If we reversed this assumption, do males not play basketball and volleyball for fear of being considered homosexual?

In a virtual reversal of Brazil's position, Sweden is one of the top four countries with the largest population of female soccer players in the world (FIFA, 2014), which is unsurprising as they significantly invest in women's soccer along with pathways for youth player to become professional through sport schools. These schools have a dual focus, firstly to combine a focus on education and high-level sport training to assist with transition into professional sport after school (Andersson and Barker-Ruchti, 2019), and secondly to enable students to have a dual career, i.e. a life after sport with a quality educational platform. Even with this dual focus, there is a high dropout rate from sport for females finishing high school, as athletes decide whether to continue both study and sport or to choose one over the other. The expectation of the dual career option during tertiary education is very demanding, and students are unwilling to take on the workload. As at the high school level, the players do not always develop equally in both fields and will prioritise soccer over education or vice versa (Andersson and Barker-Ruchti, 2019). To fully investing in soccer as a full-time career may fall second to education for Swedish youth as currently this is not an economically viable option. We observe a similar system set-up in North America, but for athletes in America who want to be professional basketball players in the Women's National Basketball Association (WNBA). The WNBA system has been specifically devised to ensure that education is achieved prior to a professional sporting career; that is, to be eligible for the draft pick, women must be at least 22 years old, a minimum of four years after graduating high school which enables them to complete a college degree (Edelman and Harrison, 2008). While WNBA policy was designed to send the message that females are capable of succeeding as a professional athlete as well as excelling academically, it signalled very different message, one that implies that women who want to become professional athletes need an education as a sports career will not ensure financial sustainability. Women's sports are not as lucrative as males, nor is there the same avenues for post sports careers in coaching or commentating. This dual entry requirement for women is not in place for males entering the National Basketball Association (NBA). Here, by virtue of the *one-and-done* requirement domestic players need only be 19 in the draft year and be at least one year out of high school. They are then eligible to choose a professional sports career over completing their college degree (Taylor et al., 2020). This ideology implies that females can and must do it all in order to meet the

Table 6.1 Proportion of Female Coaches in Female Competitions

Female coach	Soccer (%)	Basketball (%)	Netball (%)	Cricket (%)
Australia	22	37.5	87.5	37.5
USA	11	33.3	–	–
UK	66	9	100	33.3

minimum requirements of the sport. By having a college degree, they can transition into a career post-sport more easily. And, only by succeeding at both will they be inspirational to young girls.

In addition to the reduction in earning capacity, it may be the case that many more young girls drop out or are less engaged than their male counterparts, because they see neither career prospects nor role models, nor are they inspired by proximity to or promotion of such career options (Aman, 2018). The underrepresentation of females in sport extends beyond the playing field and includes lowers levels of females in any head coaching roles but becomes especially relevant when there is a lack of females coaching in female sports (Kane and LaVoi, 2018). We observe significant variations across countries and sporting codes when it comes to hiring female coaches; for example, we examined the webpages (2020) for the national women's sporting competitions for soccer: FA W-SL (UK), W-League (AUS) and WNSL (USA); basketball: WBBL (UK), WNBL (AUS) and WNBA (USA); netball: Super Netball (AUS) and Netball Super League (UK); and cricket: WBBL (AUS) and ECB Super League (UK). See Table 6.1 for an overview.

One of the solutions put forward to correct for this lack of female involvement has been the establishment of female competitions by many of the governing bodies, in order to provide women with platforms to advocate for equal opportunities that are offered to their male counterparts, such as remuneration, resources and employment security. However, it is very likely that there is a lag in the system due to the lack of former female players that could be called upon to take up coaching roles as there was no former elite competition that women could compete in for there to be former players. Even when compared to other industries where gender inequalities are rampant, the sports industry has not done well.

Winner-takes-all equilibriums?

Frank and Cook (2010) argued that sports are prime examples of winner-takes-all markets that can result in inefficient allocation of human labour resources, and there is a noticeable upside for sports. As the number of individuals wishing to make it into the elite ranks of sport increases, the competitive skill levels must also increase, which in turn forces all these individuals to exert maximum effort in skills training. By doing so, it reduces the size of the skill gap between players which makes the sport much more competitive.

This does not remove the inefficient allocation problem from the over-subscription of players (male) incentivised by the very large payoff for being a winner. While the lower payoffs faced by female players act as a disincentive resulting in less of inefficient allocation problem, the lower number of players this generates, creates the potential for weaker competition as there are lower numbers of players competing for spots. This helps to create a bigger skill gap between players. The 2012 Australian Tennis Open finals provided a perfect example of this, where the Women's Final was won by Victoria Azarenka over Maria Sharapova with the score of 6:3 and 6:0 in just over 1 hour 22 min, whereas the men match between Novak Djokovic (winner) and Rafael Nadal went for almost 6 hours with a final score of 5:7, 6:4, 6:2, 6:7 and 7:5 (Krumer et al., 2016). The skill gap argument is supported by the betting odds for both the men's and women's finals, as Djokovic was only slightly favoured at 4/6 while Nadal was listed at 6/5. But the odds showed a clear advantage towards Azarenka at 37/50 and Sharapova at 11/10.[7] It is much easier to observe this effect in individual rather than team sports, especially in sports that are played by both males and females that are incentivised differently (tennis). Weaker competitions make it less interesting for fans to support and attend, making it less likely that it gets coverage in other avenues making it even less attractive to watch, looping back to the sponsorship and broadcasting problems.

If the lower number of players who compete in competition does create larger skill gaps between players, and those larger skill gaps between players results in less close competition; i.e., this should generate more certainty in outcomes and a lower amount of variation in winners in the men's game. For example, we observe this in the Tennis Grand Slam (Australian Open, French Open, US Open, Wimbledon) winners since 2000 – where there is less variation in the men (19 winners) as opposed to the women (31 winners). However, it may seem somewhat ironic that women's sport may actually be a more efficient allocation of human capital (players) of what is normally thought of as an inefficient winner-takes-all market – and the solution to reducing the skill gaps in women's sports may be to create intentional inefficiencies with larger incentives to attract more women into sport. The lack of incentives or pathways to elite sportswomen results in the preferences of women to be placed elsewhere. What we would expect to see is that at the lower ranks, such as the amateur or recreational level, there would be more participation than we would observe but the semi-professional and professional levels. This is much different to the highly congested ranks of men sport but would see a much greater number of players at all levels (see Figure 6.1). What we observe in male competitions conforms to Frank and Cook's (2010) expectations of human capital misallocation in winner-takes-all competitions, where large incentive payoffs incentivise a larger number of individuals than would be efficient to enter and compete in this market space.

Not only would we expect that there are significant differences in the levels of engagement in sport at all levels of professionalism between males and females, but absolute numbers of players engaged at the upper levels of sport

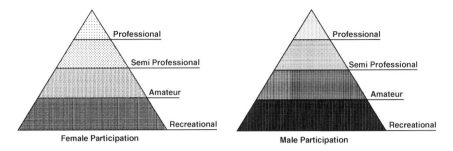

Figure 6.1 Distribution of Male and Female Players at All Levels of Sport.

are also much reduced in women's sport. The lower number of pathways into professional sports and the lack of visibility result in lesser numbers at all levels, but this is especially important for the top end (semi-professional and professional) as this could result in less competition and bigger skill gaps between players.

Given the low number of spaces that are available for women in the elite sporting competitions and the very much lower salaries paid to those women who do compete, one must conclude that this is not a competitive market. Normally, we would consider sports leagues to be monopsonies, that is there is a single employer of the professional level. This would be the case with women sports. And, there may or may not be countervailing monopoly players organisation (or union) for women sport. As such, it makes sense to consider that the labour market for women at this level could be considered to be one with a price (wage) ceiling, one that is driven by the lack of funding, sponsorship and the low number of positions that are available. In a free market, we will assume that an equilibrium could be reached such that the wage level would reflect the quantity of labour demanded. However, the low levels of funding have seen salary caps put in place to enable the sustainability of the competition rather than free market forces that will allow players to be paid they're worth – this results in lower numbers of women being willing to supply the labour because of the prevailing disincentives even if there is the potential for a higher number of places made available through the demand of labour from the competition.

Market disequilibriums and wage discrimination

Obviously a major disincentive for female athletes is the pay discrepancies between male and females, and while pay inequality is virtually universal across all labour markets, we do observe some of the largest and most inequitable outcomes in the sports market. The biggest elephant in this particular room is the $370 million wage gap between the Men's and Women's FIFA World Cup, and the stupefying underpayment of one of the most successful sports teams in modern history – the USA Women's Football Team. The prize pool for the 2018 Men's World Cup was an impressive $400 million (USD), while the following year the women competed for a paltry $30 million (USD) – which was $8 million less than the payout for the men's winner at $38 million (McCarthy, 2019). The most successful team in FIFA World Cup history is Brazil (male), who have had five wins and been the runner-up twice; the second place is a three-way tie between Germany (male), Italy (male) and the USA (female) with four World Cup wins.[8] The American women's team are the second most successful football team in history. Given that the women achieved this from a total of 8 events (since 1991) while the men competed in 21 iterations (since 1930) of the tournament –women clearly have a much higher rate of success. The women's team received $1.8 million for winning the 2015 World Cup while the men's team received $2.5 million just for qualifying. This can be directly linked to the size and value of the sponsorship, i.e. $529 million, compared to $17 million. The women have consistently outperformed the men but still get paid significantly less.

This inequity was further supported by estimates of the Australian Bureau of Statistics (2013) of a median wage gap of $24,752 between male ($67,652) and female ($42,900) sportspersons, i.e. athletes from all levels who earn money from their sport. While some sports have better gender equity, the gaps in others are profound; for example, in Australia female cricketers have minimum contracts at $87,609 while their male counterparts receive around $313,000. This also holds for soccer where minimum contracts in the W-League (women's soccer) are $12,287, while in the men's A-League they start at $64,113. A major impact of this wage discrepancy for female athletes is that many women need to take second jobs in order to earn sufficient income to continue playing sport – this makes it a particularly unattractive career prospect for young girls to aspire to. Thus, it is unsurprising that so many young women choose to discontinue pursing sport as a serious career option due to the perceived lack of career paths available and financial uncertainty that goes with it. This includes that the majority of female athletes playing in traditionally male-dominated sports as the competitions on offer for females are not to the extent of males, which means females become semi-professional athletes or part-time (Taylor et al., 2020).

A recent example of a new league that only offers females part-time employment is the National Rugby League Women's (NRLW), which began in 2018. In this competition, there are four teams, and the competition consists of four rounds which allow each team to compete against each other once and includes the grand finale (NRLW, 2020). While this league provides a step forward in the sport industry, this sport only offers minimal salaries and employment. Therefore, females in this sport have to juggle their sport alongside their family, work and study commitments. The unequal opportunities for females to participate in sport either in playing or coaching, suggests that sport is not a viable career option. From the part-time employment on offer, the athletes involved in NRLW reported that trying to balance playing/

Table 6.2 Career Incentives for Women

	High human capital (C_H)	Low human capital (C_L)
Sport	$60,000	$60,000
Non-sport	$100,000+	$50,000

training and personal commitments caused them significant stress. Stress was evident among players who reported having supportive families and employers, as the economic strain restricted the number of hours they reduced from work to increase training before the season started. The balancing act was not the only reason for stress; these athletes received negative comments from social/public media. These comments largely revolve around physical appearance, and sexuality (Taylor et al., 2020).

The knock-on effect of the wage problem is that many female sports players will opt out of a career in sports but rather choose a higher paying career option. This choice can actually create a large disequilibrium in the player talent for women sport if we consider those with the comparative or an absolute advantage over other players. If we consider two types of players – one with a high human capital (C_H) and the other with a lower capital (C_L) – the major difference between these two players is the number of options that the capital would enable each type (see Table 6.2). For simplicity, we assume that athletes would receive the same pay rates in sports regardless of their level of human capital – although it is possible that individuals with higher levels of human could have a greater level of ability (more skilled) and receive higher pay.

Women with higher levels of human capital are more likely to have a broader range of skills and be more likely to have multiple career choices with outside options that would pay well. Therefore, even if they are world-class athletes there are large financial incentives not to become or remain an athlete. That is, even with an absolute advantage as a sportsperson, the low wages and high uncertainty of a sports career would mean that those with high levels of human capital would need to forgo a large amount of money from the career option perspective. Alternatively, women with lower levels of human capital are likely to have less career options and potentially ones that would result in lower wages. As such, there may not be as large a financial difference between a sporting career and the outside option in this case, where women are characterized by a lower level of human capital stock. In this case, athletes with a lower human capital would have a comparative advantage to stay in sports rather than opt for a career outside of sports. This is not to say that the end result is not that the best players do not opt for a sporting career, but it does demonstrate that the disincentive structure of women's sport does force women to consider outside options. While this may be true for both male and female athletes, the outcomes are exacerbated by the gendered wage disequilibriums in both the sport and every other field, such that the relative payoffs might be similar and the absolute differences are clear (see Table 6.3).

Table 6.3 Career Incentives for Men

	High human capital (C_H)	Low human capital (C_L)
Sport	$120,000	$120,000
Non-sport	$200,000+	$100,000

While Table 6.3 is also a simplified example of the options being faced by men, we have included an increased payoff for men across the board (doubled) which is not indicative of the true size of the gender wage gap.

This particular wage discrepancy issue also comes up for many female athletes in the less popular sporting fields, in sports we consider to be second tier when it comes to broadcast coverage, popularity and the numbers of players. In these second-tier sports, we would expect to find much lower wages than we would observe in the "premier" sports, and as a result, those women who do wish to pursue a sporting career in these fields are regularly forced to do so on a part-time basis in order to support themselves. In order to be competitive, these part-time athletes are forced to put in much longer hours as the focus can no longer be purely on training. But athletes need to work enough hours a week to earn a liveable wage. This limits the time that can be expended on training and related activities. These part-time athletes also suffer in the long run as the earnings from their sporting career do not offset the forgone wages and promotion opportunities they will experience in the career option. This is also not to mention the fact that women are already receiving lower salary rates than their male counterparts across most industries, which results in lower savings and investments and much lower retirement savings. All told, the lack of competitive wages in the sporting industry has the effect of punishing women twice: once during the sports career and then during the remainder of their working life.

Market failures and disorganisation

A consistent problem plaguing many women's sporting organisation is that they are run as either separate organisations or in parallel with the men's organisations rather than being run as a single sporting entity. For example, even though it is counted as one of the most successful governing bodies in women's sport, the Women's Tennis Association (WTA), which successfully lobbied for and gained equal access to facilities and conditions to the men, only managed to achieve pay equity at the British (Wimbledon) and French (Roland-Garros) Opens in 2007. If one of the world's most successful women's sporting organisations has only recently achieved pay parity with men, then the outcome for women's sports relying on the male-dominated governing body of a male-dominated sport to support the growth and development of women's sports is even less likely to result in an optimal outcome. A prime example of this was the English Football Association (FA) handling of women's soccer which has a history of actively resisting women from participating in football, as evident in their 1971 ban on females from playing football on their grounds. The FA's continued mishandling of the Women's Super League (WSL) competition continued up until 2009 when announced the launch of the new competition. The creation of the WSL is important as it mirrored the male competition step away from the FA in order to form their own elite league – the English Premier League (EPL). This loss forced the FA into taking action as they wanted to regain control and the competition was marketed as the promotion of women in sport and a way to increase participation of families at the grassroots level (Woodhouse et al., 2019). While the FA may not have been completely altruistically motivated, the loss of control over the EPL did result in a clear win for the WSL and women's sport in general.

Women's professional basketball in the USA has had a similar turbulent history. While women have been playing basketball since it was invented in 1891, it was not until 1976 that the first female league was even planned. Even then women had to wait until 1978 until the first Women's Basketball League (WBL) was delivered, but the lack of support and funding saw it fold up three seasons later. Finally, in 1997 two competing competitions came to life with the American Basketball League (ABL) and the WNBA. Unlike the previous attempts, this time the WNBA had the backing of their male counterpart and have remained a viable competition.[9] This situation is not unique to America as women in Australia experienced a similar fate playing cricket, where Lily Poulett-Harris created her own league in 1894, but it has only been recently that women have seen anything resembling a professional league. In an uncommon move at the time, Women's Cricket Australia (WCA) merged with their male counterpart the Australian Cricket Board (ACB) in 2003 to form a unified board (Cricket Australia) that oversees all aspects of both the men's and women's game – this has included movement towards equality in contacts, pay and promotion, but more importantly a major success for the women's team. However, in the last few years we have observed a significant increase in the interest of women's sports through broadcast and sponsorship.[10] This is often because female sports occupy a better social branding position than male sports, as they are seen as more inspiring, more family-orientated, more socially responsible, more inclusive and less aggressive (Nielsen, 2019). In Australia, we have seen the launch of the Women's Big Bash League (WBBL) cricket competition in 2015, the Women's Australian Rules Football League (AFLW) in 2017 and the Super Netball in 2017 with wide-ranging broadcast and sponsorship deals. While the starting position of women sports is negatively affected by the prior focus of resources being concentrated in male sports, the long term sustainability of women's professional sporting leagues has begun to noticeably change for the better even within the leagues. What women continue to lag behind is the benefits males experience participating in professional sport leagues. Other stand-alone governing bodies may have been less successful overall because by having separate organisations for men and women they both end up competing for the same set of limited resources, i.e. funding, sponsorship and facilities. Furthermore, the entrenched gender inequality in the sports domain results in the funding for women falling further behind the already well-established male competitions as potential sponsors often decide that the more entrenched competitions would better promote their brand.

Conclusions

We need to solve the ongoing gender inequality we observe in sport. However, this should not be about tearing down men's sport to enforce equality with women; rather, this needs to be about building up systems and mechanisms to enable women to complete on an equal playing field. This requires an equitable distribution of resources. We have already observed arguments that Title IX has caused lasting damage to the men's sports programme in the NCAA. For example, many colleges have cut wrestling programmes in order to "accommodate" or fund the female sports programmes. However, in this case the blame falls on cutting resources to 'wrong' male sports programmes. Cuts could have made to an already bloated football programme. Squad size could have been reduced, for example, by removing the third- and fourth-string quarterbacks. But many colleges chose to keep their bloated football programmes intact and cut soft targets such as wrestling. This approach might very well have been a strategic choice and one intended to maximise partisan (male) anger and provoke sexist pushback against women's sports in general and Title IX, by trying to demonstrate that Title IX sporting equity could only be achieved by sacrificing male sports.

There is little doubt that significant resources are generated through the male sporting programmes around the world, and these have a long-term benefit for future male athletes. However, a significant part of this success in male sports was achieved due to the absence of or the diversion of resources away from women's sports. The modern era has seen the construction of massive sporting institutions, which have been largely built around male sports. The lack of resources and the legal obstacle to women sports has disincentivized women in sports and reduced the human capital investment by women in sports. Apparent underperformance of women in sports or female sports is often a byproduct of women's sports being historically underfunded.

The obvious underfunding and underdevelopment of female sports create additional problems downstream, as eventually it feeds back into the image of female sports, which further limits its development. Simply taken at face value, this would imply that fans are less interested or less excited to watch or attend sports of this nature, and the knock-on effect is that sponsors are less interested in providing financial support for sports with low numbers of supporters and fans. This then affects the potential value for broadcast deals, as the broadcasters must consider the revenue streams from advertising and the size of the audience. This lack of revenue and exposure flows back into the female sports in terms of lower salaries, less exposure and less ground-level players and associations which, in the long run, act as a serious disincentive for women who would otherwise seek a career as an elite athlete.

Notes

1. UN estimates that for every 100 females, there are 101.7 males or 49.58% of the world population is female; this was accessed from https://population.un.org/wpp/Download/Standard/Population/ on 16 March 2021.
2. Statistics were obtained from the Olympics organisations' web reports on Women in the Olympics, available at https://www.olympic.org/women-in-sport/background/statistics, accessed on 16 March 2021.
3. This is despite the fact that "working-class" English women have been engaging in prize fighting since at least the 1700s (Hargreaves, 1997), contrary to the notions of gentility and ladylike behaviour.
4. A common anecdotal story was that women could not be real sports broadcasters as they would have to enter into the men's locker rooms for interviews – where they would be "exposed" to inappropriate male behaviours, so for their own good, it would be best to not have female reporters (rather than correct the male behaviours).
5. Sourced from the Global World Index Trends Report by Chase Buckle (2019), "Understanding the Women's World Cup Audience," available at https://blog.globalwebindex.com/trends/understanding-womens-world-cup-audience/.
6. For additional discussions and comments about female commentators/comments, see https://www.insidethegames.biz/articles/1075178/alan-hubbard-experts-or-eye-candy-is-it-tv-tokenism-as-football-shows-its-feminine-side? and https://www.nytimes.com/2016/04/29/sports/more-than-mean-women-journalists-julie-dicaro-sarah-spain.html.
7. Historical odds obtained from https://www.sportsbettinglines.com/2012-australian-open-tennis-womens-singles-futures-odds/ and https://www.gambling911.com/sports/novak-djokovic-vs-rafael-nadal-betting-odds-2012-australia-open-mens-final-012812.html.
8. It should be noted that the best result of the USA men's team was a third place in 1930, but the team failed to qualify between 1954 and 1990 and failed to qualify again in 2018, resulting in only ten appearances from 21 tournaments, one of which was an automatic qualification in 1994 for being the host nation.
9. The American Basketball League (ABL), like the WBL, filed for bankruptcy after three seasons (Staffo, 1998).
10. See the Nielsen Report "Girl Power: Measuring the Rise of Women's Sport in Australia" (Nielsen, 2019) at https://www.nielsen.com/au/en/insights/article/2019/girl-power-measuring-the-rise-of-women-s-sport-in-australia/.

References

Aman, M. P., Yusof, A., Ismail, M., and Mohamed Razali, A. B. (2018). Pipeline problem: Factors influencing the underrepresentation of women in the top leadership positions of sport organisations. *Malaysian Journal of Movement, Health & Exercise*, 7(2), 151–166.

Andersson, R., and Barker-Ruchti, N. (2019). Career paths of Swedish top-level women soccer players. *Soccer & Society*, 20(6), 857–871.

Australian Bureau of Statistics. (2013). Women in Sport: The State of Play 2013 Perspectives on Sport Data Block 4156.0.55.001. Accessed December 2019, available through https://www.abs.gov.au/ausstats/abs@.nsf/Products/4156.0.55.001~June+2013~Main+Features~Women+in+Sport+The+State+of+Play+2013

Australian Sports Commission. (2001). *Body image and participation in sport*. [Canberra]: Australian Sports Commission.

Bernstein, A. (2002). Is it time for a victory lap? Changes in the media coverage of women in sport. *International Review for the Sociology of Sport*, 37(3–4), 415–428.

Borland, J., and MacDonald, R. (2003). Demand for sport. *Oxford Review of Economic Policy*, 19(4), 478–502.

Braithwait, R. (1994). *The English gentleman*. Bristol: Thoemmes Press.

Button, K. J., and Weyman-Jones, T. G. (1992). Ownership structure, institutional organization and measured X-efficiency. *The American Economic Review*, 82(2), 439–445.

Caple, H., Greenwood, K., and Lumby, C. (2011). What league? The representation of female athletes in Australian television sports coverage. *Media International Australia*, 140(1), 137–146.

Caruso, R., Di Domizio, M., and Savage, D. A. (2017). Differences in national identity, violence and conflict in international sport tournaments: Hic sunt leones! *KYKLOS*, 70(4), 511–545.

Clark Blickenstaff, J. (2005). Women and science careers: Leaky pipeline or gender filter? *Gender and Education*, 17(4), 369–386.

Colander, D., and Woos, J. W. (1997). Institutional demand-side discrimination against women and the human capital model. *Feminist Economics*, 3(1), 53–64.

Cooky, C., Messner, M. A., and Hextrum, R. H. (2013). Women play sport, but not on TV: A longitudinal study of televised news media. *Communication & Sport*, 1(3), 203–230.

Da Costa, L. M. (2014). Beauty, effort and talent: A brief history of Brazilian women's soccer in press discourse. *Soccer & Society*, 15(1), 81–92.

Davies, S. G., and Deckert, A. (2019). Pretty strong women: Ingenious agency, pink gloves and Muay Thai. *Sociology of Sport Journal*, 36, 213–223.

Drewes, M. (2003). Competition and efficiency in professional sports leagues. *European Sport Management Quarterly*, 3(4), 240–252.

Dupas, P., Modestino, A., Niederle, M., and Wolfers, J. (2020). Gender and the Dynamics of Economics Seminars. In presentation at lunchtime seminar, *Economic Society of Australia*.

Eastman, S. T., and Billings, A. C. (2001). Biased voices of sports: Racial and gender stereotyping in college basketball announcing. *Howard Journal of Communications*, 12(4), 183–201.

Edelman, M., and Harrison, C. K. (2008). Analyzing the WNBA's mandatory age/education policy from a legal, cultural, and ethical perspective: Women, men, and the professional sports landscape. *Northwestern Journal of Law and Social Policy*, 3(1), 1–28.

Espinosa, L. (2011). Pipelines and pathways: Women of color in undergraduate STEM majors and the college experiences that contribute to persistence. *Harvard Educational Review*, 81(2), 209–241.

Farh, C. I., Oh, J. K., Hollenbeck, J. R., Yu, A., Lee, S. M., and King, D. D. (2020). Token female voice enactment in traditionally male-dominated teams: Facilitating conditions and consequences for performance. *Academy of Management Journal,* 63(3), 832–856.

FIFA. (2014). Women's Football Survey. Retrieved from https://resources.fifa.com/image/upload/fifa-women-s-football-survey-2522649.pdf?cloudid=emtgxvp0ibnebltlvi3b&fbclid

FIFA. (2019). FIFA Women's World Cup France 2019. Global Broadcast and Audience Report. Retrieved from fifa.com/womensworldcup/news/fifa-women-s-world-cup-2019tm-watched-by-more-than-1-billion

Frank, R. H., and Cook, P. J. (2010). *The winner-take-all society: Why the few at the top get so much more than the rest of us.* New York: Random House.

Franks, S., and O'Neill, D. (2016). Women reporting sport: Still a man's game? *Journalism,* 17(4), 474–492.

Hardin, M., and Shain, S. (2006). Feeling much smaller than you know you are: The fragmented professional identity of female sports journalists, *Critical Studies: Media Communication,* 23(4), 322–338.

Hargreaves, J. (1997). Women's boxing and related activities: Introducing images and meanings. *Body and Society,* 3(4), 33–49.

Hull, K. (2017). An examination of women's sports coverage on the Twitter accounts of local television sports broadcasters. *Communication & Sport,* 5(4), 471–491.

Jenkel, L. (2021). The FA's ban of women's football 1921 in the contemporary press– a historical discourse analysis. *Sport in History,* 41 (2), 1–21.

Jones, D. (2006). The representation of female athletes in online images of successive Olympic Games. *Pacific Journalism Review,* 12(1), 108–129.

Kane, M. J., and LaVoi, N. (2018). An examination of intercollegiate athletic directors' attributions regarding the underrepresentation of female coaches in women's sports. *Women in Sport and Physical Activity Journal,* 26(1), 3–11.

Kim, M.-C., and Hong, E. (2016). A red card for women: Female officials ostracized in South Korean football. *Asian Journal of Women's Studies,* 22(2), 114–130.

Krumer, A., Rosenboim, M., and Shapir, O. M. (2016). Gender, competitiveness, and physical characteristics: Evidence from professional tennis. *Journal of Sports Economics,* 17(3), 234–259.

Leibenstein, H. (1966). Allocative efficiency vs. "X-efficiency". *The American Economic Review,* 56(3), 392–415.

Lumby, K., Caple, H., and Greenwood, K. (2010). *Towards a level playing field: Sport and gender in Australian media, January 2008-July 2009.* Canberra: Australian Sports Commission.

McCarthy, N. (2019). The Gender Pay Gap at the FIFA World Cup Is $370 Million, Forbes Online, June 11 available at https://www.forbes.com/sites/niallmccarthy/2019/06/11/the-gender-pay-gap-at-the-fifa-world-cup-is-370-million-infographic/?sh=234559b12751

Messner, M. A. (1988). Sports and male domination: The female athlete as contested ideological terrain. *Sociology of Sport Journal,* 5, 197–211.

Miloch, K. S., Pedersen, P. M., Smucker, M. K., and Whisenant, W. A. (2005). The current state of women print journalists: An analysis of the status and careers of females in newspapers sports departments, *Public Organization Review,* 5, 219–232.

Morgan, A. (2019). An examination of women's sport sponsorship: A case study of female Australian Rules football. *Journal of Marketing Management,* 35(17–18), 1644–1666.

Nielsen Report (2019). Girl Power: Measuring the Rise of Women's Sport in Australia. Accessed December 2019, available at https://www.nielsen.com/au/en/insights/article/2019/girl-power-measuring-the-rise-of-women-s-sport-in-australia/

NRLW. (2020). Women's Rugby League. NRLW Premiership. Retrieved from https://www.nrl.com/womens/nrlw-premiership/

Rogers, R. (2020). Boys in the booth: The impact of announcer gender on audience demand. *Journal of Sports Economics*, 1527002520921231.

Rowe, D., and Brown, P. (1994). Promoting women's sport: Theory, policy and practice. *Leisure Studies*, 13, 97–110.

Staffo, D. F. (1998). The history of women's professional basketball in the United States with an emphasis on the old WBL and the new ABL and WNBA. *The Physical Educator*, 55(4), 187–198.

Taylor, T., Fujak, H., Hanlon, C., and O'Connor, D. (2020). A balancing act: Women players in a new semi-professional team sport league. *European Sport Management Quarterly*, doi: 10.1080/16184742.2020.1815821.

Trolan, E. J. (2013). The impact of the media on gender inequality within sport. *Procedia - Social and Behavioral Sciences*, 91, 215–227.

Tuggle, C. A., and Owen, A. (1999). A descriptive analysis of NBC's coverage of the centennial Olympics: The "games of the woman"? *Journal of Sport and Social Issues*, 23(2), 171–182.

Sherry, E., Osborne, A., and Nicholson, M. (2016). Images of sports women: A review. *Sex Roles*, 74, 299–309.

Whiteside, E., and Hardin, M. (2011). Women (not) watching women: Leisure time, television, and implications for televised coverage of women's sports. *Communication, Culture & Critique*, 4(2), 122–143.

Wilson, E. O. (2000). *Socio-biology: The new synthesis* (25th Anniversary Ed). Cambridge: Harvard University Press.

Women in Sport. (2018). Where Are All the Women. Shinning a light on the visibility of women's sport in the media. Retrieved from https://www.womeninsport.org/wp-content/uploads/2018/10/Where-are-all-the-Women-1.pdf

Wood, D. (2018). The beautiful game? Hegemonic masculinity, women and football in Brazil and Argentina. *Bulletin of Latin American Research*, 37(5), 567–581.

Woodhouse, D., Fielding-Lloyd, B., and Sequerra, R. (2019). Big brother's little sister: The ideological construction of women's super league. *Sport in Society*, 22(12), 2006–2023.

7 Winner alright? New evidence on high-stakes bidding and returns to ownership in the thoroughbred horseracing industry

David Butler and Robert Butler

Introduction

While there is substantial literature considering auction bidding behaviour experimentally (Kagel & Levin, 2002), field studies addressing the sale of goods tending towards a common value are much rarer in the literature. This chapter seeks to address this by taking advantage of the unique conditions of thoroughbred horseracing in Great Britain and Ireland. Given the data available on sales and productivity, this is a field context where it is possible to explore auction behaviour and outcomes. It is yet another aspect of sport where an economic lens can provide useful insights into human behaviour.

We conduct an ex post productivity evaluation of 1,681 thoroughbred foals sold between 2007 and 2008 in Great British and Irish public auctions who have now concluded their racing careers. Fundamentally, this method is a 'first-pass' test of efficiency (Burger & Walters, 2008). These auctions took place at Goffs and Tattersalls (auction houses), both of which are reputable sellers that regularly convene bloodstock sales. This approach can offer various insights concerning thoroughbred ownership that are specific to the industry. More generally, by carrying out this analysis, we can make a new contribution to the topic of owner motivations in sport. This remains an underdeveloped topic of empirical inquiry.

From a behavioural perspective, few if any other auction environments cleanly offer the *combination* of unique conditions we present here. First, our auction context offers an opportunity to study competitive bidding behaviour at high stakes. Our analysis shows that on average, winning bids exceed €42,000. This is a non-trivial sum. Second, each thoroughbred's lifetime winnings provide a precise measure of each asset's output on the track. This allows one to determine the productivity of these assets ex post, when their career on the racetrack concludes (Smith, Staniar & Splan, 2006; Langlois & Blouin, 2007). In general, having a determinate single measure of output is a rare feature of auction environments. Third, as thoroughbred sales are

DOI: 10.4324/9781003080824-9

recurring events, the auction environment is populated with bidding agents who have ample opportunity to learn.

Finally, the informational features on offer are rarely, if ever, represented in other naturally occurring auctions – foal auctions provide restricted informational conditions that can approximate laboratory environments. Given each asset's infantile status, there are minimal disparities in information across potential buyers. No knowledge of their training or earnings potential is available at the time of sale to a bidder at auction as foals are usually only 'broken in' as yearlings (a process known as halter-breaking). Thus, the potential for information differences between buyers is significantly reduced when compared to yearling markets where information leakages can occur. If sellers have additional and valuable information later in a thoroughbred's life cycle – for instance, knowledge relating to medical history, physical attributes or psychological profile – adverse selection problems can emerge (Chezum & Wimmer, 1997). At the time of the auctions studied in this chapter, all potential buyers only have access to a foal's pedigree and past veterinary reports. Thus, foal auctions offer a clean but naturally occurring information structure.

Although few studies have considered this auction context, fewer still have evaluated the returns to the assets sold or considered alternative economic and psychological explanations for the patterns observed. Besides analysing thoroughbreds from their earliest sales point, we offer two further steps forward. The first is methodological – the sample evaluated is not restricted by thoroughbred bloodline or gender. Moreover, we access data on thoroughbreds that are sold but do not appear on the racetrack. This sampling strategy offers a clearer picture of the industry's operations. Next, the dataset facilitates a basic exploration of two arguments proposed to explain the findings: principal-agent problems arising between owners/trainers and diversification strategies adopted by owners. To date, neither of them have been empirically explored as a route to explain returns in horseracing.

A further unique feature of our contribution is that it concentrates on the horseracing industry in the British Isles. While the basic sporting operations of thoroughbred horseracing are alike on either side of the Atlantic, the traditions and institutional features of the industry have evolved differently. So far, this topic has been studied in the context of American thoroughbred horseracing only (Gamrat & Sauer, 2000; Gamrat & Sauer, 2001; Ray, 2001; DeGennaro, 2003). We understand that a detailed assessment of bidding efficiencies has yet to be conducted for thoroughbred horseracing in Great Britain and Ireland. Thus, the findings presented here offer a basis for comparison and can provide a practical guide for those developing bidding strategies within the industry.

To preview the analysis, we provide empirical weight to a commonly held belief – a high percentage of thoroughbreds sold at auction incur net negative returns. We show that the scale of losses is amplified as winning auction bids increase. Once winning bids exceed approximately €20,000 on average, losses are incurred. If one is to assume that bidding power is a measure of an owner's status, the evidence implies that absolute risk aversion decreases with wealth. As the results reveal break-even points, the findings have implications for those formulating bidding strategies within the industry. Given the extent of losses observed, this study can also inform a wider debate relating to the motivations of owners in sport.

The next section offers a brief introduction to the workings of the industry in Great Britain and Ireland, focusing on the means of purchasing thoroughbreds and their maturation process. Section 'Background' provides a background to past research. Section 'Empirical framework' introduces the empirical framework, specifying the auction details and productivity data. Section 'Analysis' conducts an analysis of ex post returns. Two previously unexplored behavioural explanations for the observed results are then addressed. Section 'Discussion' discusses the results, and section 'Conclusion' concludes the chapter.

A primer on the Great British and Irish thoroughbred industry

Horseracing in Great Britain and Ireland and can be traced back centuries. The earliest known steeplechase, over a distance 4.5 miles, was run in County Cork in 1752. The Epsom Derby can be traced back to 1780. The historical connections between the two islands – economically, politically and socially – have resulted in the administration of the sport being split between Great Britain and the island of Ireland. Normally, the administration of sport on the island of Ireland is split between north and south (Northern Ireland and the Republic of Ireland) or the Republic of Ireland and the United Kingdom (with includes Northern Ireland). Horseracing is an exception. The two racecourses in Northern Ireland – at Down Royal and Down Patrick – are administered by Horse Racing Ireland based in County Kildare in the Republic of Ireland, rather than the British Horse Racing Authority in London.

There are now more than 1,800 race meetings run annually in Great Britain and Ireland at 86 different racecourses (60 in Great Britain and 26 in Ireland). A race meeting normally consists of between seven and nine individual races, run at intervals of about 30 minutes apart. In total, a meeting normally lasts between three and four hours and can consist of a combination of flat, hurdle and steeplechase races. Flat racing does not require the jumping of obstacles during a race and is normally run over shorter distances – between a minimum of 5 furlongs and maximums in excess of about 2.5 miles – when compared to both hurdle and steeplechase races. The horses considered in the data section in this chapter generally spent their entire racing careers as flat racehorse and represent an elite group of thoroughbred animals.

In order for owners to compete at the track with a thoroughbred, ownership of a horse is required. There are multiple ways to purchase a thoroughbred racehorse. Thoroughbreds can be acquired through (i) a claiming race –

where all horses running are for sale; (ii) leasing agreements – where there is no commitment required from the buyer to purchase the asset; (iii) a private purchase – where a buyer negotiates a price and is sold the asset directly from a stud farm, breeder or trainer; and finally, (iv) an auction. These auctions constitute the most common sales mechanism and are usually organised by the age of the animal for sale and, in the case of foals, occur late in the calendar year.

All foals are registered with the same birth date (1 January). The animals range in weight from approximately 31.8 kg to 65.5 kg at birth. They are suckled by their dam, in most cases for six months; grow quickly; and reach 90% of their adult size by the time they are two years old (Horse Racing Ireland, 2009). Importantly, a limited but equal information set is available to all interested parties at foal auctions. For buyers, decision-making is commonly directed by the heritage of the foal. While heritable traits act as important indicators to buyers, genetic evidence suggests that only 35% of variation in a thoroughbred's performance is attributed to genetic lineage (Gaffney & Cunningham, 1988). The Irish horseracing body publicly discloses this uncertainty to potential buyers, suggesting that the attribution to genetics can even be as low as 9% (Horse Racing Ireland, 2009, p. 32). Therefore, regardless of the quality of a thoroughbred's genes, there is no guarantee of success based on breeding characteristics alone. Lineage provides a loose guide.

Initially, auction companies list each foal in internationally published catalogues approximately one month prior to an auction. These catalogues provide access to each foal's pedigree, veterinary reports, date of birth and the performance data of their relatives on the racetrack. Therefore, during an auction all potential buyers have access to a foal's pedigree, past veterinary reports and the performance data of their relatives on the racetrack. Potential buyers are also permitted to vet the foal before it enters the sales ring. This allows potential buyers to subjectively evaluate the conformation of a foal, in addition to assessing its bone structure, movements and other factors that allow necessary due diligence. Buyers may also assess a foal for psychological characteristics such as temperament.

The auctions for foals considered here are conducted in the format of an *English* auction where the highest current bid assumes the position of the standing bid. In this format, the bid of every interested party is known during the auction. By dropping out, one is disclosing their maximum valuation of the asset for sale. Owners who win an auction can be individuals, partnerships (which consist of between two and four people) and syndicates (which consist of up to 20 members).

By the age of two, far more information is known about the potential quality of the thoroughbred. After being sold, the thoroughbreds are 'broken in' (usually as yearlings). This is an initial step in their preparation to race and compete for prize money. Later, they are prepared for racing by a trainer. The training process usually involves detailed attention to the thoroughbred's dietary requirements and exercise routines.

The winning bidder at auction is not permitted to race their asset until it is two years old. Once a thoroughbred reaches two years of age (and is appropriately trained), they are eligible to enter races where there is an opportunity to earn significant prize money to recoup the initial purchase price. Given the distribution of racing talent, thoroughbreds are grouped into similar racing classes to safeguard competitive balance. The best thoroughbreds are those that win the highest amount of prize money, often by performing in lucrative races known as the *Classics* such as the *1,000 Guineas Stakes*, the *Epsom Derby* and the *St. Leger Stakes*. In addition to this, other *Group 1* races offer substantial prize money to successful entrants. In most races, prize money is offered in a descending scale from the first horse to placed horses that finish second or third in a race. On occasion, prize money is offered to entrants ranked lower. In general, an inverse relationship exists between the class of race and the prize money on offer.

Depending on the ability of the thoroughbreds, they can have alternative career lengths and can run in different types of races. Generally, thoroughbreds that are recognised for their speed participate in more lucrative 'flat' races. Flat horses usually begin their career at two, with some of the most lucrative races taking place when they are three. These flat horses commonly peak between the ages of four and five and can retire as young as four years old.

Horses that are not recognised for their speed often participate in National Hunt races, which involve jumping hurdles and fences. National Hunt thoroughbreds usually only begin a career after significantly more maturation, usually at about four years of age. These thoroughbreds have longer careers than flat horses and, in some cases, can race up to the age of 13. They generally peak between seven and eight years of age.

Given the distribution of prize money attached to races, long careers do not translate to higher earnings – often elite horses must be selective about the races they enter. Trainers and owners may act strategically, attempting to maximise a thoroughbred return while minimising the likelihood of fatigue or injury. Once their career is complete, *elite* horses commonly retire to stud to breed future offspring.

Background

Several previous studies have examined economic issues in horse racing. Fernie and Metcalf (1999), Coffey and Maloney (2010) and Butler, Butler and Simmons (2020) all examine jockey performance under various contractual arrangements with owners. While past research has also explored pricing models for thoroughbreds (Parson & Smith, 2008; Robert & Stowe, 2016), sire stud fees (Stowe, 2013) and the impact of disclosures on pricing (Plant & Stowe, 2013), analyses of bidding efficiencies or adverse selection effects have been rare and are restricted to the American thoroughbred industry (Chezum & Wimmer, 1997; Wimmer & Chezum, 2003). A series of contributions and replies at the turn of the century are the only analysis of the topic (Gamrat & Sauer, 2000; 2001; Ray, 2001; DeGennaro, 2003).

Gamrat and Sauer (2000) initiated a discussion of returns to thoroughbred investment by showing that owners pay a greater sum for an asset than its expected present value of cash flows. Less than half of their sample of 805 fillies recoup their initial cost. While this is a behavioural trait that a rational investor interested in maximising returns should avoid, the authors interpret the difference between mean returns and auction price as a measure of the non-pecuniary utility of ownership. They propose that the data support a participation premium model (Gamrat and Sauer, 2000). The extent of losses could be explained as a cost of owning thoroughbreds and 'playing the game'. This contrasts with a pure championship model, where one would assume a causal relationship between the fee paid for a thoroughbred and probability of success on the track.

The insights of Gamrat and Sauer (2000) were subject to discussion, particularly in terms of their sampling strategy. The data accessed were restricted to a sample of fillies only and did not take account of environmental factors relating to performance (Ray, 2001). Further comment on Gamrat and Sauer (2000) is provided by DeGennaro (2003). DeGennaro (2003) suggests that a non-linear relationship may exist between the distribution of thoroughbred prices and the expected returns of a horse. In turn, this poses challenges to distinguishing between a championship model and a participation model; as the distribution of talent is highly skewed, few thoroughbreds sold at auction will become elite horses.

To date, no additional evidence has been provided. While this chapter does not attempt to solve the challenging problem posed by DeGennaro (2003), several of the sampling issues raised by Ray (2001) are addressed here and a superior dataset to that of Gamrat and Sauer (2000) is constructed.

Empirical framework

The empirical section of this chapter focuses on the net returns of foals auctioned between 2007 and 2008 at sales on Great Britain and Ireland. Information on the thoroughbreds is captured at two points in time: firstly, when an auction sale took place; and secondly, when a thoroughbred's flat career concluded.

The monetary return of each asset, that is their net profit or loss, is treated as the dependent variable. As opposed to win ratios, the net return of a thoroughbred adjusts for the quality of races entered. As one cannot simply model how a buyer will form expectations about a foal at time period 1, evaluating the ex post productivity of the asset at time period 2 is the most logical manner to proceed.

Auction procedures and data

The dataset for this study is assembled manually through online resources. Data are accessed for foal sales from four auctions in Ireland (two) and England (two) between 2007 and 2008. These dates are chosen as many foals sold at these auctions had completed their careers by the end of the 2015 racing season. The data for these auctions are accessed from the Racing Post Bloodstock Sales Database. Table 7.1 summarises the key details of the auctions.

Goffs and *Tattersalls* are the auction houses that organised the sales. All auctions occurred over a five-day period and followed an ascending bid or *English* auction format. At the time of bidding, it is assumed that all potential owners are aware of the possible rewards available to these foals once they have matured. Owners in Western Europe have their own interest group (AIRO) that is established to protect these financial interests. The group has specific goals that include maintaining and increasing prize money in races.

The clearance rates for the four auctions ranged from 40.1% to 57.1%. For each auction, a percentage of total lots are either withdrawn or not sold. This regularly occurs as a foal may fail to reach a reserve price. From the remaining sales, a proportion of foals auctioned are unregistered. These are not named at the time of sale and could not be identified. Additionally, a proportion of lots sold are removed from the sample for one of two reasons. Firstly, an observation is removed if a thoroughbred's career had not concluded as their total productivity was only subject to partial measurement. The most common reason for a thoroughbred not to have finished their (flat) career was because they also competed in National Hunt horseracing. Thoroughbreds that have a dual registration normally compete for a longer time period than horses that solely run in flat races. Secondly, observations are removed if there was incomplete information concerning the thoroughbred's earnings over the course of their career. For instance, thoroughbreds may enter races in countries outside of Ireland and Great Britain where no earnings data were accessible. All foals that remained in the sample concluded their careers between 9 October 2009 and 23 September 2015.

Table 7.1 Auction Details

Date	Auction house	Lots	Withdrawn	Sales	Unregistered	Removed	N
17–21 November 2008	Goffs	1253	750	503	136	60	307
25–29 November 2008	Tattersalls	1251	688	563	123	51	389
18–22 November 2007	Goffs	1270	603	667	189	48	430
27 November–1 December 2007	Tattersalls	1390	597	793	190	48	555

Source: Racing Post Bloodstock Sales Database.

Information is available on the characteristics of 1,681 individual lots. Data on physical attributes were collected on each of the foals, such as their colour (black 73%, chestnut 19%, grey 5%, brown 3%), sex (62.6% colts; 37.4% fillies) and relations (205 sires, 1580 dams). In addition, information regarding the specific lot is recorded; data are available on each foal's breeder (1062), sales vendor (567), new owner (1102) and future trainer (665). Thirty-one owners are defined as syndicates (which consist of up to 20 members). Importantly, the winning auction bid for each foal is recorded. All winning bids are converted to euros, and historical exchange rates are used to standardise the values.[1] The average winning bid is €42,047.52 (Std. Dev. = €58,631.31). The lowest winning bid was €991.03, while the highest winning bid was €655,192.10.

Productivity data

The productivity measure of lifetime earnings for each lot is accessed from the Irish Racing database. Irish Racing is a website owned by The Irish Times Ltd and provides comprehensive statistics on Irish, British and major international horseracing. In addition, data are collected on each lot's number of starts during their career, number of wins, place finishes (second–third) and career length in days. Table 7.2 provides descriptive statistics for the thoroughbreds.

The minimum days active for any lot was zero. This occurred if a horse only had one race in their career. Thus, a racehorse's career start and end occurred at the same point in time. This was true for 142 lots in the sample. Thirty-seven lots (2%) of the sample, despite being successfully auctioned, never became active or had the opportunity to produce a return. This outcome is not surprising, however, and is indicative of the challenging process of preparing foals to race.

Analysis

This section provides a descriptive account of the net returns at an aggregate level and details the asset's returns along alternative dimensions such as the gender and bidding range. Second, alternative behavioural explanations that can be controlled for are given due consideration.

Table 7.2 Productivity Details

Productivity 2008–2015 (n = 1,681)	Mean	Std. Dev.	Min	Max
Starts	12.75	13.62	0	83
Wins	1.37	2.06	0	13
Places	2.60	3.64	0	22
Career length (days active)	25	579	0	2346

Source: Irish Racing.

Average returns

Table 7.3 considers the average returns of the entire sample of auctioned thoroughbreds and gender-specific subsamples. Consistent with Gamrat and Sauer (2000), on average, the net returns for the sample are negative. As gender is an important determinant of performance in horseracing, it is worthwhile to analyse the returns of the thoroughbreds by sex. While fillies do incur greater losses than colts, the monetary differences are not substantial. The median net losses observed for the entire sample are −€14,375.15. For the colt sample and filly sample, these net losses are −€14,763.78 and −€13,855.44, respectively. It is of note that these statistics abstract from any returns generated by insider information in the betting market, something which cannot be measured.

Figure 7.1 presents the unconditional net returns (indicated in black) and the restricted net returns (indicated in grey) in ascending order for the 1,681 lots in the sample. The unconditional net returns represent a straightforward analysis contingent on winning auction bids and returns. The restricted net returns measure controls for two further cost-side factors: (i) the annual average cost of a thoroughbred's upkeep which is estimated at €15,200 per annum by AIRO, adjusted for each thoroughbred's career length; and (ii) costs associated with commissions and jockey bonus fees, estimated to reduce reported earnings by approximately 10% (Gamrat & Sauer, 2000).

For the unconditional measure, the frequency of negative returns across auctions ranges from 74.35% of the sample (Goffs, 2008 auction) to 83.96% (Tattersalls, 2007 auction). For the complete sample, 1,342 thoroughbreds (79.8%) realised negative returns and conclude their career in the domain of losses. A total of 339 thoroughbreds (20.2%) returned a profit. Adopting the second criterion, which is sensitive to further cost-side measures,

Table 7.3 Ex Post Analysis

Ex post efficiency evaluation	Mean	Std. Dev.	Min	Max
Winning bid (N = 1,681)	€ 42,047.52	€ 58,631.31	€ 991.03	€ 655,192.10
Lifetime winnings (N = 1,681)	€ 18,337.91	€ 68,328.62	€ 0.00	€ 1,206,376.00
Net returns	−€ 23,709.61	€ 85,967.64	−€ 644,685.10	€ 1,191,376.00
Winning bid colt (N = 1,053)	€ 44,248.27	€ 61,757.08	€ 991.03	€ 655,192.10
Lifetime winnings colt (N = 1,053)	€ 22,149.20	€ 76,560.23	€ 0.00	€ 1,206,376.00
Net returns	−€ 22,099.07	€ 94,707.53	−€ 644,685.10	€ 1,191,376.00
Winning bid filly (N = 628)	€ 38,357.42	€ 52,820.09	€ 991.03	€ 545,067.60
Lifetime winnings filly (N = 628)	€ 11,947.33	€ 51,086.77	€ 0.00	€ 1,004,890.00
Net returns	−€ 26,410.09	€ 68,855.84	−€ 545,067.60	€ 902,971.10

Source: Irish Racing.

deflates returns further. A total of 1,610 thoroughbreds (95.7%) realised negative returns and conclude their career in the domain of losses. Seventy-one thoroughbreds (4.3%) returned a profit. As the returns estimated from the restricted sample are derived from relatively unsophisticated measures, the forthcoming inferential statistical assessment treats the first unconditional returns measure as the dependent variable.

Given the distribution of the bidding and earnings data, we distinguish between alternative ranges of winning bids. To investigate this relationship, Figure 7.2 represents the average returns for winning bids in nine alternative bidding ranges (€991–€4,999, n = 249; €5,000–€9,999, n = 211; €10,000–€19,999, n = 307; €20,000–29,000, n = 207; €30,000–39,999, n = 155; €40,000–59,000, n = 177; €60,000–€79,000, n = 113; €80,000–€99,000, n = 85; >€100,000, n = 177). A monotonically decreasing relationship is observed (a phenomenon robust to altering the parameters of the bidding ranges). Low winning bids, on average, produce net positive returns. Increases on average in winning bids correspond to net returns entering the domain of losses after the third bidding category (approximately €20,000). Once winning bids reach this value, on average, the asset's productivity fails to recoup the initial investment. Considering the distribution of the categories in Figure 7.2 and assuming bidding power is a measure of an owner's wealth status, the monetary distances between the categories suggest that absolute risk aversion decreases with wealth.

Comparing mean ranks in alternative bidding categories reports a statistically significant difference between the groups identified in Table 7.4

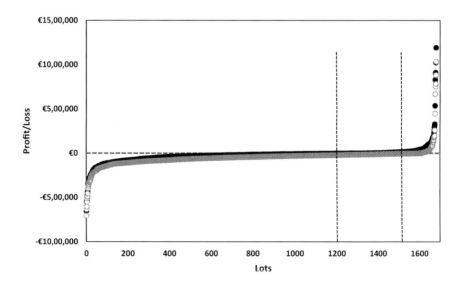

Figure 7.1 Returns by Lots in Ascending Order.

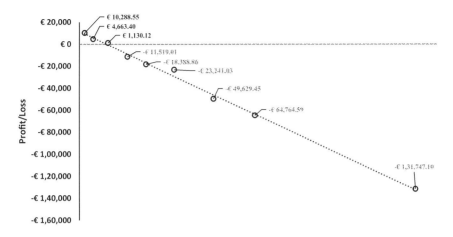

Figure 7.2 Average Net Returns for Alternative Bidding Ranges.

(KW: χ^2 =1015.59, p = 0.00). The specific differences between the bidding categories are identified in Table 7.4 along with the pairwise comparisons of means using the Bonferroni correction technique. Once bidding is greater than €100,000, negative returns are amplified. These results add further insight to the nature of bidding efficiencies in the industry. In bidding conditions with relatively low winning bids, positive returns on average exist. These positive averages are, for the most part, produced by horses sold for low winning bids that unexpectedly earn significant prize money. No statistically significant pairwise correlations are observed between lower bidding ranges, where positive returns on average are recorded.

Alternative behavioural explanations

The thoroughbred horseracing industry is complex and involves multiple interacting parties. While the non-pecuniary motivations' interpretation of the inefficiencies provided by Gamrat and Sauer (2000) offers a plausible explanation for these data, other logical behavioural interpretations may exist.

A first explanation to explain the presence of significant losses appeals to the potential for misaligned incentives that can arise between owners (principals) and trainers (agents). From the data collected, it is possible to control for moral hazard that could emerge from misaligned incentive structures. One can identify the returns of thoroughbreds that are owned and trained by the same individual (incentive-compatible condition) compared to the rest of the sample (moral hazard condition). A total of 228 sales occurred where the trainer held full ownership over the foal or had a stake in its ownership or the owner was directly related (through family name) to the trainer. In these circumstances, one could assume that the trainer had a greater interest in

Table 7.4 Pairwise Correlations of Bidding Categories

Pairwise correlations	Bidding group								
	1	2	3	4	5	6	7	8	9
€991–€4,999 (n = 249)	–								
€5,000–€9,999 (n = 211)	1.00	1.00							
€10,000–€19,999 (n = 307)	1.00	1.00	1.00						
€20,000–€29,000 (n = 207)	0.07	0.14	0.31	1.00					
€30,000–€39,999 (n = 155)	0.07	0.01**	0.021**	1.00	1.00				
€40,000–€59,000 (n = 177)	0.00***	0.00***	0.00***	0.01***	0.03**	0.13			
€60,000–€79,000 (n = 113)	0.00***	0.00***	0.00***	0.00***	0.00***	0.01***	1.00		
€80,000–€99,000 (n = 85)	0.00***	0.00***	0.00***	0.00***	0.00***	0.00***	0.00***	1.00	
>€100,000 (n = 177)	0.00***	0.00***	0.00***	0.00***	0.00***	0.00***	0.00***	0.00***	–

Statistical significance: *** at the 1% level; and ** at the 5% level.

ensuring a thoroughbred performed to the best of its ability. The net returns for both the moral hazard and incentive-compatible conditions are negative. Interestingly, losses are greater for thoroughbreds in the incentive-compatible condition. The average net losses for thoroughbreds owned and trained by the same party are −€31,045 and −€22,492 in the moral hazard subsample. This finding suggests that principal-agent dynamics are not an influencing factor on net returns. On the contrary, trainers, with future incomes in mind, may pay more attention to horses they do not have a stake in.[2]

Equally, owners who also trained thoroughbreds show a tendency to have similar bidding strategies; no distinct differences exist between the maximum amount training owners and non-training owners are willing to bid to win an auction. As a corollary of this argument, one could argue that ownership structures defined as syndicates may earn even lower returns; increasing the size of the ownership arrangement of a thoroughbred may detach a trainer further from achieving elite performance. There is no evidence to suggest that syndicates return disproportionately greater losses. The 31 owners classified as syndicates returned average losses of −€26,571.63.

A second behavioural explanation to account for the losses could appeal to owners adopting a diversification strategy when purchasing foals. Fully aware that some will return losses, owners could be confident that high profits from one successful thoroughbred will insure the losses of others. Like the moral hazard argument, the dataset facilitates an empirical examination of this reasoning. Table 7.5 displays the 18 owners in the dataset who purchased five or more thoroughbreds across the four auctions. Considering the winning bids, only two of the buyers return positive earnings.

As Table 7.5 reveals, no systematic evidence exists to suggest that buying multiple foals can return a profit on average. As one would expect these owners to have a detailed knowledge of the industry, the losses posted are noteworthy. Additional ownership costs outside of the purchase price, coupled with the fact that the winning sums are not solely distributed to owners, would only serve to diminish these returns further.

Discussion

Thoroughbred auctions are public contests where non-trivial monetary sums are committed by experienced buyers. The evidence reported here confirms an intuition that the majority of thoroughbreds purchased via this mechanism incur net negative returns. Two questions are worthy of discussion. The first is 'why are these losses accrued?' The second is 'what are the implications of these results?'

The first line of argument, consistent with that of Gamrat and Sauer (2000), suggests that the industry is one where the motivation of profit maximisation is questionable. This is not an uncommon occurrence in sport where *win* maximisation, rather than *profit* maximisation, is the ultimate objective of the owners. If utility maximisation (with this realised through wins) is the goal

Table 7.5 Alternative Behavioural Explanations – Returns to Diversification

Owner	No. ≥ 5	Mean bid	Mean returns	Profit/loss
Andrew Tinkler	5	€ 51,935.44	€ 35,483.38	−€ 16,452.06
Dr Marwan Koukash	10	€ 26,851.99	€ 54,890.24	€ 28,038.25
Godolphin	15	€ 93,492.38	€ 43,214.21	−€ 50,278.17
Habton Farms	5	€ 21,121.54	€ 4,620.64	−€ 16,500.89
Hamdan Al Maktoum	18	€ 111,458.32	€ 17,480.08	−€ 93,978.25
Highclere Thoroughbred Racing	6	€ 33,691.88	€ 67,841.54	€ 34,149.67
HRH Princess Haya of Jordan	5	€ 38,757.86	€ 15,400.65	−€ 23,357.21
Jaber Abdullah	14	€ 27,356.84	€ 4,912.69	−€ 22,444.14
M Khan X2	5	€ 41,993.24	€ 7,655.13	−€ 34,338.11
Mark T Gittins	5	€ 25,226.77	€ 3,586.00	−€ 21,640.77
Michael Tabor	8	€ 213,804.10	€ 138,594.24	−€ 75,209.86
Mrs H Steel	7	€ 58,708.29	€ 27,157.26	−€ 31,551.03
Mrs J Wood	7	€ 56,681.07	€ 8,814.26	−€ 47,866.81
Mrs John Magnier	6	€ 96,584.84	€ 55,969.41	−€ 40,615.43
Saeed Manana	11	€ 32,979.24	€ 8,268.37	−€ 24,710.88
Saleh Al Homaizi and Imad Al Sagar	5	€ 103,476.50	€ 709.18	−€ 102,767.32
Sheikh Ahmed Al Maktoum	18	€ 80,217.00	€ 27,435.01	−€ 52,781.99
Sheikh Majid bin Mohammed Al Maktoum	5	€ 144,654.13	€ 30,903.35	−€ 113,750.78

Source: Racing Post Bloodstock Sales Database and Irish Racing.

of owners, the extent of losses could be interpreted as a form of (conspicuous) consumption as opposed to an investment or as an entry fee to participating in the sport. Akin to affluent individuals buying yachts or football clubs, thoroughbred horseracing could be viewed as another domain where costly signalling takes place. We hypothesise that the sustained nature of the losses incurred rests on an owner's ability to cross-subsidise from other business interests (i.e. the losses are absorbed elsewhere). This purchasing activity could also offer further insights to a 'collector' style of behaviour (Apostolou, 2011). While it would be naïve to imply that every owner is indifferent to losses, the extent of negative returns has implications for the use of profit-maximising models used to study this industry. This point is particularly relevant for owners with a greater number of purchases.

A second line of argument, previously unexplored, relates to the potential for decision-making errors to arise from the auction environment. While Ray (2001) suggests that evidence of overbidding may be due to an incorrect assessment of thoroughbred abilities, no research has considered whether an interaction between estimation failures *and* the auction mechanism is a potential cause of negative returns. The evidence presented here, while consistent with the idea of non-pecuniary motivations or a version of conspicuous consumption, is also *generally* consistent with a winner's curse hypothesis (Capen, Clapp & Campbell, 1971; Thaler, 1988). This is the tendency for individuals to overbid or follow naïve bidding strategies when the true value of an asset is unknown. This concept has been previously applied to other sports labour markets (Cassing & Douglas, 1980; Burger & Walters, 2008; Massey & Thaler, 2013). Given the uncertainty attached to a thoroughbred foal's productivity and an expected variance in bidder estimates, the possibility of a winner's curse may increase in likelihood in this industry. At a minimum, a premium associated with winning the auction may inflate loses. As no information can be accessed on bidder characteristics, this argument is evidently tentative and conjectural in nature.[3] Despite this, the tendency for bidders to estimate an extreme value at these auctions and subsequently overbid is a logical argument worthy of consideration.

Conclusion

This chapter takes advantage of the unique characteristics of thoroughbred horseracing auctions, where the 'cost of thinking' is high, to evaluate bidding strategies under unique informational conditions. By analysing a new dataset, with improved sampling, we make a novel contribution to the topic of ownership motivations in sport and highlight informational biases that are consistent with the patterns observed. Conducting an ex post efficiency evaluation of thoroughbred foals, we show that a high percentage sold via public auctions in Ireland and Great Britain incur net negative returns over their career. When foals are grouped into specific bidding categories, a monotonically decreasing relationship is observed. Once a winning bid increases above approximately €20,000 on average, the assets enter the domain of losses. This scale of losses is amplified as winning bids increase beyond this break-even threshold. Incompatible incentives between owners and trainers and diversification strategies on behalf of owners fail to explain the level of inefficiencies observed.

When one considers the restricted estimates associated with ownership such as bonus payments, commissions, entry costs and training fees, there is a high level of inefficient bidding *if* owners are assumed to be profit-maximising agents. The results show that increases in winning bids have a negative relationship with returns across alternative estimations, a result which has practical implications for those within the industry seeking to formulate optimal bidding strategies. Consistent with Gamrat and Sauer (2000), on average thoroughbreds fail to recoup their value. While this study does not attempt to identify the alternative motivations of owners, several of the methodological improvements relating to sampling strategies are addressed.

It is important to highlight the limitations. Firstly, we are cognisant of missing information that cannot be accessed and restricts a complete measurement of returns. This study has purposely focused on accessible valuation and productivity information. Other than basic estimates, it was not possible to collect data on the transaction costs or management costs associated with owning thoroughbreds (e.g. training fees, commissions, entry fees and veterinary bills). These are heterogeneous expenses that will amplify negative returns and dampen positive returns. Equally, limited information is available on residual revenue streams from these assets, most importantly a thoroughbred's stud fees. Although foals are bred for the purpose of racing, a thoroughbred could recoup their initial investment if they are selected to breed. Stud fees are often negotiated privately and are frequently undisclosed. While this is a limitation, it should be noted that only select thoroughbreds are used in stud farms; the dataset accessed here contains information of foals sired by just 205 colts. Hence, holding a substantial residual value is reserved for elite thoroughbreds who perform well on the racetrack. Several of these thoroughbreds already successfully recouped their initial cost on the track prior to entering stud.

Secondly, bidding inefficiencies could be tapered if industry-specific informal mechanisms exist to allow bidders to recoup investment. While we are aware of no such informal mechanisms other than 'pinhooking',[4] prospective research may identify subtle informal contracts, buyback arrangements or resale tactics. Finally, isolating the heterogeneous motivations of owners could serve to distinguish between different owner types and address the concerns that multiple interpretations can explain the observed pattern. While interpreting the results reported here through the lens of 'conspicuous consumption' or collector behaviour may offer insights to explain the trend, it would be naïve to assume that owners are indifferent to efficiency. Documenting the specific strategies of owners can form the basis of future research.

Notes

1 Bids in Great British foal auctions are occasionally made in Guineas. These bids are converted to pounds sterling, and subsequently euros, at the given exchange rates for the dates of the auction. A guinea was historically equal to one pound and one shilling (£1.05). Sales companies still use guineas, although most have switched to pounds.
2 Subsamples (*n* = 228) were also randomly drawn to investigate this further given the skewed distribution of the data. All random subsamples had negative returns ranging from −€10,801 to −€32,387.
3 The presence of additional or competing biases is also plausible. For example, bidders may be overconfident in their assessment of potential or underestimate the variability in returns. Alternative psychological conjecture raises questions for future studies if access to bidder data per auction becomes available.
4 A strategy of a small group of buyers is an activity referred to as 'pinhooking'. This is when investors purchase thoroughbreds solely for the purpose of resale. While individual 'pin-hookers' can earn significant profits following this strategy, this study focuses on the unconditional net returns on the assets rather than the distribution of gains and losses and every effort was made to identify thoroughbreds resold.

References

Apostolou, M. (2011). Why men collect things? A case study of fossilised dinosaur eggs. *Journal of Economic Psychology*, 32(3), 410–417.

Burger, J. D., & Walters, S. J. (2008). The existence and persistence of a winner's curse: New evidence from the (baseball) field. *Southern Economic Journal*, 75(1), 232–245.

Butler, D., Butler R., & Simmons, R. (2020). Contracts and bonuses in the sport of kings – new evidence on jockeys' pay and performance. *Working Paper Series*. University College Cork.

Capen, E. C., Clapp, R. V., & Campbell, W. M. (1971). Competitive bidding in high-risk situations. *Journal of Petroleum Technology*, 23(06), 641–653.

Chezum, B., & Wimmer, B. (1997). Roses or lemons: Adverse selection in the market for thoroughbred yearlings. *Review of Economics and Statistics*, 79(3), 521–526.

Coffey, B., & Maloney, M. T. (2010). The thrill of victory: Measuring the incentive to win. *Journal of Labor Economics*, 28(1), 87–112. https://doi.org/10.1086/648318

DeGennaro, R. P. (2003). The utility of sport and returns to ownership. *Journal of Sports Economics*, 4(2), 145–153.

Fernie, S., & Metcalf, D. (1999). It's not what you pay it's the way that you pay it and that's what gets results: Jockeys' pay and performance. *Labour*, 13(2), 385–411.

Gaffney, B., & Cunningham, E. P. (1988). Estimation of genetic trend in racing performance of thoroughbred horses. *Nature*, 332(6166), 722–724.

Gamrat, F. A., & Sauer, R. D. (2000). The utility of sport and returns to ownership evidence from the thoroughbred market. *Journal of Sports Economics*, 1(3), 219–235.

Gamrat, F. A., & Sauer, R. D. (2001). Reply: "The utility of sport and returns to ownership: Evidence from the thoroughbred market". *Journal of Sports Economics*, 2(2), 204–205.

Horse Racing Ireland. (2009). *Racing the Irish way – A guide to racing in Ireland*. Available at URL: https://www.goracing.ie/pics/hri/racing_the_irish_way.pdf

Horse Racing Ireland. (2015). *Horse racing Ireland - Irish champion flat racehorse trainers 1950–2011*. Available at URL: http://www.goracing.ie/HRI/Racing-Statistics/Trainer-Statistics/ [Accessed: 20 DEC 16].

Kagel, J., & Levin, D. (2002). *Common value auctions and the winner's curse*. Princeton, NJ: Princeton University Press.

Kahane, L. H. (2010). Returns to skill in professional golf: A quantile regression approach. *International Journal of Sport Finance*, 5(3), 167–180.

Langlois, B., & Blouin, C. (2007). Annual, career or single race records for breeding value estimation in race horses. *Livestock Science*, 107(2), 132–141.

Massey, C., & Thaler, R. H. (2013). The loser's curse: Decision making and market efficiency in the national football league draft. *Management Science*, 59(7), 1479–1495.

Parsons, C., & Smith, I. (2008). The price of thoroughbred yearlings in Britain. *Journal of Sports Economics*, 9(1), 43–66.

Plant, E. J., & Stowe, C. J. (2013). The price of disclosure in the thoroughbred yearling market. *Journal of Agricultural and Applied Economics*, 45(02), 243–257.

Ray, M. A. (2001). The utility of sport and returns to ownership: Evidence from the thoroughbred market. *Journal of Sports Economics*, 2(2), 201–203.

Robert, M., & Stowe, C. J. (2016). Ready to run: Price determinants of thoroughbreds from 2 year olds in training sales. *Applied Economics*, 48(48), 4690–4697.

Smith, A. M., Staniar, W. B., & Splan, R. K. (2006). Associations between yearling body measurements and career racing performance in Thoroughbred racehorses. *Journal of Equine Veterinary Science*, 26(5), 212–214.

Stowe, C. J. (2013). Breeding to sell: A hedonic price analysis of leading thoroughbred sire stud fees. *Applied Economics*, 45(7), 877–885.

Stachurska, A., Pięta, M., Łojek, J., & Szulowska, J. (2007). Performance in racehorses of various colours. *Livestock Science*, 106(2), 282–286.

Thaler, R. H. (1988). Anomalies: The winner's curse. *Journal of Economic Perspectives*, 2(1), 191–202.

Vincent, C., & Eastman, B. (2009). Determinants of pay in the NHL: A quantile regression approach. *Journal of Sports Economics*, 10(3), 256–277.

Wimmer, B. S., & Chezum, B. (2003). An empirical examination of quality certification in a "lemons market". *Economic Inquiry*, 41(2), 279–291.

Part 3
Momentum and reference points in sports behaviour

8 Does psychological momentum differ for home and away teams? Evidence from penalty shoot-outs in European cups

Alex Krumer

Introduction

In the context of the European Cups tournaments in professional soccer, penalty shoot-outs provide a good opportunity to test the effect of psychological momentum on performance. The reason is that in these tournaments it is possible for a shoot-out to occur despite one team having just won the game in regular time and the other team having lost; this suggests that the winning team has a momentum advantage over the losing team.[1] Thus, it allows us to test whether winning in regular time has an effect on the probability of winning the shoot-out and whether this effect differs between home and away teams.

However, first, it is important to disentangle the two types of momentum that exist in contests. Strategic momentum is generated by strategic incentives inherent in the contest (Klumpp and Polborn, 2006).[2] In this paper, however, we discuss another type of momentum: psychological momentum. Cohen-Zada, Krumer, and Shtudiner (2017) defined psychological momentum as "the tendency of an outcome to be followed by a similar outcome not caused by any strategic incentive of the players" (p. 66). In that regard, penalty shoot-outs allow us a clear view of psychological momentum, since both teams have no strategic incentives to reduce efforts during penalty kicks as may appear in other, mostly multi-stage, contests.

Evidence regarding the effect of psychological momentum is mixed. For example, Malueg and Yates (2010) investigated best-of-three-set tennis matches between equally skilled players. They found that, as predicted by strategic momentum theory, the winner of the first set had a higher probability of winning the second set, but – contrary to psychological momentum theory – if the match reached the third and final set, the winner of the second set did not have a significantly higher probability of winning that set. Based on the latter finding, the authors concluded that psychological momentum does not play a significant role in contests. The laboratory results of Mago, Sheremeta, and Yates (2013) support these findings. Similarly, Morgulev, Azar, and Bar-Eli (2019), as well as Morgulev et al. (2020), found that momentum played no significant role in overtimes of NBA games.

DOI: 10.4324/9781003080824-10

On the other hand, Cohen-Zada et al. (2017) investigated bronze medal fights in professional judo, which is a one-stage contest without strategic considerations, where psychological momentum is easily identified. The authors showed that competing after previous win increases the probability of winning compared to competing after a previous loss. However, that result was only significant among men.[3] In addition, Rosenqvist and Skans (2015) showed that golf players who succeeded marginally in one tournament performed better in the following tournament than those players who just marginally failed. Similarly, Jetter and Walker (2015) found that an additional win in ten recent tennis matches increased the likelihood of winning the next match. In addition, being more likely to succeed again after a successful action seems to be an evolutionary feature that goes beyond just humans. This effect was observed among insects (Adamo and Hoy, 1999), rats (van de Poll et al., 1982), and birds (Drummond and Canales, 1998).

Mixed evidence about the hypothesis that success breeds success also occurs in the literature on the "hot hand" that is well connected to the literature on momentum. In a seminal article, Gilovich, Vallone, and Tversky (1985) coined the term "the hot hand fallacy", according to which the hot streaks in performance of basketball players are most likely due to random variation and are only a cognitive illusion and a general misconception of chance. Several follow-up articles in sports psychology agreed with the fallacy statement (for example, Koehler and Conley, 2003; Avugos et al., 2013). However, by using statistical measures with superior identifying power over previous studies, Miller and Sanjurjo (2014) and later Miller and Sanjurjo (2018) contradicted these findings, showing that the hot hand is not an illusion.

It is also worth mentioning three recent studies on the effect of scoring a goal just before half-time in soccer. All three papers had different results. On the one hand, Gauriot and Page (2018) found that scoring just before half-time had no effect on subsequent performance. On the other hand, Meier et al. (2020) showed that the scoring team benefits from a goal just before half-time, while Baert and Amez (2019) found that scoring a goal just before the half-time is actually detrimental for the home team.

Those heated debates on existence of psychological momentum create fertile soil for further research on psychological momentum. As discussed, a penalty shoot-out in a situation where one team had just won the match allows a clear view on the effect of psychological momentum in real-tournament settings. To that end, we examined 214 shoot-outs between the 1970/1971 season and the 2017/2018 season from the most prestigious European Cups tournaments (UEFA Champions League/Champions Cup, Europa League/ UEFA Cup, and the Cup Winners' Cup). We find that any additional goal scored beyond the opponent in the second leg (game) has a positive effect on the probability of winning the shoot-out, but only for away teams. Our results suggest that a margin of every additional goal in favor of the away team in regular time increases its probability of winning by 12.5% points. We find that the winning home teams in regular time have a 50% chance of winning a shoot-out, regardless of the difference in goals in the second game.

This result regarding the absence of momentum effect among home teams may relate to the literature on "choking" under high expectations. This is because home teams that win in regular time may experience higher expectations from the local crowd. In that regard, Baumeister, Hamilton, and Tice (1985) showed that high audience expectations created additional psychological pressure that harmed the performance of students when solving anagrams. In another experimental study, Butler and Baumeister (1998) demonstrated that participants performed worse in front of a supportive audience in skill-based math and video game tasks.

Choking in front of a supportive audience has also been documented in sports-related studies. For example, Dohmen (2008) found that players in the German soccer Bundesliga missed the target significantly more when shooting penalties in home games. In the same spirit, Harb-Wu and Krumer (2019) found that biathletes from the highest ability distribution missed significantly more shots when competing in their home country. Similarly, Böheim, Grübl, and Lackner (2019) showed that NBA basketball players missed significantly more free throws the larger the audience when they play at home.

These results suggest that high expectations of performing well in front of a friendly audience prompt individuals to choke. An additional reason for choking may relate to the inability of home teams to take advantage of hosting the second game before the shoot-outs, which is a well-known phenomenon in European soccer (Page and Page, 2007; Krumer, 2013). Thus, it is possible that a home team may gain a momentum advantage by winning in regular time, but choke during the penalty shoot-out due to higher expectations from the home crowd. These two forces may cancel each other; however, away teams that have just won in regular time do not experience high expectations from the local crowd, benefitting only from psychological momentum.

The remainder of the paper is organized as follows. Section "Description of penalty shoot-outs in the European cups" describes the penalty shoot-out setting. Section "Data and variables" presents the data and descriptive results, before Section "Estimation strategy and results" presents the estimation strategy and results. Finally, we offer concluding remarks in Section "Conclusion".

Description of penalty shoot-outs in the European cups

A penalty shoot-out normally takes place in elimination-type tournaments, where a winner advances to the next stage and the loser is eliminated. This structure appears in European Cups tournaments where teams (usually from different countries) compete against each other in a two-leg tie, with each team playing once at home.

A shoot-out only takes place in the second leg and only if both teams have scored the same overall number of goals and both games have ended in exactly the same result in regular time (90 minutes) of each game without scoring in the extra time (additional 30 minutes) that occurs in such cases. Before the advent of shoot-outs, games that ended in a draw were decided by the toss of a coin or by a replay. In 1968, Yosef Dagan, the Israel Football Association's secretary at the time, proposed penalty shoot-outs after his team lost at the 1968 Olympics by the drawing of lots. The International Football Association Board (IFAB) approved the proposal in 1970.

Each team takes turns shooting at goal from the penalty spot, with the goal only defended by the opposing team's goalkeeper. Five different kickers from each team are selected to take penalties; a player from one team takes a kick, then a player from the other team, and so on. If the score is still tied after five pairs of kicks, each team must kick one more time each, with new players, until one of the teams wins.[4]

Data and variables

Data

To estimate the effect that momentum and playing at home have on the probability of winning a shoot-out, we used data on second games of two-leg ties in which a home team played on its usual stadium. We utilized data from games in the three European tournaments: the UEFA Champions League (previously known as the Champions Cup), Cup Winners' Cup (that later merged with the UEFA Cup), and the UEFA Europa League (previously known as the UEFA Cup). Table 8.1 describes the relevant competitions and the years. In total, 225 penalty shoot-outs took place in these competitions between the 1970/1971 season and the 2017/2018 season.[5] For all of these games, information is available regarding the names of the teams, the location, the round of the game in the tournament, the total number of rounds in the tournament, and the ranking of a teams' country on the official UEFA rankings.

Variables

For each match in our dataset, we randomly picked one of the teams and denoted it as *Team A* and the other team as *Team B*. Thus, our outcome variable

Table 8.1 Description of the Dataset

Competition	Seasons	Observations
Champions Cup/Champions League	1970/71–2016/17	46
Cup Winners' Cup	1970/71–1998/99	32
UEFA Cup/Europa League	1971/72–2017/18	136
Total		214

Note: Starting from the 1992/93 season, the Champions Cup became the UEFA Champions League. In the 2009/10 season, the UEFA Cup changed its name to the UEFA Europa League. The Cup Winners' cup ceased to exist in 1998/99.

takes the value of one if *Team A* won the shoot-out and zero otherwise. Table 8.2 shows that a random *Team A* won 52.3% of the shoot-outs.

We use the goal difference between the teams in regular time of the second game to estimate the effect of momentum on probability of winning the shoot-out. As discussed, the shoot-outs take place only if the results of both games were identical, so a larger goal difference in the second leg represents a larger comeback and possibly stronger momentum. In other words, we assume that a win by a margin of two goals in regular time of the second leg represents greater psychological momentum than a win by a margin of one goal.

The variable that indicates *Team A* having a home advantage receives the value of one if *Team A* competes at home and zero otherwise. Our next variable is the interaction term between goal difference and the home advantage of *Team A*. This variable is close to 0.3, suggesting that a home team scores more goals than the away team in the regular time. This is in line with the home advantage, a well-known phenomenon in sports in general and in soccer in particular.[6] We also use a variable that indicates the ratio between the round of the game and the total number of rounds in the tournament.

Following Krumer (2020), who found that teams from higher divisions have a higher probability of winning shoot-outs in domestic cups of the top five soccer European countries, we use the country ranking of the respective teams to calculate the standardized coefficient of each team as a proxy of ability. Countries' rankings are published by the UEFA and based on the performance of the teams of each country in the European Cups in the preceding several years. The higher the ranking, the better the performance of the country's teams. More specifically, we followed Szymanski and Smith's (1997) methodology and calculated the standardized ranking as $-\ln\left(\frac{p}{t+1-p}\right)$,

Table 8.2 Descriptive Statistics

	Mean	Standard deviation	Min	Max
Variable name				
Team A wins	0.523	0.500	0	1
Goal difference (Goals Team A-Team B in game 2)	0.005	1.235	−3	3
Team A home advantage	0.505	0.501	0	1
Goal difference*Team A home advantage	0.299	0.847	−3	3
Relative round	0.393	0.209	0.1	1
Country standardized coefficient Team A	1.104	1.400	−2.833	3.989
Country standardized coefficient Team B	1.038	1.407	−2.833	3.989
Observations	214			

Table 8.3 Comparison of Teams' Pre-treatment Characteristics

	Team A	Team B	Difference	P-value
	(1)	(2)	(3)	(4)
Team wins	0.523	0.477	0.046	0.496
Home advantage	0.504	0.495	0.009	0.892
Goals scored in game 2	0.864	0.859	0.005	0.956
Home advantage*Goal difference	0.299	0.294	0.005	0.956
Country's standardized coefficients	1.104	1.038	0.066	0.572

Notes: Columns 1 and 2 present the average value of each of the characteristics of *Teams* A and B, respectively. The differences between these values appear in Column 3. Column 4 reports the P-values of paired *t*-test.

where p is the ranking of a team's country in the UEFA official ranking in the respective year, and t is the total number of participating countries in the respective season. The higher the coefficient, the better the performance of the teams from the specific country in European Cups tournaments.

We randomized the identity of *Teams* A and B, so they are not expected to be different in any of their characteristics. Table 8.3 compares the means of each characteristic of the two teams and tests whether the difference between them is significant. In Columns 3 and 4 of Table 8.3, we report the difference and the *P-values* of the paired *t-test*, respectively. We can see that *Teams* A and B do not differ in any of their characteristics, implying that the randomization process was successful.

Estimation strategy and results

Psychological momentum

Since our outcome variable is a binary one, we estimate a logit model of the probability of *Team A* winning the shoot-out as a function of goal difference between the teams in the second leg. Our basic set of controls includes a dummy variable for whether each of the teams has a home advantage, the relative round of the tournament, standardized coefficients, and competition dummies. Formally, this specification takes the form:

$$Log\left(\frac{\pi_{ABg}}{1-\pi_{ABg}}\right) = \beta_0 + \beta_1 \cdot GoalDiff_{ABg} + \beta_2 \cdot X_{ABg} + \varepsilon_{ABg} \quad (1)$$

where the dependent variable is the probability of *Team A* to defeat *Team B* in game g, X_{ABg} is our set of controls, and ε_{ABg} is an error term. As described above, if the psychological momentum has a positive effect on probability of winning the shoot-out, then β_1 would have a positive sign.

Column 1 of Table 8.4 presents the results, from estimating Equation (1) without a list of controls. Standard errors appear in parentheses. The results show that the coefficient β_1 is positive and significant at the 1% level. This suggests that every additional goal (without conceding a goal) during regular time of *Team A* increases its probability of winning the shoot-out by 6.9 percentage points. Next, we add the home advantage and the relative round. Column 2 shows that a margin of one goal in favour of *Team A* increases its probability of winning by 6 percentage points with a significance level of 5.1%. The results are robust to including standardized coefficients and tournament types, as appear in Columns 3 and 4, respectively. Moreover, *GoalDiff* is the only significant variable in all the specifications, suggesting that the psychological momentum gained during the regular time carries over to the penalty shoot-outs. This result replicates the finding of Cohen-Zada et al. (2017), Rosenqvist and Skans (2015), and Jetter and Walker (2015), who found a positive effect of psychological momentum in men's judo, golf, and tennis, respectively.

It is important to note that in this specification, the effect of scoring an additional goal without conceding on the probability of *Team A* winning the shoot-out is $2\beta_1$. To illustrate the magnitude of this estimate, the probability of each of two equal teams that drew the second leg (*GoalDiff* = 0) winning the shoot-out is 50%. However, according to the results in Column 4, a team that scores one goal more than its opponent increases its probability of winning to 56.6%, which is 13.2% points higher than the probability of the other team winning (56.6% relative to 43.4%).

Another interesting result is that playing at home has no effect on the probability of winning the shoot-out, which contradicts the well-known phenomenon of home advantage (Moskowitz and Jon Wertheim, 2011). Similar results on the

Table 8.4 Logit Average Marginal Effect of Momentum on the Probability of Winning a Penalty Shoot-Out

	(1)	(2)	(3)	(4)
GoalDiff	0.069***	0.060*	0.067**	0.066**
	(0.027)	(0.031)	(0.031)	(0.031)
Team A home		0.049 (0.075)	0.044 (0.076)	0.046 (0.076)
Relative round		0.049 (0.161)	0.206 (0.201)	0.193 (0.205)
Country standardized coefficient Team A			−0.022 (0.027)	−0.018 (0.028)
Country standardized coefficient Team B			−0.028 (0.028)	−0.026 (0.028)
Champions Cup				−0.066 (0.084)
Cup Winners' Cup				0.058 (0.099)
Number of obs.	214	214	214	214

Note: *GoalDiff* is defined as the difference between the scored goals of *Team A* and *Team B* in the regular time of the second leg. Standard errors are in parentheses. *, **, and *** denote significance at the 10%, 5%, and 1% levels, respectively.

absence of home advantage in penalty shoot-outs have been shown by Apesteguia and Palacios-Huerta (2010); Arrondel, Duhautois, and Laslier (2019); and Kocher, Lenz, and Sutter (2008). The possible reason for the absence of home advantage in penalty shoot-outs is referee bias that may be present during regular time (Garicano, Palacios-Huerta and Prendergast, 2005; Downward and Jones, 2007; Page and Page, 2010; Pettersson-Lidbom and Priks, 2010; Dohmen and Sauermann, 2016). However, referees have no significant involvement during shoot-outs in the period covered in our paper (before the introduction of VAR). The second possible explanation for the absence of home effect during shoot-outs is choking in front of the home crowd. In the next sub-section, we investigate the possible heterogeneity that is driven by the home variable.

Home effect

Following Dohmen's (2008) finding on higher share of missing the target at home in penalty kicks in the German Bundesliga, as well as Harb-Wu and Krumer (2019), and Böheim et al. (2019) who found a negative effect of performing at home on shooting accuracy in biathlon and basketball, respectively, our aim is to test whether momentum has a different effect at home compared to away games. For that, we add to Equation (1) the variable *GoalDiff* * *Home*, which is an interaction term between *GoalDiff* and a dummy variable for *Team A*'s home advantage. The interpretation of the *GoalDiff* * *Home* is by how much the probability of winning the shoot-outs differs between the home and the away teams as a result of an additional unit in *GoalDiff*.

Column 1 of Table 8.5 shows that *GoalDiff* is positive and significant at the 1% level. The interpretation of that variable is by how much the probability of the *away* team winning is affected by a change in one unit of *GoalDiff*. Thus, the results suggest that each additional goal of the away team (without conceding) in regular time increases its probability of winning by 12.5% points. To calculate the effect of goal difference when competing at home on the probability of winning the shoot-out, we total the coefficients of *GoalDiff* and *GoalDiff* * *Home*. The coefficient of the interactive term *GoalDiff* * *Home* is negative and very close to the absolute value of *GoalDiff*. This means that a one-goal margin in favour of the home team in regular time has a negative effect on the probability of winning compared to the similar margin in favor of the away team. Thus, the total effect of scoring an additional goal (without conceding one) by a home team on its probability of winning the shoot-out is 0.004 (0.125−0.121) and highly insignificant (p-val = 0.907). Thus, the home teams that win in the regular time have a 50% probability of winning a shoot-out regardless of the goal difference in their favour in regular time.

Our results are robust to adding information on relative round, countries' standardized coefficients, and tournament types as shown in Columns 2 and 3, respectively. In Column 4, we remove the games that ended with a draw in which *GoalDiff = 0*. We find that no other variables except for the *GoalDiff* and *GoalDiff* * *Home* are significant in all the specifications. The results in

Table 8.5 Logit Average Marginal Effect of Momentum on the Probability of Winning a Penalty Shoot-Out at Home and Away

	(1)	(2)	(3)	(4)
GoalDiff	0.125★★★ (0.046)	0.140★★★ (0.046)	0.141★★★ (0.046)	0.156★★★ (0.049)
Team A home (Home)	0.041 (0.076)	0.036 (0.076)	0.038 (0.076)	−0.025 (0.101)
GoalDiff★Home	−0.121★ (0.062)	−0.132★★ (0.062)	−0.135★★ (0.062)	−0.147★★ (0.066)
Relative round		0.260 (0.202)	0.248 (0.207)	0.261 (0.240)
Country standardized coefficient Team A		−0.024 (0.027)	−0.020 (0.027)	−0.042 (0.032)
Country standardized coefficient Team B		−0.034 (0.027)	−0.033 (0.028)	−0.027 (0.033)
Champions Cup			−0.071 (0.083)	−0.044 (0.110)
Cup Winners' Cup			0.062 (0.099)	0.009 (0.112)
H_0: GoalDiff + GD★Home (p-val)	0.004 (0.907)	0.008 (0.847)	0.006 (0.877)	0.009 (0.837)
Number of obs.	214	214	214	147

Note: *GoalDiff* is defined as Goals of Team A-Goals of Team B before shoot-outs in game 2. Columns 1–3 represent all data. Column 4 represents games that did not end in a draw before the shoot-outs. Standard errors are in parentheses. ★, ★★, and ★★★ denote significance at the 10%, 5%, and 1% levels, respectively.

Column 4 suggest that winning a game in regular time by one goal increases the away team's probability of winning by 15.6% points. However, the home team's probability of winning is not affected by goal difference in regular time. The reason for such a difference may be that, in general, momentum has a positive effect on performance, but this momentum is cancelled by additional choking when performing at home (Baumeister et al., 1985; Butler and Baumeister, 1998; Dohmen, 2008; Böheim et al., 2019; Harb-Wu and Krumer, 2019). Thus, while winning home teams have a momentum advantage, higher expectations from the home crowd can provoke choking. In sum, it is possible that these two forces cancel each other out.

An additional control that would be worth adding is the identity of the first kicking team. For example, Apesteguia and Palacios-Huerta (2010) found that the first kicking team had a significant margin of 21% points over the second kicking team. However, Kocher et al. (2012) and Arrondel et al. (2019) challenged that result, while Palacios-Huerta (2014) reproduced this first-mover advantage using a significantly larger sample size than in the two challenging papers (including the entire data of Kocher et al. (2012)). Therefore, omitting the identity of the first-kicking team may bias the results.

However, it was not possible to obtain information on the identity of the first-kicking team in games that took place in the period of more than 40 years. Nevertheless, based on a very plausible assumption that a random home Team A that wins in regular time did not have a significantly larger probability of being the first-kicking team, our results remain unbiased.

There are several additional explanations to our findings. For example, a winning team in regular time simply turned out to be a better team on that day and won the shoot-out because of its higher ability. However, in such a case, we would expect a higher probability of the home teams winning as well. It is also possible that a team that won in regular time exerted more efforts, so its players were more tired. However, we would then expect the away winning team to lose more often in shoot-outs, which is not the case.

Finally, our results emphasize the importance of the heterogeneity analyses. Looking only at the results in Table 8.4, we could conclude that momentum has a similar effect on the probability of winning for the home and away teams. However, a closer look at each type of team shows that the effect is twice as much for the away teams compared to the results presented in Table 8.4 and zero effect for the home teams.

Conclusion

In this study, we have found that scoring more goals than one's opponent in the second leg of the European Cups tournaments has a positive effect on the probability of winning the shoot-out, but only for the away teams. This result confirms the positive effect of psychological momentum, as well as the negative effect of performing in front of a supportive audience.

The findings of this study may help coaches and players prepare better for shoot-outs. For example, coaches of the away teams may increase the confidence of their players by emphasizing the negative role of the crowd and positive role of momentum in case the away team won. On the other hand, the coaches of the home team should reduce the pressure from their players by reducing the level of expectations.

Finally, further research may be in place to test the effect of momentum in penalty shoot-outs in domestic cups, which are likely to involve lower stakes and pressure than the more prestigious European Cups tournaments.

Notes

1 In these tournaments, teams play each other twice, once at each team's home field. If both teams have scored the same number of goals after two games, on aggregate, and the result was identical in both games (for example, each team won once with the same result), the teams will compete in a penalty shoot-out to determine the winner. For additional details on the rules, see Section 2.
2 For example, Klumpp and Polborn (2006) described the so-called New Hampshire effect, according to which a winner of the first state in the primary elections generates momentum that helps him/her become the final candidate for

the USA presidential elections. The mechanism behind strategic momentum is that the loser of the first stage will have a lower incentive to exert costly effort in the second stage, thereby yielding an increased probability that the winner of the first stage will win again.
3 See also Gauriot and Page (2019), who used professional tennis to find again that only men are affected by momentum. In addition, Page and Coates (2017) found that, among men, the winner of a closely fought tie-break had a significantly higher probability of winning the second set.
4 See Dohmen (2008) and Apesteguia and Palacios-Huerta (2010) for additional details on the rules of penalty kicks.
5 Note that we removed 11 shoot-outs in which the home team did not play at its usual stadium and one final game that was in the form of a one-leg tie.
6 Courneya and Carron (1992) defined home advantage as "the consistent finding that home teams in sports competitions win over 50% of the games played under a balanced home and away schedule" (p. 13). Moskowitz and Jon Wertheim (2011) surveyed 19 different sports leagues covering more than 40 countries between 1871 and 2009 and showed that the within-league home-field advantage "is almost eerily constant through time" (p. 113). The percentage of games won by the home teams in these leagues varied between 53.3% and 69.1%.

References

Adamo, S.A. and Hoy, R.R., 1995. Agonistic behaviour in male and female field crickets, Gryllus bimaculatus, and how behavioural context influences its expression. *Animal Behaviour*, 49(6), pp. 1491–1501.
Apesteguia, J. and Palacios-Huerta, I., 2010. Psychological pressure in competitive environments: Evidence from a randomized natural experiment. *The American Economic Review*, 100(5), pp. 2548–2564.
Arrondel, L., Duhautois, R. and Laslier, J.F., 2019. Decision under psychological pressure: The shooter's anxiety at the penalty kick. *Journal of Economic Psychology*, 70, pp. 22–35.
Avugos, S., Köppen, J., Czienskowski, U., Raab, M. and Bar-Eli, M., 2013. The "hot hand" reconsidered: A meta-analytic approach. *Psychology of Sport and Exercise*, 14(1), pp. 21–27.
Baert, S. and Amez, S., 2018. No better moment to score a goal than just before half time? A soccer myth statistically tested. *PloS One*, 13(3), p. e0194255.
Baumeister, R.F., Hamilton, J.C. and Tice, D.M., 1985. Public versus private expectancy of success: Confidence booster or performance pressure? *Journal of Personality and Social Psychology*, 48(6), p. 1447.
Böheim, R., Grübl, D. and Lackner, M., 2019. Choking under pressure–Evidence of the causal effect of audience size on performance. *Journal of Economic Behavior & Organization*, 168, pp. 76–93.
Butler, J.L. and Baumeister, R.F., 1998. The trouble with friendly faces: Skilled performance with a supportive audience. *Journal of Personality and Social Psychology*, 75(5), p. 1213.
Cohen-Zada, D., Krumer, A. and Shtudiner, Z., 2017. Psychological momentum and gender. *Journal of Economic Behavior and Organization*, 135, pp. 66–81.
Courneya, K.S. and Carron, A.V., 1992. The home advantage in sport competitions: A literature review. *Journal of Sport & Exercise Psychology*, 14(1), pp. 13–27.

Dohmen, T. and Sauermann, J., 2016. Referee bias. *Journal of Economic Surveys*, 30(4), pp. 679–695.
Dohmen, T.J., 2008. Do professionals choke under pressure? *Journal of Economic Behavior & Organization*, 65(3–4), pp. 636–653.
Downward, P. and Jones, M., 2007. Effects of crowd size on referee decisions: Analysis of the FA Cup. *Journal of Sports Sciences*, 25(14), pp. 1541–1545.
Drummond, H. and Canales, C., 1998. Dominance between booby nestlings involves winner and loser effects. *Animal Behaviour*, 55(6), pp. 1669–1676.
Garicano, L., Palacios-Huerta, I. and Prendergast, C., 2005. Favoritism under social pressure. *Review of Economics and Statistics*, 87(2), pp. 208–216.
Gauriot, R. and Page, L., 2018. Psychological momentum in contests: The case of scoring before half-time in football. *Journal of Economic Behavior & Organization*, 149, pp. 137–168.
Gauriot, R. and Page, L., 2019. Does success breed success? A quasi-experiment on strategic momentum in dynamic contests. *The Economic Journal*, 129(624), pp. 3107–3136.
Gilovich, T., Vallone, R. and Tversky, A., 1985. The hot hand in basketball: On the misperception of random sequences. *Cognitive Psychology*, 17(3), pp. 295–314.
Harb-Wu, K. and Krumer, A., 2019. Choking under pressure in front of a supportive audience: Evidence from professional biathlon. *Journal of Economic Behavior & Organization*, 166, pp. 246–262.
Jetter, M. and Walker, J.K., 2015. Game, set, and match: Do women and men perform differently in competitive situations? *Journal of Economic Behavior & Organization*, 119, pp. 96–108.
Klumpp, T. and Polborn, M.K., 2006. Primaries and the New Hampshire effect. *Journal of Public Economics*, 90(6–7), pp. 1073–1114.
Kocher, M., Lenz, M. and Sutter, M., 2008. Performance under pressure–The case of penalty shootouts in football. In Andersson, P., Ayton, P., and Schmidt, C., eds. *Myths and facts about football: The economics and psychology of the world's greatest sport* (pp. 61–72). Cambridge, UK: Cambridge Scholars Publishing.
Kocher, M.G., Lenz, M.V. and Sutter, M., 2012. Psychological pressure in competitive environments: New evidence from randomized natural experiments. *Management Science*, 58(8), pp. 1585–1591.
Koehler, J.J. and Conley, C.A., 2003. The "hot hand" myth in professional basketball. *Journal of Sport and Exercise Psychology*, 25(2), pp. 253–259.
Krumer, A., 2013. Best-of-two contests with psychological effects. *Theory and Decision*, 75(1), pp. 85–100.
Krumer, A., 2020. Pressure versus ability: Evidence from penalty shoot-outs between teams from different divisions. *Journal of Behavioral and Experimental Economics*, 89, p. 101578.
Mago, S.D., Sheremeta, R.M. and Yates, A., 2013. Best-of-three contest experiments: Strategic versus psychological momentum. *International Journal of Industrial Organization*, 31(3), pp. 287–296.
Malueg, D.A. and Yates, A.J., 2010. Testing contest theory: Evidence from best-of-three tennis matches. *The Review of Economics and Statistics*, 92(3), pp. 689–692.
Meier, P., Flepp, R., Ruedisser, M. and Franck, E., 2020. The advantage of scoring just before the half-time break – pure myth? Quasi-experimental evidence from European football. *Journal of Sports Economics*, 21(5), pp. 548–565.
Miller, J.B. and Sanjurjo, A., 2014. A cold shower for the hot hand fallacy. mimeo.

Miller, J.B. and Sanjurjo, A., 2018. Surprised by the hot hand fallacy? A truth in the law of small numbers. *Econometrica*, 86(6), pp. 2019–2047.

Morgulev, E., Azar, O.H. and Bar-Eli, M., 2019. Does a "comeback" create momentum in overtime? Analysis of NBA tied games. *Journal of Economic Psychology*, 75, pp. 102–126.

Morgulev, E., Azar, O.H., Galily, Y. and Bar-Eli, M., 2020. The role of initial success in competition: An analysis of early lead effects in NBA overtimes. *Journal of Behavioral and Experimental Economics*, 89, p. 101547.

Moskowitz, T. and Wertheim, L.J., 2011. Scorecasting: The hidden influences behind how sports are played and games are won. Crown Archetype.

Page, L. and Coates, J., 2017. Winner and loser effects in human competitions. Evidence from equally matched tennis players. *Evolution and Human Behavior*, 38(4), pp. 530–535.

Page, L. and Page, K., 2007. The second leg home advantage: Evidence from European football cup competitions. *Journal of Sports Sciences*, 25(14), pp. 1547–1556.

Page, K. and Page, L., 2010. Alone against the crowd: Individual differences in referees' ability to cope under pressure. *Journal of Economic Psychology*, 31(2), pp. 192–199.

Palacios-Huerta, I., 2014. Psychological pressure on the field and elsewhere. Chapter 5 in Beautiful game theory: How soccer can help economics. Princeton University Press.

Pettersson-Lidbom, P. and Priks, M., 2010. Behavior under social pressure: Empty Italian stadiums and referee bias. *Economics Letters*, 108(2), pp. 212–214.

Rosenqvist, O. and Skans, O.N., 2015. Confidence enhanced performance? – The causal effects of success on future performance in professional golf tournaments. *Journal of Economic Behavior & Organization*, 117, pp. 281–295.

Szymanski, S. and Smith, R., 1997. The English football industry: Profit, performance and industrial structure. *International Review of Applied Economics*, 11(1), pp. 135–153.

Van de Poll, N.E., De Jonge, F., Van Oyen, H.G. and Van Pelt, J., 1982. Aggressive behaviour in rats: Effects of winning or losing on subsequent aggressive interactions. *Behavioural Processes*, 7(2), pp. 143–155.

9 Reference point behavior and sports

Tim Pawlowski[1]

Introduction

In order to account for several anomalies in observed (economic) behavior under risk and uncertainty which are not in line with expected utility theory, Daniel Kahneman and Amos Tversky introduced Prospect Theory more than 40 years ago.[2] Their theory distinguishes between two phases in the choice process, i.e., editing and evaluation. A major operation of the editing phase is coding of outcomes. Based on some empirical evidence, Kahneman and Tversky (1979, 274) reasoned that "people normally perceive outcomes as gains and losses, rather than as final states of wealth or welfare. Gains and losses, of course, are defined relative to some neutral reference point." As such, reference points represent a core concept in Prospect Theory with the proposed hypothetical value function being defined on deviations from the reference point.[3] In summary, the value function is concave for gains and convex for losses, capturing the phenomenon of diminishing sensitivity. Moreover, it is steeper for losses than for gains, capturing the phenomenon of loss aversion (Kahneman & Tversky, 1979).

In their main analysis, the authors assume that a common reference point is the (i) status quo or one's current asset. However, they already acknowledge that situations exist "in which gains and losses are coded relative to an expectation or aspiration level that differs from the status quo" (p. 286). In fact, more recent literature has empirically explored a number of alternative reference points including, for instance, (ii) expectations; (iii) aspirations, goals, and targets; (iv) initial purchase or yearly high prices; (v) contracts; (vi) fair wages and bonuses; or (vii) round numbers (for an overview, see Markle et al., 2018, or Weingarten et al., 2019). Since most decisions involve multiple reference points, gains and losses can be defined either relative to one of these reference points at a time (as argued for instance by March & Shapira, 1992), to some weighted average of such a set of reference points (as argued for instance by Winer, 1986), or simultaneously to each of the possible reference points (as argued by Kahneman, 1992).

Kahneman and Tversky (1979) already stated in their seminal work that Prospect Theory and the concept of reference point behavior are readily

DOI: 10.4324/9781003080824-11

applicable to choices in various areas of life. In this chapter, I discuss the recently growing empirical evidence about the occurrence and relevance of reference points and reference point behavior in sports. While this review is not exhaustive, it follows the objective to cover at least the seminal works exploring the relevance of *different* reference points in *different* sport settings and (eventually) revealing some controversial findings. As such, I propose a structure along two distinct research lines. The first part is focused on *athletes and coaches* (Section "Reference Point Behavior of Athletes and Coaches"). The second part is focused on *fans* (Section "Reference Point Behavior of Fans"). Section "Conclusion" concludes.

Reference point behavior of athletes and coaches

Previous studies empirically testing reference point behavior of athletes and coaches have either focused on effort provision, managerial decisions, and performance (2.1), or performance evaluation and happiness (2.2).

Effort provision, managerial decisions, and performance

Empirical studies exploring the effects of reference point behavior on effort provision and performance of athletes have focused either on *current performance*, *past performance*, *expectations*, or *round numbers* as reference points, while studies exploring reference point behavior of coaches have exclusively focused on *expectations*.

Current performance: "The important thing in the Olympic Games is not to win, but to take part." This famous quote by Pierre de Coubertin,[4] initiator of the modern Olympic Games, might be questioned in times when professional sports have become a multi-billion-dollar business with an extremely skewed income distribution toward successful teams and athletes, i.e., a "winner-takes-it-all" market. Winning does matter, not only for the sake of glory, but because (partly) huge financial rewards are involved. Consequently, a number of papers have already empirically explored whether current relative performance might act as a reference point. For instance, Berger and Pope (2011) use data coming from 18,000 National Basketball Association (NBA) games, as well as 45,000 collegiate games, in order to explore reference point behavior in basketball. They find that being *slightly* behind (i.e., one point) at halftime increases the team's chance of winning the game significantly. In a follow-up study, Goldman and Rao (2017) use in-play NBA data covering 2.5 million possessions to test whether win-probability-related reference points adjust in response to relative performance during the game. They find that players of a team falling behind run several extra feet per minute. Moreover, these teams achieve more points per hundred possessions. However, in contrast to Berger and Pope (2011), they do not find adjusting of reference points during games (e.g., at halftime).

Genakos and Pagliero (2012) generally confirm the relevance of intermediate results with round-by-round panel data from international weight lifting competitions. By analyzing 41,550 individual stage-specific weight announcements and lift outcomes of overall 3,762 athletes, they find that athletes lagging behind take greater risks and have a higher probability of a successful lift conditional on the chosen weight. Importantly, however, the relationship between risk taking and intermediate rank is inverted U-shaped, i.e., announcements increase only from first to sixth place suggesting a *discouraging effect* when *considerably* lagging behind. Moreover, and in contrast to Berger and Pope (2011) as well as Goldman and Rao (2017), they show that athletes systematically underperform when ranked closer to the top suggesting some *choking under pressure*.

It is remarkable that such kind of psychological pressure might be introduced just by the order of contestants. In a seminal work, Apesteguia and Palacios-Huerta (2010) analyze 269 penalty shoot-outs with overall 2,820 penalty kicks from all main international and various national cup competitions in soccer between 1970 and 2008. They exploit the fact that it had been decided by the referee tossing a coin (and as such fully randomly) who takes the first kick until July 2003.[5] Overall, they reveal that the intermediate score, i.e., the score at the time a player shoots, acts as a reference point and that teams taking the first kick win the penalty shoot-out 60.5% of the time. In a follow-up study, however, Kocher, Lenz, and Sutter (2012) could not find any significant effect when analyzing an extended sample of 540 (instead of 129) shoot-outs. Moreover, a study by Kassis et al. (2021) suggests that the order of kicks does not matter per se. Rather, winning the toss and being able to determine whether to take the first or second kick (and start with the own goalkeeper) seems to matter. Finally, Cohen-Zada, Krumer, and Shapir (2018) show that any effect may diminish when an alternative format is introduced.[6] By analyzing 1,701 men's and 920 women's tiebreak games from different top-tier tennis tournaments between 2012 and 2015, they do not find that serving first significantly influences winning probabilities, when the order of the first two serves is a mirror of the next two serves.[7]

Past performance: Closely related to the literature about current performance are studies looking at past performance as a reference point. By analyzing 133 million chess games, Anderson and Green (2018) find that *peak* past performance, i.e., a player's *personal best*, acts as a reference point in this setting. Players exert extra effort to set new personal bests and quit at higher rates and for longer spells after setting a new personal best. The latter finding is suggestive of loss-averse behavior. In addition to this paper, there is a substantial amount of studies exploring the effects of success or failure on subsequent performance, i.e., *momentum*, since several settings in sports are considered to offer a unique opportunity for disentangling between momentum generated by strategic incentives and psychological momentum. While the evidence is generally mixed, some studies confirm the existence of path dependency in performance and as such the relevance of past performance as a reference point (e.g., Malueg & Yates (2010) or Gauriot & Page (2019) in tennis as well as Cohen-Zada, Krumer, & Shtudiner (2017) in judo).[8]

Expectations: Pope and Schweitzer (2011) use performance data from PGA Tours covering over 2.5 million putts[9] of professional golfers. They find evidence that professional golfers adopt par[10] within each whole as a reference point. Likewise, golfers develop rational expectations for their performance by adopting average performance on holes by the entire field as a further reference point. Overall, results suggest that professional golfers exhibit loss aversion since they hit birdie[11] putts less accurately and less hard than par putts. This pattern is confirmed in a follow-up analysis conducted by Elmore and Urbaczewski (2020). They exploit a natural experiment, i.e., the fact that the same hole at two courses hosting the US Open has been rated as a par-5 in some years and as a par-4 in other years without any substantial differences regarding the architecture (such as lengthening or shortening the holes) between years. By analyzing overall 31,710 unique hole scores across four US Opens, they find evidence that professional golfers tend to score lower when the same hole is rated as a par-4 (instead of a par-5). This finding suggests that golfers try harder when playing to avoid losing a stroke on a par-4 hole.

Riedl, Heuer, and Strauss (2015) explore whether reference point behavior of players and coaches might explain the controversial empirical findings about the impact of introducing the three-point rule in soccer. By analyzing more than 118,000 match results from the domestic first soccer divisions in 24 countries over 20 seasons, they find that awarding three instead of two points for a win slightly reduces the number of draws per season. Importantly, however, this reduction is not large enough to push the fraction of draws to its statistically expected value. In contrast, the authors find evidence that manipulating incentives for losses yields a reduction at or even below the statistically expected value. While Riedl et al. (2015) conclude that this finding is in line with the phenomenon of loss aversion, they are unable to further disentangle whether the finding is driven by loss-averse players and/or coaches.

Bartling, Brandes, and Schunk (2015) combine a measure of expectations based on preplay betting odds with in-play event information for 8,200 football matches played in the German Bundesliga and the English Premier League. They find reference point behavior for both players and coaches. While players receive more cards per minute, coaches implement more offensive strategy adjustments if their team is behind one goal and was expected to win the match. Since further analysis reveals that both types of behavior worsen the ultimate match outcome, the authors conclude that being behind expectations may induce irrational behavior. Urschel and Zhuang (2011) confirm reference point behavior of coaches by analyzing 2,592 kickoffs during the 2009 National Football League (NFL) regular and playoff seasons. They observe diminishing sensitivity to changes in scoring outcomes when moving further away from zero points (i.e., the reference point). Moreover, they find evidence for loss aversion in this setting. Likewise, Pedace and Smith (2013) analyze reference point behavior of managers in Major League

Baseball (MLB) by using 15,880 player-team-year observations between 1976 and 2005. They find that managers have a tendency to "hold on losers" who they hired and that new coaches have a higher probability to divest poor-performing players when they were acquired by the prior manager. Moreover, they provide evidence that the immediate past manager's tendency to "hold on losers" can be explained by an irrational aversion to admit mistakes.

Round numbers: Pope and Simonsohn (2011) were the first to provide empirical evidence for the existence of round number reference points in sports. By using seasonal information about 8,817 players in MLB, they find that a batting average[12] of 0.300 may serves as a goal that influences behavior. For instance, players just below 0.300 adjust their behavior on the last play of the season in order to successfully hit the ball. Moreover, they are less likely to be substituted. Allen et al. (2017) examine reference point behavior using data regarding almost 10 million marathon finishing times. They find bunching just ahead of round number finishing times, such as 3h or 4h, confirming the relevance of round number reference points in sports. Further analysis suggests that the effect is psychological in nature rather than being caused by extrinsic rewards (such as financial incentives or qualifying for the Boston Marathon), peer effects, or institutional features (such as pacesetters). With data coming from almost 4,000 finishers of California's venerated Western States 100 (WS100), Grant (2016) confirms the existence of a round number reference point (i.e., 24h) in ultramarathoning. Likewise, Lusher, He, and Fick (2018) find evidence that the performance of professional basketball players bunches at round numbers. By analyzing almost 3 million shot attempts during NBA games, they find that players significantly improve free throw accuracy and take significantly more shots closer to the hoop when shooting to make their individual game stats a round number.

Summing up, while previous studies confirm reference point behavior in sports related to *expectations* and *round numbers*, the evidence about (current or past) *performance* as a reference point is less conclusive. This might be caused by some overlapping effects which are hard to reveal and disentangle in these settings.

Performance evaluation and happiness

Empirical studies exploring the effects of reference point behavior on performance evaluation and happiness of athletes have focused either on *counterfactual thinking, round numbers,* or *performance goals beyond round numbers* as reference points and provide unambiguous findings.

Counterfactual thinking: Already, in 1995, Medvec, Madey, and Gilovich analyze the emotional reactions of bronze and silver medalists at the 1992 Summer Olympic Games in Barcelona, as well as the 1994 Empire State Games in Syracuse.[13] In line with previous psychological research on the effects of counterfactual thinking, they find that bronze medalists appear to be happier than silver medalists. This can be attributed to the fact that bronze medalists refer to the non-medal fourth place rank as a reference point, whereas silver medalists reflect the "loss" of the gold medal as a reference point.

Round numbers: Markle et al. (2018) confirm the existence of (multiple time) goal reference points using official performance data in combination with data coming from 1,801 runners who had been surveyed before and after 15 of the largest U.S. marathons. Their analysis suggests that satisfaction by athletes is a function of relative performance measured as the difference between the targeted / the best / the last marathon times and her/his actual finishing time. Moreover, it was found that satisfaction exhibits a jump at the reference point and that losses loom larger than gains, reflecting the classical loss aversion phenomenon.

Performance goals beyond round numbers: Heath, Larrick, and Wu (1999) confronted participants with scenarios about goals in workout plans (i.e., the number of sit-ups) and information about the achievement (or not) of these goals by different (fictitious) individuals. The participants were asked to list the emotion they believe each of these individuals would be experiencing. Overall, they find that *single* goals inherit the properties of the value function of Prospect Theory, including diminishing sensitivity and loss aversion. In a follow-up project, Weingarten et al. (2019) look at multiple goals as reference points. In one of their studies, they also confronted participants with workout plans and information about the achievement (or not) of these goals by different (fictitious) individuals. In contrast to Heath et al. (1999), however, they focused on two different exercises, i.e., push-ups and lunges. Overall, they confirm that also *multiple* goals inherit the aforementioned properties of the value function, i.e., diminishing sensitivity and loss aversion. However, additivity is not supported since failure in the push-up goal and success in the lunges goal (or vice versa) are perceived as less pleasurable than the sum of the separate feelings would predict. As such, they conclude that "one failure makes everything else feel worse" (see also the paper's title).

Reference point behavior of fans

The second research line is focused on expectations by *fans* and exploits the fact that (average) expectations as reference points can be directly inferred from the betting market.[14] Next to the literature looking at the effects of (un)expected outcomes on *sports demand* (3.1), several empirical studies have already explored the effects of emotional cues (i.e., upset losses or upset wins) from watching sporting events and the corresponding behaviors that translate to *other areas beyond sports*, such as stock markets (3.2).

Sports demand

More than six decades ago, Rottenberg (1956) and Neale (1964) provided some anecdotic evidence suggesting that fan interest increases with increasing uncertainty about game and league outcomes. It took quite a long time, before this so called "Uncertainty of Outcome Hypothesis" (UOH) was formalized in theoretical models considering reference-dependent preferences. Coates, Humphreys, and Zhou (2014) introduced a model for live game attendance where the UOH emerges when the marginal utility of an unexpected win (gain) exceeds the marginal utility of an unexpected loss. According to this model, the UOH does not hold for loss-averse spectators. In fact, many empirical studies do not find support for the UOH at the level of a single game (see Pawlowski (2013) or Nalbantis & Pawlowski (2016) for recent overviews). At the same time, however, these studies do not provide direct support for the existence of loss-averse spectators given the underidentification problem of the implemented empirical models as noted already by Humphreys and Zhou (2015).

A different approach incorporating more indirectly the basic idea of the UOH is presented by Ely, Frankel, and Kamenica (2015). They introduced the concepts of suspense and surprise for (in-play) entertainment demand by modeling the belief paths of agents. In this regard, suspense measures the variance of the next period's beliefs, while surprise relates in-play events to anterior beliefs. Bizzozero, Flepp, and Franck (2016) provide the first study empirically testing both concepts in a sport setting by combining in-play betting odds and minute-by-minute TV viewing figures from 80 men's single tennis matches at Wimbledon. Overall, they find evidence that both greater suspense and surprise are driving demand. Buraimo et al. (2020) provide a further empirical test by analyzing in-play TV audience figures from 540 English Premier League matches. They confirm the relevance of surprise and suspense, as well as the difference between pre-match and current game outcome probabilities (referred to as "shock"). Summing up, there are already some empirical studies confirming a relationship between reference points and fan interest, although their explicit (theoretical and empirical) modeling just started few years ago.[15]

Behavior in other areas beyond sports

Stock market reactions: By analyzing the investors' behavior at the stock market, Edmans, García, and Norli (2007) were the first to empirically explore the effects of sports sentiment on behavior in other areas beyond sports. In order to measure sports sentiment, they collected data on outcomes of more than 2,000 international matches played during several decades in different team sports, i.e., soccer, cricket, rugby, ice hockey, and basketball. Overall, they find that losses by the national teams are associated with negative domestic stock market reactions, particularly for soccer; however, they do not find any evidence for a response to wins. Moreover, they do not find any relationship between ex-ante probabilities to win and stock market re-actions. As such, they cannot directly confirm reference point behavior in this setting.

Crime: By linking data on family violence as reported in the National Incident-Based Reporting System (NIBRS) with team records for local franchises in the National Football League and betting odds data covering around 1,000 games, Card and Dahl (2011) were the first to study the effects of emotional cues from unexpected game outcomes on crime. They find evidence for both reference-dependent behavior and loss aversion. While *upset* losses lead to a significant increase in family violence, neither *expected* losses nor *upset* wins unfold any significant effects on family violence. Several papers followed the idea exploring the link between crime and emotional cues associated with upset game outcomes. Two of them directly follow the approach proposed by Card and Dahl and also use NIBRS data. Cardazzi et al. (2020) use NIBRS data in combination with NBA game-level and betting odds data, as well as detailed information about the correctness of calls and non-calls by referees in the last two minutes of close basketball games. They find evidence that call correctness is negatively correlated with fatigue. At the same time, differences in fatigue by referees explain most of the variance in family violence caused by unexpected losses of an NBA team. As such, Cardazzi et al. (2020) confirm the finding by Card and Dahl (2011) on the effect of emotional cues on family violence in a different sport setting. Moreover, they provide suggestive evidence that the mechanism might work via referee accuracy. Lindo, Siminski, and Swensen (2018) combine NIBRS data with college football game data and find that upset wins by teams playing in the highest division of colleague football, i.e. Division 1A, increase excessive partying and alcohol consumption, as well as reports of rape on match day. In contrast, however, to the findings on family violence by Card and Dahl (2011) as well as Cardazzi et al. (2020), the corresponding effects on alcohol consumption and rape are not significant for upset losses.

Next to these papers, Munyo and Rossi (2013) analyze the effects of emotional cues on violent crime in Montevideo, the capital of Uruguay, by combining a database covering all thefts and robberies between January 2002 and December 2010 from the local police department with data on soccer results and betting odds for around 300 games played by two popular local soccer teams, Nacional and Peñarol. Following an event-study approach, they report a significant increase by 70% in robberies right after an unexpected (compared to an expected) loss but do not observe any effects on thefts. Likewise, they report a significant decrease by 42% in robberies right after an unexpected (compared to an expected) win but do not observe any effects on thefts. Marie (2016) uses hourly recorded data at the borough level from the Metropolitan Criminal Statistics System (MCSS) in combination with data for 1,147 games of all nine London football teams in the top two divisions in England between October 1994 and March 1997. While he does not directly test for reference point behavior in this setting, his finding that violent behavior increases only during derbies provides at least some suggestive evidence for the relevance of the emotional state of fans in this regard. Finally, Ge, Sarmiento Barbieri, and Schneider (2020) use granular spatial information on vehicle thefts and robberies in the Brazilian city São Paulo in order to replicate and extent the study by Munyo and Rossi (2013). While they observe too few upset wins in their data in order to estimate any credible effect, they confirm that upset losses as well as derby games significantly increase total property crimes within the 1-mile radius around a stadium. However, this effect is mostly driven by an increase in thefts, which was found to be insignificant in the study by Munyo and Rossi (2013).

Court judge behavior: Eren and Mocan (2018) explore the effects of emotional cues on judicial decisions of juvenile court judges in the state of Louisiana between 1992 and 2012 by combining defendant data obtained from the Louisiana Department of Public Safety and Corrections, Youth Services, Office of Juvenile Justice (OJJ), with game-level information about the Louisiana State University (LSU) football team. They find that the disposition (sentence) lengths imposed by judges significantly increase after an unexpected loss of the LSU team in a Saturday game. This effect even persists throughout the whole work week.

Tipping behavior: Finally, Ge (2018) studied the link between taxi passengers' tipping behavior and emotional cues associated with unexpected wins and losses by a professional basketball team (i.e., the New York Knicks). Based on the analysis of overall 268 home game days at the Madison Square Garden, Ge finds support for reference-dependent preferences, i.e., tipping amounts, are driven by deviations from expected game outcomes. However, loss aversion appears to be subdued due to the presence of social norms in this setting.

Conclusion

This chapter provides a structured overview on the recently growing literature empirically testing reference point behavior of athletes, coaches, and fans. Overall, the studies confirm that the athletes' level of effort provision as well as their performance and performance evaluation is commonly related to certain reference points. As such, *expectations* and *round numbers* were found to serve as reference points while the evidence about (current or past) *performance* is less conclusive. Moreover, *expectations* were found to influence decision-making by coaches and to shape the fans' interest in sports as well as their behavior in other areas beyond sports. Remarkably, emotional cues from watching sporting events were found to influence investment and judging decisions as well as tipping behavior and criminal conduct.

Many of these studies were published in leading field journals in economics (such as *American Economic Review, American Economic Journal: Applied Economics, Econometrica, Journal of Political Economy, Quarterly Journal of Economics,* or the *Journal of Finance*), management (such as *Management Science*), and psychology (such as *Psychological Review* or *Psychological Science*), documenting the relevance and opportunities of using data from sport settings for exploring reference point behavior in sports and beyond.

For future research, it appears very promising to further exploit the rich (in-play) data available in sport settings by taking advantage of some recent developments in statistical (learning) techniques for analysis in order to address some core topics of reference point behavior. Such topics include disentangling team and individual reference points in team (sport) settings or exploring the relevance of social pressure as a moderator / mediator. Likewise, sports data might offer the possibility to study more general issues such as updating of reference points or exploring how multiple reference points compete and combine. The latter issue was already raised by Kahneman (1992) three decades ago but remains, by and large, a rather unexplored topic of research.

Notes

1 Tim Pawlowski is also affiliated with the LEAD Graduate School & Research Network as well as the Interfaculty Research Institute for Sports and Physical Activity in Tuebingen. This chapter informs the empirical work of a project funded by the Deutsche Forschungsgemeinschaft (DFG, German Research Foundation) under Germany's Excellence Strategy – EXC number 2064/1 – Project number 390727645. I would like to thank Alex Krumer, Travis Richardson, and Dominik Schreyer for helpful comments and suggestions. All errors are mine.
2 Their seminal work was published in 1979 in *Econometrica*. Twenty-three years later, Kahneman was awarded the Nobel Memorial Prize in Economic Sciences for his achievements in this field of studies.
3 The concept of cognitive reference points goes back to Wertheimer (1938) who suggested *"that among perceptual stimuli, there are certain 'ideal types' which act as the anchoring points for perception"* (Rosch, 1975, 532).
4 https://libquotes.com/pierre-de-coubertin/quote/lbq2m0c, accessed on November 4, 2020.
5 Note that this is fundamentally different compared to the procedure that was implemented in July 2003 where *"the team whose captain wins the toss decides whether to take the first or second kick"* (http://web.deu.edu.tr/atiksu/ana23/fifason.pdf, accesses on November 4, 2020 (p. 36) as quoted by Apesteguia and Palacios-Huerta (2010) on p. 2551).
6 Imagine two players / teams, A and B. The sequence in penalty should-outs in soccer is ABAB or BABA. In tennis tiebreaks, however, the sequence is always ABBA or BAAB.
7 The literature on causes and consequences of *ahead-behind asymmetry* in sports contests is vast. For a recent review of the literature on *order effects*, see Joustra, Koning, and Krumer (2020). For a recent review of the literature on *discouragement effects*, see Iqbal and Krumer (2019).
8 For a review of the literature on path dependency in performance, see Gauriot and Page (2019). A much related topic is the *hot hand phenomenon* according to which success might breed success and failure might breed failure (Gilovich, Vallone, & Tversky, 1985). The literature empirically testing this phenomenon in sports is vast and inconclusive (for a review, see Bar-Eli, Avugos, & Raab, 2006). Quite recently, Miller and Sanjurjo (2018) showed that parts of this confusion might be caused by a subtle but substantial streak selection bias:

> Upon correcting for the bias, we find that the data that had previously been interpreted as demonstrating that belief in the hot hand is a fallacy, instead provide substantial evidence that it is not a fallacy to believe in the hot hand. (p. 2032)

9 "The hitting of the golf ball on or near the green using the putter. Putting takes up approximately 40% of all shots during a round of golf." (https://www.golfonline.co.uk/golf-glossary#P, accessed on October 23, 2020).

10 "Each hole on a golf course has a designated score that is used to represent its difficulty. Pars range from 3 to 5 normally, although some courses have par 6 holes. A par of three means that the golfer is meant to hit the ball from tee to the hole in 3 strokes." (https://www.golfonline.co.uk/golf-glossary#P, accessed on October 23, 2020).
11 "A score of one under the par of the hole." (https://www.golfonline.co.uk/golf-glossary#B, accessed on October 23, 2020).
12 The batting average measures the number of balls hit successfully divided by the number of at bats (http://m.mlb.com/glossary/standard-stats/batting-average, accessed on October 23, 2020).
13 The Empire State Games are a regional amateur athletic event which took place in Syracuse in 1994. Overall, more than 5,000 athletes from across New York State (including Olympic gold medalists and NBA stars) participated in this event (Medvec, Madey, & Gilovich, 1995).
14 Pawlowski, Coates, and Nalbantis (2018) provide survey evidence that "average" expectations about game outcomes derived from betting markets are highly correlated with individual expectations.
15 For a detailed literature review, see Budzinski and Pawlowski (2017) or Pawlowski and Nalbantis (2019).

References

Allen, E. J., Dechow, P. M., Pope, D. G., & Wu, G. (2017). Reference-dependent preferences: Evidence from marathon runners. *Management Science, 63*(6), 1657–1672.

Andersen, A. & Green, E. A. (2018). Personal bests as reference points. *Proceedings of the National Academy of Sciences of the United States of America, 115*(8), 1772–1776.

Apesteguia, J. & Palacios-Huerta (2010). Psychological pressure in competitive environments: Evidence from a randomized natural experiment. *American Economic Review, 100*(5), 2548–2564.

Bar-Eli, M., Avugos, S., & Raab, M. (2006). Twenty years of "hot hand" research: Review and critique. *Psychology of Sport and Exercise, 7*, 525–553.

Bartling, B., Brandes, L., & Schunk, D. (2015). Expectations as reference points: Field evidence from professional soccer. *Management Science, 61*(11), 2646–2661.

Berger, J. & Pope, D. (2011). Can losing lead to winning? *Management Science, 57*(5), 817–827.

Bizzozero, P., Flepp, R., & Franck, E. (2016). The importance of suspense and surprise in entertainment demand: Evidence from Wimbledon. *Journal of Economic Behavior & Organization, 130*, 47–63.

Budzinski, O. & Pawlowski, T. (2017). The behavioural economics of competitive balance – Theories, findings and implications. *International Journal of Sport Finance, 12*(2), 109–122.

Buraimo, B., Forrest, D., McHale, I. G., & Tena, J. D. (2020). Unscripted drama: Soccer audience response to suspense, surprise, and shock. *Economic Inquiry, 58*(2), 881–896.

Card, D. & Dahl, G. B. (2011). Family violence and football: The effect of unexpected emotional cues on violent behavior. *Quarterly Journal of Economics, 126*, 103–143.

Cardazzi, A. J., McCannon, B. C., Humphreys, B. R., & Rodriguez, Z. (2020). Blaming the ref: Interpreting the effect of unexpected emotional cues on family violence. *West Virginia University, Econ. Faculty Working Papers Series, 52*.

Coates, D., Humphreys, B., & Zhou, L. (2014). Reference-dependent preferences, loss aversion, and live game attendance. *Economic Inquiry, 52*(3), 959–973.

Cohen-Zada, D., Krumer, A., & Shapir, O. M. (2018). Testing the effect of serve and order in tennis tiebreak. *Journal of Economic Behavior & Organization, 146*, 106–115.

Cohen-Zada, D., Krumer, A., & Shtudiner, Z. (2017). Psychological momentum and gender. *Journal of Economic Behavior & Organization, 135*, 66–81.

Edmans, A., García, D., & Norli, O. (2007). Sports sentiment and stock returns. *The Journal of Finance, 112*(4), 1967–1998.

Elmore, R. & Urbaczewski, A. (2020). Loss aversion in professional golf. *Journal of Sports Economics*, doi: 10.1177/1527002520967403.

Ely, J., Frankel, A., & Kamenica, E. (2015). Suspense and surprise. *Journal of Political Economy, 123*(1), 215–260.

Eren, O. & Mocan, N. (2018). Emotional judges and unlucky juveniles. *American Economic Journal: Applied Economics, 10*(3), 171–205.

Gauriot, R. & Page, L. (2019). Does success breed success? A quasi-experiment on strategic momentum in dynamic contests. *Economic Journal, 129*(624), 2107–3136.

Ge, Q. (2018). Sports sentiment and tipping behavior. *Journal of Economic Behavior & Organization, 145*, 95–113.

Ge, Q., Sarmiento Barbieri, I., & Schneider, R. (2020). Sporting events, emotional cues and crime: Spatial and temporal evidence from Brazilian soccer games. *Economic Inquiry*, doi:10.1111/ecin.12950.

Genakos, C. & Pagliero, M. (2012). Interim rank, risk taking, and performance in dynamic tournaments. *Journal of Political Economy, 120*(4), 782–813.

Gilovich, T., Vallone, R., & Tversky, A. (1985). The hot hand in basketball: On the misperception of random sequences. *Cognitive Psychology, 17*, 295–314.

Goldman, M. & Rao, J. M. (2017). Loss aversion around a fixed reference point in highly experienced agents. *SSRN Working Paper*, doi.org/10.2139/ssrn.2782110

Grant, D. (2016). The essential economics of threshold-based incentives: Theory, estimation, and evidence from the Western States 100. *Journal of Economic Behavior and Organization, 130*, 180–197.

Heath, C., Larrick, R. P., & Wu, G. (1999). Goals as reference points. *Cognitive Psychology, 38*, 79–109.

Humphreys, B. R., & Zhou, L. (2015). The Louis-Schmeling paradox and the league standing effect reconsidered. *Journal of Sports Economics, 16*(8), 835–852.

Iqbal, H. & Krumer, A. (2019). Discouragement effect and intermediate prizes in multi-stage contests: Evidence from Davis Cup. *European Economic Review, 118*, 364–381.

Joustra, S., Koning, R., & Krumer, A. (2020). Order effects in elite gymnastics. *De Economist*, doi.org/10.1007/s10645-020-09371-0

Kahneman, D. (1992). Reference points, anchors, norms, and mixed feelings. *Organizational Behavior and Human Decision Processes, 51*, 296–312.

Kahneman, D. & Tversky, A. (1979). Prospect theory: An analysis of decision under risk. *Econometrica, 47*(2), 263–292.

Kassis, M., Schmidt, S. L., Schreyer, D., & Sutter, M. (2021). Psychological pressure and the right to determine the moves in dynamic tournaments – Evidence from a natural field experiment. *Games and Economic Behavior, 126*, 278–287.

Kocher, M. G., Lenz, M. V., & Sutter, M. (2012). Psychological pressure in competitive environments: New evidence from randomized natural experiments. *Management Science, 58*(8), 1585–1591.

Lindo, J., Siminski, P., & Swensen, I. D. (2018). College party culture and sexual assault. *American Economic Journal: Applied Economics, 10*(1), 236–265.

Lusher, L., He, C., & Fick, S. (2018). Are professional basketball players reference-dependent? *Applied Economics, 50*(36), 3937–3948.

Malueg, D. & Yates, A. (2010). Testing contest theory: Evidence from best-of-three tennis matches. *Review of Economics and Statistics, 92*(3), 689–692.

March, J. G. & Shapira, Z. (1992). Variable risk preferences and the focus of attention. *Psychological Review, 99*(1), 172–183.

Marie, O. (2016). Police and thieves in the stadium: Measuring the (multiple) effects of football matches on crime. *Journal of the Royal Statistical Society: Series A (Statistics in Society), 179*(1), 273–292.

Markle, A., Wu, G., White, R., & Sackett, A. (2018). Goals as reference points in marathon running: A novel test of reference dependence. *Journal of Risk and Uncertainty, 56*, 19–50.

Medvec, V. H., Madey, S. F., & Gilovich, T. (1995). When less is more: Counterfactual thinking and satisfaction among Olympic medalists. *Journal of Personality and Social Psychology, 69*(4), 603–610.

Miller, J. B. & Sanjurjo, A. (2018). Surprised by the hot hand fallacy? A truth in the law of small numbers. *Econometrica, 86*(6), 2019–2047.

Munyo, I. & Rossi, M. A. (2013). Frustration, euphoria, and violent crime. *Journal of Economic Behavior & Organization, 89*, 136–142.

Nalbantis, G., & Pawlowski, T. (2016). *The demand for international football telecasts in the United States*, edited by W. Andreff and A. Zimbalist. Houndmills, UK: Palgrave.

Neale, W. C. (1964). The peculiar economics of professional sports: A contribution to the theory of the firm in sporting competition and in market competition. *Quarterly Journal of Economics, 78*(1), 1–14.

Pawlowski, T. (2013). Testing the uncertainty of outcome hypothesis in European professional football: A stated preference approach. *Journal of Sports Economics, 14*(4), 341–367.

Pawlowski, T. & Nalbantis, G. (2019). Competitive balance: Measurement and relevance. In P. Downward, B. Frick, B. R. Humphreys, T. Pawlowski, J. Ruseski, & B. P. Soebbing (eds.), *The sage handbook of sports economics*, 154–162. Thousand Oaks, CA: SAGE Publications Ltd.

Pawlowski, T., Nalbantis, G., & Coates, D. (2018). Perceived game uncertainty, suspense and the demand for sport. *Economic Inquiry, 56*(1), 173–192.

Pedace, R. & Smith, J. K. (2013). Loss aversion and managerial decisions. Evidence from Major League Baseball. *Economic Inquiry, 51*(2), 1475–1488.

Pope, D. G. & Schweitzer, M. E. (2011). Is tiger woods loss averse? Persistent bias in the face of experience, competition, and high stakes. *American Economic Review, 101*, 129–157.

Pope, D. & Simonsohn, U. (2011). Round numbers as goals: Evidence from Baseball, SAT takers, and the lab. *Psychological Science, 22*(1), 71–99.

Riedl, D., Heuer, A., & Strauss, B. (2015). Why the three-point rule failed to sufficiently reduce the number of draws in soccer: An application of prospect theory. *Journal of Sport & Exercise Psychology, 37*, 316–326.

Rosch, E. (1975). Cognitive reference points. *Cognitive Psychology, 7*(4), 532–547.

Rottenberg, S. (1956). The baseball players' labor market. *Journal of Political Economy, 64*(3), 242–258.

Urschel, J. D. & Zhuang, J. (2011). Are NFL coaches risk and loss averse? Evidence from their use of kickoff strategies. *Journal of Quantitative Analysis in Sports*, 7(3), Article 14.

Weingarten, E., Bhatia, S., & Mellers, B. (2019). Multiple goals as reference points: On failure makes everything else feel worse. *Management Science*, 65(7), 3337–3352.

Wertheimer, M. (1938). Numbers and numerical concepts in primitive peoples. In W. D. Ellis (ed.), *A source book of Gestalt psychology* (265–273). New York: Harcourt, Brace, & Co.

Winer, R. S. (1986). A reference price model of brand choice for frequently purchased products. *Journal of Consumer Research*, 13(2), 250–256.

10 The importance of the serve in winning points in tennis

A Bayesian analysis using data for the two winners of the 2019 French Open singles

Vani K. Borooah

Introduction

The Reverend Thomas Bayes, an 18th-century Presbyterian minister, proved what, arguably, is the most important theorem in statistics.[1] Bayes' theorem states that the probability of a hypothesis being true (event T), *given that the data have been observed* (event A), is the probability of the hypothesis being true, *before any data have been observed*, times an "updating factor". The theorem is encapsulated by the well-known equation:[2]

$$P(T \mid A) = \frac{P(A \mid T)}{P(A)} \times P(T) \qquad (1)$$

where $P(T)$ represents the *prior* belief that the hypothesis is true *before the data have been observed*; $P(A)$ is the probability of observing the data, *regardless of whether the hypothesis is true or not*; $P(A|T)$ is the probability of observing the data, given that the hypothesis is true; and $P(A|T) / P(A)$ is the Bayesian "updating factor" which translates one's *prior* (that is, *before* observing the data) belief about the hypothesis's validity into a *posterior* (that is, *after* observing the data) belief.[3]

Bayes' theorem has been extensively applied in law and in medicine. For example, in the area of law it has shed light on the so-called "prosecutor's fallacy" whereby a prosecutor argues that since the probability of observing a particular piece of evidence (say, blood type identical to that found at the scene of the crime), *under the assumed innocence of the defendant*, is very small (that is, $P(A|T)$ is low), the probability of the defendant being innocent, *given that his blood type matches that at the crime scene*, must also be very small (that is, $P(T \mid A)$ must also be low). This fallacious reasoning stems from assuming that the ratio $P(T) / P(A)$ in Equation (1) is equal to unity (Aitken, 1996; Thompson and Schumann, 1987). If, however, the prior belief that the defendant is innocent ($P(T)$), relative to the probability of finding a blood type identical to that found at the scene of the crime, is high, then $P(T \mid A)$ could be high even though $P(A \mid T)$ was low.

In medicine, the theorem has, for example, been used to analyse the efficacy of breast screening. Proponents of screening would argue, on the basis of

DOI: 10.4324/9781003080824-12

the "screening fallacy", that because the probability of the screen returning a positive result, *given that the patient has cancer*, is large (that is, $P(A\,|\,T)$ is high), the probability of the patient having cancer, *given that the screen returns a positive result*, must also be large (that is, $P(T\,|\,A)$ must also be high). This fallacious reasoning again stems from assuming that the ratio $P(T)\,/\,P(A)$ in Equation (1) is equal to unity. If, however, the proportion of persons with cancer in the population, relative to the proportion of positive screen results, is small (i.e., $P(T)\,/\,P(A)$ in Equation (1) is low), then $P(T\,|\,A)$ could be appreciably smaller than $P(A\,|\,T)$. The size of this difference represents cancer "over diagnosis" and has recently been estimated at 10% (Zackrisson et al., 2006). In effect, 1 in 10 women diagnosed with breast cancer would not require treatment.

In this paper, we apply these ideas to examining the importance of the serve – specifically, the first serve (FS) and the second serve (SS) – in winning a point. Excluding double faults, we assume that for the player serving for a particular point there are two possible options: the FS was "good" (event A) or the FS was "bad" or a fault (event $\tilde{A}$). Because the possibility of double faults has been excluded, event $\tilde{A}$ is synonymous with the SS being good. In this paper, we distinguish between the probabilities of two events: (i) the probability that a winning point was *preceded* by a good FS or, in other words, what is the probability that if the FS is good the point would be won? (ii) the probability that a good first service would be *succeeded* by a winning point or, in other words, what is the probability that a winning point would be result of a good first service?

However, the question of interest is not about the likelihood that, if a point was won, it would have been *preceded* by a good FS – that is, (i) above – but, rather, the likelihood that a "good" FS will be *succeeded* by a winning point – that is point (ii) above. It is important to emphasise that conceptually these are separate questions in much the same way that the probability that a test for cancer will report positive, *if one has cancer*, is conceptually different from the probability that one has cancer *if the test for cancer is positive*.

Similarly, the question of interest is not about the likelihood that a losing point will have been *preceded* by a "bad" FS, but, rather, it is the likelihood that a "bad" FS would be *succeeded* by a losing point. Again, it is important to emphasise that these are two separate questions in much the same way that the probability that a test for cancer will report negative, *if one does not have cancer*, is conceptually different from the probability that one does not have has cancer *if the test for cancer is negative*. The strength of Bayes' theorem is that it is able to provide an answer to the second set of questions by linking it, via Equation (1) above, to the first set.

The performance of tennis players has been the subject of considerable statistical analysis (Cross and Pollard, 2009; *inter alia* Cui et al., 2018; Moss and O'Donoghue, 2015; O'Donoghue, 2012; O'Donoghue and Brown, 2008, 2009) and, in particular, the importance of the serve has been extensively examined. Furlong (1995) found that serve was more important on grass than on clay and more important in men's than in women's singles while Hugh and Clarke (1995) found that serve was more important at Wimbledon than in the Australian Open. O'Donoghue and Ingram (2001) showed that the duration of a rally depended on service speed while O'Donoghue and Ballantyne (2004) and Unierzyski and Wieczorek (2004) showed, respectively, how service speed and placement could be used to improve the effectiveness of the service.

More recently, O'Donoghue and Brown (2008) studied the rate at which the service advantage decayed as the rally progressed: in men's tennis, the advantage persisted for three to four shots after the first serve but, in women's, the advantage of the first serves was lost after two shots. Notwithstanding the richness of the literature on the importance of the serve in tennis, to the best of our knowledge, a Bayesian analysis of the type articulated in this paper has not been attempted and that is this paper's raison d'être.

The data for this paper are from website www.rolandgarros.com. The existence of this data is due to analytics provided by Roland Garros's new technology partner, Infosys. According to the Infosys press release, "the collaboration is aimed at enriching the game by providing fans, players and coaches with a new experience leveraging Infosys' expertise in digital technologies such as artificial intelligence, big data and analytics, mobility, virtual and augmented reality".[4]

Bayesian analysis of the outcomes of service points

The first question of interest is that if a player won a service point (event T occurred), what is the probability that it would have been *preceded* by a good FS, event A? To put it slightly differently, what is the probability that event A occurs, *conditional on event T having occurred*? This probability is written as $P(A|T) = \alpha$, for some real number $0 \leq \alpha \leq 1$. The *sensitivity* of the first serve is defined by α: the more sensitive the first serve, the greater the likelihood that a point won will have been *preceded* by a "good" FS.

Similarly, the *specificity* of the first serve, β, is defined as the likelihood that a point *lost* will have been preceded by a "bad" FS: $P(\tilde{A}|\tilde{T}) = \beta$. Following from this, *1-specificity* = $1 - \beta = 1 - P(\tilde{A}|\tilde{T}) = P(A|\tilde{T})$ is the probability of a *false positive*: the probability that a point *lost* (false) will have been preceded by a "good" FS (positive). Similarly, *1-sensitivity* = $1 - \alpha = 1 - P(A|T) = P(\tilde{A}|T)$ is the probability of a *true negative*: the probability that a point won (true) would have been preceded by a "bad" FS (negative). These four possibilities are set out in Table 10.1.

As discussed above, Bayes' theorem states that the probability of a theory being true (event T: a player wins a point), *given that the data have been observed* (event A: her FS was "good"), is given by Equation (1), above. After the data have been observed, the Bayesian "updating factor" in Equation (1), $P(A|T)/P(A)$, translates one's *prior* belief about the theory's validity into a *posterior* belief which, in the context of tennis, translates one's *prior* belief

Table 10.1 The Reliability of the Service in Winning a Point

True positive (sensitivity): $P(A\|T)=\alpha$	True negative (1-sensitivity) $P(\tilde{A}\|T)=1-\alpha$
False positive (1-specificity): $P(A\|\tilde{T})=1-\beta$	False negative (specificity): $P(\tilde{A}\|\tilde{T})=\beta$

T is the event that the first serve was good while $\tilde{T}$ is the event that the first serve was a fault (but the second serve was good). A is the event that the point was won, while $\tilde{A}$ is the event that the point was lost.

about a player winning a service point into a *posterior* belief about winning the point after the data were observed.

The probability of a "good" FS is the weighted sum of the probabilities of a "true positive" (a player wins the point [true] with a good FS [positive]) and a "false positive" (a player loses the point [false] with a good FS [positive], the weights being the strength of one's prior belief, $P(T)$, where $P(\tilde{T}) = 1 - P(T)$:

$$P(A) = P(A \cap T) + P(A \cap \tilde{T}) = P(T) \times \underbrace{P(A|T)}_{\text{prob of a true positive}} + P(\tilde{T}) \times \underbrace{P(A|\tilde{T})}_{\text{prob of a false positive}}$$

where $\tilde{T}$ is the event that the player loses the point and $P(\tilde{T}) = 1 - P(T)$. By analogous reasoning:

$$P(\tilde{A}) = P(\tilde{A} \cap T) + P(\tilde{A} \cap \tilde{T}) = P(T) \times \underbrace{P(\tilde{A}|T)}_{\text{prob of a true negative}} + P(\tilde{T}) \times \underbrace{P(\tilde{A}|\tilde{T})}_{\text{prob of a false negative}} \quad (3)$$

Equation (3) says that the probability of a "bad" FS is the weighted sum of the probabilities of a "true negative" (a player wins the point [true] with a bad FS [negative]) and a "false negative" (a player loses the point [false] with a "bad" FS [negative], the weights being the strength of one's prior belief, $P(T)$.

Substituting the expression in (2) into Equation (1) yields:

$$P(T|A) = \frac{P(T) \times P(A|T)}{P(T) \times P(A|T) + P(\tilde{T}) \times P(A|\tilde{T})} = P(T) \times \frac{P(A|T)}{P(A)} \quad (4)$$

In an analogous manner, one can also enquire about $P(T | \tilde{A})$, the probability of winning a point after a second serve, by substituting Equation (3) into Equation (1):[5]

$$P(T|\tilde{A}) = \frac{P(T) \times P(\tilde{A}|T)}{P(T) \times P(\tilde{A}|T) + P(\tilde{T}) \times P(\tilde{A}|\tilde{T})} = P(T) \times \frac{P(\tilde{A}|T)}{P(\tilde{A})} \quad (5)$$

190 Vani K. Borooah

Now suppose that *prior* to a match being played, a particular player is expected to win 60% of the points for which she is serving, that is, $P(T) = 0.6$. Suppose also that if the serving player *wins* a point, the chances are 70% that it will be on a first serve: in other words, using the terminology developed earlier, the player's serve has a sensitivity, $\alpha = P(A|T) = 0.70$. Similarly, suppose that if the serving player *loses* the point, the chances are 85% that it will be on her second serve: in other words, again using the earlier terminology, the player's serve has a specificity, $\beta = P(\tilde{A}|\tilde{T}) = 0.85$; this implies that the probability of a false positive – the probability of the serving player's losing point being *preceded* by a "good" first serve – is $1 - \beta = P(A|\tilde{T}) = 0.15$.

Substituting these assumed values into Equation (4) yields:

$$P(T|A) = \frac{0.6 \times 0.7}{0.6 \times 0.7 + 0.4 \times 0.15} = 0.88 \tag{6}$$

or, in other words, there is a 88% chance that a good first serve would be *succeeded* by a winning point. Similarly, substituting these assumed values into Equation (5) yields:

$$P(T|\tilde{A}) = \frac{0.6 \times 0.3}{0.6 \times 0.3 + 0.4 \times 0.85} = 0.35 \tag{7}$$

or, in other words, there is a 35% chance of that the second serve would be *succeeded* by a winning point.

Estimates using data for Barty and Nadal from the 2019 French Open

This paper puts empirical flesh on the analysis set out in the previous section by considering the aggregate performance of Ashleigh Barty and Rafael Nadal, respectively, the French Open women's and men's champions in 2019, against successive opponents from Round 1 of the tournament to the final. The performance data for Barty and Nadal, against their various opponents, are set out in Tables 10.2 and 10.3, respectively.

Table 10.2 shows that in the eight matches Barty played for her title, excluding 15 double faults, she served 450 times of which 268 first serves were good and the remaining 182 first serves were "bad" (that is, resulted in a second serve). Consequently, in the notation adopted in this paper, $P(A) = 268/450 = 59.6\%$ and $P(\tilde{A}) = 40.4\%$ for Barty. Table 10.3 shows that in the eight matches Nadal played for his title, excluding 15 double faults, he served 575 times of which 403 first serves were good and the remaining 172 first serves were "bad" (that is, resulted in a second serve). Consequently, in the notation adopted in this paper, $P(A) = 403/575 = 70.1\%$ and $P(\tilde{A}) = 29.9\%$ for Nadal. One difference between Nadal and Barty is that, compared to Barty, a greater proportion of Nadal's first serves were good: 70.1% versus 59.6%.

Table 10.2 Performance Statistics of Ashleigh Barty vis-à-vis Successive Opponents: Women's Singles French Open 2019

Name	Round	Aces	Double faults	Serves	First serves	Win on first serve	Second serves	Win on second serve	Receiving points	Win on receiving	Total points won	Total points lost	Duration (minutes)
Barty Vondrousova	Final	3	1	54	37	23	17	13	64	33	69	49	70
Barty Anisimova	SF	5	3	93	49	34	44	20	97	49	103	87	113
Barty Keys	QF	4	1	60	36	29	24	15	60	24	68	52	69
Barty Kenin	4R	11	3	73	47	36	26	13	82	37	86	69	90
Barty Petkovic	3R	8	3	50	29	23	21	12	49	23	58	41	60
Barty Collins	2R	4	2	65	34	25	31	17	54	26	68	51	78
Barty Pegula	1R	3	2	55	36	21	19	9	47	28	58	44	60
Barty	All	38	15	450	268	191	182	99	453	220	510	393	540

Source: Stats+ from rolandgarros.com.

Table 10.3 Performance Statistics of Rafael Nadal vis-à-vis Successive Opponents: Men's Singles French Open 2019

Name	Round	Aces	Double faults	Serves	First serves	Win on first serve	Second serves	Win on second serve	Receiving points	Win on receiving	Total points won	Total points lost	Duration (minutes)
Nadal	Final	3	0	106	78	57	28	18	92	41	116	82	111
Thiem													
Nadal	SF	3	1	88	72	49	16	9	93	44	102	79	104
Federer													
Nadal	QF	3	3	69	50	38	19	10	74	40	88	55	111
Nishikori													
Nadal	4R	6	1	76	54	40	22	13	82	39	92	66	110
Londero													
Nadal Goffin	3R	5	5	96	56	44	40	28	105	43	115	86	115
Nadal	2R	3	3	72	46	34	26	16	74	40	90	56	112
Maden													
Nadal	1R	5	2	68	47	39	21	13	84	42	94	58	112
Hanfmann													
Nadal	All	28	15	575	403	301	172	107	604	289	697	482	985

Source: Stats+ from rolandgarros.com.

First serve analysis

Barty won 191 points from the 268 first serves and she won 99 points from her 182 second serves, and so, over the eight matches she played, she won a total 290 points from her service games. In addition to these points won on her service, Barty also won 220 of the 453 points on which she received service. Consequently, Barty won a total of 510 points in the singles of the 2019 French Open: 191 on her first serve, 99 on her second serve, and 220 points when she was the receiver.

Nadal, on the other hand, won 301 points from the 403 first serves and he won 107 points from his 172 second serves, and so, over the eight matches he played, he won a total 408 points from his service games. In addition to these points won on his service, Nadal also won 289 of the 604 points on which he received service. Consequently, Nadal won a total of 697 points in the 2019 French Open: 301 on his first serve, 107 on his second serve, and 289 points when he was the receiver.[6]

In other words, 191 and 99 of Barty's points were preceded, respectively, by first and second serves so that, in terms of the notation used earlier, $P(A|T) = 191/290 = 0.659$ and $P(\tilde{A}|T) = 99/290 = 0.341$ where T is the event that Barty won a point in a service game. The *prior* belief was that 60% of these 450 services would result in a point being won: $P(T)=0.6$; in fact, 64.4% of these services (290 out of 450) resulted in a winning point.

In contrast, 301 and 107 of Nadal's points were preceded, respectively, by first and second serves so that, in terms of the notation used earlier, $P(A|T) = 301/408 = 0.738$ and $P(\tilde{A}|T) = 107/408 = 0.262$ where T is the event that Nadal won a point in a service game. The *prior* belief was that 60% of Nadal's 575 services would result in a point being won: $P(T) = 0.6$; in fact, 70.1% of these services (408 out of 575) resulted in a winning point.

Substituting the values detailed above for Barty into Equation (4) yields the probability that a "good" first serve by her would be *succeeded* by a winning point as:

$$P(T|A) = 0.6 \times \frac{P(A/T)}{P(A)} = 0.6 \times \frac{0.659}{0.596} = 0.6 \times 1.11 \qquad (8)$$

In other words, the *Bayesian updating factor* in respect of the prior belief that Barty would win a point on her service (in this case, 60%) was $0.659 / 0.596 = 1.11$. *Whatever the prior belief* that Barty would win a point in a service game ($P(T)$), it would have been raised after the data had been observed (which is that Barty's first serve was "good").

Similarly, substituting Nadal's values detailed into Equation (4) yields the probability that a "good" first serve by him would be *succeeded* by a winning point as:

$$P(T|A) = 0.6 \times \frac{P(A/T)}{P(A)} = 0.6 \times \frac{0.738}{0.711} = 0.6 \times 1.04 \qquad (9)$$

194 Vani K. Borooah

In other words, the *updating factor* in respect of the prior belief that Nadal would win a point on her service (in this case, 60%) was 0.738 / 0.711 = 1.04. *Whatever the prior belief* that Nadal would win a point in a service game (*P(T)*), it would also have been raised after the data had been observed (which is that his first serve was "good").

The upper panel of Table 10.4 sets out the calculations discussed above in tabular format.

It is important to note that the Bayesian updating factor for Nadal was *lower* than that for Barty: 1.04 versus 1.11. The Bayesian updating factor is computed as the ratio of the likelihood of the data being observed when the theory is true ((*P(A|T)*: the probability that a winning point is preceded by a "good" first serve) to the likelihood of the data being observed (*P(A)*: the first serve was "good"). Although for Nadal the likelihood of a winning point being preceded by a "good" first serve was greater than for Barty (73.8% versus 65.9%), the likelihood that Nadal put in a "good" first serve was also higher (71.1% versus 59.6%): a greater disproportionality between these two values for Barty meant that her Bayesian updating factor was higher than Nadal's.

Second serve analysis

Of the 290 points that Barty won on her service games, 99 points were won on her second serve. Consequently, $P(\tilde{A}|T) = 99/290 = 0.341$. At the same time, the probability of a second serve was $P(\tilde{A}) = 182/450 = 0.404$ so that, after substituting these values in Equation (5), the probability that a second serve by Barty would be *succeeded* by a winning point is:

$$P(T|\tilde{A}) = 0.6 \times \frac{P(\tilde{A}/T)}{P(\tilde{A})} = 0.6 \times \frac{0.341}{0.404} = 0.844 \tag{10}$$

In other words, the *updating factor* in respect of the prior belief that Barty would win a point on her service (in this case, 60%) was 0.341 / 0.404 = 0.844. *Whatever the prior belief* that Barty would win a point in a service game (*P(T)*), it would have been lowered after the data had been observed (which is that Barty's first serve was "bad").

Of the 408 points that Nadal won on his service games, 107 points were won on his second serve. Consequently, $P(\tilde{A}|T) = 107/408 = 0.262$. At the same time, the probability of a second serve was $P(\tilde{A}) = 172/575 = 0.299$ so that, after substituting these values in Equation (5), the probability that a second serve by Barty would be *succeeded* by a winning point is:

$$P(T|\tilde{A}) = 0.6 \times \frac{P(\tilde{A}/T)}{P(\tilde{A})} = 0.6 \times \frac{0.262}{0.299} = 0.876 \tag{11}$$

In other words, the *updating factor* in respect of the prior belief that Nadal would win a point on his service (in this case, 60%) was 0.262 / 0.299 = 0.876. *Whatever the prior belief* that Nadal would win a point in a service game (*P(T)*),

Table 10.4 Bayesian Calculations for Barty and Nadal in the 2019 French Open Singles Championship

First serve analysis (%)

	Barty	Nadal
Prior probability that a point will be won on a service game: $P(T)$	60	60
Probability of a good first serve: $P(A)$	59.6	70.1
Probability that a winning point would be preceded by a first serve: $P(A\|T)$	65.9	73.8
Updating factor computed from Equations (8) and (9)	1.11	1.04
Ex-post probability that a good first serve would be succeeded by a winning point: $P(T\|A)$	66.6	62.4

Second serve analysis (%)

	Barty	Nadal
Prior probability that a point will be won on a service game: $P(T)$	60	60
Probability of a second serve: $P(\tilde{A})$	40.4	29.9
Probability that a winning point would be preceded by a second serve: $P(\tilde{A}\|T)$	34.1	26.2
Updating factor computed from Equations (10) and (11)	0.844	0.876
Ex-post probability that a good second serve would be succeeded by a winning point: $P(T\|\tilde{A})$	50.6	52.6

Source: Own calculations using data from rolandgarros.com.

it would have been lowered after the data had been observed (which is that his first serve was "bad").

The lower panel of Table 10.4 sets out the calculations discussed above in tabular format.

Now, it is important to note that the Bayesian updating factor for Nadal was *higher* than Barty's: 0.876 versus 0.844. As mentioned earlier, the Bayesian updating factor is computed as the ratio of the likelihood of the data being observed when the theory is true $(P(\tilde{A}|T))$ (the probability that a winning point is preceded by a "bad" first serve) to the likelihood of the data being observed $(P(\tilde{A})$: the first serve was "bad"). Although for Nadal the likelihood of a winning point being preceded by a "bad" first serve was lower than for Barty (26.2% versus 34.1%), the likelihood that Nadal put in a bad first serve was also lower (29.9% versus 40.4%): a greater disproportionality between these two values for Nadal meant that his Bayesian updating factor was higher than Barty's.

Conclusions

Matthews (2005) lists Bayes' theorem as one of the 25 big ideas of science. It is a way of turning evidence into insight and "is now being recognised as the most reliable way of making sense of evidence. From scientists, to jury members, to code-breakers, to consumers, everyone can benefit from its powers" (p. 86). This paper represents an attempt to enable tennis analysts to benefit from its powers. It is does so by transforming the answer to question what is the likelihood that if a point is won, it will have been preceded by a first service (the probability that if the theory is true, the data will be observed) to a more interesting and relevant question: if the first serve is good, what is the probability that the point will be won (the probability that if the data are observed, the theory will be true).

Empirical flesh was put on Bayes' theorem by studying the performance of the winners of the men's and singles titles at the 2019 French Open: Rafael Nadal and Ashleigh Barty. Whatever the prior likelihood that they would win a point on their service game, this had to be revised upward for both players if the data showed that their first serve was "good" and had to revised downward if the point required that they serve again. On the assumption that the prior probability was 60%, this then allows the analyst to deduce that the probabilities of winning a point on the first service were 65.9% for Barty and 73.8% for Nadal. Similarly, it could be deduced that the probabilities of winning a point on the second service were 34.1% for Barty and 26.2% for Nadal. The contribution of the paper lies in showing how in tennis evidence can be turned into insight for service games.

Notes

1 See *The Economist*, "In Praise of Bayes", 28 September 2000, https://www.economist.com/science-and-technology/2000/09/28/in-praise-of-bayes.
2 P in this term represents probability, and the symbol | denotes that the event following | has already occurred.
3 The updating factor is the ratio of the probability of observing the data when the theory is true, to that of observing the data regardless of whether the theory is true or false: $P(A) = P(A|T)P(T) + P(A|\bar{T})P(\bar{T})$, $\bar{T}$ being the event that the theory is false.
4 Infosys and Roland Garros Partner for Digital Innovation, Infosys Press Release 20 March 2019. https://www.infosys.com/newsroom/press-releases/Pages/digital-innovation-partner-roland-garros.aspx (accessed 25 June 2019).
5 Note that $\tilde{A}$ is the event that the FS was "bad" and, since double faults are excluded, it is the event that the SS was "good".
6 Nadal played a total of 1,179 points (697 won and 482 lost) over 985 minutes of play implying that the average point lasted 50 seconds. Barty, on the other hand, played 903 points (510 won and 393 lost) over 540 minutes of play implying that the average point lasted 39 seconds.

References

Aitken, C. (1996), "Lies, Damned Lies, and Expert Witnesses", *Mathematics Today*, **32**: 76–80.
Cross, R. and Pollard, G. (2009), "Grand Slam Men's Singles Tennis: Serve speeds and Other Related Data", *Coaching & Sport Science Review*, **16**: 8–10.

Cui, Y., Gomez, M.-A., Goncalves, B. and Sampaio, J. (2018), "Performance Profiles of Professional Female Tennis Players in Grand Slam Finals", *PLOS ONE*, **13**: 1–18.

Furlong, J. (1995), "The Service in Lawn Tennis: How Important Is It?", in T. Reilly, M. Hughes, and M. Lees (edited), *Science and Racket Sports*, London: Taylor & Francis, 266–71.

Hughes, M. and Clarke, S. (1995), "Surface Effect on Elite Tennis Strategy", in T. Reilly, M. Hughes, and M. Lees (edited), *Science and Racket Sports*, London: Taylor & Francis, 272–78.

Matthews, R. (2005), *25 Big Ideas: The Science That Is Changing the World*, Oxford: One World.

Moss, B. and O'Donoghue, P. (2015), "Momentum in US Open Men's Singles Tennis", *International Journal of Performance Analysis in Sport*, **15**: 884–96.

O'Donoghue, P. and Ballantyne, A. (2004), "The Impact of Speed of Service in Grand Slam Singles Tennis", in A. Lees, J. Kahn, and I. Maynard (edited), *Science and Racket Sports III*, London: Routledge, 179–84.

O'Donoghue, P. and Brown, E. (2008), "The Importance of Service in Grand Slam Singles Tennis", *International Journal of Performance Analysis in Sport*, **8**: 70–78.

O'Donoghue, P. and Brown, E. (2009), "Sequences of Service Points and the Misperception of Momentum in Elite Tennis", *International Journal of Performance Analysis in Sport*, **9**: 113–27.

O'Donoghue, P. and Ingram, B. (2001), "A Notational Analysis of Elite Tennis Strategy", *Journal of Sports Sciences*, **19**: 107–15.

Thompson, W.C. and Schumann, E.L. (1987), "Interpretation of Statistical Evidence in Criminal Trials: The Prosector's Fallacy and the Defense Attorney's Fallacy", *Law and Human Behavior*, **11**: 167–87.

Unierzyski, P. and Wieczorek (2004), "Comparison of Tactical Solutions and Game Patterns in the Finals of Two Grand Slam Tournaments", in A. Lees, J. Kahn, and I. Maynard (edited), *Science and Racket Sports III*, London: Routledge, 169–74.

Zackrisson, S., Andersson, I., Janzon, L., Manjer, J. and Garne, J.P. (2006), "Rate of Over-Diagnosis of Breast Cancer 15 Years after End of Malmo Mamographic Screening", *British Medical Journal*, **33**: 689–92.

Part 4
Heuristics, sports, behaviour and outcomes

11 Beauty, preferences and choice exemplified in the sports market

Hannah Josepha Rachel Altman, Morris Altman, Benno Torgler and Stephen Whyte

Introduction

Beauty has been used as a positive fast and frugal heuristic, and therefore as an important determinant of choice and reward, as highlighted in research by Hamermesh (2013).[1] Beauty is assumed to be a proxy for objective characteristics in a world of asymmetric and costly information. The argument is that beauty is used as a fast and frugal heuristic because it is a profitable endeavour. On average, this yields an income premium to "beautiful" people. In sports and the health and fitness industry, a correlate of beauty, sexiness, has been used to choose trainers or even to select the athletes expected to perform best (Wainwright 2018). Here too, it is assumed that beauty or sexiness is a proxy for objective characteristics that yield positive outcomes for the organization. Also, sexiness (for both men and women) is used as a signifier for marketability of the output produced or co-produced by the athlete. Fans follow sports due to aesthetic factors (Smith 1988).[2]

Additionally, in sports, we argue that beauty can be defined with regards to the ideal characteristics (anthropomorphic characteristics) of a prospect, which are expected to yield optimal productivity outcomes. A beautiful athlete, for example, would be a person who has certain physical characteristics which are expected to serve her or him well when competing, and this individual would be more likely to be selected or prepared to compete. This might be supplemented with psychological attributes.

A fast and frugal heuristic here would use these characteristics of beauty or sexiness to select our athletes, trainers, physiotherapists, coaches, etc. One theoretical narrative suggests that such a heuristic should generate superior outcomes to more nuanced, calculating and time-consuming decision-making tools, which are more in line with conventional neoclassical economics methodology (Gigerenzer 2007). But evidence suggests that the beauty heuristic often generates sub-optimal results with regards to performance, by excluding individuals who are better in terms of outcomes than the beauty heuristic (Altman and Altman 2015a, 2015b).

We argue that beauty or sexiness can be a good or bad heuristic depending on the objective relationship between beauty and what it proxies.

DOI: 10.4324/9781003080824-14

For example, when beauty is a proxy for the revenue-generating power of an athlete, related to consumer demand, this can be a valid proxy (good heuristic) given consumer preferences. Our discussion of the beauty heuristic in sports, we argue, helps to illustrate the conditions under which a heuristic yields optimal results. We argue that optimality is conditional on circumstance, and different circumstances require different types of heuristics (Kahneman 2003, 2011). In this contribution, we argue that – all too often – the beauty or sexiness heuristic yields sub-optimal results in terms of performance or productivity and/or quality of outcomes. Moreover, in this case, when athletes, trainers and others in sports-related organizations receive a beauty premium in terms of their income, but one not warranted by economic outcomes, this can represent a form of economic discrimination analogue to Becker's coefficient of discrimination; wherein women or Blacks receive a lower rate of pay than men or Whites – even though men or Whites are no more productive (Becker 1957). This is simply an outcome of whether male or White employers have a distaste for female or Black employees embedded in their preference function. Such a premium can undermine the economic sustainability of the organization.

There are two points that need to be addressed here. One relates to beauty or sexiness as a heuristic where the employer believes that the beautiful are more productive. The other specifically relates to the utility maximizing employers who are most concerned about less beautiful/sexy employees being penalized for not being beautiful or sexy, or the more beautiful and sexy employees being awarded simply on the basis of beauty and sexiness. This raises the question of how such sub-optimal decisions can persist over time, a topic we address in this chapter.

Finally, we show how beauty or sexiness as a sub-optimal heuristic (bad heuristic) can persist over time. The beauty heuristic need not be optimal to persist over time. Of particular importance is the market for sports team output (performance) or that of health and fitness outlets and how bad heuristics impact on the survival of these organizations. This builds upon an understanding of how sub-optimal or inefficient organizations can survive over time. It also relates to how understanding imperfect information can serve to protect a bad beauty heuristic from being identified as the cause of poor performance outcomes. There can be an expected trade-off for a rational utility maximizing employer between beauty and revenue, depending on the preferences of the employer and the competitiveness of the market. Beauty as a heuristic in the sports and health and fitness industries exemplifies how and why fast and frugal heuristics need not generate the best possible outcomes, even given bounded rationality.

Beauty and sexiness as a fast and frugal heuristic

The concept of fast and frugal heuristics was developed by Gerd Gigerenzer (2007, 2011) and his colleagues at the Center for Adaptive Behavior and Cognition (ABC) at the Max Planck Institute for Human Development in Berlin. The argument put forth is a simple one. Given bounded rationality (as developed by Simon 1955, 1979, 1987), it is inefficient to use the highly calculating, non-emotive and technical decision-making procedures thought be most effective by conventional economic theory. In the real world of bounded rationality, unlike in the neoclassical world, information is asymmetric and costly. One cannot project the outcomes of current decisions and related choices into the future, and individuals do not have the natural capability to process and understand the information that they do have access to. Therefore, it is more efficient to adopt decision-making shortcuts to engage in the decision-making process. Gigerenzer favours heuristics that are not only frugal, but also fast. He argues that such heuristics yield better (closer to optimal) outcomes than generated by conventional decision-making tools. They evolve from the experiences of decision-makers, based on effective decision-making tools given the decision-making environment. These heuristics are, therefore, deemed to be ecologically rational (Smith 2003, 2005).

One decision-making shortcut makes decisions based on the beauty or sexiness of a prospect, wherein beauty is a proxy for other desired characteristics. But one of the issues that we address is whether beauty as a heuristic in sports organizations – and, relatedly, health and fitness organizations – is a bad heuristic, despite the fact that using the beauty or sexiness heuristic is not only common practice amongst decision-makers in these organizations, but also fast and frugal.

The concept of procedural rationality, developed by Simon, allows us to model the extent to which a heuristic is optimal without adopting neoclassical behavioural norms as a benchmark for optimality. This point is discussed in some detail in this book's chapter "Sports Performance, Procedural Rationality and Organizational Inefficiency." Procedural rationality is a pragmatic approach to better understanding optimal decision-making in the real world. Simon (1986, p. S211) argues that

> ...if we accept the proposition that knowledge and the computational power of the decision maker are severely limited, then we must distinguish between the real world and the actor's perception of it and reasoning about it ... we must construct a theory (and test it empirically) of the processes of decision. Our theory must include not only the reasoning processes but also the processes that generate the actor's subjective representation of the decision problem, his or her frame ... The rational person of neoclassical economics always reaches the decision that is objectively, or substantively, best in terms of the given utility function. The rational person of cognitive psychology goes about making his or her decisions in a way that is procedurally reasonable in the light of the available knowledge and means of computation [it is context dependent].

Procedural rationality assumes that decision-makers or economic agents are smart in the context of bounded rationality (Altman 2017c). They have objectives or goals such as winning a game or championship or making more profit on the margin. Given these objectives, decision-makers attempt to realize these objectives within the decision-making environment and their decision-making capabilities. Decisions and choices must be made to achieve their end, and this will involve the use of heuristics or decision-making shortcuts. The decision-makers, it is assumed, will attempt to optimize in the context of bounded rationality. But these efforts might fail. We argue that this can be the consequence of adopting bad heuristics that the decision-makers believe to be optimal or best practice based on what other organizations or respected leaders have done in the past. One possible cause for individuals or organizations doing less well than they should is the unwitting adoption of bad decision-making heuristics. We argue that the beauty or sexiness heuristic is often a bad heuristic which can yield sub-optimal outcomes. It is important to identify the circumstances in which the beauty or sexy heuristic can be expected or predicted to generate sub-optimal results in sports organizations and why such heuristics would nevertheless be adopted.

Two components of the beauty or sexy heuristic and premium

One component of the beauty heuristic relates to the beauty or sexiness heuristic yielding a revenue premium. Individuals are willing to pay more because an athlete or sports physio, for example, is beautiful or sexy. This applies to both male and female employees. Having a beautiful athlete might attract more fans and more advertising income.[3] If a trainer is beautiful this would attract more clients, and these might even be willing to pay higher fees given that they are being serviced by a relatively beautiful individual, which yields them a higher level of utility. If employers believe that there is this type of beauty or sexiness premium paid by clients or fans, then employers will engage some athletes/employees who are beautiful or sexy. Beauty or sexiness becomes a heuristic here to identify revenue and, more importantly, profit enhancing employees. This assumes that the beautiful person is at least as qualified/productive/profit generating as the less beautiful individual. This can yield a premium being paid to such individuals. If this assumption proves to be false, then this beauty premium is not matched by a compensating premium in terms of revenue – marginal revenue will exceed marginal cost. If more is paid based on beauty or sexiness, but these individuals are relatively less productive, the beauty or sexiness premium must at least cover the relatively lower income generated by the lower level of productivity. When beauty or sexiness proves to be a bad heuristic, one must identify why it is adopted in the first place and how it might be sustainable over time.

The Russian ex-tennis star Anna Kournikova, for example, became one of the most photographed and highest paid sporting celebrities, listed in 2002 by a monthly British men's lifestyle magazine as the "Sexiest Woman in the World,"[4] despite failing to win a WTA title (Meier and Konjer 2015). Pfister (2015) uses the notion of "Kournikova syndrome" to reflect the resemblance to other stars and starlets in the entertainment business who generate income via self-marketing to capitalize on their looks and appearance.[5] Konjer et al. (2019) refer to "erotic capital," stressing that it might be more important for female athletes. Erotic capital[6] has been conceptualized as a fourth personal asset next to economic, cultural and social capital (Hakim 2010), becoming one of the factors that affect social positioning in modern societies (Konjer et al. 2019). The Kournikova syndrome suggests that erotic capital in high-performance sport can be translated into economic capital via attracting public attention, sponsors and advertisers (Mutz and Meier 2016).[7]

When beauty or sexiness is used as a selection criterion, with full knowledge that the employee will be less productive than the less beautiful or sexy alternative, such selection and the payment of the beauty premium can only be related to the additional utility that the employer garners from employing what he or she perceives as a beautiful or sexy employee. This should not be confused with a heuristic. It is not the same thing as using beauty or sexiness as a decision-making shortcut heuristic to identify more productive, revenue-generating employees. But it is analogous, as mentioned above, to Gary Becker's coefficient of discrimination wherein a racist or sexist employer will hire a man over a woman or a White person over a Black person – or will only hire women or Blacks at a lower rate of pay – because the employer experiences disutility from the employment of women or Blacks. The lower rate of pay compensates the employer for the disutility incurred. We discuss how this coefficient of discrimination or, relatedly, a beauty sexiness premium can persist over time.[8]

A second component relates to beauty or sexiness as a proxy for performance as an athlete, trainer, physio, etc. An important issue that needs to be addressed is whether there should be a positive causal relationship between beauty or sexiness and productivity. This is separate and apart from component one above, wherein beauty and sexiness are assumed to drive revenue growth independent of any productivity differential between beautiful and less beautiful employees. In this latter case there is simply a premium on beauty. For the purposes of component two, one has the beauty heuristic where beauty and sexiness is defined traditionally – referencing the beauty or sexiness of the individual – and employers use this heuristic as a proxy for productivity. This heuristic can be used simply as a screening device to screen in prospective more beautiful and sexy athletes, trainers and coaches. But if it is anticipated that the more beautiful or sexy employee will be more productive, yielding higher revenue, then in this instance the heuristic is productivity-based even though it can also generate a beauty premium. It is a premium on relatively higher productivity. However, when beauty and sexiness is a bad heuristic, there is no systematic relationship between beauty and sexiness and productivity. This raises the question of the extent to which this type of bad heuristic can persist over time – and perhaps more importantly – if it does persist, it is necessary to understand how this might affect the performance of other employees and of the organization.

We also introduce the concept of beauty or sexiness as referencing certain characteristics of an individual that are supposed to be indicative of that individual's current and near future productivity (referred to as anthropomorphic characteristics). This is not the "classic" beauty or sexiness referred to above. This type of heuristic is used to select athletes and employees in the health and fitness industry and has been subject to criticism, for example, in the *Moneyball* narrative (Lewis 2003). A bad or failed heuristic is one where the beauty heuristic, as defined above (anthropomorphic-related beauty), fails as a proxy for productivity. Here too, one has a bad heuristic since it results in the hiring of sub-optimal, relatively poor-performing employees (athletes and trainers, for example).

Sports inefficiency and the persistence of a bad beauty heuristic

In conventional economics, inefficiency (apart from allocative inefficiency), is assumed to be eliminated through market forces or through the hard-wired preferences of decision-makers to maximize profits. Therefore, there cannot be any big bills lying on the sidewalk, by assumption (Olson 1996). But if the beauty or sexiness heuristic is a bad heuristic and fails as a proxy for productivity or another measure of success, then it would contribute to the existence of inefficiency and there *would* be big bills lying on the sidewalk. Relatedly, a failed heuristic would result in a less successful sports organization, the selection of athletes that are not optimal in performance now or in the future, and trainers and other sports professionals whose services are sub-optimal (yielding sub-optimal outcomes). These are related to the existence of inefficiency. However, in behavioural economics modelling, especially evidence-based modelling pioneered by Herbert Simon, inefficiency is recognized as a very real possibility. Therefore, one must specify the circumstances wherein inefficiency is likely and where it was not. Some of these specifications are noted in this book's chapter "Sports Performance, Procedural Rationality and Organizational Inefficiency."

Simon (1979, 509) underlines the importance of the existence of inefficiency or sub-optimal performance for the modelling of decision-making and of the firm:

> The presence of something like organizational slack in a model of the business firm introduces complexity in the firm's behavior in the short run. Since the firm may operate very far from any optimum, the slack serves as a buffer between the environment and the firm's decisions. Responses to environmental events can no longer be predicted simply by analyzing the "requirements of the situation," but depend on the specific

decision processes that the firm employs. However well this characteristic of a business firm model corresponds to reality, it reduces the attractiveness of the model for many economists, who are reluctant to give up the process-independent predictions of classical theory, and who do not feel at home with the kind of empirical investigation that is required for disclosing actual real world decision processes. But there is another side to the matter. If, in the face of identical environmental conditions, different decision mechanisms can produce different firm behaviors, this sensitivity of outcomes to process can have important consequences for analysis at the level of markets and the economy. Political economy, whether descriptive or normative, cannot remain indifferent to this source of variability in response.

Once inefficiency can persist over time or in the long run, then bad heuristics and other forms of sub-optimal behaviours can persist in the long run. Simply the adoption of the beauty or sexiness heuristic cannot be taken as evidence that it is optimal. The latter is sometimes implied in the fast and frugal narrative (Altman 2017b; Gigerenzer 2007). This point is elaborated upon by Leibenstein (1966) in his X-efficiency theory of the firm. In the latter, organizational slack[9] persists (hence, inefficiency) because product markets are imperfect (a realistic assumption) and, therefore, inefficient firms or organizations are protected from market forces.[10] This protection is required because market force changes are very costly. Such firms supplement the protection afforded to them by market imperfections with the successful lobbying of government for support in the form of protection and subsidies. For Leibenstein, firms are sub-optimal because economic agents, especially management, are not working as hard or smart as they potentially could. In other words, economic agents are not maximizing their effort in the production process, as they would in the conventional economic model.[11] Moreover, effort is a variable in the production function. This argument can be extended to all economic agents within the firm (Altman 2006).

With respect to the use of bad or sub-optimal heuristics, sports organizations are not doing as well as they can because they are employing individuals based on perceived beauty and sexiness – and this results sub-optimal performance. A better heuristic would result in the employment of better performing individuals. This is not x-inefficiency in terms of sub-optimal effort inputs. Rather, bad heuristics results in a type of misallocation of labour resources in the economy through the employment of individuals who are not the best fit (sub-optimal) in terms of their performance, in both quantity and quality dimensions. Bad heuristics can, therefore, result in what would be traditionally referred to as lower productivity. Ceteris paribus, bad heuristics contribute to the making of inefficient organizations.

These inefficient organizations can persist in the long run if consumers, clients and fans are willing to pay higher prices for the output of the relatively inefficient organizations so that they can meet their costs and their target rate of return. In this way, organizations can earn acceptable levels of profits or rates of return even if they are inefficient (if they are performing suboptimally), in this case using bad heuristics to engage athletes or employees. Bad heuristics results in sub-optimal performance or lower levels of quality. This sub-optimal selection or promotion decision-making heuristic can also be compensated for by reducing costs in the organization. But this can be operationalized only if such cuts are not resulting in economic agents responding by becoming less productive. This would be expected, when effort is variable and employees retaliate by reducing the quality or quantity of their effort input (Akerlof 1982; Altman 2006; Leibenstein 1966).

The generalized model is of fundamental importance, as there can be multiple equilibria across less efficient-to-more efficient organizations (Altman 2017a). Both efficient and inefficient firms can earn an acceptable rate of return through appropriate changes in product price and input costs. There is no economic imperative towards some X-efficient optimum as would be the case in the conventional economic modelling (Altman 2006; Simon 1979). Bad heuristics can be sustainable both in the short and the long run. Of significance here is the importance of the willingness of consumers to a pay higher price for output and the ability to cut costs (without negatively impacting efficiency) when the beauty or sexiness heuristic is a bad or suboptimal heuristic.

Bad heuristics can also persist when the source of sub-optimal performance cannot easily be identified. This is particularly the case given costly and asymmetric information, which characterizes a boundedly rational decision-making environment. This decision-making environment can protect sub-optimal decision-making even if it comes at a cost to the sports organization's or individual athlete's performance. Such inefficient outcomes can drive a sports organization into bankruptcy, but this need not drive a change in decision-making heuristics, if bad or sub-optimal heuristics cannot be identified. But to reiterate, such an organization can survive if clients (or fans) are willing to pay for outputs of poorly performing or X-inefficient organizations. Some of these points are illustrated in Figure 11.1.

0a represents the target, competitive, acceptable rate of return to our sports organization. The rate of return is given by some measure surplus (total revenue minus total cost) divided by costs. Total revenue is affected by price. In the conventional model, applying the best or optimal decision-making heuristics yields the highest rate of return, ceteris paribus. In our case, this is given by *0a*. When this heuristic becomes increasingly sub-optimal, the rate of return diminishes as one hires individuals whose performance falls increasingly below the optimal level, in terms of quantity and quality. This is given by *ab*. This diminishing rate of return is given by lower productivity and by a drop in price for an inferior output/performance. This drop in the rate of return is a function of the beauty or sexiness heuristic not selecting the athletes and health and fitness professionals that are best. If the measure of the application of a bad heuristic is a measure of "badness" at *0c* with the gap

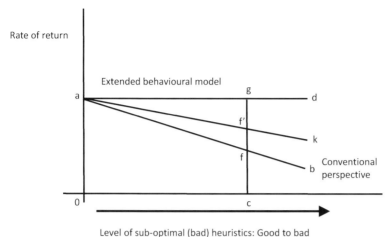

Figure 11.1 Bad and Good Heuristics and Multiple Equilibria.

between the target and the actual rate of return being *fg*, this gap can be filled by increasing price or by reducing costs sufficiently. Customers, clients and fans would have to be quite sensitive to a particular perception of beauty or sexiness if they were to pay a sufficiently higher price for sub-optimal output. Decreasing costs cannot be negated by negative productivity effects, which is what would be predicted by efficiency wage theory. When price increases and costs fall, this pivots our sub-optimal rate of return line from *ab* to *ak*.

Some implications of beauty and sexiness as a bad heuristic

In the selection of athletes in professional sports, beauty or sexiness is not a proxy for excellence in performance and can yield sub-optimal performance or x-inefficiency in sports performance. Given the real world of bounded rationality, this can result in an error in decision-making; based on a false mental model (Altman 2014) as to the relationship between beauty and performance. The latter can be reinforced by herding wherein a decision-maker, in a world of asymmetric and costly information, adopts a heuristic (even if it turns out to be a bad heuristic) because other decision-makers, especially respected and leading decision-makers, adopt this heuristic. If one assumes smart, boundedly rational individuals who seek towards optimizing on performance outcomes, then one would expect that errors in decision-making would be corrected once underperformance is recognized and the source of this underperformance is identified. But obstacles to correcting errors in decision-making would include confirmation, self-serving and sunk cost biases where the latter is related to the endowment effect, loss aversion and status quo biases. Failure to abandon a bad heuristic would then result in continued underperformance by the sports organization. This is not sustainable unless customers are willing to pay a sufficiently higher price for a sub-optimal sports output.

Proposition One: Our model suggests that a bad beauty heuristic is unlikely to persist in the long run within an organization and errors in decision-making are likely to be corrected in this domain.[12]

If the beauty or sexiness heuristic is used in the selection of sports professionals such as trainers, physiotherapists and exercise scientists and does not result in the selection of the most qualified professionals, it can generate sub-optimal outcomes that can even yield injuries to clients or customers with immediate negative consequences to the organization. *If the employers' preferences are oriented towards providing the best possible service* (whilst meeting profit targets), then the sub-optimal outcomes can be expected to generate a correction to the error in decision-making which, in this instance, would be a by-product of adopting the beauty or sexiness heuristic. Otherwise, the beautiful or sexy employees can damage the profitability of the employer organization. What becomes of critical importance is the ability of employers to identify the sources of harm caused by inadequately qualified individuals (Altman 2020). Beauty or sexiness is, for example, not a component of due qualification for health and fitness professionals.

Proposition Two: If the employer of a health and fitness organization has the *provision of quality service, whilst maintaining a target rate of return* as her or his objective, using the beauty or sexiness heuristic will cease once the decision-maker realizes that this heuristic yields sub-optimal results. Therefore, one can predict that this heuristic should not persist over time.

If beauty and sexiness is used as a heuristic by clients in the health and fitness industry for excellence in service provision, this can result in sub-optimal outcomes when this heuristic is unrelated to the provision of quality service. But in a world of asymmetric and costly information, clients may not be able to identify if their beautiful health and fitness professionals are the source of the receipt of sub-optimal services. In this case, rational substandard health and fitness professionals will continue to provide their services to rational clients and generate sub-optimal health and fitness outcomes (Altman 2020).

Proposition Three: A bad beauty or sexiness heuristic used by clients can persist over time in a world of bounded rationality unless objective, easily identifiable and respected standards/qualifications are required by health and fitness professionals (Altman 2020). If such requirements are in place, clients can identify beautiful or sexy health and fitness professionals who deliver sub-optimal services. In this instance, if the provision of high-quality services is the highest ranked preferred characteristic for the client, a beautiful or sexy health and fitness professional would only be chosen if she/he can be identified as providing high-quality services. Under these conditions, one would expect that the beauty or sexiness heuristic would no longer be used as a heuristic to identify providers of the highest quality service.

The self-employed in the health and fitness industry might use beauty and sexiness as a method of selling their services. This is not the same thing as beauty and sexiness as a decision-making heuristic. But beauty or sexiness might signal to some the quality of service where clients use the beauty heuristic, as in the above, to identify quality health and fitness professionals. This heuristic can work for the self-employed in a world of asymmetric and costly information where clients cannot easily identify sub-optimal service providers. We are assuming here that there are clients who prefer the services provided by those who they identify as beautiful or sexy, conditional upon their services being of high quality.

Proposition Four: The self-employed can be expected to use beauty and sexiness to sell their services even if these services are sub-optimal, unless there are easily objective, easily identifiable and respected standards/qualifications in place given bounded rationality.

Anthropometric characteristics (which we argue are similar to the beauty or sexy heuristic) as a heuristic for the athlete selection and to position athletes (in team sports) can persist in the long run, even if it is not an optimal heuristic on its own for identifying optimal potential performance, given bounded rationality. This is the case when, in a world of bounded rationality, it is difficult to identify superior heuristics and the inappropriate use of anthropometric characteristics (in a narrow and isolated manner), and may then be a cause for sub-optimal sports performance. This point is similar to that made regarding Proposition One above, and discussed in detail in this book's chapter "Moneyball and Decision-Making Heuristics: An Intersection of Statistics and Practical Expertise." As discussed above, with reference to Proposition One, once this heuristic is in place, decision-makers who favoured the use of this heuristic would be reluctant to change their preference for anthropometric characteristics as a core heuristic for athlete selection and positioning. Above we referenced the confirmation, self-serving and sunk cost biases, the endowment effect, loss aversion and status quo biases. However, one would expect that rational (smart, boundedly rational) decision-makers with a preference for optimizing sports performance would revise their decision-making heuristic when made aware of alternative heuristics. This amounts to improving their information set.

To the extent that anthropometric athlete selection and positioning yields sub-optimal results, this can be corrected for by providing decision-makers with alternative and superior heuristics. This requires a decision-making environment that is receptive to different approaches to athlete selection and positioning in the sports team. Improving decision-makers' information set is a necessary, but not sufficient condition for change to occur.

Proposition Five: Beauty or sexiness defined relative to anthropometric characteristics is assumed by many experts to be an optimal heuristic even if it is not. But this bad heuristic can persist when it cannot easily be identified as a cause of relatively poor performance.[13] Given this, the leaders' decision-making biases contribute to the persistence of such a bad, sub-optimal heuristic. Policy that identifies the flaws in this heuristic can contribute towards positioning anthropometric characteristics into a more effective decision-making framework.

In some instances, beauty or sexiness of athletes or health and fitness professionals can be expected to yield higher income for their employers. This would be a type of beauty premium referenced by Hamermesh (2013). But in this instance, we are referring to a beauty premium to the sports organization. The beauty premium modelling requires a ceteris paribus caveat wherein one is assuming that performance of the beautiful or sexy athlete, for example, is *no less* "productive" compared with her or his less beautiful or sexy counterpart. Put another way, one is assuming that the marginal product of the beautiful or sexy athlete is equal to that of the less beautiful or sexy athlete. In this case, a rational employer would hire beautiful or sexy athletes or health and fitness professionals up to the point that there is no marginal net benefit from so doing. Such hiring would not amount to discrimination in the sense that it is based on the predicted premium earned (and generated) by prospective beautiful or sexy athlete or employee. In this case, the beautiful or sexy prospect generates additional income to the organization. This could result in beautiful or sexy individuals dominating the sports market, which we know is not the case.

Proposition Six: If there is a market-based beauty or sexiness premium associated with being beautiful or sexy and one controls for productivity or performance outcomes, one would expect or predict that rational employers will engage the relatively more beautiful or sexy athletes or health and fitness professionals until the beauty or sexiness premium is dissipated. But the payment of this market-based premium becomes complex, given that it is difficult to disentangle the marginal revenue product contribution of each individual when productivity or performance is a function of the team. A beautiful or sexy individual might be generating the additional revenue only because she or he is part of a very productive team. If there is no such team, the productivity or performance level would fall, and it would be less likely that clients, customers or fans would pay a beauty premium in this instance.

Proposition Seven: One should not expect a beauty or sexiness premium to be paid on *economic grounds* if a beautiful or sexy athlete or health and fitness professional does not generate a premium in terms of marginal revenue product.

Non-economic aspects of a beauty or sexy premium: a matter preferences

It is important to differentiate sports based on the individual athlete, such as tennis or golf, from team sports such as rugby, football (soccer), hockey and baseball. With the former, it is easier (low cost) to identify whether and the extent to which an individual earns a beauty and sexiness premium. However, it is also important not to confuse correlation with causation. A beautiful or sexy athlete or employee might generate a relatively high marginal revenue product. This might be because of their superior performance, not their beauty or sexiness. Hence, it is critically important to control for productivity or performance differences between beautiful and sexy and relatively less beautiful and sexy athletes and health and fitness professionals. Customers, clients or fans might be paying not for beauty or sexiness, but rather for the quality of the output, be it an outstanding team performance or an outstanding service from a health and fitness professional. As discussed above, when discussing the economic viability of a beauty or sexiness premium it is critically important to control for the productivity of the economic agent.

Proposition Eight: What might appear to be a beauty or sexiness premium might actually be payment for superior performance or service. It is, therefore, important to control for productivity when determining if what appears to be a premium for beauty or sexiness is truly a reward for superior performance.

There are other aspects of the beauty or sexiness premium that are unrelated to the productivity or performance of the athlete or the health and fitness professional. One relates to customers of health and fitness professionals who are willing to pay a higher price for the services provided by beautiful health and fitness professionals even if the service provided is of relatively low quality. The other aspect relates to employers willing to pay a higher price or premium for poorer performing athletes simply because they are regarded as beautiful or sexy. In both above cases, the marginal revenue product is below the marginal cost. From a narrow economics perspective this would be irrational since one is paying more than one should, based on fundamental economic criteria. The provision of this type of beauty or sexiness premium begs the question, discussed above, about the economic sustainability of the payment of such a premium when it is known to be economically inefficient.

The payment of a sub-optimal (from an economics point of view) beauty or sexiness premium can be modelled similarly to Gary Becker's modelling of his coefficient of discrimination; i.e., there is nothing irrational here. In our case, one simply has decision-makers whose utility is maximized by hiring beautiful or sexy people at a premium or paying health professionals at a premium even *when it is known* that their performance is sub-optimal. But how can paying individuals a non-productivity-based premium be consistent with the survival of an organization? As we discussed above, an organization can survive on the market if customers, clients or fans are willing to pay more (consistent with covering the premium) to maximize their utility where their preferences incorporate an "eye" for beauty and sexiness. There would be an anticipated trade-off of more beauty or sexiness for poorer performance, but the strength of such a preference needs to be tested empirically.

With respect to the health and fitness industry, for example, clients would be willing to pay more for the prospect of being served by a beautiful or sexy (female or male) health and fitness professional – and risk injury. There is no evidence that this is the case, but it is a question worthy of further empirical investigation. It is more likely that one has highly skilled beautiful or sexy professionals who receive a beauty or sexiness premium (e.g. via a selection effect). But here, as discussed above, one is not sacrificing on the quality of service. Related to this point, there is no widespread evidence that individuals are willing to pay a premium to a beautiful or sexy professional who is less skilled than a less beautiful and sexy professional. But the point we are making here is that if a client has a preference for beauty or sexiness one can expect a beauty premium to be paid, controlling for quality of service. This is part and parcel of the client's utility maximizing exercise. Once again, what is critically important is that a person might be willing to pay more for beauty or sexiness, if quality is not being sacrificed (too much) and therefore is good enough (satisfied with the quality). Beauty or sexiness here is, basically, an additional desired characteristic of a service being paid for (Becker and Murphy 1993).

Proposition Nine: A beauty or sexiness premium can be paid without any relationship productivity or revenue generation, based on the utility function or preferences of the employer, client or customer. However, the sustainability of this approach very much depends on the extent to which the payer is willing to self-sacrifice to achieve this end or the extent to which such a beauty premium can be subsidized by others.

One way to subsidize a beauty or sexiness premium is to underpay the less beautiful and sexy athletes and health and fitness professionals. If one assumes that effort input is fixed, this type of scenario is possible only if the lower paid but equally productive are unable to relocate to other firms who are willing to pay these individuals at a rate higher than they were paid in the firm that de facto discriminates by paying them below their marginal revenue product to subsidize the less productive but relatively more beautiful or sexy individuals. As in the Becker model, discrimination would result in a movement of the underpaid economic agents to higher paying positions, at least in the longer run, undermining the subsidies to the more highly paid beautiful or sexy athletes and health and fitness professionals. This requires the existence of an adequate supply of non-discriminatory employers.

Another point to note here is that given the existence of effort discretion – a reasonable real-world assumption – if the relatively less beautiful or sexy people are paid less than their more beautiful or sexy counterparts, this utility maximizing act of discrimination can result in the discriminated parties reducing their effort input to their organization (Altman 1995). This is an efficiency wage effect. This response reduces the performance of the sports organization as the discriminated individuals retaliate against the discriminators. This type of "fairness"-based behaviour is elaborated upon by Akerlof (1982). But once this occurs, the beauty or sexiness premium is no longer subsidized by the equally productive (but less beautiful or sexy) members of the sports organization. Discrimination here can only persist with customers, fans and clients willing to pay more for the product or service. But even with such customer support, if this type of discriminatory behaviour results in upsetting the performance of other members of the sports organization and, therefore, of the quality of service or performance provided, it is unlikely that the beauty or sexiness premium will be sustainable.

As discussed above, in this scenario, customers must be willing to pay for an increasingly substandard product for discriminating firms to survive. This could be especially harmful to clients in the health and fitness industry where injuries are more likely to occur (Altman 2020). At the same time, the market would be supplying a higher quality product at a lower price due to non-discriminating sports organizations, where no beauty or sexiness premium exists.

Proposition Ten: If the beauty or sexiness premium is subsidized by paying the less beautiful or sexy firm members at below their marginal revenue product, the expected efficiency wage effect related to being treated unfairly will undermine this type of subsidy.

Conclusion

We examine the hypothesis that beauty or sexiness can be used as an efficient fast and frugal heuristic in selecting the most potentially productive members of a sports organization and for clients to select best-practice health and fitness professionals. We also examine this hypothesis with respect to beauty as defined in relation to andromorphic characteristics of prospective members of a sports organization. We argue that much depends upon the revenue-generating potential of such individuals. And, to the extent that this is an inefficient or bad heuristic, this will damage the organization that employs her or him, or the clients that contract the services of such an individual. This heuristic is sustainable to the extent that individuals cannot, at low cost, identify the objective performance of the relatively beautiful or sexy individuals. In a world of imperfect and asymmetric information this requires policy that better identifies the objective potential and performance prospective and actual members of a sports organization.

The beauty premium (Hamermesh 2013) is related to the beauty or sexiness heuristic and has become a well-researched topic in economics. The payment of such a premium implies that in many instances beauty – and, one can extend this to sexiness – may yield a higher rate of pay to an employee or an economic agent within an organization. In this chapter, we explore this hypothesis from a theoretical and behavioural economics perspective, with regards to athletes, health and fitness professionals and sports organizations. We bring to this analytical narrative a discussion of the conditions under which a beauty or sexiness premium can persist over time. We also introduce bounded rationality, efficiency wage and X-efficiency to enrich the latter discussion and to better understand how a beauty or sexiness coefficient that is perceived to be discriminatory or unfair can negatively affect the quality and level of individual and organization performance. We also exploit

Becker's theory of discrimination to better understand the beauty or sexiness premium as a function of the preferences of employers, clients, customers and fans, and how this impacts the persistence and possible demise of this premium.

We argue that the beauty or sexiness premium is most likely to persist when it is consistent with the economic viability of a sports organization. At an individual level, this premium's longevity is causally linked with a client's willingness to pay. In both cases, the quality of output produced by the relatively beautiful or sexy individuals is of critical importance. Persistence is enhanced – even when output is sub-optimal – when employers, clients, customers and fans cannot easily make causal links between such sub-optimal performance and the beautiful or sexy individuals who are being paid a beauty or sexiness premium. This identity problem is most likely given bounded rationality and various decision-making "biases" identified in this chapter, such as confirmation and status quo biases.

We argue that to isolate the importance of the beauty or sexiness premium, it is essential to control for productivity, quality and the level of performance. It is unlikely that the typical employer, client, customer or fan will pay a beauty or sexiness premium when output is known to be sub-optimal. In other words, one would expect a beauty or sexiness premium to be paid by individuals with a particular set of preferences as long as they are not sacrificing optimality of performance. To avoid situations where the beauty or sexiness premium is being paid under false pretences (sub-optimal performance) it is important for policy to be designed and implemented to provide quality and trustworthy information to employers, customers, clients and fans on the level and quality of performance generated by the perceived relatively beautiful and sexy members of sports organizations. This would also increase the probability that the beauty or sexiness heuristic will not be applied when it is objectively sub-optimal.

Finally, the beauty and sexiness premium results in relative underpayment of those members of the sports organization who are perceived less beautiful and sexy. This is a form of Beckerian discrimination. We argue that when this form of differential payments is perceived to be unfair, the expected result is reduced productivity in both its quality and quantity dimension, damaging the competitiveness of the pertinent sports organization. The beauty and sexiness premium as a form of discriminatory and unfair treatment of members of a sports organization creates an incentive environment wherein this type of premium becomes increasingly unsustainable.

To reiterate, the beauty and sexiness premium is most sustainable when those in receipt of such a premium are generating the revenue sufficient to sustain this premium whilst performing optimally or at least as well as other members of the sports organization. In this manner, the premium is being subsidized through the income sacrificed by individuals whose utility is increased by viewing or engaging the services of those they perceive to be relatively more beautiful or sexy.

Notes

1 See also Dion, Berscheid, and Walster (1972); Eagly et al. (1991); Etcoff (1999); Kanazawa and Still (2018); Langlois et al. (2000); Li, Zhang, and Laroche (2019); Meier and Konjer (2015); Rosenblatt (2008); Ryall (2016); Stephan and Langlois (1984); Lorenzo et al. (2010); Stoll, VanMullem, Ballestero and Brown (2017); and Varian (2006). In sports, Hoegele, Schmidt and Torgler (2016) find that beauty has an influence on how fans perceive football players (assigning higher scores to personality, behaviour and skills to more attractive players). In academia, social scientists benefit from a beauty premium in the speaking fee market whilst natural scientists gain from unattractiveness (Bi, Chan and Torgler 2020).

2 This can also have negative side effects. In aesthetic sports such as figure-skating or gymnastics, eating disorders are more commonly observed amongst athletes (Krentz and Warschburger 2011); for example, Nelson (2009) explores beauty amongst female athletes. She stresses that in figure-skating,

> [a]thletes in sequins and 'sheer illusion sleeves' glide and dance, their tiny skirts flapping in the breeze. They achieve, but without touching or pushing anyone else. They win, but without visible signs of sweat. They compete, but not directly. Their success is measured not by conformation with an opponent, nor even by a clock or a scoreboard. Rather, they are judged as beauty contestants are judged: by a panel of people who interpret the success of the routines. Prettiness is mandatory. Petite and groomed and gracious, figure skaters – like cheerleaders, gymnasts, and aerobic dancers – camouflage their competitiveness with niceness and prettiness until it no longer seems male or aggressive or unseemly.
> (p. 529)

She emphasizes that in the 1990s, figure-skating was the most televised women's sport:

> in 1995 revenue from skating shows and competitions topped six hundred million dollars. In the seven months between October 1996 and March 1997, ABC, CBS, NBC, Fox, ESPN, TBS, and USA dedicated 162.5 hours of programming to figure skating, half of it in prime time. Kerrigan earns up to three hundred thousand dollars for a single performance.
> (p. 529)

3 The role fans play in sports is well articulated by Simons (2013).
4 FHM's 100 Sexiest Women (UK) – Wikipedia.
5 As other examples, she mentions the gymnast Magadalena Brzeska or the boxer Regina Halmich.
6 For a discussion on the erotic in sports, see Guttmann (1997).
7 Evidence indicates that both attractiveness and athletes' expertise are positively related to endorsement-event fitness or appropriateness (Cunningham et al. 2008; Fink et al. 2004). On the other hand, Meier and Konjer (2015) report evidence that does not support the idea that attractiveness compensates for lower sporting expertise (looking at German TV ratings for tennis games).
8 Mobius and Rosenblat's (2006) lab experiment looking at the labour market identified a sizable beauty premium that is affected by the available information, showing that controlling for confidence, physically attractive workers are wrongly considered more able by employers despite punishing employers in case of mis-predicting the employees' performances (lower earnings).
9 However, organizational slack can act as a buffer when the environment becomes less favourable (Cyert and March 1992). Tan and Peng (2003) in an empirical study undertaking in China find an inverse U-shaped relationship between slack and performance.

10 Leibenstein (1966) refers to x-inefficiency as being less productive than is practically possible given existing traditional factor inputs, holding technology constant. Maximizing productivity given traditional factor inputs yields X-efficiency in production.
11 Here, it is assumed that effort inputs are fixed at some maximum.
12 A bad beauty heuristic may survive in specific niches as long as organizations are not challenged by a competitor. As Herbert (1997) points out, "survival only requires meeting the competition. In a system in which there are innumerable rents, of long-term and short-term duration, even egregious sub-optimality may permit survival" (p. 283). However, learning from sub-optimal past decisions means that we adapt and revise our heuristics in response to negative feedback (Lo 2019). Organizations therefore learn from unfolding of events around them (Simon 1996).
13 There are also endogenous elements. Better-looking athletes may get more attention from their support staff. If trainers expect better-looking athletes to outperform others, they will devote more attention to them (kernel-of-truth hypothesis; see Eagly et al. 1991).

References

Akerlof, George (1970). "The Market for Lemons: Quality Uncertainty and the Market Mechanism," *Quarterly Journal of Economics*, 84: 488–500.

Akerlof, George A. (1982). "Labor Contracts as Partial Gift Exchange," *Quarterly Journal of Economics*, 97: 543–569.

Akerlof, George A., and Rachel E. Kranton (2010). *Identity Economics: How Our Identities Shape Our Work, Wages, and Well-Being*. Princeton, NJ: Princeton University Press.

Alter, Adam (2013). "Does Beauty Drive Economic Success?" *The New Yorker*. Accessed at: https://www.newyorker.com/business/currency/does-beauty-drive-economic-success.

Altman, Hannah (2020). *The Behavioural Economics of Organisational Inefficiency: The Example of the New Zealand Fitness Industry*. Master of Philosophy Thesis, Queensland University of Technology. Brisbane: Australia.

Altman, Hannah, and Morris Altman (2015a). "Sport Economics and Performance Inefficiencies," in Morris Altman (ed.) *Real World Decision Making: An Encyclopedia of Behavioral Economics*. New York: Praeger, ABC-CLIO: 410–412.

Altman, Hannah, and Morris Altman (2015b). "Sports Economics and Economic Psychology," in Morris Altman (ed.) *Real World Decision Making: An Encyclopedia of Behavioral Economics*. New York: Praeger, ABC-CLIO: 412–415.

Altman, Morris (1995). "Labor Market Discrimination, Pay Inequality, and Effort Variability: An Alternative to the Neoclassical Model," *Eastern Economic Journal*, 21: 157–169.

Altman, Morris (2006). "What a Difference an Assumption Makes: Effort Discretion, Economic Theory, and Public Policy," in Morris Altman, ed., *Handbook of Contemporary Behavioral Economics: Foundations and Developments*. Armonk, New York: 125–164.

Altman, Morris (2014). "Mental Models, Bargaining Power, and Institutional Change," World Interdisciplinary Network for Institutional Research, Old Royal Naval College, Greenwich University. London, UK, September 11–14.

Altman, Morris (2017a). "Policy Consequences of Multiple Equilibria and the Indeterminacy of Economic Outcomes in a Boundedly Rational World: Closing the System with Non-Economic Variables," *Forum for Social Economics*, 64: 234–251.
Altman, Morris (2017b). "A Bounded Rationality Assessment of the New Behavioral Economics," in Roger Frantz, Shu-Heng Chen, Kurt Dopfer, Floris Heukelom, and Shabnam Mousavi (eds.) *Routledge Handbook of Behavioral Economics*. London and New York Routledge: 179–193.
Altman, Morris, ed. (2017c). *Handbook of Behavioural Economics and Smart Decision-Making: Rational Decision-Making within the Bounds of Reason*. Cheltenham, UK: Edward Elgar.
Becker, Gary S., and Kevin M. Murphy (1993). "A Simple Theory of Advertising as a Good or Bad," *Quarterly Journal of Economics*, 108: 941–964.
Becker, Gary S. (1957). *Economics of Discrimination*. Chicago: University of Chicago Press.
Becker, Gary S. (1996). *Accounting for Tastes*. Cambridge and London: Harvard University Press.
Bi, Weilong, Ho Fai Chan, and Benno Torgler (2020). "'Beauty' Premium for Social Scientists but 'Unattractiveness' Premium for Natural Scientists in the Public Speaking Market," *Humanities and Social Sciences Communications*, 7: 1–9.
Cunningham, George B., Janet S. Fink, and Linda Jean Kenix (2008). "Choosing an Endorser for a Women's Sporting Event: The Interaction of Attractiveness and Expertise," *Sex Roles*, 58: 371–378.
Cyert, Richard M., and James G. March (1992). *A Behavioral Theory of the Firm*. Oxford: Blackwell Publishers Inc.
Dion, Karen, Ellen Berscheid, and Elaine Walster (1972). "What Is Beautiful Is Good," *Journal of Personality and Social Psychology*, 24: 285–290.
Eagly, Alice H., Richard D. Ashmore, Mona G. Makhijani, and Laura C. Longo (1991). "What Is Beautiful Is Good, but…: A Meta-analytic Review of Research on the Physical Attractiveness Stereotype," *Psychological Bulletin*, 110: 109–128.
Etcoff, Nancy (1999). *Survival of the Prettiest: The Science of Beauty*. New York: Anchor Books/Doubleday.
Fink, Janet S., George B. Cunningham, and Linda Jean Kensicki (2004). "Using Athletes as Endorsers to Sell Women's Sport: Attractiveness vs. Expertise," *Journal of Sport Management*, 18: 350–367.
Gigerenzer, Gerd (2007). *Gut Feelings: The Intelligence of the Unconscious*. New York: Viking.
Gigerenzer, Gerd (2011). "The Recognition Heuristic: A Decade of Research," *Judgment and Decision Making*, 6: 100–121.
Guttmann, Allen (1997). *The Erotic in Sports*. New York: Columbia University Press.
Hakim, Catherine (2010). "Erotic Capital," *European Sociological Review*, 26: 499–518.
Hamermesh, Daniel S. (2013). *Beauty Pays: Why Attractive People Are More Successful*. Princeton, NJ: Princeton University Press.
Hoegele, Daniel, Sascha L. Schmidt, and Benno Torgler (2016). "The Importance of Key Celebrity Characteristics for Customer Segmentation by Age and Gender: Does Beauty Matter in Professional Football?" *Review of Managerial Science*, 10: 601–627.
Kahneman, Daniel (2003). "Maps of Bounded Rationality: Psychology for Behavioral Economics," *American Economic Review*, 93: 1449–1475.

Kahneman, Daniel (2011). *Thinking, Fast and Slow.* New York: Farrar, Straus and Giroux.

Kanazawa, Satoshi, and Mary C. Still (2018). "Is there Really a Beauty Premium or an Ugliness Penalty on Earnings?" *Journal of Business and Psychology,* 33: 249–262.

Krentz, Eva M., and Petra Warschburger (2011). "Sports-Related Correlates of Disordered Eating in Aesthetic Sports," *Psychology of Sport and Exercise,* 12: 375–382.

Langlois, Judith H. et al. (2000). "Maxims or Myths of Beauty? A Meta-analytic and Theoretical Review," *Psychological Bulletin,* 126: 390–423.

Leibenstein, Harvey (1966). "Allocative Efficiency vs. X-efficiency," *American Economic Review,* 56: 392–415.

Lewis, M. (2003). *Moneyball: The Art of Winning an Unfair Game.* New York: W.W. Norton.

Li, Yaoqi, Chun Zhang, and Michel Laroche (2019), "Is Beauty a Premium? A Study of the Physical Attractiveness Effect in Service Encounters," *Journal of Retailing and Consumer Services,* 50: 215–225.

Lo, Andrew W. (2019). *Adaptive Markets: Financial Evolution at the Speed of Thought.* Princeton: Princeton University Press.

Lorenzo, Genevieve L., Jeremy C. Biesanz, and Lauren J. Human (2010). "What Is Beautiful Is Good and More Accurately Understood: Physical Attractiveness and Accuracy in First Impressions of Personality," *Psychological Science,* 21: 1777–1782.

March, James G. (1978). "Bounded Rationality, Ambiguity, and the Engineering of Choice," *Bell Journal of Economics,* 9: 587–608.

Meier, Henk Erik, and Mara Konjer (2015). "Is there a Premium for Beauty in Sport Consumption? Evidence from German TV Ratings for Tennis Matches," *European Journal for Sport and Society,* 12: 309–340.

Mobius, Markus M., and Tanya S. Rosenblat (2006). "Why Beauty Matters," *American Economic Review,* 96: 222–235.

Mutz, Michael, and Henk Erik Meier (2016). "Successful, Sexy, Popular: Athletic Performance and Physical Attractiveness as Determinants of Public Interest in Male and Female Soccer Players," *International Review for the Sociology of Sport,* 51: 567–580.

Nelson, Mariah Burton (2009). "I Won. I'm Sorry," in Sonia Maasik and Jack Solomon (eds.) *Signs of Life in the U.S.A.* Boston: Bedford/St. Martin's: 569–579.

Olson, Mancur (1996). "Distinguished Lecture on Economics in Government: Big Bills Left on the Sidewalk: Why Some Nations Are Rich, and Others Poor," *Journal of Economic Perspectives,* 10: 3–24.

Rosenblat, Tanya (2008). "The Beauty Premium: Physical Attractiveness and Gender in Dictator Games," *Negotiation Journal,* 24: 465–481.

Ryall, Emily (2016). "Sport Is Not Just about Athleticism: Beauty Matters Too," *Aeon.* Accessed at: https://aeon.co/ideas/sport-is-not-just-about-athleticism-beauty-matters-too.

Simons, Eric (2013). *The Secret Lives of Sports Fans: The Science of Sport Obsession.* London: Overlook Ducklook.

Simon, Herbert A. (1955). "A Behavioral Model of Rational Choice," *Quarterly Journal of Economics,* 69: 99–118.

Simon, Herbert A. (1979). "Rational Decision Making in Business Organizations," *American Economic Review,* 69: 493–513.

Simon, Herbert A. (1986). "Rationality in Psychology and Economics," *Journal of Business,* 59: S209–S224.

Simon, Herbert A. (1987). "Behavioral Economics," in John Eatwell, Murray Milgate, and Peter Newman (eds.) *The New Palgrave: A Dictionary of Economics.* London: Macmillan, 221–225.

Simon, Herbert A. (1996). *The Science of the Artificial.* Cambridge: MIT Press.

Simon, Herbert A. (1997). *Models of Bounded Rationality*, Vol. 3. Cambridge: MIT Press.

Smith, Garry J. (1988). "The Noble Sports Fan," *Journal of Sport and Social Issues*, 12: 54–65.

Smith, Vernon L. (2003). "Constructivist and Ecological Rationality in Economics," *American Economic Review*, 93: 465–508.

Smith, Vernon L. (2005). "Behavioral Economics Research and the Foundations of Economics," *Journal of Socio-Economics*, 34: 135–150.

Stephan, Cookie W., and Judith H. Langlois (1984). "Baby Beautiful: Adult Attributions of Infant Competence as a Function of Infant Attractiveness," *Child Development*, 55: 576–585.

Stoll, Sharon K., Heather VanMullem, Nicole Ballestero, and Lisa Brown (2017). "Beauty and the Beast: Perception of Beauty for the Female Athlete," in Lisa Brown and Martha Peaslee Levine (eds.) *Beauty and the Beast: Perception of Beauty for the Female Athlete.* intechopen.com, 159–171.

Tan, Justin, and Mike W. Peng (2003). "Organizational Slack and Firm Performance during Economic Transitions: Two Studies from an Emerging Economy," *Strategic Management Journal*, 24: 1249–1263.

Varian, Hal. R. (2006). "The Beauty Premium: Why Good Looks Pay," *New York Times.* Accessed January 22, 2021, Available at: https://www.nytimes.com/2006/04/06/business/worldbusiness/06iht-beauty.html.

Wainwright, Giselle (2018). "Meet the Personal Trainers Who Sleep with Their Clients," *Cosmopolitan.* Accessed March 1, 2021. Available at: https://www.cosmopolitan.com/uk/body/fitness-workouts/a15913399/personal-trainers-who-sleep-with-clients/.

12 Moneyball and decision-making heuristics

An intersection of statistics and practical expertise

Hannah Josepha Rachel Altman and Morris Altman

Introduction

This chapter is motivated by a critically important and practical decision-making issue raised in the book and movie *Moneyball* (Lewis 2003). These narratives relate to how a baseball manager, Billy Beane of the Oakland A's, adopts a particular heuristic, the use of statistics, to determine which players he'll draft as well as where he'll position these players in the roster. Ultimately, this heuristic helps to inform the manager how best to organize the team so as to maximize their probability of winning. *Moneyball* demonstrates how statistics and sports statisticians can be core to a particular team's success and highlights how, in many cases, statistics can serve as a substitute for the 'instinct' embedded in scouts, managers, or coaches. Certainly, as a narrative, it makes the case that the sports statisticians should overrule the old-fashioned expert.

Counterpose this message to the one advanced in another film, *Trouble with the Curve* (Scott 2012). In this story, Gus Lobel with his experienced baseball scout's wisdom (accumulated human capital), and his instinct honed over many years in the game, generates superior results for the Atlanta Braves to those produced by young university diploma stats gurus. Is there a common theme in both these stories? Both narratives highlight the use of important decision-making heuristics (shortcuts) and stand in opposition to other more time-intensive decision-making tools (Gigerenzer 2007; Gladwell 2005; Kahneman 2011).

We argue that that decision-making in sports teams benefits from using both heuristic approaches, statistics, and the accumulated knowledge and related intuition embedded in scouts, managers, and coaches. But achieving best outcomes requires that decision-makers not take a strictly binary approach to any heuristic. As Nobel Laureate Herbert Simon (1977, 1979, 1997) articulates in a narrative on bounded rationality, data and computational and computer-facilitated data analytics can be a vital compliment to the decision-making process adopted by a sport team's decision-makers, but not a substitute. Moreover, it is a myth that decision-makers in the past did not make use of data. Today, however, we have access to much more sophisticated, nuanced, and powerful software, machines, and data to enhance the

DOI: 10.4324/9781003080824-15

decision-making process, and this can make it more efficient and effective. The theme expounded in *Moneyball*, in and of itself, is not the panacea for optimal decision-making in sports.

We make the case that the quality of decision-making in sport teams that impacts outcomes is heavily dependent on the nature of the decision-making heuristics adopted by team decision-makers. Only optimal heuristics generate optimal results, but optimality, we point out, is not inevitable in either the short or long run. Indeed, according to Simon (1977, 1978, 1987), optimality in any decision space is largely unobtainable in real-world decision-making environments given the existing mismatch between the complex decision-making environment agents operate within and the limited decision-making capabilities of decision-makers. These two variables constitute what Simon refers to as bounded rationality, and decisions are bounded and affected by the limits created by existing environmental and capability factors. In conventional economic approaches, such bounds are largely assumed away unlike with bounded rationality where the competitive environment within which decision-makers and their organizations are embedded becomes important. Decision-makers make the best possible choices given their preferences and the constraints they face in these environments (Altman 2017b; Gigerenzer 2007). Most importantly, these preferences, given the reality of constraints, need not be focused on optimal outcomes.

Simon (1987) refers to the best possible outcomes that result from constrained circumstances as satisficing behaviour. Compare this to the more conventional economic approach which stresses optimal or best possible outcomes that necessarily emanate from choice behaviour. A key critical consideration in this chapter, therefore, will be to explore what factors help decision-makers improve on their satisficing decisions when their focus is on sports teams and their outcomes. This is particularly important given that sports teams are not by definition, and invariably by dint of market forces, optimal in terms of their performance.

Given a bounded rational decision-making environment, we model conditions under which sport team-related decisions can be improved on (improve outcomes) with respect to the intersection of intuition or experience and statistics or data analytics-based heuristics (referred to as sabermetrics). We assume a type of optimality frontier that is achievable, but not yet realized, given a particular set and combination of heuristics already in place. The optimality frontier is affected by technological change in the decision-making space, such as with the development of calculators, computers, statistical packages, and video hardware and software. This, therefore, speaks to the potential use and application of statistics to sports decision-making. But approaching the optimality frontier is a function of the skill sets (and related experience and the quality of experience—quantity and quality of human capital formation) embedded in decision-makers, such as managers, coaches, and trainers, as well as sports statisticians. Approaching the frontier is also a function of how organizations are managed. From our perspective in this chapter, it becomes important to separate movements in the optimality frontier, movements to or away from the frontier and the determinants thereof.

We make the case that best-practice satisficing behaviour, one which allows organizations to approach optimality given bounded rationality, is best achieved by using a combination of heuristic devices, taking advantage of sport statistics and sports statisticians as well as the experience and related intuition of informed decision-makers. Ideally, each different type of expert is informed by the other. Managers, coaches, and trainers, who are or should be the ultimate decision-makers, should be informed by sports statistics and sport statisticians. But this requires that they understand the statistics and the statistical analysis at hand. On the other hand, the quality of sports statistical analysis must be informed by the knowledge of the sport for which the statistical analysis is rooted in. Otherwise, the sports statistician is apt to generate results that will yield errors in decision-making. But even if the statistical analysis is done well, we argue that sports statistics are not a substitute for the experience/intuition heuristic. Rather, they are a compliment that, when appropriately adopted into the decision-making process, can facilitate improved outcomes for sports organizations.

Sub-optimal performance and economic inefficiency

Conventional economics, by assuming that organizations are efficient, tends to pay little attention to how decision-making actually takes place inside of the organization. Decisions are assumed to be made in a manner consistent with optimizing the organization's (such as a sport team's) outcomes. This behaviour is assumed to be either a product of innate, hard-wired, 'neoclassical' rational behaviour or by dint of highly competitive market forces (Alchain 1950; Altman 1999; Friedman 1953). A fundamental assumption in behavioural economics is that market inefficiencies are pervasive and, therefore, decision-makers, economic agents, can capture economic gains by locating these inefficiencies (Altman 1996, 2005; Leibenstein 1966; Shiller 2000; Simon 1987). In addition, these pervasive inefficiencies are consistent with rational or smart behaviour by economic agents. These inefficiencies are not of the sort related to price distortions (which generate deadweight losses). They are related to firm's performing sub-optimally given relative prices. Leibenstein (1966) refers to this type of inefficiency as x-inefficiency, specifically organizational x-inefficiency. The assumption of pervasive inefficiencies in sports teams is a critical one in both *Moneyball* and *Trouble with the Curve* with their focus on baseball, but it is generalizable to other sports organizations.

A basic assumption of many behavioural economists is that markets are typically not competitive, at least not competitive enough, to force optimal behaviour across organizations. Therefore, relatively inefficient organizations can exist and persist over time. Moreover, inefficient organizations can be protected through government support such as subsidies and tax breaks and by protection from global or even regional competition.

Simon argues (1986, p. 223):

> In the biological world at least, many organisms survive that are not maximizers but that operate at far less than the highest achievable efficiency. Their survival is not threatened as long as no other organisms have evolved that can challenge the possession of their specific niches. Analogously, since there is no reason to suppose that every business firm is challenged by an optimally efficient competitor, survival only requires meeting the competition. In a system in which there are innumerable rents, of long-term and short-term duration, even egregious sub-optimality may permit survival.

This does not mean that competition has no bearing on the extent of x-inefficiency. Ceteris paribus, more competition should result in less x-inefficiency. But in the real world, organizations have the ability to make x-inefficient choices without risking the wrath of the market and, therefore, bankruptcy. Even if being x-inefficient results in higher average costs or lower profit, this does not necessarily translate into sufficient incentives to make choices that are conducive to more x-efficient, lower average cost production.[1] This is the case when a higher cost or lower profit organization can survive in the market. Therefore, it is possible to have organizations with different levels of average costs and rates of profit capable of surviving on the market. There is a type of multiple equilibria (Altman 1999, 2017a). For example, rational agents with different preferences with regard to what is an acceptable (or satisficing) average cost or rate of profit can make sub-optimal choices in terms of x-inefficiency (sub-optimal choices) consistent with 'maximizing' their utility given their unique preference function. In the first instance, firms can be protected from market forces by subsidies and by the ability to charge higher prices to compensate for x-inefficient behaviour (Leibenstein 1966).

For any sports organization, what allows for the organization's survival in the market is not simply or necessarily maximizing wins per season, championships per decade, achieving high league rankings, or points per game. A financially sustainable sports organization/team can even be a loser on the board if fans are loyal and purchase sufficient tickets to the game and buy sufficient quantities of team merchandise, and/or if the team can sell sufficient advertisements, and if the team and/or its league can sell sufficient TV rights, for example. Losers can be winners on the financial side, and winners need not be winners on the financial side. This provides a degree of protection to team decision-makers that make persistent sub-optimal choices. As long as sub-optimal or x-inefficient choices are consistent with the sports organization meeting its target rate of profit, for example, such sub-optimal choices are sustainable. It is important not to equate a sports team's performance with the profitability of the organization within which the team is embedded.

Therefore, as long as a relatively poorly performing team meets some target rate of return or some other financial target set by firm owners, there is no market imperative for choice behaviour to change. This reality is reinforced if sub-optimal choices by management are consistent with the preferences of management. Other teams can perform better, in terms of financial returns as well as in terms of their performance on the 'field,' but this need not drive the management of the less well-performing sports organizations to change their choice behaviour.

Some of these points are illustrated in Figure 12.1. In the conventional economic wisdom, organizational inefficiency should generate a lower rate of return as in line segment, Con, ceteris paribus. What we argue is that this need not be the case. It is possible for the target of return to be constant across different levels of organizational inefficiency, illustrated by line segment Ad. This is the case when sports teams can generate surplus income even if they are not the best they can be on field. But being relatively more efficient need not yield higher returns—it need not result in more surplus income yielding higher rates of return. Winning games, scoring more points, and even winning more championships need not generate higher rates of return. More to the point, if the organization's owners are largely interested in a target rate of return, as long as this is achieved, organizational inefficiency can persist over time. But further increases in organizational efficiency can, eventually, result in higher rates of return as illustrated in line segment dOE.

From our perspective in this chapter where we critically examine the *Moneyball* and *Trouble with the Curve* narratives where sports outcomes such as wins and league standings are critically important, we pay special attention to the determinants of sub-optimal and optimal sports outcomes. As we've already pointed out, being sub-optimal in this domain is not inconsistent with the sports organization being financially sustainable. Making choices that are optimal from the perspective of somehow maximizing sports outcomes are, therefore, not inevitable. But one can conceptualize choices that would 'maximize'

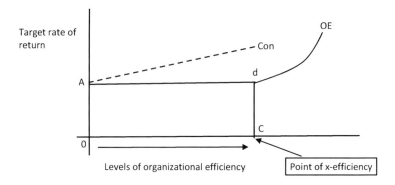

Figure 12.1 Levels of Organizational Efficiency and Target Rates of Return.

the probability of maximizing sports outcomes. For such choices to be realized, they must be consistent with the decision-makers' preferences. Moreover, these decision-makers must be aware of the specific choices that would facilitate their maximization of outcomes. Therefore, even if decision-makers prefer to maximize sports outcomes, this won't happen if decision-makers are not aware of the choices they need to make for this to happen. This awareness need not necessarily exist in world of imperfect and asymmetric information (Akerlof 1970; Altman 2020). This type of world populates Simon's narrative of bounded rationality. Therefore, better understanding the relationship between sports statistics, statistical analysis, and more conventional approaches to decision-making is critically important in informing us as to what bundle of decision-making tools is needed to improve and, indeed, maximize sports outcomes. But then decision-makers must also be aware of which tools they might need and understand their effectiveness.

This type of analytical approach to decision-making is very much part and parcel of Simon's analytical behavioural economics narrative wherein he argues for deconstructing the black box of the organization in order to determine how performance can be inefficient or sub-optimal and how performance, through choice behaviour, can be improved. Simon's notion of procedural rationality stands in opposition to the conventional economics notion of rationality which assumes efficiency as an analytical starting point. Simon (1978, p. 9) writes:

> [In a complex and dynamic world i.e. the real world] we must give an account not only of substantive rationality-the extent to which appropriate courses of action are chosen-but also *procedural* rationality-the effectiveness in light of human cognitive powers and limitations, of the *procedures* used to choose actions. As economics moves out toward situations of increasing cognitive complexity, it becomes increasingly concerned with the ability of actors to cope with the complexity, and hence with the procedural aspects of rationality.

In this chapter, we make the following assumptions: there is a complex decision-making environment with asymmetric information coupled with imperfect human agents wherein a subset of these decision-makers within sports organizations are striving to achieve optimal outcomes. Some of these agents can be smart (and rational in this sense), but they can be procedurally irrational because they fail to achieve what is possible even in the face of all the constraints before them. In the *Moneyball* narrative, for example, what we refer to as procedural irrationality would be a product of deliberately ignoring sports data analytics as a driving force for smart decision-making. But then what the *Moneyball* narrative ignores is the potential importance of intuition/experience, highlighted in *Trouble with the Curve*, where the scouts' experience (which is based on data but not on data analytics) outperforms the sports statisticians.

Machine learning, data analytics, and sports decision-making

A fundamentally important assumption made in *Moneyball* is that organizational inefficiencies existed in baseball's Oakland A's and that these could be and ultimately were dramatically reduced through the introduction and application of sports statistics and analysis by trained statisticians. Of course, the existence and persistence of organizational or x-inefficiencies has always been a critical component of behavioural economics (Leibenstein 1966; Shiller 2000). But the *Moneyball* narrative further assumes that sport data analytics should have a pre-eminent role in determining decision-making within sport teams as these analytics play the key role in eliminating sports outcome inefficiencies. This then would allow teams with lower levels of financial resources to be competitive with the better resourced teams, as was the case with the Oakland A's. What this narrative fails to address, however, is how this happens when all sports teams adopt sports data analytics as their engine of decision-making.

In the *Moneyball* narrative, the assumed traditional focus on the intuition of scouts, coaches, and managers in driving decision-making is considered to be misplaced because it is assumed that this approach is not evidence based. Moreover, this traditional approach is also assumed to be the main source of sports inefficiencies. The focus on inefficiencies is related to the team's performance (points, wins, rankings, etc.) as opposed to some target rate of return, although the former is expected to impact on the latter. And, at times, the two are assumed to be the same. Following the popularity of the Moneyball narrative, many experts have generalized the specific conclusions and learnings emanating from this book on the Oakland A's to other teams in baseball and to other sports whatever they might be.

It bears repeating that the importance of data and statistical analysis was well articulated by Simon when formulating the theoretical framework of bounded rationality. The mind, Simon argues, is a scarce resource. This limits our computational abilities. Computational machines provide a means to expand the computation capabilities of the mind, facilitating improvements in our decision-making capabilities and allowing for more efficient decision-making, much akin to technological change. This point is especially important because the conventional economics simplifying assumption positing the extreme calculating capabilities of economic agents is fundamentally wrong. Rather, it is innovations within the domain of decision-making capabilities which allows the economic agent to approach the neoclassical ideal of the human as an efficient and effective calculating machine.

Simon writes (1977): 'The direct economic effects of introducing computers as numerical calculators and decision-makers are like those of introducing any new form of capital that raises productivity and improves the quality of the product.'

Simon elaborates with regard to the potential impact of computers to decision-making (1978, p. 8):

> In the precomputer era, for example, it was very difficult for managers in business organizations to pay attention to all the major variables affected by their decisions.
>
> Company treasurers frequently made decisions about working capital with little or no attention to their impact on inventory levels, while production and marketing executives made decisions about inventory without taking into account impacts on liquidity. The introduction of computers changed the ways in which executives were able to reach decisions: they could now view them in terms of a much wider set of interrelated consequences than before. The perception of the environment of a decision is a function of-among other things-the information sources and computational capabilities of the executives who make it.

From the perspective of the arguments forwarded in this chapter, Simon's computers are akin to the introduction of computer-/software-assisted statistical analysis in the *Moneyball* narrative to the decision-making process, thereby expanding the decision-making capabilities of their decision-makers. This should allow for better decision-making outcomes to transpire—closer to some optimal. But the introduction of computer-/software-assisted statistical analysis is not a seamless/costless process. This point is underlined by Robert Solow (1987) writing at the time when the use of relatively inexpensive computers and computer-related machines and accompanying software was spreading rapidly. While the consensus among the experts was that this should have yielded significant and persistent increases in productivity, it didn't, at least not initially.

Solow remarks in his famous quip (1987):

> What this means is that [computer and tech advocates] are somewhat embarrassed by the fact that what everyone feels to have been a technological revolution, a drastic change in our productive lives, has been accompanied everywhere, including Japan, by a slowing-down of productivity growth, not by a step up. You can see the computer age everywhere but in the productivity statistics.

Thus, it becomes clear that it is how computers are used, how well they are used, how well they are integrated into an organization's structure, and relatedly, how experienced and knowledgeable the human agents making use of them are, which best explains better outcomes. This relates directly to the complexity which underlies any decision-making heuristic and how it is operationalized (related to procedural rationality). The effectiveness of a heuristic ultimately depends on the capabilities of the human agent who makes use of a heuristic, in the case of the *Moneyball* narrative the computer-/software-assisted statistical analysts or sabermetricians.

From this perspective, going beyond the Simon narrative, it would be incorrect to predict that computers + software + data should yield improvements in specific outcomes. Rather, one would require computers + software + data + human agent capabilities in this domain informed by organizational specific knowledge to improve outcomes. In other words, computers and related instruments serve to improve productivity or other pertinent outcomes only under specific conditions. Sports statisticians making use of computers require specific data and understanding of those data to facilitate and contribute to improvements in sports-related outcomes such as wins, points scored, league standings, and championships won.

These points can be illustrated in Figure 12.2, below, with production possibility curves (PPF). For Simon, there is a theoretically optimal production possibility curve given perfect information and the perfect computational capabilities of decision-makers. But theoretical optimum can't be achieved without decision-making aids that will improve the information quality available to decision-makers and their decision-making capabilities. One can assume that Y'X' is one such optimum. But in the real world, one can only aspire to this optimum. Reality could be represented by YX. Technical change in decision-making aids, such as computers and software, can be represented by shifts in the PPF from YX to Y'X', in the Simon narrative. But, we argue, in line with Solow, that this movement from YX to Y'X' is conditional upon the decision-making capabilities of those making use of the decision-making aids. With regard to sabermetrics, movements in a sports team's PPF are conditional upon the technology, the quality of the data, its relevance, and the capabilities of the sports statistician.

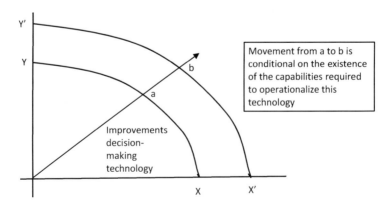

Figure 12.2 Improvements to Decision-Making Outcomes through Decision-Making Technical Change.

The *Moneyball* narrative suggests that sport statisticians are the drivers of optimal decision-making in the organization, this being exemplified by the 'transformation' of the Oakland A's under the management of Billy Beane. In this case, it is the computer + data + statistician that are said to be key to improved decision-making and that computer + data + statistician is a substitute for the traditional more intuitive/experience-based efforts at optimal decision-making. Therefore, in *Moneyball* little attention is paid to sports experts, such as scouts, coaches, and managers, who are informed by experience, as an important determinant of improved sports outcomes.

But the evidence suggests otherwise (Barra 2011; Burns 2016; Cooper 2015; Gerard 2020; Hirsch & Hirsch 2011; Hugland 2011; Kin et al. 2021; Roberts et al. 2021; Scott 2012; Steinberg 2015; Wade 2010). Sports statisticians allow for improvements in decision-making when they complement traditional approaches. This is consistent with Simon's arguments on the importance of computers in enhancing the decision-making capabilities of the human agent in the real world of bounded rationality. But it is also consistent with the argument Solow forwarded of the apparent initial ineffectiveness of computer-related technology in positively affecting outcomes, in and of itself. Therefore, predicting that introducing sports statisticians (computer + data + statistician) will improve performance would be incorrect. The relationship between sports statisticians and performance is nuanced and much depends on how sports statistics, sports statisticians, and sports analytics are operationalized within the sports organization.

The evidence supports the hypothesis that sports statistics, sports statisticians, and sports analytics, combined, are but one important input into the decision-making process. Ignoring this input would contribute towards generating sub-optimal outcomes. But focusing on this input alone is misplaced, yielding problematic (sub-optimal) decisions and outcomes.

This point is illustrated in Figure 12.3, below. Optimal sports outcomes can only be achieved if one brings into the decision-making mix both sports statistical analysis and the more conventional intuitive approach of decision-makers resulting in a dynamic interaction between the two. Sub-optimal outcomes will result if decision-making stems exclusively from either sabermetrics or traditional approaches. Sub-optimal outcomes would also follow if one replies on sports statisticians to make the final decision. Instead, one would argue that the final decision should be left to the sports experts, with significant and meaningful input from the sabermetricians.

Problems with the *Moneyball* narrative

On the positive side, Haglund (2011) argues, for example, that finding and reducing market inefficiencies in sports teams can contribute towards making relatively under-resourced sports teams more competitive. The better resourced teams can buy their way towards more competitive outcomes, be they wins, league rankings, and championships, for example. He further argues,

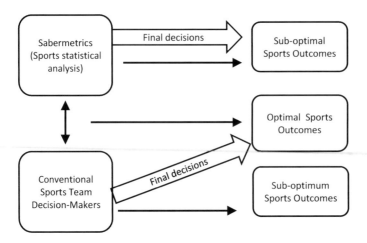

Figure 12.3 Determinants of Optimal Decision-Making.

agreeing with Lewis, that all too often decision-makers pay too much attention to the wrong set of data points, such as the athleticism (and the 'look') of the player. This might be at the expense of the player's actual overall performance—looks becomes a proxy or decision-making heuristic for performance. Moreover, referring to baseball, decision-makers might focus on batting average, paying little or no attention to on-base percentage (OBP), where the latter is an important input to team success. This is the ratio of the number hits, walks, and being hit by the ball (which means that you get on base) to the number of times at the plate. Batting average only covers one method of getting on base. However, it gets much the press. It has a better *look*, it's *sexier*, than a walk or being hit by the ball. But they can have the same effect on the team's performance. Lewis and sports statisticians blame such errors in decision-making on scouts, coaches, and managers. To a large degree, these problems can be fixed, Lewis holds, by allowing sports statisticians, with their focus on data, to replace the intuitive decision-makers, thereby reducing the extent of inefficiencies in decision-making and, thereby, in performance.

But Hugland points out that empirically *Moneyball* misses the point or is, in the very least, somewhat misleading in that a key to the Oakland A's success was actually recruiting star players through traditional (experience-based) scouting. Hugland (2011)) finds that

> ...the main reason the A's were successful in the early 2000s was that four of the high draft picks they were awarded after lousy seasons in the late 1990s all turned fairly quickly into top-notch players [a fifth player was recruited by a scout].... In 2002, those were Oakland's five best players ... Oakland could afford these five because Major League Baseball's salary structure severely limits how much young players can make.

Thus, the engine of Oakland A's successes was largely unrelated to the application of sports data analytics or sabermetrics.

Hugland (2011) points out another flaw with *Moneyball's* exclusive sabermetrics approach. 'Having grabbed the reins of his team, Beane mostly ignored his scouts in the 2002 draft and took a bunch of hitters based on their numbers alone.' But although Oakland returned to the payoffs in 2003 and 2006, this was the last of its great successes. Some have suggested that this is because Beane's innovations were adopted by competitors elsewhere, thereby eliminating Oakland's advantage (a type of Schumpeterian process wherein the rents from innovation are eventually eliminated). But Hugland argues that Oakland's main problem has been that it has been unable to replace the five great players who were recruited through scouting—part of the traditional approach to decision-making. Also, the pitchers they obtained over the years were not kept in good health. So even if and when sports statisticians or sabermetricians are successful, statistical analysis can't speak to the importance of keeping players healthy for the longer term. This can become a critical missing variable.

But focusing on statistics alone appears to be a heuristic that fails as sabermetrics can't speak to which variables to assess and analyse. A sports statistician can select the wrong variable generating significant errors in decision-making. This highlights another shortcoming with relying on the *Moneyball* narrative as a road map to success as it pays much too little attention to the training required in the field, and this has little to do with sabermetrics in and of itself.

Barra finds (2011):

> Each year Oakland demonstrated that they had the talent to win more games than the big guys, but each time they couldn't play the "small ball" required to clench the key games that would have given them the series. You can call it a crapshoot, but all this is reflective of talents that Beane was largely indifferent to, namely fielding and base running, the kind of small things that get overlooked when a general manager is obsessed with large concepts like on-base percentage. And yet they are skills that don't require a great deal of money to work on.

Sub-optimal decisions can be very much a product of poor decisions with regard to training in the field, where such inefficiencies can exist with or without sabermetrics. Even if sabermetrics were fundamentally important to reducing certain errors in decision-making (in this case, it would be a necessary condition), sabermetrics would not be sufficient in and of itself in reducing such errors. Training on the field is vital as would be training off the field, and the latter also does not feature in the *Moneyball* narrative.

The importance of farm teams in building up top teams' talent pool is also missing from Lewis' *Moneyball* and sabermetrics narrative. Farm teams in the minor leagues feed players into the major leagues. If well developed, farm teams provide a pool of talent and tried and tested players who can be called upon when needed. Major league teams' experts, such as scouts, would have major insight (inclusive of data) on their minor league players. Major league teams without this depth of strength emanating from strong farm teams can be disadvantaged (Barra 2011). Sports statisticians, one can argue, can play a role in selecting players to move from the farm team to the majors. But without a strong farm team or teams, the role of sabermetrics would be beside the point. Only with a strong farm team system can sports statisticians make important contributions to improving their team's performance.

Also obscured in the *Moneyball* narrative are other sources of data, more qualitative in nature, that are based on the lived experience of scouts, coaches, and managers as we witness with Gus Lobel in *Trouble with the Curve*. Such experiential data that can be recorded and even assessed are derived from the experience and experience-based interaction of scouts, coaches, and managers with athletes. These data can be as important as the data gleaned by the sports statisticians in making optimal decisions. There are also the more precise data recorded by scouts, coaches, and managers as well as by trainers, including the use the videos of athletes' performance and data provided by trainers, physios, nutritionists, and sports psychologists, for example. These data are useful in selecting and also in helping train players, thereby improving their performance.

Any statistical analytical approach to decision-making which pays little attention to the concrete process of statistical analysis should be suspect. The *Moneyball* narrative with its exclusive focus on hits is an excellent example. Statistical analysis is as good as the variables and their related data that are incorporated into the analysis. Missing variables and problematic data invariably results in misleading statistical results and can convolute correlation with causation. The sabermetrician needs to be well versed in the sport that he or she is analysing. As importantly, the sports statistician's analysis improves through her or his collaboration with the sports experts, the often maligned scouts, coaches, and managers.

Making reference to hockey, Cooper argues (2015):

> But what's increasingly clear in hockey, as in all areas that are being transformed by big data [such as baseball], is that data don't apply themselves. Concepts like repeatability, sustainability and sample size are useful, but only if you understand how and when to apply them. To do that, it takes a good qualitative understanding of whatever subject you're studying (in my case hockey), constant attention to whether the data are relevant to the hypothesis you're testing, and the creativity and analytical chops to interpret whatever your scatter plot, histogram or regression model *might* be telling you.

Cooper reiterates the significance of collaboration across decision-makers with sports statisticians to make best use of sabermetrics. Absent this collaboration, errors in statistical analyses are bound to occur. But with this collaboration, sabermetrics can improve the decision-making process and outcomes.[2]

The significance of *Moneyball* for decision-making

As Bill Gerrard (2020) points out: 'The real lesson of *Moneyball* is the value of an evidence-based approach. This goes beyond the immediate context of player recruitment in pro baseball to embrace all coaching decisions in all sports.' Statistical analysis has promise when the statisticians are part of the team and actually understand the team, its players, and the sport. Gerrard (2020) writes: '…data analytics only really works when there is full engagement between the coaches and the data analysts.' They become a member of the coaching team. They provide one important input into the decision-making process.

Sabermetricians should not be regarded as substitutes for scouts, coaches, and managers. They are compliments. They input into the scouts', coaches', and managers' decision-making. Therefore, experience counts, but experience-based decision-making is enriched by sports data analytics. In addition, the latter can provide a check on scouts, coaches, and managers making decisions that are inconsistent with the evidence, such as allowing the look of the athlete to trump the objective potential of the athlete. In this manner, traditional decision-makers are also not threatened by the sabermetricians. Hence, making use of data analytics will not be part of a power play between the sabermetricians and the conventional or traditional decision-makers, but rather the adoption of data analytics could then be regarded as consistent with the latter's preference of maximizing team performance.

Sabermetrics allows for more effective decision-making. It is a tool and an additional argument in the production function. Therefore, as in the Simon narrative, it can contribute to increasing productivity, in our case improving sports performance. But as the evidence suggests, it is not at all clear that sabermetrics is what drove the Oakland A's to significant improvements. Other factors also played an important role. These include traditional decision-making related to sports experience-based heuristics. The *Moneyball* narrative focuses attention on how statistical analysis can improve on decision-making in sports, but unfortunately it does so while diminishing the role of other factors in optimizing decision-making.

But this focus on data and statistical analysis is an important one that it highlights one potentially critical input into the decision-making process given the reality of bounded rationality. Notwithstanding the critiques of the *Moneyball* narrative with regard to the factors underlying the success of the Oakland A's and other sport teams, this should not distract us from the positive potential importance of data and statistical analysis for improved decision-making in sports teams. Sabermetrics is now widespread among sports teams. It is considered as a must have in the teams' decision-making arsenal. But within the framework of the bounded rationality approach to behavioural economics, a critical question remains as to how best (optimally) to integrate sabermetrics into the decision-making process. This requires a nuanced understanding of a team's overall decision-making process. Behavioural economics, modelled in terms of multiple equilibria, which includes sustainable sub-optimal outcomes, recognizes that simply adopting sabermetrics is no guarantee of success. But integrating sabermetrics into the decision-making process appears to be a necessary condition for improved decision-making and improved team performance.

Conclusion

The *Moneyball* narrative challenged the conventional wisdom in sports that intuitive-based decision-making had the highest probability of a sports team achieving the best possible outcomes—what is referred to in behavioural economics as satisficing outcomes. According to this narrative, statistics plus statisticians plus computers and pertinent software is what generates relatively optimal outcomes and should dominate the decision-making process. Sabermetrics should allow decision-makers to identify inefficiencies or suboptimal decisions and choices creating opportunities for smarter and wiser team managers and owners to pick up 'big bills lying on the sidewalk.' This would allow the financially weaker teams to be competitive with the financially more robust teams who, it is assumed, are, and will continue to be, relatively inefficient.

The *Moneyball* narrative sheds light and provides important focus on the role of the use of data and data analysis (sabermetrics) to improving the quality of decision-making in sports and, thereby, improving sports outcomes. This focus is consistent with Simon's bounded rationality narrative wherein decision-making technology can significantly improve decision-making outcomes in the *real world* where information is costly and asymmetric and the brain (or mind) is a scarce resource with regard to locating, collating, and analysing data. But, even from a theoretical perspective, this approach is overly simplistic. *Moneyball* distracts from other critical decision-making inputs without which sabermetrics could not improve upon decision-making outcomes. As in the story of old baseball scout Gus Lobel in *Trouble with the Curve*, the complex human agent needs to be factored in. The bounded rationality approach with its focus on computational/machine innovations also does not pay sufficient heed to the non-machine side, the human side, of the computing/data analytics process. The latter must, in itself, be efficient for machine-side innovations to be optimized with regard to decision-making outcomes. This speaks to the importance of process rationality, wherein the importance of identifying the best-practice decision-making process specific to an organization and a decision problem is emphasized. In other words, what transpires inside of the 'black box' of the organization is of critical importance to better understand the actual decision-making process and what constitutes optimality in terms of outcomes. This is what Leibenstein called the micro-microeconomics of the firm.

From a theoretical perspective, we argue that to best understand how 'machine' and software innovations can improve decision-making outcomes, one must understand how computers, software, and data fit into the decision-making process. Technology is ultimately operationalized by humans, and it is the human agent who determines whether and to what extent the decision outcomes are optimized. This takes the 'machine' component of bounded rationality one step beyond the original Simon perspective. Integrating the 'machine' with the human agent is vital to better understand how the introduction of sabermetrics can improve the decision-making process and related outcomes in sports organizations.

We argue that sabermetrics can improve decision-making outcomes only if it's part and parcel of a cooperative and collaborative decision-making environment. Statisticians must not dominate the decision-making process for decision-making to be optimized. They represent but one input. The evidence suggests that this input must be informed by sports experts who have accumulated specific human capital and have a nuanced and in-depth understanding of the sport, which includes intuition which is experience based.

Even though *Moneyball* is strongly suggestive of sabermetrics being fundamentally instrumental to the success of the Oakland A's, this appears to be an oversimplification. The more traditional modes of decision-making played an instrumental role. But this should not distract from the fact that sabermetrics or sports data analytics can play a fundamentally important role in improving performance outcomes when part of a more holistic decision-making environment. On the other hand, dismissing sabermetrics as being of little importance has no empirical bearing. What's critical is how it is employed in the decision-making process.

We also argue that, given that performance inefficiency or sub-optimal sports performance is sustainable (losing teams can be profitable), there is no market imperative that would force sports organizations to adopt best practices to maximize the probability of achieving performance efficiency. Given this modelling, one can expect or predict that there would be a variety of heuristics that are in place among sports organizations, many of which are inefficient, but are sustainable in equilibrium over time. This can be for reasons of lack of information or misleading information on best practices. Or, it can be because the preferences of lead decision-makers have a present bias for existing heuristics irrespective for how inefficient they might be, as long as they are consistent with the viability of their organization.

We argue, however, that it should be possible to identify a set of decision-making heuristics and principles that would facilitate maximizing the probability of achieving the best possible outcomes given available resources. This would be specific to the sports organization that one is analysing. Simon's process rationality narrative makes this critical point wherein the focus is on what's required to achieve particular goals (in our case, wins, points, league standing, and championships) in an organization. We argue that the *Moneyball* narrative is important because it pays special attention to the role of statistics and data analytics (particularly) to realizing optimal outcomes in sports organizations. But it detracts attention from the conventional decision-makers and decision-making heuristics that have been and remain critically important to the realization of optimal outcomes.

Ignoring more conventional human heuristics is bound to generate suboptimal outcomes. Data analytics (sabermetrics) and conventional heuristics (which also rely on data) must be viewed as compliments, not as substitutes. And, sabermetrics is certainly not a substitute for conventional approaches to decision-making. Appreciating the dynamic synergies between the two is key achieving optimal sports outcomes.

Notes

1 The relationship between average cost, labour productivity, and labour and related costs can be illustrated in the following equation where, for simplicity, one has one factor input: $AC = w/(Q/L)$, where AC is the average cost, w is the wage rate, and Q/L is the labour productivity. Organizational inefficiency, a form of x-inefficiency, reduces productivity and, thereby, increases the average cost. Ceteris paribus, a higher or lower average cost can result in lower or higher rates of profit, respectively.
2 For further discussion on the Moneyball narrative, see Burns (2016), Hirsch and Hirsch (2011), Steinberg (2015), and Wade (2010).

References

Akerlof, G. (1970). "The Market for Lemons: Quality Uncertainty and the Market Mechanism," *Quarterly Journal of Economics*, 84: 488–500.

Alchain, A. A. (1950). "Uncertainty, Evolution and Economic Theory," *Journal of Political Economy*, 58, 211–221.

Altman, H. (2020). *The Behavioural Economics of Organisational Inefficiency: The Example of the New Zealand Fitness Industry*. Master of Philosophy Thesis, Queensland University of Technology. Brisbane: Australia.

Altman, H. and M. Altman (2015a). "Sport Economics and Performance Inefficiencies," in Morris Altman (ed.) *Real World Decision Making: An Encyclopedia of Behavioral Economics*. New York: Praeger, ABC-CLIO: 410–412.

Altman, H. and M. Altman (2015b). "Sports Economics and Economic Psychology," in Morris Altman (ed.) *Real World Decision Making: An Encyclopedia of Behavioral Economics*. New York: Praeger, ABC-CLIO: 412–415.

Altman, M. (1996). *Human Agency and Material Welfare: Revisions in Microeconomics and their Implications for Public Policy*. Boston, Dordrecht, London: Kluwer Academic Publishers.

Altman, M. (1999). "The Methodology of Economics and the Survivor Principle Revisited and Revised: Some Welfare and Public Policy Implications of Modeling the Economic Agent," *Review of Social Economics*, 57, 427–449.

Altman, M. (2002). "Economic Theory, Public Policy and the Challenge of Innovative Work Practices," *Economic and Industrial Democracy: An International Journal*, 23, 271–290.

Altman, M. (2005a). "Behavioral Economics, Rational Inefficiencies, Fuzzy Sets, and Public Policy," *Journal of Economic Issues*, 34, 683–706.
Altman, M. (2009). "A Behavioral-Institutional Model of Endogenous Growth and Induced Technical Change," *Journal of Economic Issues*, 63, 685–713.
Altman, M. (2017). "Policy Consequences of Multiple Equilibria and the Indeterminacy of Economic Outcomes in a Boundedly Rational World: Closing the System with Non-Economic Variables," *Forum for Social Economics*, 64: 234–251.
Barra, A. (2011). "The Many Problems with 'Moneyball'", *The Atlantic*. Accessed September 6, 2020 at https://www.theatlantic.com/entertainment/archive/2011/09/the-many-problems-with-moneyball/245769/.
Burns, E. (2016). "Sports Data Analytics Isn't Always a Slam Dunk," *SearchBusinessAnalytics.com*. Accessed September 6, 2020 at https://searchbusinessanalytics.techtarget.com/opinion/Sports-data-analytics-isnt-always-a-slam-dunk?vgnextfmt=print.
Cooper, I. (2015). "The Dangerous Data Fetishes of Sports Analytics," *Wharton Magazine*. Accessed September 6, 2020 at https://magazine.wharton.upenn.edu/digital/the-dangerous-data-fetishes-of-sports-analytics/.
Cyert, R. M. and J. C. March (1963). *A Behavioral Theory of the Firm*. Englewood Cliffs, NJ: Prentice-Hall.
Friedman, M. (1953). "The Methodology of Positive Economics," in M. Friedman, *Essays in Positive Economics*. Chicago: University of Chicago Press, pp. 3–43.
Gerrard, B. (2020). "The Real Lessons of Moneyball," *Winning with Analytics*. Accessed September 6, 2020 at https://winningwithanalytics.com/2016/09/07/blog-8-the-real-lessons-of-moneyball/.
Gigerenzer, G. (2007). *Gut Feelings: The Intelligence of the Unconscious*. New York: Viking.
Gladwell, M. (2005). *Blink: The Power of Thinking without Thinking*. New York: Little, Brown and Company.
Hirsch, S. and A. Hirsch (2011). *The Beauty of Short Hops: How Chance and Circumstance Confound the Moneyball Approach to Baseball*. Jefferson: McFarland and Company.
Hugland, D. (2011). *"More Moneyball, Same Problems," Slate*. Accessed September 6, 2020 at https://slate.com/culture/2011/09/moneyball-movie-the-numbers-are-good-but-the-story-is-still-bunk.html.
Kahneman, D. (2003). "Maps of Bounded Rationality: Psychology for Behavioral Economics," *American Economic Review*, 93, 1449–1475.
Kahneman, D. (2011). *Thinking Fast and Slow*. New York: Farrar, Strauss, Giroux.
Kim, J., C. Dibrell, E. Kraft and D. Marshall (2021). "Data Analytics and Performance: The Moderating Role of Intuition-based HR Management in Major League Baseball," *Journal of Business Research*, 122, 204–216. ISSN 0148–2963, https://doi.org/10.1016/j.jbusres.2020.08.057.
Leibenstein, H. (1966). "Allocative Efficiency vs. 'X-efficiency'," *American Economic Review*, 56, 392–415.
Leibenstein, H. (1979). "A Branch of Economics Is Missing: Micro-Micro Theory," *Journal of Economic Literature*, 17, 477–502.
Lewis, M. (2003). *Moneyball: The Art of Winning an Unfair Game*. New York: W.W. Norton.
Roberts, A., D. Greenwood, M. Stanley, C. Humberstone, F. Iredale and A. Raynor (2021). "Understanding the "Gut Instinct" of Expert Coaches during Talent Identification," *Journal of Sports Sciences*, 39(4), 359–367, doi:10.1080/02640414.2020.1823083.

Scott, A. O. (2012). "Rooting for One Player in Baseball Politics: Dad," *The New York Times*. Accessed October 16, 2020 at https://www.nytimes.com/2012/09/21/movies/trouble-with-the-curve-with-clint-eastwood-and-amy-adams.html.

Shiller, R. J. (2000). *Irrational Exuberance*. New York: Random House.

Simon, H. A., G. B. Dantzig, R. Hogarth, C. R. Plott, H. Raiffa, T. C. Schelling, K. A. Shepsle, R. Thaler, A. Tversky and S. Winter (1987). "Decision Making and Problem Solving," *Interfaces*, 17, 11–31.

Simon, H. A. (1977). "What Computers Mean for Man and Society," *Science*, 195, 1186–1191.

Simon, H. A. (1978). "Rationality as a Process and as a Product of Thought," *American Economic Review*, 70, 1–16.

Simon, H. A. (1979). "Rational Decision Making in Business Organizations," *American Economic Review*, 69, 493–513.

Simon, H. A. (1987). "Behavioral Economics," in *The New Palgrave: A Dictionary of Economics*, eds. J. Eatwell, M. Millgate and P. Newman. London: Macmillan, 266–267.

Simon, H. A. (1997). *Models of Bounded Rationality. Empirical Grounded Economic Reasons*, Vol. III. Cambridge, MA: MIT Press.

Steinberg, L. (2015). "Changing the Game: The Rise of Sports Analytics," *Forbes*. Accessed June 1, 2020 at https://www.forbes.com/sites/leighsteinberg/2015/08/18/changing-the-game-the-rise-of-sports-analytics/.

Thaler, R. H., and C. Sunstein (2008). *Nudge: Improving Decisions about Health, Wealth, and Happiness*. New Haven and London: Yale University Press.

Wade, D. (2010). "The Good Face, the Halo, and Projectability," *The Hardball Times*. Accessed September 6, 2010 at https://tht.fangraphs.com/tht-live/the-good-face-the-halo-and-projectability/.

Part 5

Fans, fan behaviour, and sports outcomes

13 Reference-dependent preferences, outcome uncertainty, and sports fan behavior – a review of the literature

Clay Collins and Brad R. Humphreys

Introduction

The uncertainty-of-outcome hypothesis (UOH) represents an important concept that differentiates research in sports economics from other fields in the discipline. The UOH predicts that attendance at games with relatively uncertain outcomes, for example, games between equally matched teams where the likelihood that either team wins is roughly 50%, will exceed attendance at games where one team appears much stronger than the other because fans derive more utility from attending games with uncertain outcomes and less utility from attending games with relatively certain outcomes.

Consumer utility does not depend on uncertainty about the consumption experience in other settings. Consumer decisions about attending a movie, buying a new pair of shoes, or dining in a new restaurant involve some uncertainty, but increased uncertainty about how comfortable a new pair of shoes will be does not increase demand for shoes. Broadway shows with uncertain entertainment value typically close after a small number of performances.

The UOH also plays a key role in economic models of outcomes in sports leagues, another topic unique to sports economics. Unlike other settings, sports leagues feature joint production of output in the form of games sold to and consumed by fans. Production of this entertainment good requires many competitors who all sell this jointly produced product separately to fans. Neale (1964) famously dubbed this the "peculiar economics" of sports and described how this leads to different outcomes than found in other industries. In the textbook "two-team" model of sports league outcomes (Fort and Quirk, 1995), team revenue first increases as team success increases, but eventually revenue begins to decline for extremely successful teams because fans lose interest in attending games that a dominant team will almost certainly win. The UOH motivates the concavity of team revenue functions in terms of team success in economic models of sports league outcomes.

Sports economists treated the UOH as an accurate description of consumer behavior for decades and exploited its clear empirical implications – attendance should be higher at games with less certain outcomes and lower at games with more certain outcomes, other things equal – as the basis for a large

DOI: 10.4324/9781003080824-17

body of empirical research beginning in the 1980s. Ready access to data on both attendance and expectations about game outcomes, mostly from sports betting markets, drove this empirical research. The fact that scarce empirical support for the UOH emerged from this research attracted little attention.

Sports economists who noted the lack of empirical support for the UOH also noted its lack of a clear theoretical underpinning. No model of consumer choice under uncertainty about game outcomes existed, despite economists' reliance on formal models to guide economic research. The first such model, developed by Coates et al. (2014), contained an interesting feature: in order to generate predictions consistent with the UOH, this model required explicitly behavioral assumptions in the form of reference-dependent preferences (RDP). Absent RDP, the model predicted that attendance increased monotonically with team success. This prediction stands in contrast to the UOH, which requires attendance to decline for dominant teams because fans lose interest in attending games played by dominant teams because of the relatively certain outcome of these games.

The model developed by Coates et al. (2014) contained a second important behavioral aspect. Loss aversion played a key role in fan attendance decisions. In this context, loss aversion refers to the negative utility experienced by fans who expect their team to have a reasonable chance to win, attend the game, and wind up sitting through a bitterly disappointing loss. The presence of fans with sufficiently strong loss aversion generated predictions exactly opposite to the UOH. Loss-averse fans attend games where their team is an underdog because of the large marginal utility generated by watching their team pull off an upset exceeds the lost utility from watching an expected loss to a stronger opponent. Loss-averse fans are less likely to attend games with an uncertain outcome, but return in large numbers to games their team is strongly favored to win.

This chapter reviews the recent theoretical literature on the UOH and discusses the existing empirical literature testing the UOH in light of this recent theoretical research. The model developed by Coates et al. (2014) generates predictions supporting the UOH and predictions consistent with the presence of fans with loss aversion who attend games where their team is an underdog, and games where their team is a strong favorite, but eschew games with uncertain outcomes. This flexibility provides a powerful lens for re-examining the existing literature, since it motivates the mixed results found in this literature. We also document a strong thread of support for the loss aversion form of the model, suggesting the need for more research on the importance of loss aversion in consumer decisions about attending or watching sporting events.

The theoretical basis for the UOH

Despite its widespread application in sports economics, the UOH lacked a formal basis in economic theory for decades. In a social science field noted for mathematical rigor and formality, sports economists simply took as self-evident that the UOH, first identified by Rottenberg (1956), briefly described in a footnote in Neale (1964), and widely applied to empirical attendance demand models, reflected an outcome predicted by some underlying model of consumer choice. A lack of clear empirical support for the UOH in many early empirical studies, as far back as the 1980s, did not seem to bother many economists studying attendance demand.

This changed when Coates, Humphreys, and Zhou (2014) (CHZ) modified the model of RDP developed by Koszegi and Rabin (2006) and extended the emotional cue application of this model developed by Card and Dahl (2011) to the case of the decision made by a representative fan to attend a sporting event with an uncertain outcome. In this model, the fan compared expected utility generated by different potential outcomes of the game to a reference level of utility obtained by not attending, and attended only if the level of expected utility exceeded the reference level.

Reference dependence represented a key aspect of this model. Absent reference dependence, the model predicted fans exhibit pure *home win preference* in that attending a game the fan believed the home team was more likely to win generated more expected utility, increasing the probability that the fan would attend. This prediction appears unsurprising. A consumer would clearly be more likely to dine in a restaurant where the actual quality of the meal served was unknown prior to eating but the expected quality of the meal was higher, perhaps as indicated by online ratings. But home win preference cannot be reconciled with the UOH, which predicts that fans will be more likely to attend a game where the perceived probability of a home team win is near 50% and less likely to attend when the perceived home win probability is large.

In the form of the model containing fans with RDP about home team win probability in games, CHZ showed that predictions consistent with the UOH emerged from the model under certain conditions. In the model with reference dependence, expected utility was a quadratic function of the perceived probability that the home team would win an upcoming game, opening the possibility that games with uncertain outcomes could potentially generate more expected utility than games with more certain outcomes, either relatively certain losses or wins. In other words, the expected utility function could be concave in home win probability, taking an inverted U form with a maximum near 50%, reflecting the common definition of the UOH.

However, the relationship between expected home win probability and expected utility depended critically on the relative consumption utility from attending wins and losses. In particular, for outcome uncertainty to dominate fan decisions, the marginal "gain–loss" utility – the change in utility generated by reference dependence – a fan receives from watching a home team win must exceed the marginal "gain–loss" utility a fan receives from watching a home team loss. Given a reference point for expected game outcomes, if fans derive more utility from watching a win than watching a loss, then fans will be more likely to attend games with uncertain outcomes. Fans with these types of preferences will be more pleasantly surprised by watching a win than unpleasantly surprised by sitting through a loss.

The second type of "gain–loss" utility in this comparison depends on the importance of loss aversion in fan decisions. Loss aversion plays an important role in behavioral economics, in particular in generating key predictions about consumer choice under uncertainty in prospect theory, first developed by Kahneman and Tversky (1979). In prospect theory, loss aversion leads consumers to systematically value expected outcomes in the loss domain differently than expected outcomes in the gain domain. Loss aversion enjoys substantial empirical support in the literature and forms the basis of important behavioral biases such as the endowment effect (Marzilli Ericson and Fuster, 2014). Given the theoretical and empirical importance of loss aversion, the idea that it affects fans' decisions on game attendance appears uncontroversial.

CHZ showed that the case where loss aversion exceeded the marginal "gain–loss" utility from seeing a home team win generated an expected utility function with a U shape where expected utility was largest when the expected likelihood of a home win was very large, reflecting "home win preference," and when the expected likelihood of a home team win was small. In other words, fans would also be likely to attend games where the home team was a large underdog, corresponding to expected home win probabilities substantially smaller than 50%. CHZ referred to this as reflecting fans' preferences for potentially watching the home team pull off an epic upset over a favored opponent. While anecdotal evidence supporting this prediction exists, this was the first theoretical prediction of fan interest in attending potential upsets in the literature. In the discussion below, we refer to this form of the model as the *loss aversion* form.

The importance of reference dependence in generating predictions supporting the UOH in the model developed by CHZ proved somewhat controversial. In subsequent work, Humphreys and Miceli (2020) developed a model of fan attendance decisions under uncertainty with no behavioral elements, but including fan heterogeneity, that also generated predictions supporting the UOH. The fan heterogeneity in this model took the form of home team fans and visiting team fans both potentially attending games played in the home team's stadium and variable cost of travel by visiting fans. This model setup also generated an aggregate expected utility function from all fans attending a game concave in home win probability, taking an inverted U form with a maximum near 50%, again reflecting the common definition of the UOH. Intuitively, visiting team fans decide not to travel to an away contest when they expect their team to be a large underdog, reducing total attendance at that game.

The existing theoretical models of sports fan attendance decisions under uncertainty can generate predictions consistent with the general understanding of the UOH. But the behavioral economics-based model developed by Coates et al. (2014) generates strikingly different predictions based on the relative size of "gain–loss" utility generated by fans watching wins or losses by the home team relative to their reference points. In practical terms, the relationship between attendance and a quadratic function of the likelihood that the home team will win a game can empirically distinguish the loss aversion form of the model and the "home win preference/upset" form of the model. Fully understanding the behavioral aspects of sports fan attendance decisions requires a thorough analysis of the existing evidence on the relationship between outcome uncertainty and attendance.

Empirical evidence on outcome uncertainty and attendance

A substantial empirical literature analyzing the relationship between outcome uncertainty and fan attendance exists. Our searches identified 57 papers analyzing this relationship published in peer-reviewed journals, dating back to Jennett (1984). This large body of research focused on many different sports, used many different proxy measures for expected home win probabilities, and considered many different types of outcome uncertainty. Szymanski (2003) identified match- or game-level outcome uncertainty, season-level outcome uncertainty, and championship outcome uncertainty as affecting fan interest and attendance.

Organizing a discussion of a literature this large requires some decisions in terms of organization. The key theoretical relationship involves the impact of fans' perceived likelihood that one team, typically the home team, will win a game, finish at the top of the league table, or win a postseason championship. Because of this, we organize papers based on the proxy variable used to represent this expected likelihood of winning. This empirical literature contains two broad approaches: papers using past outcomes in terms of game results, league standings, or final season standings and papers using betting odds to estimate outcome probabilities, including the Theil index to reflect inequality of expected outcome likelihoods. Papers using the Theil index all focus on game outcome uncertainty in football (soccer in North America), since football matches take three discrete outcomes (home win, draw, and away win) rather than two (home win and away win). We also discuss a catch-all category of papers using proxy variables that do not fit this taxonomy.

Research using league standings and past outcomes

Some of the earliest and relatively basic empirical UOH research used a team's position in the league standings, or the difference in league standings for home and visiting teams, as the primary proxy measure for outcome uncertainty. These papers assume that fans assess the likelihood that the home team will win a game based on observable past performance of the two teams involved. However, the mapping from actual past performance to fan's perceptions of the likelihood of a win in an upcoming game may be inexact and may reflect behavioral biases. Also, empirical researchers face difficulties identifying past outcomes salient to fans' perceptions about expected future outcomes. Perhaps due to these factors, mixed support for the UOH exists in papers that use league standings compared to papers that use other measures of uncertainty.

In an early, comprehensive 36-season (1950–1986) study of Australian Rules Football (ARF) attendance, Borland (1987) used "average games behind the league leader measured at four points in the season" (pg. 224) to proxy for game outcome uncertainty. Borland (1987) claimed to find evidence supporting the UOH, even though their parameter estimates of interest were not statistically different from zero at conventional significance levels. In another ARF study, Borland and Lye (1992) found that game uncertainty, measured by the difference in league standings (current position on the league table) over the 1981–1986 seasons, was a significant determinant of game attendance. Falter and Pérignon (2000) used the difference in league standing as a measure of uncertainty in their study of game attendance in the French Premiere Division football (soccer) league for the 1997/1998 season, finding no evidence supporting the UOH. In a similar study of Brazilian football (soccer) over four seasons (2003–2006), Madalozzo and Berber Villar (2009) found that difference in league position had no effect on game attendance.

In an analysis of game attendance for Spanish First Division football (soccer) over four seasons (1992/1993–1995/1996), García and Rodríguez (2002) used the difference in league position between teams, the difference in league position squared, and a measure of "closeness" of league position. The authors find evidence supporting the UOH, as higher attendance was found in games against closely ranked opponents. However, a U-shaped relationship was not found. Benz et al. (2009) also incorporated difference in league standing in their analysis of game attendance from season ticket holders for a German Bundesliga (soccer) club over five seasons (1999/00–2003/2004), finding it generally insignificant. Meier et al. (2016) attempt to use difference in league rank in their study of game attendance for Frauen-Bundesliga women's soccer games over 14 seasons (1998/1999–2011/2012), but omit the variable due to multicollinearity concerns. Instead, the authors generate dummy variables for "David" or "Goliath" matchups, when the home team is more than five league places behind or ahead of their opponents, respectively. They find the parameter estimate on this variable statistically insignificant.

Rascher and Solmes (2007) found evidence supporting the UOH based on results from a censored regression model using NBA game attendance from the 2001/2002 regular season. Rascher and Solmes (2007) estimated the probability that the home team would win each game based on the home and visiting teams' current winning percentages. Their regression model included this home win probability, and the probability squared, and the parameters on these variables supported the UOH. However, similar results were not found in a probit model of game sellouts, reducing confidence in the results.

In a 30-year (1980–2011) study of international test cricket match attendance, Sacheti et al. (2014) used the difference in ICC quality ratings between teams as a measure of uncertainty. In addition, the authors also employed a ratings squared variable "to distinguish impacts of small and large increases in uncertainty of outcome" (pg. 2036). The parameter estimates on both measures were not statistically different from zero. Schreyer et al. (2017) used difference in FIFA rankings as an uncertainty measure in their study of television audiences for 21 years (1993/1994–2013/2014) of international football (soccer) games. They conclude that "spectators do generally care about game outcome uncertainty. In particular, we find that the demand for international friendlies is positively affected by the closeness of the game outcomes" (pg. 43). However, they find no evidence supporting the UOH in terms of attendance at World Cup or UEFA European Championship matches.

Another important approach taken by Jennett (1984) proposed that "attendances are generated not solely by the probability of victory of either club in any one game, but by the significance of the game in the overall championship race" (pg. 179). Their paper, as a result, employs the "Home and away team championship significance" (pg. 185) to measure outcome uncertainty. The author found "championship uncertainty" to be a significant factor explaining variation in attendance at Scottish Football (soccer) League games. This evidence of "championship uncertainty" spawned a separate line of research (see, e.g., Roy (2004), Lee and Fort (2008), and Pawlowski and Nalbantis (2015)), which, while interesting, lies outside the focus of this chapter.

A variation of the league standing papers uses differences in points earned by participating teams to date as an uncertainty measure. Paul and Weinbach (2013) used the difference in team's total points accrued to date as a measure of outcome uncertainty in their analysis of television audience size for Major League Soccer (MLS) and National Hockey League (NHL) matches for single seasons in 2011. They found larger differences in points earned by the home and visiting teams to date, in other words less evenly matched teams, associated with smaller television audiences. This result supports the UOH. Paul and Weinbach (2013) also included a measure of the total number of points accrued by both teams as both an uncertainty measure and a way to identify marquee matches. They found that the sum of points generated a positive effect larger in magnitude than the difference-in-points variable.

In a study of game attendance for the Malaysian Semi-Pro Football (Soccer) League from 1989 to 1991, Wilson and Sim (1995) also employed the absolute points difference between home and away teams, as well as the absolute difference squared. Models including both measures contained insignificant parameter estimates on these variables.

In general, the empirical literature analyzing the relationship between outcome uncertainties proxied by various prior performance variables contains mixed evidence supporting the UOH. Many papers find no relationship between outcome uncertainty proxy variables and attendance. Moreover, papers using this approach often use linear measures of outcome uncertainty that cannot directly address the key UOH prediction that attendance declines at home games played by dominant teams.

Research using outcome probabilities estimated from betting markets

Generating home win probabilities from betting odds represents the most common approach to quantifying fans' perceived outcome probabilities. Research clearly shows that betting markets efficiently aggregate information, and odds set on the outcomes of sporting events accurately predict outcomes. However, considerable variation exists in this literature in terms of functional form as well as the number of outcomes analyzed. Some papers use home win probability, while others use home win probability and home win probability squared.

Papers using data from sports where draws exist sometimes use the difference in home and away win probabilities as a proxy for outcome uncertainty. The Theil index (Theil, 1967) represents another common approach used to analyze data from sports with many draws, in particular football (soccer in North America), because it easily accommodates more than two discrete outcomes. The Theil index, or nearly identical measures used in information theory such as Shannon entropy measures (Štrumbelj, 2016), conveys very similar information about the relationship between the likelihood the home team wins an upcoming game and fans' expected utility from attending as a quadratic function of the home team win probability.

For these entropy measures, maximum uncertainty occurs when all outcomes are equally likely. Peel and Thomas (1992) described calculating Theil index values based on football odds but noted "these uncertainty measures were found to be, essentially, a quadratic function of HP" (pg. 326) and used a quadratic function of home win percentage in place of the Theil index. In regressions containing the Theil/Shannon measures, a significant, positive sign on the parameter on this variable supports the UOH and a significant, negative sign supports the loss aversion form of the CHZ model.

A few papers used untransformed betting odds, without calculating win probabilities from these odds. Though primarily concerned with testing the efficient market hypothesis on handicap betting odds, Peel and Thomas (1997) also made contributions to the understanding of the UOH in their study of Rugby League game attendance in the 1994/1995 season. The authors found a negative relationship between the absolute value of handicap betting odds and game attendance, providing evidence in support of the UOH. Pawlowski and Anders (2012) generated a dummy variable for games where the home team was favored in their analysis of German Bundesliga match attendance in the 2005/2006 season, finding the parameter estimate on this variable insignificant.

In a study of game attendance at National Football League (NFL) games played over the 1985–2008 seasons, Coates and Humphreys (2010) used point spreads as a game uncertainty measure, finding evidence contrary to the UOH. Games with high points spreads (thus more likely to be home victories) were associated with more viewers. The authors also employed a squared points spread term, which was not important for explaining variation in game attendance.

In a study of UFC mixed-martial arts pay-per-view buys, Reams and Shapiro (2017) found that betting odds were not associated with increased purchases. However, in a more recent GLM study of UFC bouts, Reams and Shapiro (2017) found that betting odds were not associated with increased pay-per-view buys. Examining television viewership for NCAA Division I FBS games played over the 2006–2010 seasons, Salaga and Tainsky (2015) used untransformed betting odds as an outcome uncertainty measure, finding that games with uncertain outcomes are associated with *lower* viewership, contrary to the UOH. In an analysis of television viewership for NCAA Division I FBS college football games in the 2014–2015 season, Brown and Salaga (2018) also used untransformed betting odds to measure outcome uncertainty, specifically the Over/Under and closing points spreads. Their findings generally failed to support the UOH.

In a study of television audiences for Spanish La Liga football (soccer) games played over the 2008/2009–2011/2012 seasons, Pérez Carcedo et al. (2017) used the natural log of "the ratio of the number of triple bets over the total number of bets placed in a particular game" (pg. 132) and the natural log of the number of triple and multiple bets placed on a game as uncertainty measures. The authors only found evidence supporting the UOH for high-profile games and concluded that "expected uncertainty of outcome may either have no effect on the TV audience or lead TV viewer behavior in different directions according to the type of match broadcast" (pg. 137).

Humphreys and Miceli (2020) offered a unique take on the UOH by developing a consumer-choice model for fan heterogeneity featuring home and visiting team fans. The authors analyzed game attendance for National Basketball Association (NBA) games over a long period, the 1979–2013 seasons, using point spreads as a measure of outcome uncertainty. Humphreys and Miceli (2020) found a negative relationship between point spreads and game attendance, but posited that outcome uncertainty might be more important to visiting team fans than home fans. They concluded that the UOH "is not necessary for league attendance to be maximized when home win probability is well below 100%" (pg. 11).

Many papers estimate home win probabilities from betting odds, occasionally including other factors reflecting outcome uncertainty in regression models. Most of these papers include both the home win probability and the square of the home win probability as measures of outcome uncertainty to produce a nonlinear relationship in order to assess the convexity or concavity of the home win probability–attendance relationship. Such results can identify evidence supporting either the UOH or loss aversion form of the CHZ model.

In addition to using the home team's position in the table, Peel and Thomas (1988) estimated home team win probabilities from betting odds in their analysis of English Football League attendance in the 1981/1982 season. The authors found increased home win probabilities associated with higher game attendance, supporting the home win preference version of the CHZ model but not the UOH.

In an early paper using an OLS regression model to explain variation in game attendance for the 1988 season in Major League Baseball's (MLB) National League, Knowles et al. (1992) found weak evidence supporting the UOH. The p-value on the positive parameter on home win probability, calculated from betting odds, was 0.56, but the p-value on the negative parameter on home win probability was 0.077. These results clearly support the "home win preference" version of the CHZ model, but the marginal statistical significance of the home win percentage squared term implies that attendance does not decline in games with strongly favored home teams, contrary to the predictions of the UOH. More recent research, discussed below, calls this result into question.

Forrest and Simmons (2002) pointed out that using betting odds alone may be problematic, as betting odds, at least in England, can be biased toward home teams. The author's solution was to incorporate the ratio of the home team's win probability to the away team's win probability as an uncertainty measure in their analysis of English Premier League game attendance in the 1997/1998 season. Forrest and Simmons (2002) find some evidence supporting the UOH from this variable.

In a study of German Bundesliga match attendance over the 1996/1997 and 1997/1998 seasons, Czarnitzki and Stadtmann (2002) also found no evidence supporting the UOH, but weak evidence supporting the loss aversion form of the CHZ model when using a quadratic function of the home team win percentage based on betting odds data. The parameter estimate on the home win probability variable was negative and significant, but the parameter estimate on the squared term was positive and borderline statistically significant.

Rather than squaring home team win probabilities, Owen and Weatherston (2004a) and Owen and Weatherston (2004b) used home win probabilities raised to the fourth power to introduce a nonlinear relationship between outcome uncertainty and attendance. In analyses of rugby union, in the form of Super 12 rugby union in New Zealand from 1999 to 2001 in the first paper and the National Provincial Championship-First Division from 2000 to 2003 in the second paper, the authors find no evidence in support of the UOH in either setting.

Lemke et al. (2010) reported evidence supporting the loss aversion version of the CHZ model in a sophisticated econometric study of data from MLB games played in the 2007 season. This paper estimated censored regression models with team fixed effects, as well as other regression models, that included the home win probability and home win probability squared. All model specifications reported by Lemke et al. (2010) reported evidence supporting loss aversion and clearly rejecting the UOH. In a study of 10,000 MLB games played over the 1985–2009 seasons, Beckman et al. (2011) derived home win probability and home win probability squared from betting lines. The authors' results, in terms of the effect of outcome uncertainty on attendance, were inconsistent, and offered no evidence supporting the UOH.

Alavy et al. (2010) used betting odds to calculate differences in home and away win probabilities, although the exact nature of this calculation is somewhat unclear. This paper used a novel data set containing minute-by-minute English Premier League television viewership from January 2002 to May 2005, and the authors also generate the probability of a draw, the squared difference of home and away win probabilities, and a series of index measures combining these probabilities. They find some evidence supporting the UOH, concluding that "Uncertainty matters in the sense that viewership is decreasing in the gap in the probabilities of each side winning, but is also decreasing in the probability of a draw" (pg. 89). However, the minute-by-minute viewership data analyzed in this paper cannot be compared to live match attendance.

Another innovation can be found in Coates and Humphreys (2012). Examining game attendance for NHL games for the 2005/2006–2009/2010 seasons, the authors derived home win probability and home win probability squared from betting odds. However, Coates and Humphreys (2012) also incorporate bands of home win probabilities. The results were mixed, with some evidence in support of UOH and some in support of loss aversion. This paper gives insight on the need for more complex regression models in this literature.

Coates et al. (2014), in a study of MLB game attendance over the 2005–2010 seasons, found strong evidence supporting the loss aversion form of the CHZ model. In an empirical test of a structural model derived directly from the CHZ model discussed above, the authors found that games where a home win was more certain generated higher attendance than games with uncertain outcome. These results were supported by the study of Humphreys and Zhou (2015), which used a similar methodology and the same data and also found evidence supporting the loss aversion form of the CHZ model.

Differences in home and away win probabilities were employed by Buraimo and Simmons (2015) in their analysis of English Premier League television viewership from the 2000/2001 to 2007/2008 seasons. Using both OLS and a Heckman selection model, the authors found no evidence supporting the UOH, and conclude that "uncertainty of outcome does not have a significant impact on television audience ratings overall" (pg. 466). Another English Premier League viewership by Scelles (2017), this one using the 2013/2014 season, also finds no evidence of UOH using the same uncertainty measure. In an analysis of spectator no-shows at German football (soccer) clubs over three seasons (2014/2015–2016/2017), Schreyer et al. (2019) also incorporated the "absolute difference in winning probability of home/away team" (pg. 585). They find slight evidence in support of UOH, but generally insignificant results.

Based on a tobit regression model, Cox (2018) found evidence of loss aversion in their study of English Premier League match attendance over the 2004/2005–2012/2013 seasons (although the paper never describes its results as such). The author found a negative relationship between home win probability and game attendance, with a positive relationship found between game attendance and home win probability squared. Cox (2018) also examined television audiences, finding generally insignificant effects of outcome uncertainty.

Humphreys and P´erez (2019) analyzed television audience size for Spanish First Division football matches played over the 2008/2009–2015/2016 seasons that aired on free television in Spain. Regression models included the home team win probability and home team win probability squared estimated from betting odds data. The presence of two dominant teams in the league, Real Madrid and FC Barcelona, generated large variation in home win probabilities in this setting. The results strongly supported the loss aversion form of the CHZ model.

Štrumbelj (2016) argued that the standard normalization procedure used to derive home win probabilities correcting for bookmaker over-round can result in biased estimates of outcome probabilities in sporting events. The author, based on OLS estimates for four seasons (2008/2009–2011/2012) of English Premier League attendance models, concluded that "the bias in probabilities derived with BN [basic normalization] also results in overestimation of the uncertainty of the outcome" (pg. 24) Instead, Štrumbelj (2016) recommended the Theil index to derive proxy variables for outcome uncertainty. However, Štrumbelj (2016) found no evidence in support of the UOH using the Theil index as an outcome uncertainty proxy.

In one of the earliest papers to develop evidence supporting the loss aversion form of the CHZ model, Peel and Thomas (1992) employed the Theil index as a measure of outcome uncertainty based on betting odds data in a study of English Football League match attendance in the 1986/1987 season. However, this method is abandoned for home win probabilities because the Theil index was "found to be, essentially, a quadratic function of HP [home-win probability]" (pg. 326). The authors found that high probability that the home team will win can drive attendance. In addition, Peel and Thomas (1992) also incorporated a squared home win probability term, revealing early evidence supporting loss aversion.

Examining English Premier League match attendance over the 2001/2002–2005/2006 seasons, Buraimo and Simmons (2008) found evidence supporting the loss aversion form of the CHZ model based on results from a tobit model accounting for censoring in attendance due to sellouts. Using home team win probability and home team probability squared variables based on betting odds as uncertainty proxy variables, the authors found that uncertainty of outcome led to lower game attendance, with the coefficient on the squared term being positive. The authors also estimated a model containing the Theil index and also found results consistent with the loss aversion of the CHZ model in this specification.

A comprehensive analysis of German Bundesliga game attendance over the 1999–2004 seasons by Benz et al. (2009) found no evidence supporting the UOH when using home win probability and home win probability squared, as well as the Theil index, as uncertainty measures. Benz et al. (2009) estimated a censored quantile regression model to account for different relationships at different points of the attendance distribution. Benz et al. (2009) used a variation of the Theil index in a response to the criticisms of Roy (2004) that the Theil index relies on all possible game outcomes. Their adjustment is to only factor in win probabilities in their analysis of German Bundesliga attendance. In a censored quantile regression, Benz et al. (2009) find no evidence of UOH from the Theil index or their adjusted index.

In an analysis of attendance at 302 German Bundesliga games in the 2005/2006 season, Pawlowski and Anders (2012) estimated a tobit model accounting for censoring in attendance including the Theil index as an outcome uncertainty proxy. The authors found evidence supporting the loss aversion form of the CHZ model but none supporting the UOH. Martins and Cró (2018) also employed the Theil index in a study of five seasons' worth of Portuguese First Division football attendance (2010/2011–2014/2015). The authors also reported evidence supporting the loss aversion of the CHZ model.

In an analysis of game attendance for four different European soccer leagues for the 2012/2013 season, Serrano et al. (2015) also used home win probabilities using the Theil index. The authors use a quantile regression and find mixed results, with evidence of UOH found in the highest quantiles. Using a non-parametric estimation of admission from season ticket holders at a Bundesliga club for the 2012/2013 season, Schreyer et al. (2016) find evidence of increased attendance in games with higher game outcome uncertainty. Their findings support the UOH. Both of these papers suggest the need for more advanced estimation methods to investigate UOH.

To measure outcome uncertainty in their analysis of television viewership for Italian Serie A football matches played over the 2008/2009–2014/2015 seasons, Caruso et al. (2019) elected to use the "Absolute difference between the home and the away team's win probabilities" as an outcome uncertainty proxy variable. These probabilities were derived from betting odds, although the exact procedure used to convert betting odds to win probabilities is unclear. Caruso et al. (2019) find little evidence in support of the UOH and conclude that fans are more interested in overall match quality than uncertainty of outcome.

In an analysis of television audience size for 210 individual pay-per-view boxing matches televised from 2006 to 2018, Butler et al. (2020) found inconclusive evidence about the impact of outcome uncertainty on pay-per-view audience size when using the Theil index applied to betting odds on the bouts. The parameter estimate on the Theil index variable took both positive and negative signs, all statistically different from zero, across different model specifications.

Betting market data represent an ideal source of data for estimating outcome probabilities for sporting events. Sports betting markets are thick, both bookmakers and bettors face strong incentives to set odds and point spreads to match future outcomes, and a large body of research shows that odds and point spreads set in these markets are informationally efficient and excellent forecasts of actual outcomes. Evidence based on outcome probabilities estimated using betting market data represents the strongest setting for analyzing the relationship between outcome uncertainty and attendance. Little research taking this approach reports evidence supporting the UOH. Indeed, a number of studies with large sample sizes report evidence supporting the loss aversion form of the CHZ model.

Research using other measures of outcome uncertainty

In addition to the two common approaches described above, several other papers employ other measures of outcome uncertainty. While not as common as the measures discussed above, these measures as a whole generate decidedly mixed evidence.

Some papers use functions of the number of points per game scored and allowed by each team as outcome uncertainty measures. Paton and Cooke (2005) employed the absolute difference in points per game between home and away teams as an uncertainty measure in their analysis of three seasons (2000–2002) of County Championship and National League cricket attendance. The authors found no relationship between uncertainty of outcome and attendance. In a study of television viewership for Danish and Norwegian league football (soccer) matches, Johnsen and Solvoll (2007) elected to use "the number of points the home team is behind the top team-the number of points the away the away team is behind the home team" (pg. 325) as a measure of uncertainty. OLS regression model results found no evidence supporting the UOH.

Forrest et al. (2005) developed an unusual alternative outcome uncertainty measure in their analysis of English Premier League television viewership over nine seasons (1993/1994–2001/2002). Their outcome uncertainty measure is described as "Home advantage plus points-per-game to date of the home team minus points-per-game to date of the away team" (pg. 654), where home advantage equals points-per-game achieved by all home teams in the previous season minus points-per-game achieved by all away teams in the previous season. Forrest et al. (2005) found some evidence in support of the UOH, but concede that more uncertain matches were more likely to be broadcast in the first place. In another study of English Premier League viewership, as well as game attendance over a shorter time period (1997/1998–2003/2004), Buraimo (2008) used the same uncertainty measure. In this case, the parameter estimate on the uncertainty-of-outcome proxy was insignificant and dropped from the final model. Benz et al. (2009) also used the Forrest et al. (2005) measure of uncertainty, but the parameter estimate on this variable, like in Buraimo (2008), was not statistically different from zero.

Another approach uses the difference in win percentage between the home and visiting teams. Meehan et al. (2007) adopted this measure in an analysis of MLB game attendance in the 2000–2002 seasons, finding strong evidence supporting the UOH. The authors conclude that "a 10-percentage point increase in the difference between the winning percentages of the two teams reduces attendance by 1,999 fans if the home team has a better record than the visiting team" (pg. 11). Similarly, in a study of television viewership for NFL Monday Night Football games played in the 1991 through 2002 seasons, Paul and Weinbach (2007) also found evidence supporting the UOH. Using the difference in win percentage between teams as an outcome uncertainty, the authors concluded that games with more uncertain outcomes generated higher viewership.

Other papers use sport-specific measures of outcome uncertainty. In a study of NFL viewership in the 2006 and 2007 seasons, Tainsky and McEvoy (2012) used a measure of outcome uncertainty based on Bill James' index of baseball game uncertainty that reflects a nonlinear function of the current and past winning percentages of the two teams involved in each game. The authors found a positive relationship between uncertainty and television viewership. In their analysis of seven seasons of Serie A football television viewership (2008/2009–2014/2015), Caruso et al. (2019) constructed an uncertainty measure of the "absolute difference between the home and the away team's relative wages, where a team relative wage is given by the team payroll divided by the seasonal average payroll" (pg. 34). The authors found evidence contrary to UOH. Matches involving large differences in wages generated higher viewership. Similar evidence was found by Schreyer and Torgler (2018) in their study of Formula One auto racing viewership in Germany from 1993 to 2014. As an uncertainty measure, the authors used the "summed difference between the qualification times of the top 3 qualifiers [later expanded to include more qualifiers]" (pg. 214). They also found evidence to the UOH in that uncertain race outcomes were associated with lower television viewership.

In a study of total spending on tickets for a single NBA team in the "2009 season" (pg. 540), Mills et al. (2016) calculated home team win probability and home team win probability squared. Only instead of deriving these from betting odds, the authors used Elo rankings of team strength, which were developed for the evaluation of chess players. However, this alternative outcome uncertainty measure did not generate results consistent with the UOH. Instead, Mills et al. (2016) found that uncertain games deterred fans from attending, consistent with the loss aversion form of the CHZ model.

Tainsky and Winfree (2010), in an analysis of MLB attendance over the 1996–2009 seasons, used a Monte Carlo simulation to predict home team win probabilities as an uncertainty-of-outcome proxy. The simulations used the home and road winning percentages and strength of schedules. However, the authors found no evidence linking this outcome uncertainty proxy to MLB game attendance.

A few of these studies generate evidence supporting the UOH, but the majority find no relationship between outcome uncertainty and attendance or television-viewing audiences. One limitation in these studies is the lack of clear nonlinearity in the outcome uncertainty–attendance relationship. Linear relationships cannot easily distinguish between the UOH and the loss aversion form of the CHZ model, since both make clear, nonlinear predictions about this relationship. The one study that uses a novel outcome proxy and a nonlinear relationship, Mills et al. (2016), finds strong evidence supporting the loss aversion form of the CHZ model.

Conclusions

A large body of empirical research analyzes the relationship between outcome uncertainty and attendance. Much of this research uses game-level data and estimates expected home win percentages based on data from betting markets. Many papers account for a nonlinear relationship that can be used to distinguish the UOH form of the CHZ model from the loss aversion version. The literature reviewed above contains a decided lack of evidence supporting UOH. Instead, much of the evidence in this literature supports the importance of loss aversion. A number of papers contain evidence supporting the home win preference form of the CHZ model, which, like the loss aversion form, cannot be reconciled with the UOH. Results in papers using large samples of games over multiple seasons and nonlinear functional forms uniformly support the importance of loss aversion in explaining variation in game attendance. Many also support the importance of home win preference. The centrality of the UOH in sports economics needs to be reassessed in future research.

The lack of widespread support for the UOH implies that the assumption of a convex relationship between team success and revenues in models of sports league outcomes needs to be reassessed. This assumption enjoys very little support in a large empirical literature. The standard two-team model developed by Fort and Quirk (1995) features downward-sloping marginal revenue curves in terms of wins or winning percentage; very successful teams in this model face negative marginal revenue from wins. The empirical support for home win preference in the existing literature argues that these downward-sloping marginal revenue curves do not reflect actual consumer decisions, calling into question the predictions made by this model.

The existing literature relies too much on the use of linear relationships between the outcome uncertainty proxy variables and attendance. Linear functional forms cannot adequately address the key nonlinear relationship between outcome uncertainty and attendance highlighted in the CHZ model. Future research should explore the role of functional form, including the use of semi-parametric methods that do not rely on parametric restrictions, to provide new evidence about this key relationship.

The existing empirical literature also features a lack of causal inference methods. While home win percentages estimated from betting market data might be plausibly exogenous to unobservable time-varying factors affecting attendance, this needs to be explored using modern causal inference methods such as instrumental variables, matching methods, or difference-in-differences methods where applicable. A handful of papers discussed above use instrumental variables, but other causal inference methods can be applied in this setting.

The importance of loss aversion clearly emerges in the theoretical and empirical literature discussed above. This underscores the need for more research on the role played by loss aversion in fan attendance decisions. The evidence summarized above shows that patterns of variation in attendance appear consistent with the presence of loss aversion, but little is known about the mechanisms through which loss aversion actually operates in this setting. Much of the existing evidence on loss aversion in other settings makes use of experimental approaches. These approaches could be applied to attendance decisions.

Survey-based research could also be a fruitful approach to better understanding the role played by outcome uncertainty in fan decisions. As an example, Pawlowski (2013) conducted a series of surveys of German Bundesliga fans during games, administered both at the stadium and at bars where games were broadcast. This paper found that "perceptions" of game uncertainty represented an important factor in fan attendance decisions, providing some evidence of UOH. Survey-based research can further investigate the role "perceived outcome uncertainty" as opposed, or complementary, to uncertainty-of-outcome measures described in section "Empirical evidence on outcome uncertainty and attendance" plays in fan attendance and television viewership decisions.

References

Alavy, K., Gaskell, A., Leach, S., and Szymanski, S. (2010). On the edge of your seat: Demand for football on television and the uncertainty of outcome hypothesis. *International Journal of Sport Finance*, 5(2):75–95.

Beckman, E. M., Cai, W., Esrock, R. M., and Lemke, R. J. (2012). Explaining game-to-game ticket sales for major league baseball games over time. *Journal of Sports Economics*, 13(5): 536–553.

Benz, M.-A., Brandes, L., and Franck, E. (2009). Do soccer associations really spend on a good thing? Empirical evidence on heterogeneity in the consumer response to match uncertainty of outcome. *Contemporary Economic Policy*, 27(2):216–235.

Borland, J. (1987). The demand for Australian Rules football. *Economic Record*, 63(3):220–230.

Borland, J. and Lye, J. (1992). Attendance at Australian Rules football: A panel study. *Applied Economics*, 24(9):1053–1058.

Brown, K. M. and Salaga, S. (2018). NCAA football television viewership: Product quality and consumer preference relative to market expectations. *Sport Management Review*, 21(4):377–390.

Buraimo, B. (2008). Stadium attendance and television audience demand in English league football. *Managerial and Decision Economics*, 29(6):513–523.

Buraimo, B. and Simmons, R. (2008). Do sports fans really value uncertainty of outcome? Evidence from the English premier league. *International Journal of Sport Finance*, 3(3):146–155.

Buraimo, B. and Simmons, R. (2015). Uncertainty of outcome or star quality? Television audience demand for English premier league football. *International Journal of the Economics of Business*, 22(3):449–469.

Butler, D., Butler, R., and Maxcy, J. (2020). New insights on the louis-schmeling paradox: Determinants of demand for subscription and pay-per-view boxing. *European Sport Management Quarterly*, 1–21. doi: 10.1080/16184742.2020.1820063.

Card, D. and Dahl, G. B. (2011). Family violence and football: The effect of unexpected emotional cues on violent behavior. *The Quarterly Journal of Economics*, 126(1):103.

Caruso, R., Addesa, F., and Di Domizio, M. (2019). The determinants of the TV demand for soccer: Empirical evidence on Italian Serie A for the period 2008–2015. *Journal of Sports Economics*, 20(1):25–49.

Coates, D. and Humphreys, B. R. (2010). Week to week attendance and competitive balance in the National Football League. *International Journal of Sport Finance*, 5(4):239–252.

Coates, D. and Humphreys, B. R. (2012). Game attendance and outcome uncertainty in the national hockey league. *Journal of Sports Economics*, 13(4):364–377.

Coates, D., Humphreys, B. R., and Zhou, L. (2014). Reference-dependent preferences, loss aversion, and live game attendance. *Economic Inquiry*, 52(3):959–973.

Cox, A. (2018). Spectator demand, uncertainty of results, and public interest: Evidence from the English premier league. *Journal of Sports Economics*, 19(1):3–30.

Czarnitzki, D. and Stadtmann, G. (2002). Uncertainty of outcome versus reputation: Empirical evidence for the first german football division. *Empirical Economics*, 27(1):101–112.

Falter, J.-M. and Pérignon, C. (2000). Demand for football and intramatch winning probability: An essay on the glorious uncertainty of sports. *Applied Economics*, 32(13):1757–1765.

Forrest, D. and Simmons, R. (2002). Outcome uncertainty and attendance demand in sport: the case of English soccer. *Journal of the Royal Statistical Society: Series D (The Statistician)*, 51(2):229–241.

Forrest, D., Simmons, R., and Buraimo, B. (2005). Outcome uncertainty and the couch potato audience. *Scottish Journal of Political Economy*, 52(4):641–661.

Fort, R. and Quirk, J. (1995). Cross-subsidization, incentives, and outcomes in professional team sports leagues. *Journal of Economic Literature*, 33(3):1265–1299.

García, J. and Rodríguez, P. (2002). The determinants of football match attendance revisited: Empirical evidence from the Spanish football league. *Journal of Sports Economics*, 3(1):18–38.

Humphreys, B. R. and Miceli, T. J. (2020). Outcome uncertainty, fan travel, and aggregate attendance. *Economic Inquiry*, 58(1):462–473.

Humphreys, B. R. and P´erez, L. (2019). Loss aversion, upset preference, and sports television viewing audience size. *Journal of Behavioral and Experimental economics*, 78:61–67.

Humphreys, B. R. and Zhou, L. (2015). The louis–schmelling paradox and the league standing effect reconsidered. *Journal of Sports Economics*, 16(8):835–852.

Jennett, N. (1984). Attendances, uncertainty of outcome and policy in Scottish league football. *Scottish Journal of Political Economy*, 31(2):176–198.

Johnsen, H. and Solvoll, M. (2007). The demand for televised football. *European Sport Management Quarterly*, 7(4):311–335.

Kahneman, D. and Tversky, A. (1979). Prospect theory: An analysis of decision under risk. *Econometrica*, 47(2):263–292.

Knowles, G., Sherony, K., and Haupert, M. (1992). The demand for major league baseball: A test of the uncertainty of outcome hypothesis. *The American Economist*, 72–80.

Koszegi, B. and Rabin, M. (2006). A model of reference-dependent preferences. *The Quarterly Journal of Economics*, 121(4):1133.

Lee, Y. H. and Fort, R. (2008). Attendance and the uncertainty-of-outcome hypothesis in baseball. *Review of Industrial Organization*, 33(4):281–295.

Lemke, R., Leonard, M., and Tlhokwane, K. (2010). Estimating attendance at Major League Baseball games for the 2007 season. *Journal of Sports Economics*, 11(3):316.

Madalozzo, R. and Berber Villar, R. (2009). Brazilian football: What brings fans to the game? *Journal of Sports Economics*, 10(6):639–650.

Martins, A. M. and Cr´o, S. (2018). The demand for football in Portugal: New insights on outcome uncertainty. *Journal of Sports Economics*, 19(4):473–497.

Marzilli Ericson, K. M. and Fuster, A. (2014). The endowment effect. *Annual Review Economy*, 6(1):555–579.

Meehan, J. W., Nelson, R. A., and Richardson, T. V. (2007). Competitive balance and game attendance in major league baseball. *Journal of Sports Economics*, 8(6):563.

Meier, H. E., Konjer, M., and Leinwather, M. (2016). The demand for women's league soccer in Germany. *European Sport Management Quarterly*, 16(1):1–19.

Mills, B. M., Salaga, S., and Tainsky, S. (2016). Nba primary market ticket consumers: Ex ante expectations and consumer market origination. *Journal of Sport Management*, 30(5):538–552.

Neale, W. C. (1964). The peculiar economics of professional sports. *The Quarterly Journal of Economics*, 78(1):1–14.

Owen, P. D. and Weatherston, C. R. (2004a). Uncertainty of outcome and Super 12 Rugby Union attendance. *Journal of Sports Economics*, 5(4):347–370.

Owen, P. D. and Weatherston, C. R. (2004b). Uncertainty of outcome, player quality and attendance at national provincial championship rugby union matches: An evaluation in light of the competitions review. *Economic Papers: A Journal of Applied Economics and Policy*, 23(4):301–324.

Paton, D. and Cooke, A. (2005). Attendance at county cricket: An economic analysis. *Journal of Sports Economics*, 6(1):24–45.

Paul, R. J. and Weinbach, A. P. (2007). The uncertainty of outcome and scoring effects on Nielsen ratings for Monday night football. *Journal of Economics and Business*, 59(3):199–211.

Paul, R. J. and Weinbach, A. P. (2013). Uncertainty of outcome and television ratings for the NHL and MLS. *Journal of Prediction Markets*, 7(1):53–65.

Pawlowski, T. (2013). Testing the uncertainty of outcome hypothesis in European professional football: A stated preference approach. *Journal of Sports Economics*, 14(4):341–367.

Pawlowski, T. and Anders, C. (2012). Stadium attendance in German professional football–the (un) importance of uncertainty of outcome reconsidered. *Applied Economics Letters*, 19(16):1553–1556.

Pawlowski, T. and Nalbantis, G. (2015). Competition format, championship uncertainty and stadium attendance in European football–a small league perspective. *Applied Economics*, 47(38):4128–4139.

Peel, D. and Thomas, D. A. (1988). Outcome uncertainty and the demand for football: An analysis of match attendances in the English football league. *Scottish Journal of Political Economy*, 35(3):242–249.

Peel, D. A. and Thomas, D. A. (1992). The demand for football: some evidence on outcome uncertainty. *Empirical Economics*, 17(2):323–331.

Peel, D. A. and Thomas, D. A. (1997). Handicaps, outcome uncertainty and attendance demand. *Applied Economics Letters*, 4(9):567–570.

P'erez Carcedo, L., Puente Robles, V., and Rodr'ıguez Guerrero, P. (2017). Factors determining TV soccer viewing: Does uncertainty of outcome really matter? *International Journal of Sport Finance*, 12:124–139.

Rascher, D. A. and Solmes, J. P. (2007). Do fans want close contests? A test of the uncertainty of outcome hypothesis in the National Basketball Association. *International Journal of Sport Finance*, 2(3):130–141.

Reams, L. and Shapiro, S. (2017). Who's the main attraction? Star power as a determinant of ultimate fighting championship pay-per-view demand. *European Sport Management Quarterly*, 17(2):132–151.

Rottenberg, S. (1956). The baseball players' labor market. *Journal of Political Economy*, 64(3):242–258.

Roy, P. (2004). *Die Zuschauernachfrage im professionellen Teamsport*. PhD thesis, Aachen: Shaker Verlag.

Sacheti, A., Gregory-Smith, I., and Paton, D. (2014). Uncertainty of outcome or strengths of teams: An economic analysis of attendance demand for international cricket. *Applied Economics*, 46(17):2034–2046.

Salaga, S. and Tainsky, S. (2015). The effects of outcome uncertainty, scoring, and pregame expectations on Nielsen ratings for bowl championship series games. *Journal of Sports Economics*, 16(5):439–459.

Scelles, N. (2017). Star quality and competitive balance? Television audience demand for English premier league football reconsidered. *Applied Economics Letters*, 24(19):1399–1402.

Schreyer, D., Schmidt, S. L., and Torgler, B. (2016). Against all odds? Exploring the role of game outcome uncertainty in season ticket holders' stadium attendance demand. *Journal of Economic Psychology*, 56:192–217.

Schreyer, D., Schmidt, S. L., and Torgler, B. (2017). Game outcome uncertainty and the demand for international football games: Evidence from the German TV market. *Journal of Media Economics*, 30(1):31–45.

Schreyer, D., Schmidt, S. L., and Torgler, B. (2019). Football spectator no-show behavior. *Journal of Sports Economics*, 20(4):580–602.

Schreyer, D. and Torgler, B. (2018). On the role of race outcome uncertainty in the TV demand for formula 1 Grands prix. *Journal of Sports Economics*, 19(2):211–229.

Serrano, R., Garc'ıa-Bernal, J., Fern'andez-Olmos, M., and Espitia-Escuer, M. A. (2015). Expected quality in European football attendance: Market value and uncertainty reconsidered. *Applied Economics Letters*, 22(13):1051–1054.

Štrumbelj, E. (2016). A comment on the bias of probabilities derived from betting odds and their use in measuring outcome uncertainty. *Journal of sports economics*, 17(1):12–26.

Szymanski, S. (2003). The economic design of sporting contests. *Journal of Economic Literature*, 41(4):1137–1187.

Tainsky, S. and McEvoy, C. D. (2012). Television broadcast demand in markets without local teams. *Journal of Sports Economics*, 13(3):250–265.

Tainsky, S. and Winfree, J. (2010). Short-run demand and uncertainty of outcome in Major League Baseball. *Review of Industrial Organization*, 1–18.

Theil, H. (1967). *Economics and Information Theory*. New York: Rand McNally.

Wilson, P. and Sim, B. (1995). The demand for semi-pro league football in Malaysia 1989–91: A panel data approach. *Applied Economics*, 27(1):131–138.

14 Moving toward behavioral stadium attendance demand research

First lessons learned from exploring football spectator no-show behavior in Europe

Dominik Schreyer[1]

Introduction

Stadium attendance demand research is firmly anchored in the literature on the economics of sports. In fact, as Fort (2005) observes, exploring the many potential determinants of spectator demand is as old as our field itself, since Rottenberg (1956), in his pioneering article on the baseball players' labor market, was first to offer a detailed demand specification, already including factors as manifold as the ticket price, potential recreational substitutes, and, perhaps most controversially, competitive balance and the resulting match outcome uncertainty. However, Melzer and Stäglin (1965), analyzing the potential correlation between the home and the away team's league position and German Bundesliga stadium attendance demand in its inaugural season 1963–1964, and later Demmert (1973) and Noll (1974), were the first to make a significant empirical contribution to the then-emerging research stream.

In fact, we sports economists, in particular, have tested both Rottenberg's (1956) original stadium attendance demand specification and its extensions extensively over the last few decades. Consequently, today, there already exists a massive body of empirical literature on the potential determinants of spectator interest in diverse professional sports, including baseball (e.g., Coates and Humphreys, 2014), European football (e.g., Pawlowski and Nalbantis, 2015), handball (e.g., Storm, Nielsen, and Jakobsen, 2018), hockey (e.g., Jones and Ferguson, 1988), and rugby (e.g., Carmichael, Millington, and Simmons, 1999), among others. Perhaps not surprisingly, this rich literature has been reviewed more than once in the past (e.g., Borland and MacDonald, 2003; Rodríguez, 2019; Villar and Guerrero, 2009). Also, Schreyer and Ansari (2021) have made an initial attempt to scope a subset of the increasingly diverse literature, though the stream's sheer volume might require additional scoping in the future.

While there exists a great interest in gradually expanding the boundaries of this important research stream by subsequently analyzing additional sports in previously unexplored markets (e.g., Rodríguez, 2019), our field's response

DOI: 10.4324/9781003080824-18

to the potential methodological challenges arising from the quasi-standard use of aggregated attendance data seems to be less dedicated (cf. Schreyer and Ansari, 2021). For example, as Forrest, Simmons, and Buraimo (2005) note, in most European professional football leagues, executives distribute a large share of all available tickets to season ticket holders (STHs) well in advance of a season.[2] Still, those published, i.e., official, aggregated attendance data routinely employed in stadium attendance demand research typically neither distinguish between the different spectator groups (e.g., Dobson and Goddard, 2011) nor indicate whether a ticket owner decided to actually attend a certain match.[3] Therefore, as Schreyer, Schmidt, and Torgler (2016) summarize, these frequently exploited data typically subsume two different, subsequent, and temporally often far-apart decisions for differing ticket products from multiple stakeholder groups, including not only paying customers but also owners of complimentary/free tickets,[4] whose short-term behavioral responses to match characteristics might differ significantly: first, an individual's decision whether to accept/purchase a ticket for a particular match; and second, the ticket holder's subsequent decision whether to attend it.[5] Hence, analyzing such aggregated attendance data is likely to result in a misjudgment of actual effect sizes (e.g., Benz, Brandes, and Franck, 2009; Chiang and Jane, 2013; Reade and Singleton, 2020), though an empirical proof is still wanting.

To address these potential methodological challenges, we, i.e., my coauthors and I,[6] have slowly begun moving toward behavioral stadium attendance research by analyzing a distinct spectator decision in the past few years: football spectator no-show behavior. That is, back in 2013, we began modeling a ticket holder's unambiguous decision whether to physically attend a football match rather than his/her behavioral intent.[7] As the resulting data generated through the stadium entrance system capture a ticket holder's distinct admission decision on matchday, we believe it is more likely to help us understand better whether factors relating to, for example, team lineups (e.g., the appearance/injury of star players), the weather (e.g., precipitation), and the winning probability of the home team, all of which are subject to change in the short term, affect spectator interest. Similarly, analyzing such data is more likely to allow us to detect behavioral responses to exogenous shocks such as dynamically spreading diseases or terrorist attacks, which might remain concealed otherwise.[8]

Summarizing our recent empirical research from exploring football spectator no-show behavior in Europe, in this book chapter, we reflect on what we have learned over these past few years and, perhaps more importantly, what we think should be addressed in future stadium attendance demand research. Accordingly, we organize the remaining chapter around seven core lessons learned from our work in the field. More precisely, we, first, disenchant a convenient myth, i.e., the myth that STHs are behaviorally loyal, before we, second, explain why we believe it is important to understand such disloyal spectator behavior better. Then, we, third, provide some additional context on the increasingly important no-show phenomenon; fourth, summarize our previous findings on the potential determinants of football spectator no-show behavior; and, fifth, summarize their robustness across different football leagues. Finally, we address potential future research avenues.

Lessons learned from exploring European football spectator no-show behavior

Below, we reflect on what we have learned from our analyses of football spectator no-show behavior over the last years and, perhaps more importantly, what we think should be addressed in future stadium attendance demand research. Accordingly, we organize our thoughts around seven key lessons. Although the sequence of these lessons follows an inherent logic, they are written to be read independently of each other.

Not all STHs are unconditionally behaviorally loyal; some of them are frequent no-shows

The idea that STHs are unconditionally behaviorally loyal, attending every home match, is relatively widespread among sports economists.[9] For example, Allan and Roy (2008) argue that STHs are unlikely to be affected by match-specific characteristics. Somewhat similarly, Benz et al. (2009) assume "that all season ticket holders attend each match within a certain season" (p. 220), referring to a sufficiently strong habit persistence. Intriguingly, this explanation is not only common in the field (e.g., Ge, Humphreys, and Zhou, 2020; Mueller, 2020; Simmons, 1996) but also initially plausible. That is, as Dobson and Goddard (2011) denote, "[t]he disincentives for season ticket holders to attend are small, unless the home team's performance is so poor that it is less painful to stay at home" (p. 323).

Whether assuming such strong behavioral loyalty from STHs may (or may not) have been previously reasonable, it is most certainly a thing of the past. For example, exploring panel data from 13,892 STHs of a German Bundesliga club during the season 2012–2013 (cf. Schreyer et al., 2016, 2018), we observe a no-show rate of about 17%, on average. In this environment, only about 3,113 STHs, i.e., roughly one in five, attended all 17 home matches. As such, STHs missed, on average, about three home matches, with roughly 3,000 of them omitting attendance for at least five times. Similarly, in a more recent discussion paper (cf. Schreyer and Torgler, 2021), analyzing panel data from 8,734 STHs of a Swiss Super League club over a significantly extended period of time covering several seasons, we observe a no-show rate of roughly 30%, on average, indicating that STHs skipped between about five and six home matches per year. In fact, additional evidence primarily generated in the related field of sports management research suggests that such no-show behavior patterns are common among most STHs (e.g., Karg and McDonald, 2011; Sampaio, Sordi, and Perin, 2015; Solberg and Mehus, 2014), as does additional anecdotal evidence generated across different sports (cf. Schreyer,

2019). This suggests that, in fact, STHs seem responsive to match characteristics and that this spectator group,[10] thus, accounts for significant variance in in-stadium attendance on a matchday that, however, has previously mostly been unobserved in the empirical literature.[11]

Understanding spectator no-show behavior is important for the sporting industry

During the (many) review processes we went through over the past years, a common argument against even considering our work on spectator no-show behavior was that understanding the phenomenon better is unnecessary because – in a nutshell – increasing stadium attendance demand is effectively about generating additional income for a sporting club. Thus, unlike a fan's purchase decision, the fan's subsequent admission decision was largely irrelevant to most, though thankfully not all, reviewers.[12]

For football executives, in contrast, understanding the antecedents and consequences of spectator no-show behavior better is increasingly important for several reasons (cf. Schreyer et al., 2020; Schreyer and Torgler, 2021). For example, as no-show behavior among STHs is a well-known antecedent of STH churn (e.g., McDonald et al., 2014), monitoring a STH's individual no-show rate can help these executives anticipate, and then perhaps lessen, future churn intentions immediately while simultaneously establishing an early warning system detecting failing product quality. More specifically, by monitoring emerging no-show habits among their STHs on a match-to-match routine, executives receive permanent feedback that otherwise would only occur once a year, i.e., during the annual season ticket renewal period. Somewhat similarly, predicting spectator no-show behavior in the preparation phase of the matchday can help those executives manage football clubs usually in strong demand, in particular to generate additional income by engaging in systematic overbooking activities (e.g., Schreyer, 2019; cf. Section 2.7),[13] while simultaneously mitigating the otherwise expectable complains from those disappointed fans on often long waiting lists.

Beyond the mere generation of additional ticket income, and the reduction of potential future season ticket churn, however, eliminating the many causes of spectator no-show behavior is necessary because as the number of no-shows is increasing, the otherwise positive effects associated with in-stadium attendances are likely to diminish, including (1) diminishing returns from catering activities,[14] merchandise sales, and issuing parking tickets, (2) prohibiting an effective matchday operation, and (3) reducing the much-discussed home-field advantage (e.g., Ponzo and Scoppa, 2018; Reade, Schreyer, and Singleton, 2020a; Sutter and Kocher, 2004).[15] Further, the resulting decrease in the stadium atmosphere that comes with an increase in empty seats is diametrically opposed to the often demanding needs of a football club's many external stakeholders, including broadcasters, corporate sponsors, investors, and also customers in the hospitality section. While these stakeholders might all benefit from an enhanced atmosphere directly on the ground (e.g., McDonald, 2010), absent TV audiences, in particular, might prescind from future stadium visits if a high no-sow rate persists (e.g., Oh, Sung, and Kwon, 2017). Also, thus football clubs increasingly diversifying their income sources (e.g., Schmidt and Holzmayer, 2018) are likely to earn less auxiliary revenues generated through, for example, club museum visits, overnight stays in club-owned hotels, and stadium tour bookings if spectator no-show behavior increases.

Although our research has initially centered around Bundesliga no-show behavior, no-shows are not a league-specific phenomenon nor is the situation in Germany particularly severe

Naturally, we began exploring spectator no-show behavior in our home market, i.e., the German football market (cf. Schreyer and Däuper, 2018).[16] In this particular environment, we initially counted, on average, about 4,107 no-shows per Bundesliga match, which equals a no-show rate of about 10%. However, as we document in a subsequent, more nuanced study (Schreyer et al., 2019), no-show rates tend to be quite different among Bundesliga clubs, with a range between roughly 5% and slightly more than 15%. Naturally, with about one in ten Bundesliga tickets remaining unused, on average, the question arises whether this observation should be a matter of concern for Bundesliga executives.

While we are unaware of any official information on comparable no-show rates across professional sporting leagues, there's increasing (anecdotal) evidence that a no-show rate of about 10% might, per se, be considered initially largely unproblematic.[17] For example, in US College Football, the no-show rate is currently said to be, on average, about 30% (Wall Street Journal, 2018). In European football, even more prominent clubs tend to observe two-digit no-show rates, in particular among their STHs (e.g., FC Business, 2018). Somewhat similarly, in Switzerland, for instance, FC Basel 1893 reports that roughly three out of ten STHs omit attendance, on average (e.g., Schreyer and Torgler, 2021). In Brazil, Sampaio et al. (2015) document a no-show rate of about 18% among Porto Alegre FC STHs during the three seasons 2008–2010.[18] Still, the management of most professional sporting clubs prefer not to report official information on their no-show rates (e.g., Deutschlandfunk, 2019).

Intriguingly, in other industries, most executives would probably be happy with a low two-digit no-show rate.[19] For example, in the health care industry, where both modeling and managing no-show behavior have a significantly longer tradition, Dantas, Fleck, Oliveira, and Hamacher (2018) note a no-show rate of 23%, on average, with some medical specialties observing no-show rates of up to 79%. Similarly, Oh and Su (2018) report that, in the hospitality industry, the no-show rate in restaurants located in large cities can be as high as 20%. In the transportation industry, American Airlines once estimated that roughly 15% of all seats on sold-out flights would be empty without overbooking (Smith, Leimkuhler, and Darrow, 1992). Still, in North America, a no-show rate of between 6% and 10% seems to be rather common among airline passengers (cf. Garrow and Koppelman, 2004; Lawrence, Hong, and Cherrier, 2003).[20]

However, having said that, there seems to be a slightly negative trend in football spectator no-show behavior that should better not be ignored. More specifically, we later observed a gradual increase in the no-show rate from about 9.25% in the season 2014–2015 to roughly 11.96% in the season 2017–2018 (cf. Schreyer, 2019). As such, Bundesliga executives, in particular, might be well advised to monitor the development closely and, where necessary, to adapt their product, i.e., the stadium experience, to meet the spectator needs better.

In Bundesliga, away team characteristics are a key driver of spectator no-show behavior

In our first two papers dedicated to the emerging phenomenon, that is, football spectator no-show behavior (Schreyer and Däuper, 2018; Schreyer, Schmidt, and Torgler, 2019), unfortunately, we failed to add the necessary nuance to our sets of explanatory variables. For example, interested in player talent's role in shaping football spectator no-show behavior, we initially just added the cumulative market value of the two adversaries' starting 11 to our models rather than including separate values for both the home team and the away team.[21] Also, we initially controlled for the stadium capacity rather than, for instance, separately adding information on both the number of complimentary/free tickets and the number of paid tickets, i.e., disaggregated into matchday and season tickets. However, as we began developing a better understanding of the phenomenon over time, and as more data became available to us, we subsequently corrected these early mistakes. Therefore, in Table 14.1, we summarize our findings from previous research on football spectator no-show behavior in Germany (see also above).

Across all our previous research on Bundesliga football no-show behavior, we observe a robust effect of those match quality aspects capturing away team characteristics. For example, we observe that football spectator no-show behavior decreases for home matches featuring an opponent with a star-studded squad (Schreyer, 2019) or a rich Bundesliga history (e.g., Schreyer et al., 2019), and also geographical derbies (e.g., Schreyer and Däuper, 2018). However, this does not mean that football spectators are not curious about promoted teams; quite contrary, they are, as the no-show rate seems to decrease for recently promoted visiting teams.[22] Further, we observe some first evidence that spectators react favorably to competitive balance and the resulting match outcome uncertainty (e.g., Schreyer, 2019).

Perhaps not surprisingly, the opportunity costs arising from physical stadium attendance also shape football spectator no-show behavior. In particular,

Table 14.1 Determinants of Football Spectator No-Show Behavior in Germany

	Bundesliga[a]							Bundesliga 2[e]
	I	II	III	IV	V	VI	No-show rate increases…	Observed effect is…
Economic aspects								
Market size				ns			…rather not (no significant effect).	…robust.
Unemployment				ns			…rather not (no significant effect).	…robust.
Quality aspects								
Home win probability	***						…if WPH increases, then decreases.[b]	
Competitive balance			***	ns		***	…if APD increases.[c]	…not robust (contrary).
Competitive intensity			ns				…rather not (no significant effect).	
Market value			***	***			…rather not (no significant effect).	…not robust (ns).
Market value, home						ns	…rather not (no significant effect).	
Market value, away						***	…if market value (away) decreases.	
Promotion, home				***		***	…if home team was not promoted.	
Promotion, away						***	…if away team was not promoted.	
Pioneer, home						ns	…rather not (no significant effect).	
Tradition, away			***	***		***	…if away team tradition decreases.	…not robust (ns).
Geographical derby			***	***		***	…if match is not a derby.	…not robust (ns).[f]
Pitch quality						ns	…rather not (no significant effect).	
Opportunity costs								
Midweek match			***	***		***	…if match is played midweek.	…not robust (ns).
Matchday			***	***		***	…until midseason, then decreases.	…not robust (ns).
First half						ns	…rather not (no significant effect).	
Holidays				ns			…rather not (no significant effect).	…robust.
Substitute, free TV			ns	ns		ns	…rather not (no significant effect).	…robust.
Temperature			***	***		***	…for extreme temperatures (low/high).	…not robust (ns).
Precipitation			***	ns		***	…if rain sets in.	…not robust (ns).

270 Dominik Schreyer

Air pressure		ns	...rather not (no significant effect).
Interval		ns	...rather not (no significant effect).
Terrorist attacks		★★★	...temporarily after an attack.
Season fixed effects	★★★	★★★	...over time. ...not robust (★★★). ...not robust (ns).
Other			
Stadium capacity	★★★	★★★	...if stadium capacity increases.
Distributed tickets		★★★	...if the number of tickets increases.
Sold tickets		★★★	...if the number of sold tickets increases.
Sold tickets, season		★★★	...if the number of season tickets increases.
Sold tickets, match		★★★	...if the number of match tickets increases.
Free tickets			...rather not (no significant effect).
Accommodation			
Ticket quantity	★★★	★★★	...if the number of tickets increases.
Ticket, standing area	★★★	★★★	...if spectator stands.
Ticket, distance to pitch	★★★	★★★	...if distance to pitch increases.
Ticket, cost	★★★	★★★	...if ticket price decreases.
Socio-demographics			
Age	★★★	★★★	...if spectator age decreases.
Gender, male	ns	Ns	...rather not (no significant effect).
Inhabitant	★★★		...if spectator lives not in host city.
Geographical distance		★★★	...if km increases, then decreases.[d]
Habit, missed match	★★★		...if spectator missed the last match.
Churn	★★★		...if spectator has already resigned.

Abbreviations, notes, and sources: Table adapted from Schreyer and Torgler (2021); insignificant/significant effect (ns/★★★); statistical significance at the 5% level (p < .05).
[a]Empirical studies numbered from I to VI are Schreyer et al. (2016: I), Schreyer et al. (2018: II), Schreyer and Däuper (2018: III), Schreyer et al. (2019: IV), Frevel and Schreyer (2020: V), and Schreyer (2019: VI).
[b]Winning probability of the home team (WPH);
[c]Absolute difference in the winning probability of home/away team (APD);
[d]Kilometer between home/stadium (KM);
[e]Schreyer et al. (2019);
[f]Effect is marginally significant, though.

we observe a robust negative effect of midweek fixtures (e.g., Schreyer and Däuper, 2018), mid-season matches, and extreme temperatures (i.e., sub-zero/high temperature and rainfall; e.g., Schreyer, 2019). Furthermore, we note a temporary, negative spectator response to an exogenous shock, i.e., a terrorist attack (cf. Frevel and Schreyer, 2020).

Earlier, by analyzing disaggregated STH data (e.g., Schreyer et al., 2016), we were already able to shed some first light on the potential role of those factors capturing both accommodation and socio-demographics in predicting football spectator no-show behavior.[23] Here, echoing our findings on the role of opportunity costs summarized above, we, for example, observe a significant, and non-linear, role of a STH's geographical distance, implying that travel time affects football spectator decision-making on matchday (e.g., Schreyer et al., 2018), as does group membership, which might increase co-ordination costs among members. In addition, we note that football spectator no-show behavior is likely to be affected by a STH's age, though, in our early research projects, we, unfortunately, did not control for potential non-linearity (cf. Schreyer and Torgler, 2021).[24]

Rare initial robustness checks reveal differences across both countries and leagues

Although we could explore football spectator no-show behavior in the German Bundesliga in some necessary detail, we, as a field, are only just beginning to examine the robustness of our previous results in other sports markets. More precisely, although we were able to compare Bundesliga and Bundesliga 2 data early (Schreyer et al., 2019), we have begun exploring Swiss football spectator data only recently (e.g., Schreyer and Torgler, 2021). Complementary, Karg, Nguyen, and McDonald (2021) have modeled individual STH attendance decisions in the Australian Football League (AFL). In contrast, Popp, Simmons, Watanabe, and Shapiro (2019) are currently working on modeling aggregated college football no-show behavior.[25]

Nevertheless, these initial robustness checks already reveal potential differences in the determinants of spectator no-show behavior across both different countries and leagues, perhaps even clubs. More specifically, as can be seen from Table 14.1, exploring a panel data set containing spectator no-show behavior information from a total of 25 Bundesliga and Bundesliga 2 clubs across the three seasons from 2014–2015 to 2016–2017, we observe that differences between the two German professional football leagues prevail, despite some few similarities. Somewhat similarly, comparing our preliminary results on STH no-show behavior in Switzerland with earlier results generated in Germany (Schreyer et al., 2016, 2018), we observe a more nuanced, i.e., non-linear, relationship between both STH age and the ticket price and STH no-show behavior (Schreyer and Torgler, 2021; cf. Section 2.4), among others.[26] Consistently, initial empirical evidence from analyzing STH behavior in the AFL (Karg et al., 2021) suggests that the determinants of spectator no-show behavior might be contextual.

To understand spectator no-show behavior better, we need to work more closely with associations and clubs

A common note in the previous literature on stadium attendance demand is that better stadium attendance data, for example, disaggregated spectator data capturing behavior/behavioral intentions by different stakeholder groups,[27] are not publicly available (e.g., Humphreys and Miceli, 2020; Paul, Weinbach, and Riccardi, 2019; Pawlowski and Nalbantis, 2015). This is certainly true.[28] However, if we, as a field, want to understand better what shapes spectator decision-making in the future, this observation should hardly serve as a perhaps convenient justification to stick to the status quo. In other words, we might need to, perhaps must, make a step toward both sports associations and sporting clubs, despite the inherent potential downsides (e.g., high coordination costs, potential dependencies, and additional/more work).[29] At least in our recent experience, the advantages of exploring unique data have largely outweighed the disadvantages, and while sporting clubs might be still reluctant to release better data to the public, most of their executives were happy to share their data, if existing, with us for academic purposes, as long as we were promising to discuss the managing implications with them in the necessary detail.

Naturally, an alternative would be exploring alternative decisions in those environments where methodological problems are existent but less pronounced. Barajas, Shakina, and Gasparetto (2019), for example, explore data from a market, i.e., Brazil, where season tickets are still rather uncommon, thus modeling a distinct decision, i.e., matchday ticket holders' intention to attend a certain match as proxied by the number of distributed tickets in advance. Similarly, some authors have begun to analyze attendance data after subtracting season tickets data, which are increasingly being available to the public (e.g., Benz et al., 2009; Bond and Addesa, 2020; Brandes, Franck, and Theiler, 2013).[30] Also, survey-based research might offer additional insights (e.g., Karg and McDonald, 2011; Schreyer, 2019; Solberg and Mehus, 2014), primarily on potential socio-demographic differences in stadium attendance demand, despite the usual reservations against it.[31]

While these approaches are certainly not without their merits, it remains unclear whether this will help the field of stadium attendance demand research to leave its largely "stationary state" (Rodríguez, 2019: 168).[32] In contrast, employing individual behavioral data from football associations and/or clubs might offer more definitive insights in the role of age, gender, and emerging no-show habits in predicting football spectator decision-making behavior (e.g., Schreyer and Torgler, 2021). Also, such data might help us, as a field, to understand related decisions such as the subsequent decision of when to enter the stadium on a matchday (e.g., Schreyer et al., 2013) or whether, and if so when, complimentary/free tickets and also the increasingly important hospitality tickets find subsequent use better.[33]

Our understanding of appropriate countermeasures is still limited at best

A common problem raised by practitioners is that while it might be interesting enough to understand the role of factors such as the away team characteristics and the weather better, the resulting managerial implications from it are largely insignificant to them. Unfortunately, without the prospect of generating such critical management implications, the interest in those research collaborations that we, as a field, need to make further progress is, however, likely to decline significantly at sports associations and clubs (cf. Section 2.6). Therefore, below, we sketch out two potential avenues for future empirical research on potential countermeasures that could be tested in cooperation with the practice, most of them experimental.[34]

Based on our observations from the research on reducing no-show behavior in other industries (e.g., the health care industry), we suggest two basic strategies to mitigate the negative consequences of spectator no-show behavior previously (cf. Schreyer, 2019), some of which are already in place at European football clubs. That is, as we illustrate in Figure 14.1, those football executives eager to decrease the no-show rate, have to choose between whether they want to treat the immediate cause of such no-show behavior or to cure the subsequent symptoms arising from it.[35]

A strategy that intends to treat the immediate cause of no-show behavior aims at nudging ticket holder behavior, thus motivating either ticket usage or its release to interested third parties. For example, to increase ticket usage among their STHs, Borussia Dortmund, a club with a packed season ticket

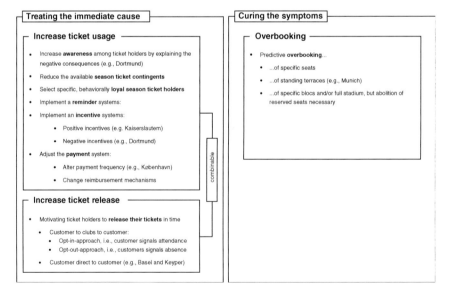

Figure 14.1 Potential Strategies to Mitigate the Negative Consequences Arising from Frequent No-Show Behavior.

waiting list, have only recently begun withdrawing their STHs, with massive no-show appearances, the right of first refusal for season tickets (Ruhr Nachrichten, 2018).[36] As similar approaches have been used in Bundesliga by clubs from Hamburg (e.g., Hamburger Abendblatt, 2017), Munich (e.g., Daily Mail, 2014), and Wolfsburg (e.g., Kicker, 2015) earlier, it would be interesting to understand the effects of implementing such negative incentive systems and their necessary framework conditions better. Previous Bundesliga club Kaiserslautern, in contrast, have experimented with employing a raffle to reduce no-show behavior among their STHs (Wochenblatt, 2019). In fact, while the use of different reminders has regularly led to decreasing no-show rates in the health care industry (e.g., McLean et al., 2016), our very own experimental exploration into the potential of reminders with such reward opportunities has been of only modest success (Schreyer et al., 2020) and, therefore, offers an interesting path for future replication and extension. Somewhat similarly, as some first football clubs, most prominently Danish club FC København (ESSMA, 2020), have begun exploring the effects of alternative, monthly subscription-based pricing models, there seems to be some value in better understanding the role of payment procedures.

In contrast, a strategy that intends to cure the symptoms of spectator no-show behavior aims at diminishing the costs of no-show behavior (cf. Section 2.2) without nudging the original ticket holder. In this context, for instance, Bayern Munich, typically selling out every single home match, is among the first Bundesliga clubs to engage in overbooking activities (cf. Smart Pricer, 2018) – a strategy that has already a long history in the transportation industry, among others.

Conclusion

While we have begun exploring one particular form of such behavior, i.e., spectator no-show behavior, in our research over the last few years, we believe that there are three potential future research avenues that we, as a field, should pursue as we move toward behavioral stadium attendance research. Largely mirroring our previous lessons, we distinguish between research on when spectator no-show behavior occurs (cf. Sections 2.3 and 2.4) and, perhaps more importantly, which potential measures might help reduce it (cf. Section 2.7).

Naturally, a first exciting avenue for future research would be to explore behavioral spectator data generated in additional markets and different sports, including often-ignored fringe, women's, and youth sports (cf. Schreyer and Ansari, 2021). More precisely, as our own empirical research has previously primarily centered around the German market, we believe that there is an initial value in the mere replication and, where necessary, extension of our early results in different environments. In fact, while spectator no-show behavior has been documented among STHs in both German (Schreyer et al., 2016, 2018) and Swiss (Schreyer and Torgler, 2021) association football/

soccer, as well as in Australian Rules football (Karg et al., 2021) previously, the phenomenon's determinants might be highly contextual, despite notable similarities (e.g., the emergence of admission/no-show habits). Further, even within a certain market, the antecedents of such decision-making might differ substantially between spectator groups, for instance, between matchday ticket holders and STHs.

Further, because our understanding of those factors relating to accommodation and socio-demographic information is still in its infancy, adding this information to existing models might help predict individual no-show behavior on matchdays better. In this context, combining survey data with information on behavioral stadium attendance demand, in particular, could offer new insights regarding the role of factors such as team identification as an antecedent of behavioral loyalty (e.g., Schreyer, 2019). In fact, although previous research has shed some first light on the potential role of such factors as age (e.g., Schreyer and Torgler, 2018), gender (e.g., Schreyer et al., 2018), and the ticket price (e.g., Karg et al., 2021) in predicting STH decision-making, it still remains unknown whether socioeconomic factors such as income, education, and occupation drive such behavioral loyalty.

Finally, we believe that future empirical research is necessary to add to our limited understanding of how to manage spectator no-show behavior better. That is, while those colleagues in related fields such as health care management have long begun experimenting with potential measures such as intervention programs (e.g., DuMontier, Rindfleisch, Pruszynski, and Frey III, 2013), no-show fines (e.g., Chariatte, Michaud, Berchtold, Akré, and Suris, 2007), or reminder systems (e.g., Milne, Horne, and Torsney, 2006), such experimental approaches – typically conducted in the field – are still largely absent from the still-emerging literature on the economics of sports. Complementary, analyzing archival spectator data provided by those sporting clubs that have already begun exploring the mechanism of potential countermeasures in the past, most notably negative incentive systems (cf. Sections 2.6 and 2.7), might generate valuable insights in the future.

Notes

1 I want to thank Payam Ansari, Tim Pawlowski, and Benno Torgler for their excellent comments and suggestions on an earlier draft of this chapter. In this context, it is, perhaps, also important to note that I allowed myself to interpret the term behavioral sports economics, i.e., the guiding theme of this book, rather freely. That is, while most readers might conceive studies in behavioral economics as the study of anomalies/paradoxes that cannot be explained by standard economic theory, and might, therefore, expect a chapter centered on potential behavioral biases in spectator decision-making, in this chapter, I'll summarize what we have learned on the economics of a particular, potentially even rational, spectator behavior recently, i.e., football spectator no-show behavior.
2 In the German Bundesliga, the most in-demand European football league in terms of the average number of tickets distributed per match (UEFA, 2019), for

instance, the relative share of distributed season tickets was, on average, about 58% in recent years (cf. Schreyer, Schmidt, and Torgler, 2020).
3 Interestingly, El Hodiri and Quirk (1975) acknowledged the potential methodological challenges that arise from the use of such public attendance data relatively early. More precisely, the two authors, reporting on attendance data for the season 1973–1974 in US sports, note that "[American f]ootball attendance data exclude 'no shows' and hence understate ticket sales relative to capacity," while both the American Basketball Association and the World Hockey Association "had incentives to overstate attendance for strategic purposes" (247). In fact, even today, employing such publicly displayed information still contains the danger that data were either unintentionally wrong or intentionally inflated, for example, to cater to investor needs. More recently, for instance, Page, Savage, and Torgler (2018), in an yet-unpublished working paper, detect clear evidence for a potential misreporting of such published attendance figures in the English Premier League (EPL), Major League Baseball, and the Nation Rugby League, indicating that "clubs inflate their attendance numbers, in particular, to declare attendance above significant thresholds in terms of thousands and tens of thousands of spectators" (2).
4 Perhaps most likely because behavioral data on stadium attendances are often still scarce, Tainsky and Winfree (2010), for example, argue that "[i]t is customary among researchers and practitioners to report the number of tickets sold as the attendance." However, it is important to note that these data, i.e., the data frequently labeled as the number of tickets sold, often also include complimentary/free tickets.
5 Using economic jargon, we could, perhaps, also differentiate between stated (i.e., the decision to accept/purchase a ticket) and revealed preferences (i.e., the subsequent decision to use it on matchday).
6 Although I am the single author of this book chapter, I prefer writing "we" over "I" because I summarize ideas that more often than not arose from conversations and/or the joint work with my dear co-authors Payam Ansari, Caroline Amberger, Daniel Däuper, Nicolas Frevel, Sascha L. Schmidt, and Benno Torgler, mentioned in alphabetical order of their last names, as well as many sport club executives operating in the field.
7 As Schreyer et al. (2020), for example, summarize, no-shows are individuals "who are expected to keep a scheduled appointment but fail to show up without notice or further arrangements (e.g., rescheduling)" (1). Thus, no-show behavior is best understood as a specific form of absenteeism, and, by this definition, no-shows are different from those arriving late or canceling last minute. Intriguingly, first empirical evidence from German football suggests that, on average, about 2% of all perfectly behaviorally loyal STHs arrive after kickoff (cf. Schreyer, Schmidt, and Torgler, 2013).
8 In their recent study on European football stadium attendance demand in the early COVID-19 pandemic, Reade and Singleton (2020), for instance, argue that

> there could have been a more significant spectator demand response in Germany [, for instance,] to the COVID–19 outbreak if it were possible to account fully for the number of people attending matches rather than the numbers of tickets sold.
> (9)

9 Intriguingly, as Schreyer and Ansari (2021) summarize, only a few of those authors exploring stadium attendance demand discuss the potential limitations related to the use of season ticket holder data, while even fewer address them (e.g., Bond and Addesa, 2020).

10 In the two manuscripts exploring STH data on the individual level, for instance, we observe a response to the accumulated away team talent and to whether a match is a geographical derby (Schreyer and Torgler, 2021), as well as to the degree of match outcome uncertainty (e.g., Schreyer et al., 2016).

11 This observation is in line with sports management research suggesting that at least some fans purchase their season tickets for other reasons than to gain a reserved seat to every home match (e.g., Karg, McDonald, and Leckie, 2019; McDonald and Stavros, 2007).

12 In practice, however, for those football club executives managing the stadium business, the opposite is the case (e.g., Borussia Dortmund, 2018).

13 As spectator no-show behavior is significantly more likely among a club's STHs (e.g., Schreyer and Torgler, 2021), those clubs continually observing stadium attendance demand that exceeds the fixed stadium capacity, in particular, lose substantial matchday income if season tickets, offered at a significant discount, remain unused but could have been otherwise sold to the public on the short term for the regular price (or sometimes even more).

14 In Europe, football spectators are currently spending about five euros, on average, per matchday on concessions (ESSMA, 2018), though there are vast differences between clubs.

15 Recently, the question of whether supportive crowds result in a home advantage has once more gained popularity as the emergence of COVID-19 accompanied by the advent of diverse protective measures, including playing football games behind closed doors, has provided our field with a natural experiment (e.g., Bryson, Dolton, Reade, Schreyer, and Singleton, 2021; Endrich and Gesche, 2020; Scoppa, 2021). Intriguingly, as Reade, Schreyer, and Singleton (2020b) summarize, most authors of these early studies, in fact, observe a general decrease in the home advantage, for instance, a significant, though modest, reduction in the total number of yellow cards awarded to the away team (e.g., Bryson et al., 2021), when football is played behind closed doors, thus implying that eliminating supportive crowds might reduce referee bias. In this context, STHs, familiar with the many rituals on a matchday, naturally play an important role in creating a supportive stadium atmosphere. However, their relative importance in creating such a home advantage is methodologically hard to quantify.

16 Quite frankly, we were not fully aware of the no-show phenomenon when we published our first attempts to model individual STH decision-making in the German football market (i.e., Schreyer et al., 2016, 2018). As such, in those manuscripts presenting our early work, we certainly lack the appropriate terminology.

17 We provide these numbers primarily to allow for a first, rough assessment of the Bundesliga's status quo. However, it is essential to note that these no-show rates might, per se, not be entirely comparable across different sports, sports leagues, and sporting clubs, all of them with differing ticketing strategies and facing varying degrees of stadium attendance demand. For instance, a data-driven sporting club engaging in protective overbooking might observe a high no-show rate, despite having all seats occupied. As such, a significantly better key performance indicator would be the effective stadium utilization, i.e., the relative share of occupied seats on matchday/the stadium admission in the stadium capacity. Unfortunately, while Schreyer (2019) reports an effective Bundesliga stadium utilization of about 79.83% in the season 2017–2018, down from roughly 82.74% in 2014–2015, this rather specific information is rarely communicated.

18 When comparing absolute numbers rather than percentages, Putsis and Sen (2000) report about 4,975 no-shows, on average, for National Football League (NFL) games during the season 1996–1997. However, as stadium capacity seems to be a key driver of both the number of distributed tickets and subsequent

no-show appearances (e.g., Schreyer, 2019), such an initially obvious comparison might be skewed.
19 As no-show rates are not even entirely comparable across different sports, sports leagues, and sporting clubs, naturally, a comparison across different industries must be interpreted with caution. Again, our intention is to allow for a rough assessment.
20 However, there seem to exist significant differences in passenger no-show behavior, depending on the form of transportation. For instance, Pérez and his co-authors (2020) note a no-show rate of only about 2.5% among scheduled paratransit services complementing the fixed-route bus system in Puerto Rico. Similarly, in the cruise industry, no-shows are typically extremely rare (e.g., Snitzer, 2020), perhaps because potential guests tend to pay their reservations well in advance.
21 As a few authors of more traditional stadium attendance demand studies have explored superstar effects on attendances now and then (e.g., Shapiro, DeSchriver, and Rascher, 2017), future research might benefit from an even more nuanced examination of the role of talent in shaping spectator no-show behavior by also exploring specific superstar effects. Somewhat related, exploring the role of a team's talent heterogeneity in more detail in the future could help us to better understand the role of stars in shaping spectator interest.
22 Also, we observe a significantly lower no-show rate for just promoted home teams, though not necessarily for Bundesliga pioneers (Schreyer, 2019).
23 Although employing such individual data can certainly improve our understanding of spectator decision-making, we have to admit that our approach in such previous studies is not without its limitations, i.e., despite adding some necessary nuance to the data. For instance, we cannot rule out the possibility that some STHs share their ticket with third parties occasionally, which could affect the reported effect sizes of those explanatory variables capturing a STH's sociodemographic profile and emerging no-show habits.
24 In fact, as the relationship between a STH's age and his/her team identification, a likely predictor of no-show behavior (Schreyer, 2019), is commonly known to be U-shaped, with a probable turning point in the 40s (Bergmann et al., 2016), expecting a similar non-linear relationship between spectator age and no-show behavior seems reasonable (cf. Section 2.5).
25 To paint a complete picture, it is worth noting that the phenomenon of spectator no-show behavior has been occasionally addressed by authors operating in the field of sports economics over the years (e.g., Siegfried and Hinshaw, 1979), primarily in the context of the introduction of the initially temporarily, but then long-tolerated anti-blackout law. While professional sporting clubs were previously granted the right to black out broadcasts of regular-season home games in the home team's territory, in 1973, Congress passed legislation prohibiting such blackouts if stadiums had been sold out three days (or more) before a match. As Siegfried and Hinshaw (1977) summarize, "NFL's opposition to the legislation [was] fundamentally based on its prediction that live televising of home games [would] increase [the number of] no-shows" (170). Analyzing the impact of the legislation on American football, the two authors observe that both the unattractive opponents and bad weather (e.g., precipitation in the form of rain or snow, below-average temperature) led to an increase in no-show behavior. In contrast, the expected competitive balance (back then proxied by the absolute distance in the two teams' league ranking position) and lifted blackouts did not. Subsequent analyses largely confirmed these previous findings (e.g., Zuber and Gandar, 1988). As such, it might, perhaps, be more appropriate to argue that those authors modeling no-show appearances

are currently contributing to a renaissance of the topic rather than entering new territory.

26 However, we also observe largely robust effects regarding the effect of gender, habit, and STH accommodation.

27 Although we advocate moving toward behavioral stadium attendance research by increasingly analyzing data capturing a ticket holder's distinct admission/no-show decision to understand better the determinants of spectator interest in the future, of course, the preceding decision, i.e., the ticket purchase decision, is still highly relevant.

28 Interestingly, as Beckman et al. (2012) reflect, it is only "since the mid-1970s, however, [that] MLB's report of box score 'attendance' is actually tickets sold and not turnstile attendance."

29 Intriguingly, a few authors were already able to employ such behavioral data in the past but modeled different spectator decisions. For example, Allan and Roy (2008), analyzing STH stadium admission in the Scottish Football League (SFL) during the season 2002–2003, among others, conclude, somewhat surprisingly, that STHs in the SFL are behaviorally loyal supporters, continuing "to attend matches irrespective of current form, whether a match is broadcast live on television, time of year, and so forth" (593). Similarly, Owen and Weatherston (2004) employed stadium admission data for 83 Super 12 rugby union matches in New Zealand between 1999 and 2001. Sacheti et al. (2016), modeling attendance demand for one-day international cricket in Australia and England between 1981 and 2015, also analyzed stadium admission data, i.e., "the number of spectators, who officially entered the venue for the match" (124) rather than mere ticket sales. Further, in the related field of sports management research, Heath McDonald and his co-authors, for instance, have frequently explored such behavioral data while exploring related concepts (e.g., Karg and McDonald, 2011), most notably STH churn, in the Australian Football League.

30 Intriguingly, as data presented by Schreyer and Torgler (2020) indicate, football spectator no-show behavior exists among matchday holders, too.

31 In the past, Karg and McDonald (2011), for instance, have already documented that STHs are likely to make false statements regarding their actual no-show behavior. However, as Pawlowski et al. (2017), modeling football fan's stated preferences to watch a game on television, argue, such false statements might be unproblematic as long as these false statements are randomly distributed.

32 In essence, Rodríguez (2019) argues that, while there have been methodological improvements in the econometric analyses of stadium attendance demand during the last decades, the basic set of explanatory variables and their approximations has not much changed recently, as most recent contributions were mere replications of existing research in new markets. To leave this stationary state, he suggests both applying and testing behavioral economics concepts. However, we believe that better data, i.e., disaggregated data capturing behavioral decision-making on the individual level, are imperative to do so.

33 In European football, for example, clubs earn, on average, about 62% of their current ticketing revenue by selling only about ten percent of their seats, i.e., their hospitality seats (cf. ESSMA, 2019).

34 Unlike when analyzing observational data or data generated through natural experiments, naturally, conducting experiments in the field would allow us to make causal claims on the effect of a certain countermeasure on subsequent no-show behavior.

35 In fact, for those clubs in high demand, nurturing no-show behavior while also combining predictive overbooking and dynamic pricing activities might be a viable strategic option, too.

36 However, as Borussia Dortmund primarily want to see a crowded stadium, those STHs listing their season ticket on the club's official secondary market platform are not punished. In fact, those STHs are, per definition, absentees rather than no-shows. Also, strategically, the club, usually observing a ticket demand that exceeds supply, employs this negative incentive system to reduce no-show behavior among their STHs and, almost equally important, make seats available to those fans longing for attendance.

References

Barajas, A., Shakina, E., & Gasparetto, T. (2019). At the stadium or at home: The effect of broadcasting matches. *Sport, Business and Management: An International Journal*, 9(5), 495–505.

Beckman, E. M., Cai, W., Esrock, R. M., & Lemke, R. J. (2012). Explaining game-to-game ticket sales for major league baseball games over time. *Journal of Sports Economics*, 13(5), 536–553.

Benz, M. A., Brandes, L., & Franck, E. (2009). Do soccer associations really spend on a good thing? Empirical evidence on heterogeneity in the consumer response to match uncertainty of outcome. *Contemporary Economic Policy*, 27(2), 216–235.

Bergmann, A., Schmidt, S. L., Schreyer, D., & Torgler, B. (2016). Age and organizational identification: Empirical findings from professional sports. *Applied Economics Letters*, 23(10), 718–722.

Bond, A. J., & Addesa, F. (2020). Competitive intensity, fans' expectations, and match-day tickets sold in the Italian football Serie A, 2012–2015. *Journal of Sports Economics*, 21(1), 20–43.

Borland, J., & MacDonald, R. (2003). Demand for sport. *Oxford Review of Economic Policy*, 19(4), 478–502.

Borussia, D. (2018). *Ticketing: Privileg nicht auf Kosten anderer ausnutzen!* [Do not use the privilege at the expense of others!]. Accessed October 30, 2020. https://bit.ly/2SnPJzH.

Brandes, L., Franck, E., & Theiler, P. (2013). The group size and loyalty of football fans: A two-stage estimation procedure to compare customer potentials across teams. *Journal of the Royal Statistical Society: Series A (Statistics in Society)*, 176(2), 347–369.

Bryson, A., Dolton, P., Reade, J. J., Schreyer, D., & Singleton, C. (2021). Causal effects of an absent crowd on performances and refereeing decisions during Covid-19. *Economics Letters*, 198, 1–5. Doi: 10.1016/j.econlet.2020.109664.

Carmichael, F., Millington, J., & Simmons, R. (1999). Elasticity of demand for Rugby League attendance and the impact of BskyB. *Applied Economics Letters*, 6(12), 797–800.

Chariatte, V., Michaud, P. A., Berchtold, A., Akré, C., & Suris, J. C. (2007). Missed appointments in an adolescent outpatient clinic: Descriptive analyses of consultations over 8 years. *Swiss Medical Weekly*, 137, 677–681.

Chiang, Y. H., & Jane, W. J. (2013). The effects of outcome uncertainties, patriotism, and Asian regionalism in the world baseball classic. *Journal of Media Economics*, 26(3), 148–161.

Coates, D., Humphreys, B. R., & Zhou, L. (2014). Reference-dependent preferences, loss aversion, and live game attendance. *Economic Inquiry*, 52(3), 959–973.

Daily Mail (2014). *Bayern may say Auf Wiedersehen to season ticket holders if they snub home matches.* Accessed October 30, 2020. http://dailym.ai/3mvokII.

Dantas, L. F., Fleck, J. L., Oliveira, F. L. C., & Hamacher, S. (2018). No-shows in appointment scheduling–a systematic literature review. *Health Policy*, 122(4), 412–421.

Demmert, H. G. (1973). *The Economics of Professional Team Sports.* Lexington, MA: Lexington Books.

Deutschlandfunk (2019). *Der Selbstbetrug bei den Zuschauerzahlen.* Accessed October 30, 2020. https://bit.ly/2DnjmKc.

Dobson, S., & Goddard, J. A. (2011). *The Economics of Football.* Cambridge: Cambridge University Press.

DuMontier, C., Rindfleisch, K., Pruszynski, J., & Frey III, J. (2013). A multi-method intervention to reduce no-shows in an urban residency clinic. *Family Medicine*, 45, 634–641.

El Hodiri, M., & Quirk, J. (1975). Stadium capacities and attendance in professional sports. *Management Science Applications to Leisure-Time Operations*, North-Holland Publishing Company, Amsterdam, 246–262.

Endrich, M., & Gesche, T. (2020). Home-bias in referee decisions: Evidence from "Ghost Matches" during the Covid19-Pandemic. *Economics Letters*, 197, 109621.

European Stadium and Safety Management Association [ESSMA] (2018). *Food and Beverage Benchmark.* Sint-Truiden, Belgium: ESSMA VZW.

European Stadium and Safety Management Association [ESSMA] (2019). *Hospitality Benchmark.* Sint-Truiden, Belgium: ESSMA VZW.

European Stadium and Safety Management Association [ESSMA] (2020). *How FC København is bringing flexibility to its season ticket holders based on the Netflix approach.* Accessed October 30, 2020. https://bit.ly/2Jj2zxx.

FC Business (2018). *Spanish Champions FC Barcelona Sees Improved Attendances at Camp Nou as They Approve New Incentives to Ticket Exchange Programme.* Accessed October 30, 2020. https://bit.ly/2R31Cbn.

Forrest, D., Simmons, R., & Buraimo, B. (2005). Outcome uncertainty and the couch potato audience. *Scottish Journal of Political Economy*, 52(4), 641–661.

Fort, R. (2005). The golden anniversary of "The baseball players' labor market". *Journal of Sports Economics*, 6(4), 347–358.

Frevel, N., & Schreyer, D. (2020). Behavioral responses to terrorist attacks: Empirical evidence from professional football. *Applied Economics Letters*, 27(3), 244–247.

Garrow, L. A., & Koppelman, F. S. (2004). Multinomial and nested logit models of airline passengers' no-show and standby behaviour. *Journal of Revenue and Pricing Management*, 3(3), 237–253.

Ge, Q., Humphreys, B. R., & Zhou, K. (2020). Are fair weather fans affected by weather? Rainfall, habit formation, and live game attendance. *Journal of Sports Economics*, 21(3), 304–322.

Hamburger Abendblatt (2017). *HSV schmeißt Hunderte Dauerkartenbesitzer raus* [HSV have banned hundreds of season ticket holders]. Accessed October 30, 2020. https://bit.ly/35NvFg7.

Jones, J. C. H., & Ferguson, D. G. (1988). Location and survival in the national hockey league. *The Journal of Industrial Economics*, 36(4): 443–457.

Karg, A. J., & McDonald, H. (2011). Fantasy sport participation as a complement to traditional sport consumption. *Sport Management Review*, 14(4), 327–346.

Karg, A., Nguyen, J., & McDonald, H. (2021). Understanding season ticket holder attendance decisions. *Journal of Sport Management*, 35(3), 239–253.

Karg, A., McDonald, H., & Leckie, C. (2019). Channel preferences among sport consumers: Profiling media-dominant consumers. *Journal of Sport Management*, 33(4), 303–316.

Kicker (2015). *Wolfsburg kämpft gegen die No-Show-Rate* [Wolfsburg fights No-shows]. Accessed October 30, 2020. https://bit.ly/1UAAU9I.

Lawrence, R. D., Hong, S. J., & Cherrier, J. (2003, August). *Passenger-based Predictive Modeling of Airline No-Show Rates*. In Proceedings of the ninth ACM SIGKDD international conference on Knowledge discovery and data mining (pp. 397–406).

McDonald, H. (2010). The factors influencing churn rates among season ticket holders: An empirical analysis. *Journal of Sport Management*, 24(6), 676–701.

McDonald, H., Karg, A. J., & Leckie, C. (2014). Predicting which season ticket holders will renew and which will not. *European Sport Management Quarterly*, 14, 503–520.

McDonald, H., & Stavros, C. (2007). A defection analysis of lapsed season ticket holders: A consumer and organizational study. *Sport Marketing Quarterly*, 16(4), 218–229.

McLean, S. M., Booth, A., Gee, M., Salway, S., Cobb, M., Bhanbhro, S., & Nancarrow, S. A. (2016). Appointment reminder systems are effective but not optimal: Results of a systematic review and evidence synthesis employing realist principles. *Patient Preference and Adherence*, 10, 479–499.

Melzer, M., & Stäglin, R. (1965). Zur Ökonomie des Fußballs – Eine empirischtheoretische Analyse der Bundesliga. *Konjunkturpolitik*, 11(11), 114–137.

Milne, R. G., Horne, M., & Torsney, B. (2006). SMS reminders in the UK National Health Service: An evaluation of its impact on "no-shows" at hospital out-patient clinics. *Health Care Management Review*, 31(2), 130–136.

Mueller, S. Q. (2020). Pre-and within-season attendance forecasting in Major League Baseball: A random forest approach. *Applied Economics*, 51(41), 4512–4528.

Noll, R. G. (1974). Attendance and price setting. *Government and the Sports Business*. Washington, DC: The Brookings Institution.

Oh, J., & Su, X. (2018). Reservation policies in queues: Advance deposits, spot prices, and capacity allocation. *Production and Operations Management*, 27(4), 680–695.

Oh, T., Sung, H., & Kwon, K. D. (2017). Effect of the stadium occupancy rate on perceived game quality and visit intention. *International Journal of Sports Marketing and Sponsorship*, 18(2), 166–179.

Owen, P. D., & Weatherston, C. R. (2004). Uncertainty of outcome and super 12 rugby union attendance: Application of a general-to-specific modeling strategy. *Journal of Sports Economics*, 5(4), 347–370.

Page, L., Savage, D. A. & Torgler, B. (2018). *Ballpark Figures: Identifying Data Manipulations from Human Biases in Random Number Generation*. Mimeo. Brisbane, Australia: Queensland University of Technology.

Paul, R., Weinbach, A., & Riccardi, N. (2019). Attendance in the Canadian hockey league: The impact of winning, fighting, uncertainty of outcome, and weather on junior hockey attendance. *International Journal of Financial Studies*, 7(1), 12.

Pawlowski, T., & Nalbantis, G. (2015). Competition format, championship uncertainty and stadium attendance in European football–a small league perspective. *Applied Economics*, 47(38), 4128–4139.

Pawlowski, T., Nalbantis, G., & Coates, D. (2017). Perceived game uncertainty, suspense and the demand for sport. *Economic Inquiry*, 56(1), 173–192.

Pérez, F. A. A., Ortiz, G. E. R., Muñiz, E. R., Sacarello, F. J. O., Kang, J. E., & Rodriguez-Roman, D. (2020). Predicting trip cancellations and no-shows in Paratransit operations. *Transportation Research Record*. Doi: 10.1177/0361198120924661.

Ponzo, M., & Scoppa, V. (2018). Does the home advantage depend on crowd support? Evidence from same-stadium derbies. *Journal of Sports Economics*, 19(4), 562–582.

Popp, N., Simmons, J., Watanabe, N., & Shapiro, S. (2019). *Why Didn't They Show Up? An Examination of Factors Influencing No Show Rates at College Football Games*. 2019 Sport Marketing Association (SMA) Conference (SMA XVII). November 7, 2019.

Putsis Jr, W. P., & Sen, S. K. (2000). Should NFL blackouts be banned? *Applied Economics*, 32(12), 1495–1507.

Reade, J. J., Schreyer, D., & Singleton, C. (2020a). Echoes: What happens when football is played behind closed doors? *SSRN Electronic Journal*. Doi: 10.2139/ssrn.3630130.

Reade, J. J., Schreyer, D., & Singleton, C. (2020b). Eliminating supportive crowds reduces referee bias. *SSRN Electronic Journal*. Doi: 10.2139/ssrn.3743972.

Reade, J. J., & Singleton, C. (2020). Demand for public events in the COVID-19 pandemic: A case study of European football. *European Sport Management Quarterly*. Doi: 10.1080/16184742.2020.1841261.

Rodríguez, P. (2019). *Economics of Attendance*. The SAGE Handbook of Sports Economics, 163–170.

Rottenberg, S. (1956). The baseball players' labor market. *Journal of Political Economy*, 64(3), 242–258.

Ruhr Nachrichten (2018). BVB will Fans die Dauerkarten kündigen, wenn sie sie nicht nutzen. Accessed October 30, 2020. https://bit.ly/2EdJr0P.

Sacheti, A., Paton, D., & Gregory-Smith, I. (2016). An economic analysis of attendance demand for one day international cricket. *Economic Record*, 92(296), 121–136.

Sampaio, C. H., Sordi, J. D., & Perin, M. G. (2015). How price bundling affects football ticket purchases and consumption behaviour. *International Journal of Sports Marketing and Sponsorship*, 16(3), 35–51.

Schmidt, S. L., & Holzmayer, F. (2018). A framework for diversification decisions in professional football. *Routledge Handbook of Football Business and Management*.

Schreyer, D. (2019). Football spectator no-show behaviour in the German Bundesliga. *Applied Economics*, 51(45), 4882–4901.

Schreyer, D., & Ansari, P. (2021). Stadium attendance demand research: A scoping review. *Journal of Sports Economics*. Doi: 10.1177/15270025211000404.

Schreyer, D., & Däuper, D. (2018). Determinants of spectator no-show behaviour: First empirical evidence from the German Bundesliga. *Applied Economics Letters*, 25(21), 1475–1480.

Schreyer, D., & Torgler, B. (2021). *Football Spectator No-Show Behavior in Switzerland: Empirical Evidence from Season Ticket Holder Behavior*. Center for Research in Economics, Management and the Arts (CREMA), CREMA Working Papers 2021–06.

Schreyer, D., Schmidt, S. L., & Torgler, B. (2013). *Any Given Sunday: How Season Ticket Holders' Time of Stadium Entrance Is Influenced by Outcome Uncertainty* (No. 2013–21). CREMA Working Paper.

Schreyer, D., Schmidt, S. L., & Torgler, B. (2016). Against all odds? Exploring the role of game outcome uncertainty in season ticket holders' stadium attendance demand. *Journal of Economic Psychology*, 56, 192–217.

Schreyer, D., Schmidt, S. L., & Torgler, B. (2018). Predicting season ticket holder loyalty using geographical information. *Applied Economics Letters*, 25(4), 272–277.

Schreyer, D., Schmidt, S. L., & Torgler, B. (2019). Football spectator no-show behavior. *Journal of Sports Economics*, 20(4), 580–602.

Schreyer, D., Schmidt, S. L., & Torgler, B. (2020). Using reminders with different reward opportunities to reduce no-show behavior: Empirical evidence from a large-scale field experiment in professional sports. *SSRN Electronic Journal*. Doi: 10.2139/ssrn.3703040.

Scoppa, V. (2021). Social pressure in the stadiums: Do agents change behavior without crowd support? *Journal of Economic Psychology*, 82, 102344.

Shapiro, S. L., DeSchriver, T. D., & Rascher, D. A. (2017). The Beckham effect: Examining the longitudinal impact of a star performer on league marketing, novelty, and scarcity. *European Sport Management Quarterly*, 17(5), 610–634.

Siegfried, J. J., & Hinshaw, C. E. (1977). Professional football and the anti-blackout law. *Journal of Communication*, 27(3), 169–174.

Siegfried, J. J., & Hinshaw, C. E. (1979). Effect of lifting television blackouts on professional football no-shows. *Journal of Economics and Business*, 32(1), 1–13.

Simmons, R. (1996). The demand for English league football: A club-level analysis. *Applied Economics*, 28(2), 139–155.

Smart Pricer (2018). FC Bayern München zählt auf Smart Pricer für die No-Show Reduzierung. Accessed October 30, 2020. https://bit.ly/2Uyv7ne.

Smith, B. C., Leimkuhler, J. F., & Darrow, R. M. (1992). Yield management at American airlines. *Interfaces*, 22(1), 8–31.

Snitzer, A. (2020). Cruise line revenue management. *Hospitality Revenue Management: Concepts and Practices*.

Solberg, H. A., & Mehus, I. (2014). The challenge of attracting football fans to stadia? *International Journal of Sport Finance*, 9(1), 3–19.

Storm, R. K., Nielsen, C. G., & Jakobsen, T. G. (2018). The complex challenge of spectator demand: Attendance drivers in the Danish men's handball league. *European Sport Management Quarterly*, 18(5), 652–670.

Sutter, M., & Kocher, M. G. (2004). Favoritism of agents–the case of referees' home bias. *Journal of Economic Psychology*, 25(4), 461–469.

Tainsky, S., & Winfree, J. A. (2010). Short-run demand and uncertainty of outcome in major league baseball. *Review of Industrial Organization*, 37(3), 197–214.

UEFA [Union des Associations Européennes de Football] (2019). *Club Licensing Benchmarking Report: Financial Year 2017*. Nyon: UEFA Club Licensing and Financial Fair Play Unit.

Villar, J. G., & Guerrero, P. R. (2009). Sports attendance: A survey of the literature 1973–2007. *Rivista di Diritto e di Economia dello Sport*, 5(2), 112–151.

Wall Street Journal (2018). *College Football's Growing Problem: Empty Seats*. Accessed October 30, 2020. https://on.wsj.com/2PlwYZB.

Wochenblatt (2019). Mit FCK und Layenberger 'uff de Betze'. Accessed October 30, 2020. https://bit.ly/2VMq4Qv.

Zuber, R. A., & Gandar, J. M. (1988). Lifting the television blackout on no-shows at football games. *Atlantic Economic Journal*, 16(2), 63–73.

Part 6
Happiness, and socioeconomics determinants of sports participation

15 The relationship of happiness and sport

Bruno S. Frey and Anthony Gullo

Introduction

An informal inquiry among a considerable number of friends and acquaintances reveals a clear picture. When asked which relationship between happiness and sport is relevant to them, almost all of them immediately answered: "Doing sport raises happiness." They pointed out that engaging in sport is good for health because it strengthens the body; induces people to enjoy fresh air; has a welcome disciplining function; and most importantly sets into motion chemical processes in the body bolstering satisfaction with life, thus increasing happiness.

But is this really true? One could also argue that the causation goes into the opposite direction: Healthy – and therefore happier – people are able to engage in sport. Persons in ill health are unable, or unwilling, to do so. Hence, greater happiness leads people to do more sport, and not the other way round.

Both directions of causation make sense, and they may exist at the same time. But it may also hold that only one of them applies, while the other does not. In this chapter, we make an effort to empirically inquire whether doing sport makes people happy, or whether happy people do more sport. It must immediately be stressed that it is most difficult, and in many cases impossible, to empirically identify the two causal links, i.e., to clearly separate the two countervailing influences. Our results should therefore be taken cautiously. More extensive and better data are needed to reach a satisfactory answer. In particular, it would be good to have more precise data on what kind of sport activity people engage in.

The econometric estimates[1] indicate that persons actively doing sport report higher happiness than those who do no sport. We find that this *correlation* between sport and reported subjective well-being is substantial. The more often people engage in sport, the higher the positive correlation with happiness. This result suggests that engagement in sport and happiness are directly related, and not only – as many people think – via the effect on physical health.

In the *causal* analysis, we find that both directions of influence matter: Sport influences happiness in a strongly positive manner, while happiness has a smaller positive impact on engaging in sport. The causal effect of sport

DOI: 10.4324/9781003080824-20

participation on happiness is considerably larger than the reversed causal effect of happiness on sports participation.

Previous empirical studies

The study of happiness research is a prime example of an interdisciplinary agenda, undertaken by various scientific disciplines such as psychology (e.g., McMahon, 2006), philosophy (e.g., Diener et al., 1999), sociology (e.g., Veenhoven, 1993), and political science (e.g., Lane, 2000). Happiness research is now widely recognized as one of the most popular fields in current economic research. Surveys on the economics of happiness have appeared as articles (e.g., Dolan et al., 2008; Frey & Stutzer, 2002a), in books (e.g., Frey, 2008; Frey & Stutzer, 2002b; Layard, 2005), and in collections of articles (e.g., Bruni & Porta, 2005; Easterlin, 2002; Frey & Stutzer, 2013). These studies identify a large number of determinants of happiness: personality factors; economic factors such as income, work, and economic development; socio-demographic factors such as age, family status, children, social relationships, health, education, culture, and religion; and political conditions, in particular the extent of democracy.

A limited number of studies explore the relationship between sport and happiness. A positive correlation has been documented in several studies with different samples (e.g., Dolan et al., 2014; Downward & Rasciute, 2011; Kavetsos, 2011; Pawlowski et al., 2011; Wheatley & Bickerton, 2017). These studies do not claim to establish a causal link between happiness and sport.

The positive relationship between active sports participation and physical health is well founded (e.g., Blacklock et al., 2007; Brown et al., 2007; Stone, 2004). Good physical health raises happiness. As a consequence, sports participation and happiness are positively related. This indirect, positive relationship between sports participation and happiness through physical health has been found in several studies (e.g., Dolan et al., 2014; Pawlowski et al., 2011). However, these studies do not include a measure of physical health in their estimates; they therefore cannot distinguish between the direct relationship between sports participation and happiness and the indirect association through physical health.

There is also a direct link between physical activity and happiness, independent of health. Sports participation provides more opportunities for social contacts, serves as a distraction from unfavorable stimuli, improves self-confidence, and helps to develop communication and cooperation skills. All these factors are closely associated with higher levels of happiness (Huang & Humphreys, 2012; Wang et al., 2012). A number of studies have explored this direct, non-health relationship between physical activity and subjective well-being (e.g., Lee & Park, 2010). They generally find a positive correlation between sports participation and subjective well-being, while holding physical health constant. Some studies also consider the frequency of engaging in sport and find a positive association with happiness (e.g., Downward & Rasciute, 2011; Wheatley & Bickerton, 2017).

Various studies make an effort to establish the causation running from sports participation to happiness, using a cross-sectional 2-stage IV approach. Huang and Humphreys (2012) use the number of sport facilities and instructors per person in the individual's country of residence; Dolan et al. (2014) make use of the respondent's perceived benefit of sports participation. Both instruments are used by Ruseski et al. (2014). According to these studies, sports participation increases happiness. However, it is questionable whether these studies are able to clearly identify the causal effect of sports participation on subjective well-being.

It may be argued that regressions using cross-sectional data only capture statistical correlations but not causality (e.g., Frey & Stutzer, 2002b; Staubli et al., 2014; Stutzer & Frey, 2006; Wang et al., 2012). The identification of causal relationships is best undertaken by using panel data. Only a few longitudinal studies identify a causal effect of sports participation on happiness (e.g., Becchetti et al., 2008). Lechner (2009) applies a matching estimator such that sports participation for individuals is initially the same. Subsequent changes over time are then analyzed. The results suggest significant positive effects of sports participation on the subjective well-being of males, and positive but statistically insignificant effects for females.

To the authors' knowledge, empirical evidence on the reverse causality running from happiness to sports participation is limited. There are some experimental studies (e.g., Bryan et al., 2007; Kiviniemi et al., 2007) seeking to capture this relationship. They find that positive affect of participants leads to higher intentions to do sport. Similarly, Ajzen and Driver (1992) find that positive moods can lead to more favorable attitudes about exercise and result in higher intentions to engage in sport. In contrast, negative moods tend to discourage individuals from participating in sport (Allen Catellier & Yang, 2013; Kwan & Bryan, 2010). These studies consider positive and negative affects to reflect people's short-run, momentary emotions, while the happiness literature typically focuses on life satisfaction, a more cognitive form of happiness (Diener et al., 1999; Frey, 2018). Becker et al. (2006) and Schneider and Becker (2005) find life satisfaction to be positively associated with active sports participation. However, since cross-sectional data are used, their findings can hardly be interpreted in a causal way.

To the authors' knowledge, (so far) there are no studies using panel data to identify the effect of happiness on the decision to participate in sport, nor are there combined analyses of both causal directions, from sport activities to happiness and from happiness to sport activities.

Theoretical approach and data

Our study deals with the relationship between happiness and sport in two steps:
The empirical connection between subjective reported life satisfaction and engagement in sport is empirically analyzed descriptively and econometrically

by using the German Socio-Economic Panel (GSOEP). The GSOEP is arguably the best data, as it measures individuals' sports participation more extensively and over a longer time period than other panel datasets.

- Employing the panel structure of GSOEP, we seek to identify the two causal links: from sport to happiness and from happiness to sport.
- As already pointed out, the respective estimation results must be interpreted with caution because the identification of two simultaneous countervailing causal relationships is a major challenge (for a more extensive analysis, including various robustness tests, see Frey & Gullo, 2021).

Following the literature, individual happiness is captured by subjectively reported life satisfaction. The terms "life satisfaction" and "happiness" are used here interchangeably, again in line with the literature. The data on life satisfaction are based on responses to the question "How satisfied are you with your life, all things considered?" Responses range from 0 ("completely dissatisfied") to 10 ("completely satisfied"). We use the data of the GSOEP as it is a representative survey of private households and persons in Germany across a time period of 35 years. The latest wave (2018) consists of more than 33'000 individuals in close to 20'000 households. The GSOEP asks a wide range of questions with regard to individual's socioeconomic status, demographic characteristics, time use, personal attitudes, and self-assessed well-being. GSOEP is a most valuable dataset because it not only captures individual happiness in a longitudinal framework but also reveals the individual's sport activity for an extended time period (Stutzer & Frey, 2004).

Sport activity is captured by a dummy variable (following, e.g., Schneider & Becker, 2005): People who do sport or exercise at least once a week are assigned the category of active (Sport active = 1). People who do sport or exercise less than once a week are assigned as inactive (Sport active = 0).

Twelve waves of the GSOEP are used in our analysis: 1992, 1994, 1996, 1997, 1999, 2001, 2005, 2007, 2009, 2011, 2015, and 2017. The omission of some intermediary years is due to the fact that some questions, in particular on sports participation, were not included. The panel is unbalanced, as the number of periods observed varies across individuals. The final dataset includes 58'368 individuals and 213'563 observations.

Empirical analysis

The average life satisfaction of the residents of Germany amounts to 7.1 (out of 10). This value is close to the value of 7.0 reported by the World Happiness Report of Helliwell et al. (2019). On average, Germans report a high life satisfaction. Thirty-two percent of the German sample population say that they regularly engage in sport (at least once per week). Sixty-two percent rarely do sport and 6% do so monthly.

Table 15.1 Descriptive Statistics of Sports Participation and Average Life Satisfaction

Variables	Average life satisfaction
Sport active	7.4
Sport inactive	6.9
Rarely doing sport	6.8
Monthly doing sport	7.3
Weekly doing sport	7.4

Table 15.1 shows the average life satisfaction in Germany for different levels of sports participation.

On average, people who are active in sport report being happier than those who are not. The difference of 0.5 is statistically significant. Regularly doing sport is associated with greater happiness. The more often people engage in sport, the happier they are on average.

The first part of the econometric analysis deals with the question of how sports participation is related to happiness, applying a pooled ordinary least squares (OLS) estimate. The partial correlation between sports participation and happiness is estimated, keeping a large number of socio-demographic, economic and social factors constant (e.g., Alesina et al., 2004; Di Tella et al., 2003; Easterlin, 2006; Frey, 2008; Stutzer, 2004):

- Age and age-squared.
- Gender: The dummy variable "male" is assigned the value 1 if the respondent is male, and 0 if female.
- Marital status according to five categories: single, married, separated, divorced, and widowed.
- Number of children (up to 16 years) according to four groups: no children; one child; two children; and three or more children.
- Place of residence: This dummy variable assigns the value 1 to residents of former West Germany and the value 0 to those of former East Germany.
- Nationality: This dummy variable takes the value 1 if the respondent is German and 0 if he or she is a foreigner.
- Education in natural logarithm of the respondent's years of education.
- Physical health according to bad health, average health, and good health.
- Household income (in natural logarithms).
- Household size (in square root): Income is shared among the household members; therefore, the square root of the household size is taken to capture a possible non-linear relationship.
- Employment status according to nine categories: full-time employed; unemployed; self-employed; some work; non-working; maternity leave; military service; in education; and retired.
- Annual working hours.

- Weekend work: This dummy variable takes the value 1 if the respondent has to work at weekends at least one a month and takes the value 0 otherwise.
- Social relationships measured by the number of meetings with friends, relatives, or neighbors in their free time: weekly, monthly, rarely (i.e., less than once a month), and no social relationships.
- Religiosity: weekly; monthly; rare; or no religious activities.

Correlational analysis

Since the dependent variable is discrete qualitative, the ranking information contained in the scaled life satisfaction should in principle be estimated by ordered probit or logit techniques. However, as shown by various happiness studies (e.g., Ferrer-i-Carbonell & Frijters, 2004; Stutzer & Frey, 2006), estimation coefficients in the OLS estimations and the average marginal effects in ordered probit estimations are quite similar. As the coefficients are easier to interpret, we opt for the OLS technique.

Our estimation model employs a dummy variable taking the value 1 if the individual is active in sport (does sport or exercise at least once a week) and 0 if he or she is not. This model aims to identify how individuals' decisions to participate in sport or not are related to happiness: Are individuals who do sport happier than those who do not? The additional interaction terms test whether the relationship between sports participation and happiness varies for different ages and health status.

Table 15.2 reports the pooled OLS estimation results. The results are only shown for the variables that are essential for the research question. In order to control for aggregate time trends, dummy variables for the 12 waves are included.

Table 15.2 illustrates the partial correlations. The coefficient of the variable "Sport active" indicates a sizeable, positive relationship between sport activity and life satisfaction: On average, people who actively engage in sport report a 0.4 points higher life satisfaction than those who do not.

The coefficients of "Age" and "Age-squared" indicate a U-shaped curve with higher levels of happiness at younger and older ages, and lower life satisfaction in middle ages for people who are inactive in sport. The positive association between sports participation and life satisfaction is stronger at younger and older ages compared to middle ages.

The coefficients of the three health categories indicate a close relationship between physical health and life satisfaction. In line with previous literature, better physical health contributes to higher life satisfaction. Especially striking is the large size of this association: Among people who do not participate in sport, individuals in bad health report 1.1 points lower life satisfaction compared to those in an average state of health, while individuals in good health report 0.8 points higher life satisfaction compared to those in an average state of health.

Table 15.2 Relationship between Sports Participation and Happiness

	Pooled OLS
Dependent variable: predictors (reference group)	Life satisfaction
Sport activity (reference: Sport inactive)	
Sport active	0.398★★★
	(0.060)
Age	−0.021★★★
	(0.002)
Age-squared	2.98e-4★★★
	(1.70e-5)
Sport active × age	−0.015★★★
	(0.003)
Sport active × age-squared	1.54e-4★★★
	(2.53e-5)
Health (reference: Average health)	
Good health	0.795★★★
	(0.010)
Bad health	−1.135★★★
	(0.011)
Sport active × good health	0.014
	(0.017)
Sport active × bad health	0.298★★★
	(0.024)
Socio-demographic factors	Included
Economic influences	Included
Year effects	Included
Constant	2.880★★★
	(0.079)
Observations	213,563
Adjusted R-squared	0.248

Notes: Standard errors in parentheses.
★★★$p < 0.01$, ★★$p < 0.05$, ★$p < 0.1$.
Variables not indicated for the socio-demographic factors: gender (male or female), marital status (four variables), children (three variables), ln (years of education), social relationships (three variables), religiosity (three variables), nationality (national or foreigner), place of residence (West Germany or East Germany), and economic influences: ln (household income), household size$^{1/2}$, and working status (eight variables).
Source: GSOEP.

The interaction terms of physical health and sport activity can be understood as differences in differences. The positive relationship between sport activity and life satisfaction turns out to be the same for people in good health compared to people in average health. However, having bad health, but still engaging in sport, is statistically significantly associated with higher life satisfaction.

The results for the socio-demographic and economic control variables (not explicitly shown in Table 15.2) are generally consistent with the empirical results from the happiness literature, extensively cited above: Higher household income, fewer household members, more children, regular social relationships, and religious activities are positively correlated with life satisfaction. Moreover, males are less happy than females, singles are less happy than married individuals but happier than divorced and separated individuals, foreigners are less happy than nationals, residents of East Germany are less happy than residents of West Germany, and full-time-employed people are happier than part-time-employed, unemployed, and self-employed people, but less happy than women on maternity leave, individuals in education, and retired people.

A related estimate takes into account how the frequency of engaging in sport is related to happiness (see Frey & Gullo, 2021). It aims to identify whether the relationship between monthly sports participation and happiness differs from the connection between rarely engaging in sport and happiness. These estimates suggest that the more frequently sport is undertaken, the stronger is the positive relation to happiness. The relationship between sports participation and happiness is increasing at a decreasing rate.

Causal analysis

The correlational analysis undertaken so far does not address the underlying *causal* mechanism: Does sports participation impact an individual's happiness or are happier people more willing to participate in sport? Part B of the empirical analysis addresses this issue by testing both causal directions.

We employ the fixed-effects model capturing causes of changes within an individual by controlling for all time-invariant unobserved differences between the individuals. Those within individual effects are averaged across individuals.

The econometric estimates are presented in Table 15.3. Results are only presented for the variables essential for our research question. Year dummies are included to account for underlying time patterns.

Effects of sports participation on happiness

The first column of Table 15.3 reports the causal determinants of happiness. The results mainly confirm the results obtained in the correlational analysis.

The coefficient of the variable "Sport active" in Model A indicates that the positive relationship between sports participation and life satisfaction found in the correlational analysis can be interpreted causally: Ceteris paribus, becoming active in sports increases life satisfaction by 0.2 points, on average.

Physical health contributes to life satisfaction. The positive effect of sports participation is larger for people whose health is worsening compared to people remaining in average health. Sports participation thus seems to be particularly beneficial to people experiencing problematic physical health.

Table 15.3 Causal Link between Sports Participation and Happiness

Dependent variable: predictors (reference group)	(A) FE-OLS life satisfaction	(B) FE-OLS sport active
Sport activity (reference: Sport inactive)		
Sport active	0.235***	
	(0.079)	
Life satisfaction		0.005***
		(0.001)
Age	−0.005	0.021***
	(0.003)	(0.002)
Age-squared	−8.03e-5**	−1.46e-4***
	(3.39e-5)	(1.41e-5)
Sport active × age	−0.014***	
	(0.003)	
Sport active × age-squared	1.92e-4***	
	(3.28e-5)	
Health (reference: Average health)		
Good health	0.429***	0.023***
	(0.011)	(0.004)
Bad health	−0.760***	−0.027***
	(0.015)	(0.004)
Sport active × good health	0.029*	
	(0.017)	
Sport active × bad health	0.124***	
	(0.028)	
Annual work hours		−1.06e-5***
		(2.79e-6)
Weekend work		−0.013**
		(0.005)
Socio-demographic factors	Included	Included
Economic influences	Included	Included
Year effects	Included	Included
Constant	5.301***	−0.658***
	(0.251)	(0.132)
Observations	213,563	125,477
Within R-squared	0.091	0.018
Overall R-squared	0.186	0.010
Number of individuals	58,368	45,808

Notes: Clustered standard errors in parentheses.
***$p < 0.01$, **$p < 0.05$, *$p < 0.1$.
Variables not indicated for the socio-demographic factors: marital status (four variables), children (three variables), ln (years of education), social relationships (three variables), religiosity (three variables), place of residence (West Germany or East Germany), and economic influences: ln (household income), household size$^{1/2}$, and working status (eight variables).
Source: GSOEP.

Effects of happiness on sports participation

Model B in Table 15.3 reports the causal determinants of sports participation. Two additional determinants of sports participation are included: annual working hours and weekend work in order to account for time limitations and the work–leisure conflict.[2] The estimate reveals a significant, but very small effect of life satisfaction on sports participation. Even if life satisfaction increases by 10 units from "completely dissatisfied" to "completely satisfied," the probability of sports participation increases by just 4.6%.

Conclusion

Our study presents new evidence on the *positive relationship* between sport and happiness: People actively participating in sport report a 0.4 points higher life satisfaction than those who do not engage in sport. This finding suggests that sports participation and happiness are not only related indirectly through its influence on physical health, but also directly.

The *causal analysis* suggests that both directions of influence matter: *Sport has a positive effect on happiness, and happiness has a positive impact on sports participation.*

On average, becoming active in sport raises life satisfaction by 0.2 points, ceteris paribus. Sports participation is particularly beneficial to people experiencing bad physical health.

Life satisfaction, in turn, has a positive effect on sport activity. However, the effect size is very small: An increase in life satisfaction by one unit increases the probability of sports participation by only 0.5%, on average.

The effect of sports participation on happiness thus dominates the reversed causality from happiness to sports participation.

The empirical results highlight the importance of sport in our societies. On the micro-level, each individual can decide to participate in sport or not, knowing that it tends to raise his or her happiness. On the macro-level, the dominant causal direction identified from sport to life satisfaction is relevant for policy interventions intending to increase happiness.

Our study is subject to various limitations, which could be accounted for in future research.

First, sport includes various aspects. For instance, it can be distinguished between team sport, sport done with others, and sport just for oneself (e.g., running, cycling). Another important difference is between active sports participation and sport spectatorship. Sports participation could be further divided into health, amateur, and professional sport. Sports spectatorship in turn includes live attendance and watching sport on TV.

Second, although fixed-effects models for panel data are widely recognized as powerful tools for causal analyses, these models also have some limitations. Fixed-effects models are not able to control for unobserved characteristics that vary over time. Fixed-effects models are also unable to capture the effect of time-invariant variables. For these reasons, difference-in-difference models (Diff in Diff) and regression discontinuity designs (RDD) have increasingly been used to identify causal effects. Both econometric methods consider the external effect a sudden, unexpected change in an explanatory variable on the dependent variable. In our case, this requires an external shock to sport, which until recently was rarely the case. However, the current global outbreak of COVID-19, producing a lockdown imposed by government of many amateur and professional sport activities, may produce such a "natural experiment." Application of these estimation techniques requires a sufficient number of data that will only be available in the future.

While the present study is subject to limitations mostly due to missing data, it expands our knowledge. It provides detailed evidence on the positive relationship between sport and happiness. It helps to fill a research gap by identifying a positive causal impact of sport on happiness, which strongly dominates the positive effect of happiness on engaging in sport.

Notes

1 The empirical estimates are based on the more extensive analysis in Frey and Gullo (2021).
2 Annual work hours and weekend work are not available for the waves 1992, 1994, 1996, 1997, 1999, and 2001, thus reducing the sample size to 45'808 individuals and 125'477 observations.

References

Ajzen, I., & Driver, B. L. (1992). Application of the theory of planned behavior to leisure choice. *Journal of Leisure Research*, 24(3), 207–224.

Alesina, A., Di Tella, R., & MacCulloch, R. J. (2004). Inequality and happiness: Are Europeans and Americans different? *Journal of Public Economics*, 88(9), 2009–2042.

Allen Catellier, J. R., & Yang, Z. J. (2013). The role of affect in the decision to exercise: Does being happy lead to a more active lifestyle? *Psychology of Sport and Exercise*, 14(2), 275–282.

Becchetti, L., Pelloni, A., & Rossetti, F. (2008). Relational goods, sociability, and happiness. *Kyklos*, 61(3), 343–363.

Becker, S., Klein, T., Schneider, S. (2006). Sportaktivität in Deutschland im 10-Jahres Vergleich. *Deutsche Zeitschrift für Sportmedizin*, 57(9), 226–232.

Blacklock, R. E., Rhodes, R. E., & Brown, S. G. (2007). Relationship between regular walking, physical activity, and health-related quality of life. *Journal of Physical Activity and Health*, 4(2), 138–152.

Brown, W. J., Burton, N. W., & Rowan, P. J. (2007). Updating the evidence on physical activity and health in women. *American Journal of Preventive Medicine*, *33*(5), 404–411.

Bruni, L., & Porta, P. L. (2015). *Economics & happiness: Framing the analysis*. Oxford: Oxford University Press.

Bryan, A., Hutchison, K. E., Seals, D. R., & Allen, D. L. (2007). A transdisciplinary model integrating genetic, physiological, and psychological correlates of voluntary exercise. *Health Psychology*, *26*(1), 30–39.

Diener, E., Suh, E. M., Lucas, R. E., & Smith, H. L. (1999). Subjective well-being: Three decades of progress. *Psychological Bulletin*, *125*(2), 276–302.

Di Tella, R., MacCulloch, R. J., & Oswald, A. J. (2003). The macroeconomics of happiness. *The Review of Economics and Statistics*, *85*(4), 809–827.

Dolan, P., Kavetsos, G., & Vlaev, I. (2014). The happiness workout. *Social Indicators Research*, *119*(3), 1363–1377.

Dolan, P., Peasgood, T., & White, M. (2008). Do we really know what makes us happy? A review of the economic literature on the factors associated with subjective well-being. *Journal of Economic Psychology*, *29*(1), 94–122.

Downward, P., & Rasciute, S. (2011). Does sport make you happy? An analysis of the well-being derived from sports participation. *International Review of Applied Economics*, *25*(3), 331–348.

Easterlin, R. A. (2002). *Happiness in economics*. Cheltenham: Edward Elgar Publishing.

Easterlin, R. A. (2006). Life cycle happiness and its sources: Intersections of psychology, economics, and demography. *Journal of Economic Psychology*, *27*(4), 463–482.

Ferrer-i-Carbonell, A., & Frijters, P. (2004). How important is methodology for the estimates of the determinants of happiness? *The Economic Journal*, *114*(497), 641–659.

Frey, B. S., & Gullo, A. (2021). Does sports make people happier, or do happy people more sports? *Journal of Sports Economics*. https://doi.org/10.1177/1527002520985667

Frey, B. S. (2008). *Happiness: A revolution in economics*. Cambridge: MIT Press.

Frey, B. S. (2018). *Economics of happiness*. Cham: Springer.

Frey, B. S., & Stutzer, A. (2002a). What can economists learn from happiness research? *Journal of Economic Literature*, *40*(2), 402–435.

Frey, B. S., & Stutzer, A. (2002b). *Happiness and economics: How the economy and institutions affect human well-being*. Princeton: Princeton University Press.

Helliwell, J. F., Huang, H., & Wang, S. (2019). Changing world happiness. In J. F. Helliwell, R. Layard, & J. D. Sachs (Eds.), *World happiness report 2019* (pp. 11–47). New York: Sustainable Development Solutions Network.

Huang, H., & Humphreys, B. R. (2012). Sports participation and happiness: Evidence from US microdata. *Journal of Economic Psychology*, *33*(4), 776–793.

Kavetsos, G. (2011). Physical activity and subjective wellbeing: An empirical analysis. In P. Rodriguez, S. Kesenne, & B. R. Humphreys (Eds.), *The economics of sport, health and happiness: The promotion of wellbeing through sporting activities* (pp. 213–222). Cheltenham: Edward Elgar Publishing.

Kiviniemi, M. T., Voss-Humke, A. M., & Seifert, A. L. (2007). How do I feel about the behavior? The interplay of affective associations with behaviors and cognitive beliefs as influences on physical activity behavior. *Health Psychology*, *26*(2), 152–158.

Kwan, B. M., & Bryan, A. (2010). In-task and post-task affective response to exercise: Translating exercise intentions into behaviour. *British Journal of Health Psychology*, *15*(1), 115–131.
Lane, R. E. (2000). *The loss of happiness in market democracies*. New Haven and London: Yale University Press.
Layard, R. (2005). *Happiness: Lessons from a new science*. New York: Penguin Press.
Lechner, M. (2009). Long-run labour market and health effects of individual sports activities. *Journal of Health Economics*, *28*(4), 839–854.
Lee, Y. H., & Park, I. (2010). Happiness and physical activity in special populations: Evidence from Korean survey data. *Journal of Sports Economics*, *11*(2), 136–156.
McMahon, D. M. (2006). *Happiness: A history*. New York: Atlantic Monthly Press.
Pawlowski, T., Downward, P., & Rasciute, S. (2011). Subjective well-being in European countries—on the age-specific impact of physical activity. *European Review of Aging and Physical Activity*, *8*(2), 93–102.
Ruseski, J. E., Humphreys, B. R., Hallmann, K., Wicker, P., & Breuer, C. (2014). Sport participation and subjective well-being: Instrumental variable results from German survey data. *Journal of Physical Activity and Health*, *11*(2), 396–403.
Schneider, S., & Becker, S. (2005). Prevalence of physical activity among the working population and correlation with work-related factors: Results from the first German national health survey. *Journal of Occupational Health*, *47*(5), 414–423.
Staubli, S., Killias, M., & Frey, B. S. (2014). Happiness and victimization: An empirical study for Switzerland. *European Journal of Criminology*, *11*(1), 57–72.
Stone, W. J. (2004). Physical activity and health: Becoming mainstream. *Complementary Health Practice Review*, *9*(2), 118–128.
Stutzer, A. (2004). The role of income aspirations in individual happiness. *Journal of Economic Behavior & Organization*, *54*(1), 89–109.
Stutzer, A., & Frey, B. S. (2004). Reported subjective well-being: A challenge for economic theory and economic policy. *Schmollers Jahrbuch : Journal of Applied Social Science Studies / Zeitschrift Für Wirtschafts- Und Sozialwissenschaften*, *124*(2), 191–231.
Stutzer, A., & Frey, B. S. (2006). Does marriage make people happy, or do happy people get married? *Journal of Socio-Economics*, *35*(2), 326–347.
Veenhoven, R. (1993). *Happiness in nations: Subjective appreciation of life in 56 nations 1946–1992*. Rotterdam: Erasmus University Press.
Wang, F., Orpana, H. M., Morrison, H., De Groh, M., Dai, S., & Luo, W. (2012). Long-term association between leisure-time physical activity and changes in happiness: Analysis of the prospective national population health survey. *American Journal of Epidemiology*, *176*(12), 1095–1100.
Wheatley, D., & Bickerton, C. (2017). Subjective well-being and engagement in arts, culture and sport. *Journal of Cultural Economics*, *41*(1), 23–45.

16 Using behavioral economics to improve health through sports participation and physical activity

Monica M. Moses and Jane E. Ruseski

Introduction

The benefits of regular participation in sport and physical activity for overall health and well-being are well documented in the clinical and public health literature. Numerous public health campaigns worldwide encourage individuals to engage in physical activity in order to enjoy these health benefits and mitigate the risks of chronic diseases, obesity, and premature death. Despite these ongoing efforts, regular participation in sport and physical inactivity falls short of the World Health Organization (WHO) guidelines in many populations. Recent data from the WHO indicate that globally 23% of adults and 81% of adolescents do not meet the WHO global recommendations on physical activity for health (World Health Organization, n.d.). According to the US Centers for Disease Control and Prevention (CDC), only one in four US adults and one in five high school students meet the WHO physical activity guidelines (Centers for Disease Control and Prevention, 2019). A recent global study using survey data from 168 countries finds that more than a quarter of adults in the world do not engage in enough physical activity for sustained health benefits (Stevens, Guthold, Riley, & Bull, 2018). This study further finds that the prevalence of insufficient activity was stable from 2001 to 2016, suggesting that little progress has been made in the collective worldwide effort to increase physical activity (Stevens et al., 2018). Such statistics lead some to conclude that physical inactivity is one of the most important global public health problems of the 21st century (Blair, 2009).

In a continued response to this global public health problem, the World Health Assembly (WHA) launched a new *Global Action Plan on Physical Activity (GAPPA) 2018–2030* that adopted a new voluntary target to reduce global physical inactivity by 10% by 2025 and by 15% by 2030 (Bull et al., 2020). As part of this resolution, the WHO updated its 2010 global recommendations on physical activity for health in 2020. Most notably, the new guidelines address, for the first time, the health impact of sedentary behavior. The primary takeaway from the guidelines is that some exercise is better than none, more exercise is better, and sedentary behavior should be limited (Bull et al., 2020).[1]

DOI: 10.4324/9781003080824-21

Improving sports participation and physical activity (SPPA) will remain an important health policy priority if the prevalence of sedentary behavior and inactivity remains sufficiently high to adversely impact health. Despite the overwhelming evidence of the beneficial impact of SPPA on reducing mortality, curbing the onset of chronic diseases, and promoting healthy growth and aging, gaps remain in the literature regarding the behavioral aspects of individual decisions about regular SPPA. Ongoing research on the determinants of SPPA is increasingly vital for informing health policy and developing successful programmatic interventions that move the needle toward achieving the WHO goals for reducing physical inactivity. In this chapter, we synthesize a growing body of literature that evaluates SPPA through the lens of behavioral economics. The objective of this review is to better understand how concepts and theories grounded in behavioral economics can widen our understanding the decision-making processes that lead to regular SPPA that ultimately improve health and well-being.

Toward this end, the chapter first provides a brief overview of the impact of regular SPPA on health and well-being. The remainder of the chapter synthesizes a large and growing conceptual literature in behavioral economics and psychology that is relevant for understanding individual decisions to initiate and maintain healthy physical activity habits. The chapter concludes with a discussion of the empirical challenges in identifying behavioral tendencies with respect to SPPA and the current state of the evidence developed in studies taking a behavioral economics approach to analyzing SPPA.

Health benefits (risks) of sports participation, physical (in)activity, and sedentary behavior

Habitual participation in sport and physical activity is now a well-established protective factor for the prevention and treatment of non-communicable diseases (NCDs). Another frequently used term for NCDs is chronic disease. Regular physical activity is associated with preventing the onset of at least 40 chronic conditions including heart disease, stroke, hypertension, diabetes, breast cancer, colon cancer, osteoporosis, and obesity (Ruegsegger & Booth, 2018). Habitual physical activity is also associated with improved mental health (Schuh et al., 2016), delay in the onset of dementia (Livingston et al., 2020), improved overall quality of life and well-being (Das & Horton, 2012), and reduced overall mortality (Livingston et al., 2020; Schuh et al., 2016; Mammen & Faulkner, 2013; Bize, Johnson, & Plotnikoff, 2007; Guallar-Castillón et al., 2014; Das & Horton, 2012). A recent systematic review of studies published between 1985 and 2007 finds that the risk for overall mortality was reduced by 31% on average for the most active individuals (Warburton, Charlesworth, Ivey, Nettlefold, & Bredin, 2010). Lack of participation in sport and physical activity can be considered either physical inactivity or sedentary behavior, both of which are modifiable risk factors for many NCDs. Physical inactivity differs in a nuanced way from sedentary behaviors. Physical inactivity refers to the non-achievement of physical activity standards, whereas sedentary behavior refers to the length of time for which an individual is expending very little energy. Sedentary behavior can occur while at work, while commuting, and during leisure time.

Sedentary behaviors are differentiated from physical inactivity based on the metabolic equivalent of task (MET). MET is the ratio of energy expended while performing some specific physical activity relative to the reference point of 1 MET. This baseline of 1 MET is roughly equivalent to the energy expended when sitting quietly. Sedentary behavior is defined as any waking behavior with an energy expenditure ≤ 1.5 METs. In contrast, moderate-intensity activities have METs between 3.0 and 6.0 while vigorous-intensity activities have METs greater than 6.0. An example of a moderate-intensity activity is walking at a moderate or brisk pace of 3–4.5 miles per hour on a level surface. Walking at a pace of 5 miles per hour or faster is an example of vigorous-intensity activity (Ainsworth et al., 1993).

The prevalence of physical inactivity and sedentary behavior varies considerably within and between countries and can be as high as 80% in some subpopulations (World Health Organization, 2018). As urbanization increases globally, and as the COVID-19 pandemic has made work-from-home technologies more accessible, we can expect an upward trajectory in trends in physical inactivity and sedentary behavior.

Chronic diseases such as cancer, heart attack, stroke, chronic respiratory problems, and diabetes are not only the leading causes of death in many nations, but they are also leading causes of disease burden and disability among the living. Almost one-third of people aged 15 and older reported living with two or more chronic conditions across many developed countries (OECD, 2019). The prevalence of NCDs is expected to rise substantially in the coming decades due to an aging and increasing global population (Bloom et al., 2011).

The economic burden of chronic disease is substantial. Macroeconomic simulations conducted in 2011 indicate a cumulative output loss of US$ 47 trillion over the next two decades from cardiovascular disease, chronic respiratory disease, cancer, diabetes, and mental health alone (Bloom et al., 2011). The US CDC estimates that $117 billion dollars in annual healthcare costs is associated with inadequate physical activity (Physical Activity – Why it Matters, 2020).

The importance of physical inactivity as a modifiable risk factor for many NCDs and overall mortality cannot be understated. NCDs disproportionately affect those aged 60 and over who also account for a higher percentage of healthcare expenditures, particularly when diagnosed with a chronic condition (Sawyer, 2019). Regular participation in sport and physical activity represents a viable prevention and treatment intervention for many chronic conditions. Its efficaciousness is by now well established with numerous studies indicating that light-to-moderate physical activity facilitates healthy aging, lowers the risk of developing chronic conditions, improves cognitive functioning and sleep, and contributes to better mental health (McAuley, 1995; Musich, 2017; Warburton, Nicol, & Bredin, 2006; Donnelly et al., 2016; Becofsky, Baruth, & Wilcox, 2016; Mummery, Schofield, & Caperchione, 2004; Heesch, Z., van Gellecum, & Brown, 2012).[2]

Examples of such studies (Cadilhac et al., 2011; Warburton, Nicol, & Bredin, 2006) estimate that a 10% reduction in physical inactivity in Australia is associated with 2,000 fewer deaths and 6,000 fewer incident cases of disease. Warburton et al. (2006) conclude that a significant number of deaths from coronary heart disease, stroke and osteoporosis, colon cancer, hypertension, type 2 diabetes, and breast cancer could be prevented in Canada through increased and regular participation in physical activity. The US CDC estimates that sufficient physical activity could prevent 1 in 10 premature deaths, 1 in 8 cases of breast cancer, 1 in 8 cases of colorectal cancer, 1 in 12 cases of diabetes, and 1 in 15 cases of heart disease (Physical Activity – Why it Matters, 2020).

The expansive literature on physical (in)activity, sedentary behavior, and health outcomes can be succinctly summarized by three "stylized facts": (1) physical inactivity is a leading and modifiable risk factor for NCDs; (2) a significant portion of the global population does not engage in sufficient physical activity for sustained health benefits; and (3) the economic burden of physical inactivity is substantial. If current documented global trends in physical inactivity continue, the WHO goal to achieve a 10% relative reduction in insufficient physical activity will not be met (Guthold, Stevens, Riley, & Bull, 2018). This reality coupled with current trends in physical inactivity indicates that progress toward achieving this goal has been too slow and underscores the urgency of prioritizing policies and programmatic interventions to increase physical activity in populations around the globe. Ongoing research is essential for monitoring levels and trends in physical activity, evaluating the impact of policy and targeted programs to reduce physical inactivity and sedentary behavior, and achieving a better understanding of factors, both individual and environmental, that influence individual decisions to engage in habitual SPPA. Future policy and program planning will benefit from analyzing SPPA through the lens of behavioral economics.

Behavioral theories for SPPA

Research about the determinants and correlates of SPPA has grown rapidly in recent decades. Much of the momentum for this research agenda stems from advances in knowledge about the importance of physical inactivity as a modifiable risk factor for NCDs. A deeper understanding of why some people are physically active and others are not is needed for developing evidence-based policies, programs, and interventions that promote regular physical activity and reduce the burden of NCDs. Theories grounded in psychology (e.g., theory of planned behavior (TPB)), behavioral economics (e.g., time inconsistency), and behavioral medicine (e.g., health behavior model) guide the research design for many studies in the SPPA domain. These theories provide frameworks for analyzing the determinants of SPPA and evaluating policies and programs, such as incentive-based programs, in moving individuals toward getting the recommended amount of physical activity for sustainable health benefits. This section reviews behavioral theories that are frequently used in the physical activity literature.

Theory of planned behavior

The TPB is an extension of an earlier theory – theory of reasoned action. TPB attempts to identify the factors that contribute to an individual's intention to engage in specific behaviors (Ajzen, 1991). Intention is the immediate determinant of action when other internal and external influences are negligible. Measures of perceived control, perception of the outside environment, social influences, pressures, attitudes, and beliefs are expected to predict intention. An important limitation of the theory of reasoned action is that demographics and personality traits are not expected to be correlated with physical activity behavior unless they influence underlying beliefs related to attitudinal and normative determinants. Only changes in information, beliefs, confidence, commitment, or goals may induce change in intentions about physical activity behavior.

TPB extends the theory of reasoned action to include automation of actions or volitional behaviors. Most behaviors can be explained as somewhere between total control and lack of control, in terms of real or perceived limitations (Godin, 1994). When behaviors are learned or memorized, they become more autonomous. TPB is frequently used to guide model specification and variable selection in studies of exercise behavior rooted in the health behavior and behavioral medicine literature (Rhodes & De Bruijn, 2011; Hashim, Jawis, Wahat, & Grove, 2014; Bourdreau & Godin, 2014; Prapavessis, Gaston, & DeJesus, 2015; Householder, Hale, & Greene, 2002).

Self-determination theory

Self-determination theory (SDT) is a metatheory used to explain the motivational factors behind the behavior of individuals. According to SDT, humans are motivated and behave according to three innate psychological needs: autonomy, competence, and relatedness (Ryan & Deci, 2000). Individuals must feel supported in these categories to initiate behaviors (Edmunds, Ntoumanis, & Duda, 2006). SDT proposes that human motivation varies based on the extent to which it is autonomous or controlling. Given these distinctions, motivation can take on one of three forms – intrinsic, extrinsic, or amotivational – that lie on a continuum ranging from high to low self-determination depending on the level of autonomy associated with each form of motivation (Edmunds, Ntoumanis, & Duda, 2006).

Several studies of interventions in the exercise domain use SDT as a theoretical framework to motivate the research design (Hagger & Chatzisarantis, 2008; Calvo, Cervelló, Jiménez, Iglesias, & Murcia, 2010; Miller & Gramzow, 2016; Gaston & Vamos, 2013). SDT also provides a suitable framework to test exercise adherence and allows for meaningful interpretation of motivational determinants that are relevant in SPPA (Wilson & Rodgers, 2004; Brooks et al., 2017).

Social cognitive theory

Social cognitive theory (SCT) is a behavioral theory developed by Bandura (1986) that emanated from social learning theory (SLT) (Bandura A., 1977). The theory posits that learning occurs in a social context featuring the dynamic and reciprocal interaction of the individual, environment, and behavior (LaMorte, 2019). The primary idea is that human behaviors are regulated by forethought (Bandura A., 1977). An important feature of SCT for understanding physical activity behavior is that it considers the unique way in which individuals acquire and maintain behavior by recognizing the importance of social influence and its emphasis on external and internal reinforcement (LaMorte, 2019). The two main constructs in SCT are self-efficacy and outcome expectations. Self-efficacy refers to the confidence an individual has to exercise control over health behaviors. Outcome expectations refer to an individual's judgments of the likely consequences of engaging or not engaging in a particular behavior (Bandura A., 2004). SCT has been widely used in analyses of the determinants of SPPA and change in physical activity behavior (see Young, Plotnikoff, Collins, Callister, & Morgan, 2014 for a systematic review analyzing the value of SCT in SPPA analysis).

Transtheoretical model

The transtheoretical model (TTM), also called the stages of change model, evolved through studies comparing the experiences of self-quitting smokers and smokers who received professional treatments to quit (Prochaska & Velicer, 1997). The TTM is of interest to the behavioral health community because it posits that behaviors, especially habitual behaviors, do not change quickly but rather change occurs over time as individuals progress through a cyclical process (LaMorte, 2019).

The TTM is comprised of five core constructs: stages of change, processes of change, decisional balance, self-efficacy, and temptation (Prochaska & Velicer, 1997). Within the first core construct, there are six stages of change: precontemplation, contemplation, preparation, action, maintenance, and termination (Prochaska & Velicer, 1997). For each stage of change, different strategies are most effective in getting an individual to the next stage of chain, and ultimately to maintenance of the behavior (LaMorte, 2019).

The TTM has been used to study several health behaviors besides smoking cessation, including exercise acquisition (Prochaska J. O., et al., 1994). An attractive feature of the TTM in identifying factors that motivate individuals to be physically active is the stages of change construct because it suggests that change in physical activity behavior is not an all-or-nothing phenomenon. Instead, it progresses gradually through the various stages of change that reflect both intention and behavior (Kosma, Ellis, & Bauer, 2012). A deeper understanding of what moves individuals through the stages of change can help in designing effective programs and policies to improve physical activity participation.

Habit formation, time-inconsistent preferences, and projection bias

Habitual exercise is necessary for harnessing the full health benefits of SPPA. For this reason, habit formation has attracted significant attention in the physical activity literature because of its potential as a mechanism, or moderator, for behavioral change. Theories about habit distinguish between habit as a behavior and habit as a process or psychological construct (Hagger M. S., 2019). Behavioral theory suggests that habit formation may occur through repetition of an activity. This is habit as a behavior. In the psychology domain, a deeper less-cognitive impulsive process regulates habits, and hence, certain learned behaviors are accomplished with less mental and physical expenditure and less consciousness (Rebar, Rhodes, & Gardner, 2019).

One view of habit formation considers four phases that lead to the learning or automation of a behavior, directed by learned cue–action associations: (1) a person makes the decision to act; (2) acts on that decision; (3) does this repeatedly; and (4) in a manner conducive to the development of cue–behavior associations (Gardner, Rebar, & Lally, 2019; Gardner & Lally, 2013). Cue triggers an impulse from a previously learned habit that then turns into action because of the non-cognitive nature of behaviors affected by habit (Gardner, Rebar, & Lally, 2019). In the absence of stronger influences, the cue trigger may determine an individual's behavior. Another view of habit formation is that habits form as a result of a behavioral process comprised of a series of phases such as the intention phase, risk perceptions, outcome expectancy, and perceived behavioral control.

Habit and habit formation are thought to play a major role in physical activity and other lifestyle behaviors. Habit can aid in SPPA and long-term maintenance by influencing individual factors and motivation to become physically active, by aiding the translation of motivation and intention into action, or by strengthening the reinforcing value of each repetition on the formation of cue–behavior associations (Gardner, Rebar, & Lally, 2020).

Although individuals often express a desire to initiate changes in health-related behaviors, such as regularly exercising, quitting smoking, and losing weight, they struggle to do so, especially over the long term. These behavioral problems with respect to habit formation have motivated a now-large literature in economics on time-inconsistent preferences (Royer, Stehr, & Sydnor, 2015). This strand of literature builds upon the general habit formation framework proposed by Becker & Murphy (1988), time-inconsistent preferences (Laibson, 1997; O'Donoghue & Rabin, 1999; O'Donoghue & Rabin, 2001), and projection bias (Loewenstein, O'Donoghue, & Rabin, 2003) to model how individuals make intertemporal decisions that require predictions about how preferences, beliefs, and constraints will change over time (Acland & Levy, 2015). These models allow for an individual's preferences to be time-inconsistent with present bias. In the context of SPPA, this means that the relative weight given to utility or disutility gained from exercise today is larger than the weight given to SPPA behavior in future periods.

Present-biased preferences lead to self-control problems, and an individual's awareness of self-control issues will influence their decisions about SPPA. O'Donoghue & Rabin (1999) argue that individuals make predictions about how their future selves will behave and those who are "sophisticated" are aware of their present bias and resultant self-control problems. On the other hand, "naïve" individuals are not aware of their present bias and will be more likely to procrastinate about undertaking an unpleasant but ultimately beneficial task. SPPA can be viewed as a potentially unpleasant task that incurs costs today but generates health benefits in the future. Identification of systematic misprediction of future behavior in the real world is challenging. As a result, the hypotheses emanating from models of time-inconsistent preferences that allow for habit formation, present bias, and projection bias have been explored through field experiments. A subset of these experiments focused on the use of financial incentives to encourage gym attendance are discussed in the final section of this chapter.

Empirical evidence of determinants and correlates of SPPA – health behavior and behavioral medicine literature

The public health priority of promoting regular physical activity and the complexity of physical activity behavior have motivated hundreds of studies on the topic. One strand of this literature is rooted in health behavior and behavioral medicine approaches. Another strand is rooted in the behavioral branches of economics, psychology, and sociology. This research is valuable from both a practical and theoretical perspective. From a practical perspective, developing consistent evidence about the determinants of SPPA over time and across populations is needed for designing effective policies and interventions. From a theoretical perspective, empirical studies motivated from alternative behavioral theories can test predictions generated from these theories. Such exercises are useful for assessing the appropriateness of applying behavioral models to SPPA and for generating empirical support or lack thereof for these theories (Bauman, Sallis, Dzewaltowski, & Owen, 2002).

Both strands of the literature on the determinants and correlates of SPPA are vast and have been systematically reviewed many times. The voluminous health behavior and behavioral medicine literature is summarized here. Findings in the sports and health economics literature are summarized in the next section.

It is now well established that many factors influence individual decisions about SPPA. A challenge in any analysis of the determinants and correlates of SPPA is variable selection. To overcome this challenge, various behavioral and ecological theories are commonly used to guide variable selection. A guiding principle of this approach is that there are multiple levels of determinants – individual, social, environmental, and policy – of physical activity that might influence decisions both on their own and interacting with each other. This complexity calls for a comprehensive, multi-level approach to analyzing determinants and correlates of SPPA.

The behavioral models most frequently used to guide variable selection in SPPA analyses are the health belief model (HBM), TPB, SCT, and TTM (Bauman, Sallis, Dzewaltowski, & Owen, 2002). Ecological models (ECO) that consider the interrelations between individuals and their social, environmental, and policy environments are also commonly used to guide study design (Bauman et al., 2012).

Trost, Owen, Bauman, & Sallis (2002) conducted a systematic review of the peer-reviewed literature of 38 new studies published between 1998 and 2000 to update the earlier review (Sallis & Owen, 1998) of approximately 300 studies. Bauman et al. (2012) and Choi, Lee, Lee, Kang, & Choi (2017) add to the work of Sallis and Owen (1998) and Trost et al. (2002) with summaries of the findings of systematic reviews of studies on the determinants and correlates of physical activity. Bauman et al. summarized the findings for 16 systematic reviews published after 1998, while Choi et al. analyzed 25 reviews published from 1999 to 2017.

Trost et al. (2002) and a companion study (Bauman, Sallis, Dzewaltowski, & Owen, 2002) provide useful tables that organize the determinants (correlates) of physical activity into several domains, identify behavioral models (if any) associated with each variable, and summarize the early evidence developed about the impact of the variables on physical activity. Tables 16.1–16.5 are adapted from these papers to provide a synthesis of the evidence from the four systematic reviews on the determinants and correlates of SPPA by domain (Sallis & Owen, 1998; Trost, Owen, Bauman, & Sallis, 2002; Bauman et al., 2012; Choi, Lee, Lee, Kang, & Choi, 2017).[3]

Table 16.1 presents a summary of the evidence about correlates of physical activity in the demographic and biological factors domain.

Age, gender, socioeconomic status (SES)/income, occupational status, and education are the most consistent demographic correlates of physical activity. Studies that included men and women with enough age diversity consistently find that participation declines as individuals aged, regardless of gender, and men are more likely to participate than women. SES/income and education

Table 16.1 Demographic and Biological Factors

Domain/determinants	Theory	Sallis & Owen[a]	Trost et al.	Bauman et al.	Choi et al.
Demographic and biological factors					
Age	None	–	–	-	-
Blue-collar occupation	None	-	-	-	-
Childless	None	+	+	NR	+ to ++
Education	None	++	++	+	+
Gender (male)	None	++	++	+	+
Genetic factors	None	++	++	NR	++
High risk for heart disease	None	-	-	NR	0
Income/socioeconomic status	None	++	++	0 to +	+
Injury history	None	+	+	NR	0
Marital status	None	0/-	-	0	0
Overweight/obesity	None	00	–	-	NR
Race/ethnicity (nonwhite)	None	–	–	-	-

Sources: Bauman, Sallis, Dzewaltowski, and Owen (2002); Trost, Owen, Bauman, and Sallis (2002); Bauman et al. (2012); and Choi, Lee, Lee, Kang, and Choi (2017).

Key: ++, consistent evidence of a positive association with SPPA; +, weak or mixed evidence of a positive association with SPPA; 00, consistent lack of association with SPPA; 0, weak or mixed evidence of no association with SPPA; -, weak or mixed evidence of a negative association with SPPA; --, consistent evidence of a negative association with SPPA; NR, not reported or included in studies; HBM, health belief model; TPB, theory of planned behavior; TTM, transtheoretical model; SCT, social cognitive theory; ECO, ecological models.
[a]The summary of findings is taken from Bauman et al. (2002) and Trost et al. (2002) which were adapted from Sallis and Owen (1998).
[b]Indicates variables not included in earlier literature reviewed in Sallis and Owen (1998). They do not have a theory or model associated with them but could easily be associated with an ecological model of SPPA.

are positively associated with sports and physical activity participation. Individuals employed in blue-collar jobs are less likely to be physically during their leisure time, although the evidence supporting this association is not as strongly established as it is for the other demographic characteristics. Empirical support for biological factors as correlates of SPPA can be characterized as mixed with the strongest evidence for a positive association between genetic factors and an inverse association between overweight/obesity and physical activity behavior.

The factors influencing SPPA in the demographic/biological domain are not associated with any behavioral theory, yet, taken together, are important determinants of physical activity behavior. This presents a challenge for future research to explore ways to logically incorporate the demographic/biological domain into existing or new behavioral theories, including economics. Such endeavors will help to identify mechanisms underlying the associations and further our understanding the interaction between the demographic/

biological domain and other domains. This new knowledge will, in turn, promote programmatic policy to reduce physical inactivity and sedentary behaviors.

Psychological, cognitive, and emotional factors

Table 16.2 summarizes the evidence developed about the association of factors in the psychological, cognitive, and emotional domain. Perhaps most noteworthy here is the strong support for the behavioral theories associated with these variables, particularly the TTM.

Self-efficacy and health (physical and mental) and fitness status are consistently the strongest correlates of SPPA in the psychological, cognitive, and emotional domain. Evidence shows changes in self-efficacy are predictive of change in physical activity and intentions (examples of such studies are as follows: Evon & Burns, 2004; Luszczynska, Mazurkiewicz, Ziegelmann, & Schwarzer, 2007; Oman & King, 1998; and Nigg et al., 2009).

Related to self-efficacy is self-motivation. SDT is often used as a context for evaluating motivation for exercise. There is support in the literature for both motivation itself and mediators for motivation such as autonomous needs as correlates for short- and long-term adherence to exercise (Dishman, Sallis, & Orenstein, 1985; Antoniewicz & Brand, 2016; Rodrigues, Teixeira, Cid, Machado, & Monteiro, 2019; Edmunds, Ntoumanis, & Duda, 2006; Calvo, Cervelló, Jiménez, Iglesias, & Murcia, 2010) and the frequency of physical activity (Markland, Hall, Duncan, & Simatovic, 2015; Hoare, Stavreski, Jennings, & Kingwell, 2017; Duncan, Hall, Wilson, & Jenny, 2010). These results suggest that individuals who internalize their exercise behaviors as part of their identity are more likely to engage in SPPA.

Other important factors that exhibit a positive association with SPPA are self-schemata for exercise, state of change, intention to exercise, control over exercise, and expected benefits (Pfeffer, Englert, & Mueller-Alcazar, 2020). Barriers to exercise and lack of time are also often associated with SPPA behavior (Hoare, Stavreski, Jennings, & Kingwell, 2017). Somewhat surprising is the lack of an effect of attitudes, health locus of control, normative beliefs, and value of exercise outcomes on physical activity behavior.

Behavioral attributes and skills

Table 16.3 identifies factors in the behavioral attributes and skills domain that are frequently included in studies of the determinants and correlates of physical activity. Like the demographic and biological domain, several variables are not associated with a health behavior model.

The SCT and TTM models receive the most support in the literature. Activity history during adulthood is associated with SCT and is consistently found to be positively associated with SPPA. Activity history during childhood is not

Table 16.2 Determinants of Physical Activity, Theories Associated with Variables, and Summary of Evidence

Domain/determinants	Theory	Sallis & Owen[a]	Trost et al.	Bauman et al.	Choi et al.
Psychological, cognitive, and emotional factors					
Attitudes	HBM, TPB	0	00	0 to 00	00
Barriers to exercise/cons	HBM, TPB, TTM	--	--	-	0 to -
Control over exercise		+	+	NR	+
Enjoyment of exercise	TPB	++	++	0	0 to +
Expected benefits/outcome expectations/pros	None	++	++	0 to +	++
Health locus of control	SCT, TTM				
Intention to exercise					
Knowledge of health and exercise		0	0	0	0
Lack of time	None	++	++	+	++
Mood disturbance	TPB	00	+	0	0 to +
Normative beliefs	HBM				
Perceived health or fitness		-	--	-	-
Personality variables	None	--	--	-	-
Poor body image	None	00	00	00	00
Psychological health	TPB	++	++	++	++
Self-efficacy	None				
Self-motivation		+	+	0	0
Self-schemata for exercise	None	-	-	NR	0
State of change	None	+	+	0 to +	0 to +
Stress	None	++	++	++	++
Susceptibility to illness/ seriousness of illness	SCT, TPB, TTM	++	++	0	0
Value of exercise outcomes	None	++	++	+	++
	None				
	TTM	++	++	+	+
	None	0	0	0 to -	0 to -00
	HBM TPB	00	00	NR	00

Sources: Bauman, Sallis, Dzewaltowski, and Owen (2002); Trost, Owen, Bauman, and Sallis (2002); Bauman et al. (2012); and Choi, Lee, Lee, Kang, and Choi (2017).

Key: ++ , consistent evidence of a positive association with SPPA; +, weak or mixed evidence of a positive association with SPPA; 00, consistent lack of association with SPPA; 0, weak or mixed evidence of no association with SPPA; -, weak or mixed evidence of a negative association with SPPA; --, consistent evidence of a negative association with SPPA; NR, not reported or included in studies; HBM, health belief model; TPB, theory of planned behavior; TTM, transtheoretical model; SCT, social cognitive theory; ECO, ecological models.
[a] The summary of findings is taken from Bauman et al. (2002) and Trost et al. (2002) which were adapted from Sallis and Owen (1998).
[b] Indicates variables not included in earlier literature reviewed in Sallis and Owen (1998). They do not have a theory or model associated with them but could easily be associated with an ecological model of SPPA.

Table 16.3 Determinants of Physical Activity, Theories Associated with Variables, and Summary of Evidence

Domain/determinants	Theory	Sallis & Owen[a]	Trost et al.	Bauman et al.	Choi et al.
Behavioral attributes and skills					
Activity history during childhood/youth	None	00	0	NR	0
Activity history during adulthood					++
Alcohol	SCT	++	++	+ to ++	
Contemporary exercise program					0 to 00
Dietary habits (quality)	None	0	0	NR	NR
Past exercise program	None	0	0	NR	
Processes for change					0 to +
School sports	None	++	++	0 to +	+
Skills for coping with barriers	None	+	++	NR	+
Smoking	TTM	++	++	+	0
Sports media use	None	00	0	NR	NR
Type A behavior pattern	SCT, TTM	+	+	NR	
Decision balance sheet					0
Intensity	None	00	–	NR	NR
Perceived efforts	None	0	0	NR	0
	None	+	+	NR	0
	TTM	+	+	NR	0
	None	–	–	NR	NR
	None	– –	– –	0 to –	

Sources: Bauman, Sallis, Dzewaltowski, and Owen (2002); Trost, Owen, Bauman, and Sallis (2002); Bauman et al. (2012); and Choi, Lee, Lee, Kang, and Choi (2017).

Key: ++ , consistent evidence of a positive association with SPPA; +, weak or mixed evidence of a positive association with SPPA; 00, consistent lack of association with SPPA; 0, weak or mixed evidence of no association with SPPA; -, weak or mixed evidence of a negative association with SPPA; --, consistent evidence of a negative association with SPPA; NR, not reported or included in studies; HBM, health belief model; TPB, theory of planned behavior; TTM, transtheoretical model; SCT, social cognitive theory; ECO, ecological models.

[a]The summary of findings is taken from Bauman et al. (2002) and Trost et al. (2002) which were adapted from Sallis & Owen (1998).

[b]Indicates variables not included in earlier literature reviewed in Sallis & Owen (1998). They do not have a theory or model associated with them but could easily be associated with an ecological model of SPPA.

routinely associated with SPPA, although some studies find a positive association between childhood varsity sports participation and current adult participation (Curtis, McTeer, & White, 1999; Dohle & Wansink, 2013).

Processes for change are a consistently strong correlate of SPPA lending support to the TTM. Risky health behaviors such as consuming alcohol and smoking are not consistently associated with SPPA, although there are some studies that find a negative association between smoking and SPPA. Some studies find a positive association between dietary habits and physical activity.

Social and cultural factors

Social support and network connections are advocated as important factors for improving physical activity participation rates. Evidence developed about the influence of factors in the social and cultural domain is summarized in Table 16.4. All of the variables, except for social isolation, are associated with SCT.

Social support from friends/peers, social support from spouse/family, and physician influence are consistently identified as important determinants of SPPA. Interventions designed to improve social support networks as a means of encouraging physical activity can be implemented in differing social contexts, for example, workplace groups, community groups, and specific cultural and social groups. The group dynamics will likely be different across contexts, resulting in differential intervention effectiveness. Regardless of the group-network setup and implementation, group dynamics are generally effective in physical activity interventions (Estabrooks, Harden, & Burke,

Table 16.4 Determinants of Physical Activity, Theories Associated with Variables, and Summary of Evidence

Domain/determinants	Theory	Sallis & Owen[a]	Trost et al.	Bauman et al.	Choi et al.
Social and cultural factors					
Exercise models	SCT	0	0	NR	NR
Past family influences	SCT	0	0	NR	NR
Physician influence	SCT	++	++	0 to +	+
Social isolation	None	-	-	NR	0
Social support from friends/peers	SCT	++	++	+ to ++	+
Social support from spouse/family	SCT	++	++	0 to +	+

Sources: Bauman, Sallis, Dzewaltowski, & Owen (2002); Trost, Owen, Bauman, & Sallis (2002); Bauman et al. (2012); and Choi, Lee, Lee, Kang, & Choi (2017).

Key: ++, consistent evidence of a positive association with SPPA; +, weak or mixed evidence of a positive association with SPPA; 00, consistent lack of association with SPPA; 0, weak or mixed evidence of no association with SPPA; -, weak or mixed evidence of a negative association with SPPA; --, consistent evidence of a negative association with SPPA; NR, not reported or included in studies; HBM, health belief model; TPB, theory of planned behavior; TTM, transtheoretical model; SCT, social cognitive theory; ECO, ecological models.
[a]The summary of findings is taken from Bauman et al. (2002) and Trost et al. (2002) which were adapted from Sallis & Owen (1998).
[b]Indicates variables not included in earlier literature reviewed in Sallis & Owen (1998). They do not have a theory or model associated with them but could easily be associated with an ecological model of SPPA.

2012; Coulon, Wilson, & Egan, 2013). Furthermore, studies have found social support in underserved neighborhoods to have a positive influence on exercise behavior (Coulon, Wilson, & Egan, 2013). A gap identified in the literature about the role of social networks and social support in the promotion of physical activity is a lack of understanding about the mechanisms underlying the positive association between social support and physical activity across subpopulations (Flórez et al., 2018). Despite this gap, the general findings suggest that interventions targeted toward improving support systems and social networks for marginalized populations may be effective in improving SPPA.

Physical environment factors

Table 16.5 summarizes the findings in the literature about the influence of factors in the physical environment domain on SPPA. It is worth noting that a more comprehensive set of variables in the physical environment domain are included in the more recent literature. Many of these factors are not associated with a health behavior or behavioral medicine theory.

Environmental factors that are consistently associated with physical activity behavior are actual access to facilities, climate, enjoyable scenery, and neighborhood safety. Perhaps surprisingly, cost of programs and satisfaction with facilities are not consistently associated with SPPA.

Empirical findings in the behavioral and experimental economics literature

Empirical evidence of the influences of participation of SPPA evolving from the behavioral literature is identified and discussed next.

Habit formation

As discussed in the *Behavioral theories for SPPA* section, habit formation has attracted significant attention in the physical activity literature because of its potential as a mechanism or moderator for behavioral change. There is now considerable interest in having a deeper understanding of the mechanisms and processes through which habit influences sports participation. Several experimental studies seek to develop causal evidence of the role of habit – either on its own or in combination with other behavioral attributes such as self-determination and self-motivation – on physical activity behavior.

A systematic review and meta-analysis of 22 studies applying a commonly used habit index, the Self-Report Habit Index, to health behaviors found that habit formation can account for around 20% of the total variance in physical activity behaviors (Gardner, de Bruijn, & Lally, 2011). Experimental studies evaluating the interaction between self-determination, self-motivation, past behavior, and habit strength (also termed automaticity) generally support a

Table 16.5 Determinants of Physical Activity, Theories Associated with Variables, and Summary of Evidence

Domain/determinants	Theory	Sallis & Owen[a]	Trost et al.	Bauman et al.	Choi et al.
Physical environment factors					
Access to facilities: actual	ECO	+	+	+ to ++	+
Access to facilities: perceived	ECO	00	+	NR	NR
Adequate lighting[b]					0
Climate/season	None	NR	0	NR	0
Cost of programs	ECO	--	--	NR	0
Enjoyable scenery[b]	SCT, ECO	0	0	NR	+
Frequently observe others exercising[b]	None	NR	+	NR	NS
Heavy traffic[b]	None	NR	+	NR	
Home equipment					0 to +
High crime in the region[b]	None	NR	0	+ to ++	0
Hilly terrain[b]	ECO	0	+	NR	0 to +
Neighborhood safety[b]	None	NR	0	0 to +	
Presence of sidewalks[b]					0
Satisfaction with facilities[b]	None	NR	+	NR	0 to −
Unattended dogs[b]	None	NR	+	0 to +	+
Urban location[b]	None	NR	0	0	0
	None	NR	+	NR	
					0
	None	NR	0	NR	0 to −
	None	NR	−	NR	

Sources: Bauman, Sallis, Dzewaltowski, and Owen (2002); Trost, Owen, Bauman, and Sallis (2002); Bauman et al. (2012); and Choi, Lee, Lee, Kang, and Choi (2017).
Key: ++, consistent evidence of a positive association with SPPA; +, weak or mixed evidence of a positive association with SPPA; 00, consistent lack of association with SPPA; 0, weak or mixed evidence of no association with SPPA; -, weak or mixed evidence of a negative association with SPPA; --, consistent evidence of a negative association with SPPA; NR, not reported or included in studies; HBM, health belief model; TPB, theory of planned behavior; TTM, transtheoretical model; SCT, social cognitive theory; ECO, ecological models.
[a]The summary of findings is taken from Bauman et al. (2002) and Trost et al. (2002) which were adapted from Sallis and Owen (1998).
[b]Indicates variables not included in earlier literature reviewed in Sallis and Owen (1998). They do not have a theory or model associated with them but could easily be associated with an ecological model of SPPA.

moderating role for self-determination in the relationship between past behaviors and current habit strength (Gardner & Lally, 2013; Radel, Pelletier, Pjevac, & Cheval, 2017; Armitage, 2005; Kaushal & Rhodes, 2015; Lally, Van Jaarsveld, Potts, & Wardle, 2010). Three main results emerge from these studies. First, individuals with strong self-determination are more likely to strengthen habit formation from past physical activity behavior relative to individuals who are less self-determined to be physically active and less likely to develop strong habits. Second, high levels of self-determination seem to be a moderating factor of SPPA rather than a mediating factor. Third, there is considerable individual heterogeneity in the rate and extent of habit development. Taken together, these results suggest that self-determination has a positive effect on both habit and physical activity, as a moderator and a predictive factor, but individuals may not all respond to habit and habit formation in the same way (Gardner & Lally, 2013). These findings have important implication for health policy, programs, and interventions.

Time inconsistency and economic incentives

Economic incentives to influence health behavior change have been used in real-life workplace settings and laboratory experiment settings for at least 20 years. According to the RAND Employer Survey, more than two-thirds of US companies with at least 50 employees and workplace wellness programs use financial incentives to encourage program uptake, and 10% used incentives tied to health-related standards (Mattke et al., 2013). The argument in favor of financial incentives stems from basic economic theory that rational individuals weigh the costs and benefits of their actions and will engage in the behavior if the perceived benefits outweigh the costs. Economic incentives have the potential to induce behavioral change by changing the cost–benefit calculus.

A substantial literature dating to the 1980s studies the effectiveness of financial incentives for promoting weight loss. An important and consistent finding is that linking incentives directly to outcomes is more effective in encouraging weight loss than linking incentives to program participation (Finkelstein, Linnan, Tate, & Birken, 2007). Finkelstein et al. (2007) add to this literature with an experiment designed to evaluate the impact of monetary rewards tied directly to weight loss in the case where program participation is not required. They found that larger financial incentives are associated with greater short-run weight loss but did not matter in the long term (Finkelstein, Linnan, Tate, & Birken, 2007).

Another stream of the economic incentives for behavioral health change literature focuses on physical activity behavior. Much of this literature consists of randomized field experiments evaluating the effectiveness of financial incentives to encourage attendance at fitness facilities.[4] These studies were perhaps motivated by DellaVigna & Malmendier (2006) who analyze the contractual choice and day-to-day attendance decisions of gym members over three years. They find that many customers made poor choices regarding their gym membership options by overestimating how often they will go to the gym and, thus, overpaying per visit. They explore several possible explanations for this finding, including behavioral explanations of time inconsistency, naiveté about time inconsistency, and learning.

Charness & Gneezy (2009) (hereafter CG) build on DellaVigna & Malmendier by testing the hypothesis that financial incentives can be used to foster good gym attendance habits. Toward this end, they undertake field experiments involving university students that pay some students to attend the gym a specified number of times per week for a specified period of time. They find that financial incentives were effective in encouraging going to the gym in the short run and in the two months following the end of the incentive program, but regular gym attendance faded as time went on. Further, financial incentives were only effective for non-regular gym goers. The financial incentives did not matter for those who were already habituated to SPPA.

Acland & Levy (2015) build on CG's experimental design to more fully investigate the potential for financial incentives to develop lasting physical activity habits and to evaluate the role of naiveté and projection bias on habit formation. Their results regarding gym use are consistent with CG in that gym attendance increased among those offered a financial incentive during and in the first few months following the incentive period. However, these effects did not persist in the long run. They also find that individuals overpredict their actual gym attendance suggesting naiveté about future self-control problems caused by present bias. They also find evidence of projection bias with respect to habit formation. These biases suggest that the prior expectations individuals develop about their own physical activity behaviors influence the take-up and maintenance of SPPA.

A consistent finding with respect to the ability of financial incentives to induce behavioral change is that they often have positive short-run effects but that the effects do not persist after the incentive program ends. Royer, Stehr, & Sydnor (2015) conduct a large-scale workplace field experiment to evaluate whether self-funded commitment mechanisms can improve the performance of an exercise incentive program. The incentive program was designed to encourage employees to use the company's on-site fitness facility with a commitment device to continue going to the gym for a period of time after the incentive program ended. Gym attendance doubled during the incentive period but the overall effects faded quickly for those who were not offered a commitment option. However, the availability of a commitment option at the end of the incentive program generated some long-run persistence in exercise behavior even two to three years after the incentive program ended.

Carrera, Royer, Stehr, & Sydnor (2018) add to the field experiments about the effect of economic incentives on exercise habits with a randomized controlled trial among new members of a gym. They hypothesize that a possible reason for relatively weak effects of incentives on developing lasting physical activity habits is that study participants were not already trying to change their physical activity behavior. This hypothesis is explored through a field experiment with new members of a gym. Motivated by the endowment effect, a unique feature of the experimental design is that some participants were offered a physical item valued at one of the monetary incentives. They find that moderately sized incentives offered to encourage regular gym attendance had only small effects during the incentive period and no effects after the incentive period ended. Several important questions would benefit from exploration in future studies of financial incentives including the optimal size of monetary incentives, the potential effectiveness of physical items rather than cash or gift cards to encourage SPPA habits, and the optimal incentive payout frequency.

Related to time inconsistency is self-control, which is the ability to bring one's responses in line with one's goals. Some individuals are better at regulating themselves than others – this is termed trait self-control, which represents the effectiveness of an individual in exerting self-control across a wide range of situations. Low-trait self-control individuals tend to stick to habit and impulse when other factors are not involved, while higher trait self-control individuals have a tendency to have higher physical activity levels (Pfeffer, Englert, & Mueller-Alcazar, 2020; Hagger, Wood, Stiff, & Chatzisarantis, 2010). Pfeffer et al. (2020) analyze stress, planning, and the intention–behavior gap, but also show that trait self-control can be useful in reducing the intention–behavior gap. Other evidence from meta-analyses confirms that changes in these self-identifying characteristics (attitudes, norms, and self-efficacy in this context) during intervention can effectively aid health behavioral change in a moderately strong and significant way (Sheeran et al., 2016).

Conclusion

This chapter explores evidence surrounding participation in sport and physical activity, while emphasizing the channels of research that may provide the most promise in helping understand SPPA behaviors and how to best improve corresponding health policy. Moving forward, the WHO has recognized the current behavioral research in this field and has applied many of these findings, such as social support and incentivization, into tangible programs and health plans in a Global Action Plan in hopes of improving physical participation across the world (World Health Organization, 2018).

Despite the body of knowledge developed through decades of research in health behavior/behavioral medicine and health and sports economics, the need for additional research is evident. An important limitation of much of the extant research is that the analyses are unconditional allowing for only an associative rather than causal interpretation. Continued evolution of research grounded in behavioral economics and causal inference methods will further improve understanding of the complex nature of SPPA. This new knowledge will inform policy, programs, and interventions designed to increase SPPA and reduce sedentary behavior, ultimately resulting in a healthier population and a reduction in the prevalence of NCDs.

All of these factors simultaneously influence and shape physical activity participation. As complex and convoluted as behaviors of SPPA may seem, focusing on a different aspect of the processes of behavior will slowly disentangle more and more the influences of SPPA, in turn improving healthy habits and lifestyles and preventative health and long-term SPPA maintenance.

Some highlights of this are in the habit formation literature, in measuring the effect of habit throughout different phases, and case studies where program characteristics are arranged to analyze specific behavioral attributes not necessarily studied ever before.

As of 2020, sedentary behaviors and physical inactivity continue to plague individuals, especially with the new work-from-home culture brought about from the COVID-19 pandemic. This potentially contributes to less activity, for example, commuting to and from work, taking the stairs, and work isolation. The importance of behavioral economics in SPPA is evident and should continue to be a priority in sports and health economics research.

Notes

1 The WHO guidelines cover different age-groups (children, adults, and older adults) and are deemed relevant for everyone irrespective of gender, cultural background, socioeconomic status, or ability. The guidelines recommend that children aged 5–17 engage in at least an average of 60 minutes per day of moderate-to-vigorous-intensity physical activity throughout the week that includes muscle- and bone-strengthening activities at least three days per week. The recommendation for adults aged 18 years and over is at least 150–300 minutes of moderate-intensity activity or at least 75–150 minutes of vigorous-intensity activity throughout the week and a minimum of two days of muscle strengthening per week. Older adults aged 65 years and older are further encouraged to do varied multicomponent physical activity that emphasizes functional balance and strength training on three or more days per week.
2 It is worth noting that the positive health benefits associated with physical activity assume an appropriate amount of energy expenditure rather than excessive energy expenditure. It is possible that over-exercising may lead to negative physical and mental health effects. The focus of this paper is on the overall and well-established positive benefits of habitual participation in sport and physical activity.
3 The factors considered and the presentation of results in Bauman et al. (2012) and Choi et al. (2017) do not map directly into the factors considered and presentation of results in Sallis and Owen (1998) and Trost et al. (2002). The summaries of the results in the Bauman et al. (2012) and Choi et al. (2017) in Tables 1–5 reflect the authors' extrapolation of the findings to allow a presentation that is consistent with the approach taken in Sallis and Owen (1998) and Trost et al. (2002).
4 See Carrera et al. (2018) for a nice review of these studies.

References

Acland, D., & Levy, M. R. (2015). Naiveté, projection bias, and habit formation in gym attendance. *Management Science, 61*(1), 146–160.

Ainsworth, B. E., Haskell, W. L., Leon, A. S., Jacobs, Jr, D. R., Montoye, H. J., Sallis, J. F., & Paffenbarger, Jr, R. S. (1993, January). Compendium of physical activities: classification of energy costs of human physical activities. *Medicine and Science in Sports and Exercise, 25*(1), 71–80. doi: 10.1249/00005768-199301000-00011

Ajzen, I. (1991). The theory of planned behavior. *Organizational Behavior and Human Decision Processes, 50*(2), 179–211.

Antoniewicz, F., & Brand, R. (2016). Dropping out or keeping up? Early-dropouts, late-dropouts, and maintainers differ in their automatic evaluations of exercise already before a 14-week exercise course. *Frontiers in Psychology, 7*, 838.

Armitage, C. J. (2005). Can the theory of planned behavior predict the maintenance of physical activity? *Health Psychology, 24*(3), 235.

Bandura, A. (1977a). Self-efficacy: toward a unifying theory of behavioral change. *Psychological Review, 84*(2), 191–215.

Bandura, A. (1977b). *Social Learning Theory*. Englewood Cliffs, N.J: Prentice Hall.

Bandura, A. (2004). Health promotion by social cognitive means. *Health Education & Behavior, 31*(2), 143–164. doi: 10.1177/1090198104263660

Bauman, A. E., Rodrigo, R. S., Sallis, J. F., Wells, J. C., Loos, R. J., & Martin, B. W. (2012). Correlates of physical activity: why are some people physically active and others not? *The Lancet, 380*(9838), 258–271. doi: 10.1016/S0140-6736(12)60735-1

Bauman, A. E., Sallis, J. F., Dzewaltowski, D. A., & Owen, N. (2002). Toward a better understanding of the influences on physical activity: the role of determinants, correlates, causal variables, mediators, moderators, and confounders. *American Journal of Preventive Medicine, 23*(2S), 5–14. doi:https://doi.org/10.1016/S0749-3797(02)00469-5

Becker, G. S., & Murphy, K. M. (1988). A theory of rational addiction. *The Journal of Political Economy, 96*(4), 675–700.

Becofsky, K., Baruth, M., & Wilcox, S. (2016). Physical activity mediates the relationship between program participation and improved mental health in older adults. *Public Health, 132*, 64–71.

Bize, R., Johnson, J. A., & Plotnikoff, R. C. (2007). Physical activity level and health-related quality of life in the general adult population: a systematic review. *Preventative Medicine, 45*(6), 401–415.

Blair, S. N. (2009). Physical inactivity: the biggest public health problem of the 21st century. *British Journal of Sports Medicine, 43*(1), 1–2.

Bloom, D. E., Cafiero, E. T., Jané-Llopis, E., Abrahams-Gessel, S., Bloom, L. R., Fathima, S., ... Weinstein, C. (2011). *The Global Economic Burden of Noncommunicable Diseases*. Geneva: World Economic Forum.

Bourdreau, F., & Godin, G. (2014). Participation in regular leisure-time physical activity among individuals with type 2 diabetes not meeting Canadian guidelines: the influence of intention, perceived behavioral control, and moral norm. *International Journal of Behavioral Medicine, 21*(6), 918–926.

Brooks, J. M., Iwanaga, K., Chiu, C. Y., Cotton, B. P., Deiches, J., Morrison, B., & Chan, F. (2017). Relationships between self-determination theory and theory of planned behavior applied to physical activity and exercise behavior in chronic pain. *Psychology, Health & Medicine, 22*(7), 814–822.

Bull, F. C., Al-Ansari, S. S., Biddle, S., Borodulin, K., Buman, M. P., Cardon, G., & Willumsen, J. F. (2020). World Health Organization 2020 guidelines on physical activity and sedentary behaviour. *British Journal of Sports Medicine, 54*(24), 1451–1462.

Cadilhac, D., Cumming, T., Sheppard, L., Pearce, D., Carter, R., & Magnus, A. (2011, September 24). The economic benefits of reducing physical inactivity: an Australian example. *International Journal of Behavioral Nutrition and Physical Activity, 8*(99). doi: 10.1186/1479-5868-8-99

Calvo, T. G., Cervelló, E., Jiménez, R., Iglesias, D., & Murcia, J. A. (2010). Using self-determination theory to explain sport persistence and dropout in adolescent athletes. *The Spanish Journal of Psychology, 13*(2), 677.

Carrera, M., Royer, H., Stehr, M., & Sydnor, J. (2018, January). Can financial incentives help people trying to establish new habits? Experimental evidence with new gym members. *Journal of Health Economics, 58*, 202–214. doi: 10.1016/j.jhealeco.2018.02.010

Centers for Disease Control and Prevention. (2019, September 25). *Lack of Physical Activity*. Retrieved from National Center for Chronic Disease Prevention and Health Promotion: https://www.cdc.gov/chronicdisease/resources/publications/factsheets/physical-activity.htm

Charness, G., & Gneezy, U. (2009). Incentives to exercise. *Econometrica, 77*(3), 909–931.

Choi, J., Lee, M., Lee, J., Kang, D., & Choi, J. (2017). Correlates associated with participation in physical activity among adults: a systematic review of reviews and update. *BMC Public Health, 17*: article # 356.

Coulon, S. M., Wilson, D. K., & Egan, B. M. (2013). Associations among environmental supports, physical activity, and blood pressure in African-American adults in the PATH trial. *Social Science & Medicine, 87*, 108–115.

Curtis, J., McTeer, W., & White, P. (1999). Exploring effects of school sport experiences on sport participation in later life. *Sociology of Sport Journal, 16*(4), 348–365.

Das, P., & Horton, R. (2012). Rethinking our approach to physical activity. *Lancet, 380*(9838), 189–190.

DellaVigna, S., & Malmendier, U. (2006). Paying not to go to the gym. *American Economic Review, 96*(3), 694–719. Retrieved from http://www.jstor.org/stable/30034067

Dishman, R. K., Sallis, J. F., & Orenstein, D. R. (1985). The determinants of physical activity and exercise. *Public Health Reports, 100*(2), 158.

Dohle, S., & Wansink, B. (2013). Fit in 50 years: participation in high school sports best predicts one's physical activity after Age 70. *BMC Public Health, 13*(1), 1–6.

Donnelly, J. E., Hillman, C. H., Castelli, D., Etnier, J. L., Lee, S., Tomporowski, P., ... Szabo-Reed, A. N. (2016, June). Physical activity, fitness, cognitive function, and academic achievement in children. *Medicine & Science in Sports & Exercise, 48*(6), 1197–1222. doi: 10.1249/MSS.0000000000000901

Duncan, L. R., Hall, C. R., Wilson, P. M., & Jenny, O. (2010). Exercise motivation: a cross-sectional analysis examining its relationships with frequency, intensity, and duration of exercise. *International Journal of Behavioral Nutrition and Physical Activity, 7*(1), 1–9.

Edmunds, J., Ntoumanis, N., & Duda, J. L. (2006). A test of self-determination theory in the exercise domain. *Journal of Applied Social Psychology, 36*(9), 2240–2265.

Estabrooks, P. A., Harden, S. M., & Burke, S. M. (2012). Group dynamics in physical activity promotion: what works? *Social and Personality Pscyhology Compass, 6*(1), 18–40.

Evon, D., & Burns, J. (2004). Process and outcome in cardiac rehabilitation: an examination of cross-lagged effects. *Journal of Consulting and Clinical Psychology, 72*(4), 605.

Finkelstein, E. A., Linnan, L. A., Tate, D. F., & Birken, B. E. (2007). A pilot study testing the effect of different levels of financial incentives on weight loss among overweight employees. *Journal of Occupational and Environmental Medicine, 49*(9), 981–989.

Flórez, K. R., Troxel, W., DeSantis, A., Colabianchi, N., Dubowitz, T., Ghosh-Dastidar, M. B., & Richardson, A. S. (2018). The power of social networks and social support in promotion of physical activity and body mass index among African American adults. *SSM - Population Health, 4*, 327–333.

Gardner, B., & Lally, P. (2013). Does intrinsic motivation strengthen physical activity habit? Modeling relationships between self-determination, past behaviour, and habit strength. *Journal of Behavioral Medicine, 36*(5), 488–497.

Gardner, B., de Bruijn, G. J., & Lally, P. (2011). A systematic review and meta-analysis of applications of the self-report habit index to nutrition and physical activity behaviours. *Annals of Behavioral Medicine, 42*(2), 174–187.

Gardner, B., Rebar, A., & Lally, P. (2019). A matter of habit: recognizing the multiple roles of habit in health behaviour. *British Journal of Health Psychology, 24*(2), 241–249.

Gardner, B., Rebar, A. L., & Lally, P. (2020). 'Habitually deciding' or 'habitually doing'? A response to Hagger (2019). *Psychology of Sport and Exercise, 47*(101539), 1–4.

Gaston, A., & Vamos, C. A. (2013). Leisure-time physical activity patterns and correlates among pregnant women in Ontario, Canada. *Maternal and Child Health Journal, 17*(3), 477–484.

Godin, G. (1994). Theories of reasoned action and planned behavior: usefulness for exercise promotion. *Medicine and Science in Sports and Exercise, 26*(11), 1391–1394.

Guallar-Castillón, P., Bayán-Bravo, A., León-Muñoz, L. M., Balboa-Castillo, T., López-García, E., Gutierrez-Fisac, J. L., & Rodríguez-Artalejo, F. (2014). The association of major patterns of physical activity, sedentary behavior and sleep with health-related quality of life: a cohort study. *Preventative Medicine*, 248–254. doi: 10.1016/j.ypmed.2014.08.015.

Guthold, R., Stevens, G., Riley, L., & Bull, F. (2018). Worldwide trends in insufficient physical activity from 2001 to 2016: a pooled analysis of 358 population-based surveys with 1.9 million participants. *The Lancet, 6*(10), 1077–1086.

Hagger, M. S. (2019). Habit and physical activity: theoretical advances, practical implications, and agenda for future research. *Psychology of Sport and Exercise, 42*, 118–129.

Hagger, M. S., Wood, C. W., Stiff, C., & Chatzisarantis, N. L. (2010). Self-regulation and self-control in exercise: the strength-energy model. *International Review of Sport and Exercise Psychology, 3*(1), 62–86.

Hagger, M., & Chatzisarantis, N. (2008). Self-determination theory and the psychology of exercise. *International Review of Sport and Exercise Psychology, 1*(1), 79–103.

Hashim, H., Jawis, M., Wahat, A., & Grove, J. (2014). Children's exercise behavior: the moderating role of habit processes within the theory of planned behavior. *Psychology, Health & Medicine, 19*(3), 335–343.

Heesch, K. C., Z, v. U., van Gellecum, Y. R., & Brown, W. J. (2012). Dose–response relationships between physical activity, walking and health-related quality of life in mid-age and older women. *Journal of Epidemiology & Community Health, 66*, 670–677. doi: 10.1136/jech-2011-200850

Hoare, E., Stavreski, B., Jennings, G., & Kingwell, B. (2017). Exploring motivation and barriers to physical activity among active and inactive Australian adults. *Sports, 5*(3), 47.

Householder, B. J., Hale, J. L., & Greene, K. L. (2002). The theory of reasoned action. In J. P. Dillard, & M. Pfau T, *The Persuasion Handbook: Developments in Theory and* Practice (vol. 14, pp. 259–286). London: Sage.

Kaushal, N., & Rhodes, R. E. (2015). Exercise habit formation in new gym members: a longitudinal study. *Journal of Behavioral Medicine, 38*(4), 652–663.

Kosma, M., Ellis, R., & Bauer, J. (2012). Longitudinal changes in psychosocial constructs and physical activity among adults with physical disabilities. *Disability and Health Journal, 5*(1), 1–8.

Laibson, D. (1997). Golden eggs and hyperbolic discounting. *The Quarterly Journal of Economics, 112*(2), 443–478. doi: 10.1162/003355397555253

Lally, P., Van Jaarsveld, C., Potts, H., & Wardle, J. (2010). How are habits formed: modelling habit formation in the real world. *European Journal of Social Psychology, 40*(6), 998–1009.

LaMorte, W. W. (2019a, September 9). *The Social Cognitive Theory*. (Boston University School of Public Health) Retrieved May 12, 2021, from Behavioral Change Models: https://sphweb.bumc.bu.edu/otlt/MPH-Modules/SB/BehavioralChangeTheories/BehavioralChangeTheories5.html

LaMorte, W. W. (2019b, September 9). *The Transtheoretical Model*. (B. U. Health, Producer) Retrieved May 12, 2021, from Behavioral Change Models: https://sphweb.bumc.bu.edu/otlt/MPH-Modules/SB/BehavioralChangeTheories/BehavioralChangeTheories6.html

Livingston, G., Huntley, J., Sommerland, A., Ames, D., Ballard, C., Banerjee, S., ... Mukadam, N. (2020). Dementia prevention, intervention, and care: 2020 report of the Lancet Commission. *The Lancet, 396*(10248), 413–446. doi: 10.1016/S0140-6736(20)30367-6

Loewenstein, G., O'Donoghue, T., & Rabin, M. (2003). Projection bias in predicting future utility. *The Quarterly Journal of Economics, 118*(4), 1209–1248.

Luszczynska, A., Mazurkiewicz, M., Ziegelmann, J. P., & Schwarzer, R. (2007). Recovery self-efficacy and intention as predictors of running or jogging behavior: a cross-lagged panel analysis over a two-year period. *Psychology of Sport and Exercise, 8*(2), 247–260.

Mammen, G., & Faulkner, G. (2013). Physical activity and the prevention of depression: a systematic review of prospective studies. *American Journal of Preventative Medicine*, 649–657.

Markland, D., Hall, C. R., Duncan, L. R., & Simatovic, J. (2015). The effects of an imagery intervention on implicit and explicit exercise attitudes. *Psychology of Sport and Exercise, 17*, 24–31.

Mattke, S., Liu, H., Caloyeras, J. P., Huang, C. Y., Van Busum, K. R., Khodyakov, D., & Shier, V. (2013). *Workplace Wellness Programs Study: Final Report*. Santa Monica: RAND Corporation. Retrieved June 2, 2021, from https://www.rand.org/pubs/research_reports/RR254.html

McAuley, E. R. (1995). Physical activity, aging, and psychological well-being. *Journal of Aging and Physical Activity, 3*(1), 67–96.

Miller, L. S., & Gramzow, R. H. (2016). A self-determination theory and motivational interviewing intervention to decrease racial/ethnic disparities in physical activity: rationale and design. *BMC Public Health, 16*(1), 1–11.

Mummery, K., Schofield, G., & Caperchione, C. (2004). Physical activity: physical activity dose-response effects on mental health status in older adults. *Australian and New Zealand Journal of Public Health, 28*(2), 188–192. doi: 10.1111/j.1467-842X.2004.tb00934.x

Musich, S. W. (2017, June 1). The frequency and health benefits of physical activity for older adults. *Population Health Management, 20*(3), 199–207. doi: 10.1089/pop.2016.0071

Nigg, C. R., McCurdy, D. K., McGee, K. A., Motl, R. W., Paxton, R. J., Horwath, C. C., & Dishman, R. K. (2009). Relations among temptations, self-efficacy, and physical activity. *International Journal of Sport and Exercise Psychology, 7*(2), 230–243.

O'Donoghue, T., & Rabin, M. (1999). Doing it now or later. *The American Economic Review, 89*(1), 103–124.

O'Donoghue, T., & Rabin, M. (2001). Choice and procrastination. *The Quarterly Journal of Economics, 116*(1), 121–160.

OECD. (2019). *Health at a Glance 2019 OECD Indicators*. Paris: OECD.

Oman, R., & King, A. (1998). Predicting the adoption and maintenance of exercise participation using self-efficacy and previous exercise participation rates. *American Journal of Health Promotion, 12*(3), 154–161.

Pfeffer, I., Englert, C., & Mueller-Alcazar, A. (2020). Perceived stress and trait self-control interact with the intention–behavior gap in physical activity behavior. *Sport, Exercise, and Performance Psychology, 9*(2), 244–260.

Physical Activity – Why it Matters. (2020, May 13). Retrieved April 1, 2021, from Centers for Disease Control and Prevention: https://www.cdc.gov/physicalactivity/about-physical-activity/why-it-matters.html

Prapavessis, H., Gaston, A., & DeJesus, S. (2015). The theory of planned behavior as a model for understanding sedentary behavior. *Psychology of Sport and Exercise, 19*, 23–32.

Prochaska, J. O., & Velicer, W. F. (1997). The transtheoretical model of health behavior change. *American Journal of Health Promotion, 12*(1), 38–48.

Prochaska, J. O., Velicer, W. F., Rossi, J. S., Goldstein, M. G., Marcus, B. H., Rakowski, W., ... Rossi, S. R. (1994). Stages of change and decisional balance for 12 problem behaviors. *Health Psychology, 13*(1), 39–46. doi: 10.1037/0278-6133.13.1.39

Radel, R., Pelletier, L., Pjevac, D., & Cheval, B. (2017). The links between self-determined motivations and behavioral automaticity in a variety of real-life behaviors. *Motivation and Emotion, 41*(4), 443–454.

Rebar, A. L., Rhodes, R. E., & Gardner, B. (2019). How we are misinterpreting physical activity intention–behavior relations and what to do about it. *International Journal of Behavioral Nutrition and Physical Activity, 16*(1), 1–13.

Rhodes, R., & De Bruijn, G. (2011). Exploring exercise behavior, intention and habit strength relationships. *Scandinavian Journal of Medicine & Science in Sports, 21*(3), 482–491.

Rodrigues, F., Teixeira, D., Cid, L., Machado, S., & Monteiro, D. (2019). The role of dark-side of motivation and intention to continue in exercise: a self-determination theory approach. *Scandinavian Journal of Psychology, 60*(6), 585–595.

Royer, H., Stehr, M., & Sydnor, J. (2015). Incentives, commitments, and habit formation in exercise: evidence from a field experiment with workers at a fortune-500 company. *American Economic Journal: Applied Economics, 7*(3), 51–84.

Ruegsegger, G. N., & Booth, F. W. (2018). Health benefits of exercise. *Cold Spring Harbor Perspectives in Medicine, 8*(7), 1–15.

Ryan, R. M., & Deci, E. L. (2000). Self-determination theory and the facilitation of intrinsic motivation, social development, and well-being. *American Psychologist, 55*(1), 68.

Sallis, J. F., & Owen, N. (1998). Determinants of physical activity. In J. F. Sallis, & N. Owen, *Physical Activity and Behavioral Medicine* (pp. 110–134). SAGE Publications.

Sawyer, B. C. (2019, January 16). *How Do Health Expenditures Vary Across the Population?* (Kaiser Family Foundation) Retrieved March 31, 2021, from Peterson-KFF

Health System Tracker: https://www.healthsystemtracker.org/chart-collection/health-expenditures-vary-across-population/#item-start

Schuch, F. B., Vancampfort, D., Richards, J., Rosenbaum, S., Ward, P. B., & Stubbs, B. (2016a). Exercise as a treatment for depression: a meta-analysis adjusting for publication bias. *Journal of Psychiatric Research*, 42–51.

Schuch, F. B., Vancampfort, D., Richards, J., Rosenbaum, S., Ward, P. B., & Stubbs, B. (2016b, June). Exercise as a treatment for depression: a meta-analysis adjusting for publication bias. *Journal of Psychiatric Research*, 77, 42–51. doi: 10.1016/j.jpsychires.2016.02.023

Sheeran, P., Maki, A., Montanaro, E., Avishai-Yitshak, A., Bryan, A., Klein, W. M., & Rothman, A. J. (2016). The impact of changing attitudes, norms, and self-efficacy on health-related intentions and behavior: a meta-analysis. *Health Psychology*, 35(11), 1178.

Stevens, G. A., Guthold, R., Riley, L. M., & Bull, F. C. (2018). Worldwide trends in insufficient physical activity from 2001 to 2016: a pooled analysis of 358 population-based surveys with 1·9 million participants. *The Lancet Global Health*, 6(10): E1077–E1086.

Trost, S. G., Owen, N., Bauman, A. E., & Sallis, J. (2002). Correlates of adults' participation in physical activity: review and update. *Medicine and Science in Sports and Exercise*, 34(12), 1996–2001.

Warburton, D. E., Charlesworth, S., Ivey, A., Nettlefold, L., & Bredin, S. S. (2010). A systematic review of the evidence for Canada's physical activity guidelines for adults. *International Journal of Behavioral Nutrition and Physical Activity*, 7(39).

Warburton, D. E., Nicol, C. W., & Bredin, S. S. (2006). Health benefits of physical activity: the evidence. *Canadian Medical Association Journal*, 174(6), 801–809.

Wilson, P. M., & Rodgers, W. M. (2004). The relationship between perceived autonomy support, exercise regulations and behavioral intentions in women. *Psychology of Sport and Exercise*, 5(3), 229–242.

World Health Organization. (2018). *Global Action Plan on Physical Activity 2018–2030: More Active People for a Healthier World*. World Health Organization.

World Health Organization. (n.d.). *Noncummunicable Diseases and Their Risk Factors*. Retrieved from https://www.who.int/ncds/prevention/physical-activity/inactivity-global-health-problem/en/

Young, M. D., Plotnikoff, R. C., Collins, C. E., Callister, R., & Morgan, P. J. (2014). Social cognitive theory and physical activity: a systematic review and meta-analysis. *Obesity Reviews*, 15, 986–995.

17 Socioeconomic and demographic correlates of sports participation in Canada

Nazmi Sari

Introduction

The positive impact of physical activity on individual health has been widely acknowledged in the academic literature where physical activity programs are considered as investments in the health of the population. The literature suggests that physically active lifestyles improve health and well-being of individuals (Humphreys and Ruseski, 2011; Humphreys et al., 2014; Sari and Lechner, 2015; U.S. Department of Health and Human Services, 1996; Warburton et al., 2006), and hence create substantial savings for society through a reduction in chronic diseases and lower utilization of healthcare services (Sari, 2009, 2010, 2011a, 2011b, 2014) and an associated increase in worker productivity and wages (see, for instance, Barron et al., 2000; Lechner, 2009, 2015; Lechner and Sari, 2015). Current investments to promote active lifestyles may also have long-term impacts on the health status of individuals. In this regard, health promotion programs can be viewed as long-term investments in individuals' health (Grossman, 1972) as they have a continuous influence over time on the resources that will be used to keep individuals healthy.

Despite various benefits of physical activity, individuals including children spend more time in sedentary activities and become physically less active. For instance, 25% of Canadian children aged 12–17 reported that they spent more than 30 hours per week in sedentary activities. Another 33% reported that their participation in sedentary activities was between 20 and 30 hours per week. Inactivity is also high among other age-groups. Two-thirds of Canadians aged 25–55 are not physically active enough to meet the Canada's Physical Activity Guidelines (Sari, 2009).

In order to avoid the negative health and healthcare consequences of physical inactivity, policymakers may be able to design incentive mechanisms to promote physically active lifestyles. These incentives could be in the form of direct or indirect subsidies for health promotion programs. For policymakers to evaluate existing policies, or to formulate new policies which would be effective in increasing physical activity, it is essential for them to have reliable estimates of the socioeconomic, demographic, and environmental

DOI: 10.4324/9781003080824-22

determinants of physical activity. There is a large body of literature focusing on the determinants of participation in physical activity. However, these studies are mainly examining the determinants of participation in leisure time physical activities. In this chapter, the focus will be on examining the determinants of participation in sports activities. In the existing physical activity literature, due to lack of data there is no a clear distinction between physical activities and sports activities. In this chapter, using a Canadian cross-sectional survey, the aim is to fill this gap and examine the socioeconomic and demographic determinants of participation in sports activities. After a brief overview of the existing literature below, the details about the survey data and the relevant sports participation variables will be discussed in section "Data and methods." The results and conclusions will be presented in sections "Results" and "Conclusion."

An overview of participation in leisure time physical activity and sports activities

The determinants of physical activity have received substantial attention in both the academic and policy worlds. The literature has focused on factors related to individual and family characteristics, other health behaviors (e.g., smoking, diet), peer, family and community influences, and environmental determinants. For instance, a large body of literature shows a consistent association between physical activity and age, gender, socioeconomic status, education, family characteristics, and occupational status (Cerin and Leslie, 2008; Kaplan et al., 2001; Pate et al., 1996; Sallis et al., 1999; Trost et al., 1996, 1997). While most of these factors (i.e., age, being male, having higher education, or having higher income) are positively associated with higher level of participation in physical activity, the association between marital status and physical activity is not consistent across different studies. Some studies reported a negative association (Kaplan et al., 2001), but others reported weak or no association between marital status and physical activity (Trost et al., 2002).

Studies have also examined the association between other behavioral attributes and physical activity. Dietary habits, past exercise behavior, and smoking status have been studied (Pate et al., 1996). Except for a few studies, the association between these health behaviors and physical activity is consistent across various studies. Some studies also show that past exercise behavior is a consistent predictor of current activity status (see Dishman et al., 1985; Kohl and Hobbs, 1998; and Trost et al., 2002 for an extensive review).

Environmental determinants of physical activity are another area studied in the literature. Studies examining components of the built environment show a positive association between physical activity-related facilities (parks, sports facilities, playgrounds, and recreational centers) and physical activity status (see Babey et al., 2008; Brownson et al., 2001; Cerin and Leslie, 2008;

Cohen et al., 2007; Saelens and Handy, 2008; Sallis et al., 1992). In a review of 18 studies on the associations of objectively assessed and perceived environmental attributes with walking, Owen et al. (2004) state that the aesthetic nature of the local environment, the convenience of facilities for walking (i.e., footpaths, trails), accessibility of places to walk to (i.e., shops, beaches), level of traffic on roads, and composites of environmental attributes are correlated with walking. There is also a large body of literature showing strong correlations between physical activity and transportation infrastructure, crime and safety, well-maintained sidewalks (see Limstrand, 2008; Kaczynski and Henderson, 2008; Kaczynski et al., 2008; Owen et al., 2004), and other factors, such as traffic noise, green space quality, land use mix, and government spending on parks and recreational centers (Brownson et al., 2001; Craig et al., 2002; Humphreys and Ruseski, 2007; Huston et al., 2003; Rodriguez et al., 2006; Saelens et al., 2003; Sallis et al., 2016). The overall conclusion from these studies shows that a favorable built environment for physical activity has a positive impact on participation in leisure time physical activity. There are two channels that the favorable built environment (i.e., density of exercise facilities, parks, and green space) encourages physical activity. First, easy access to the facilities and availability of favorable built environment create a direct effect by reducing physical barriers associated with exercise in the form of reduction in travel time cost and traffic-related stress. Second, favorable built environment has also an indirect effect since individuals living close to this environment will be observing physically active people more frequently, and therefore, this may strengthen the perception of active lifestyle to be the norm (Sallis et al., 1990). If there exist complementarities (i.e., increase in marginal utility of physical activity due to an increase in other individuals' physical activity level) between the individual choice and average choices by others, living close to a favorable built environment creates a boost in exercise levels for individuals through this channel. As suggested in Bernheim (1994), as long as the consumption complementarities are strong enough, individuals may conform to a homogeneous standard of behavior even though the individuals may have heterogeneous preferences. Among family members, it is plausible to expect that this type of consumption complementarities is even much stronger.

As briefly summarized above, there exists a wide range of studies focusing on the determinants of participation in physical activity. However, there is a limited set of studies studying a similar issue for participation in sports activities (Downward et al., 2014; Kokolakakis et al., 2011). Almost all studies mentioned above primarily focus on leisure time physical activities and their determinants without making a clear distinction between physical activities and sports activities. While few studies made an explicit effort to clarify the difference, others are not focusing on the difference between sports versus physical activities. For instance, Kokolakakis et al. (2011) list 40 physical activities (excluding walking and running, but including biking for recreational and health purposes) and use data from Spain and England to study the determinants of sports activities. This particular study uses the same definition of sports activities as widely used in studies from Europe. As concluded in Kokolakakis et al., while being male, having higher education, and holding a professional occupation are positively associated, age is negatively associated with sports participation. Overall conclusion from other studies based on European data is also similar to the conclusion from physical activity literature mentioned above. This chapter will complement the studies based on European data sets and provide additional estimates of determinants of sports participation. The data set used in this chapter and its relevant details are presented in the following section.

Data and methods

This section below presents the details about Canadian General Social Survey (GSS) data set and relevant variables and methodology to estimate the determinants of sports participation.

General Social Survey

The Canadian GSS is a cross-sectional survey started in 1985. It is a random sample of Canadians aged 15 and older living in private households in ten provinces. Its primary objective is to collect specific data on social issues affecting Canadians' living conditions and well-being, and to inform specific social policy issues in the country. Each cycle of the survey has a core theme and a rich set of socio-demographic information including age, sex, education, income, household composition, race, and immigration status (Statistics Canada, 2020a).

While earlier cycles of the survey have a sample size of approximately 10,000 persons, it has been increased in 1999 to a target of 25,000. These surveys are conducted over a 6- to 12-month period through a 40- to 45-minute-long interview. One member of each household is randomly selected to complete the questionnaire (Statistics Canada, 2020b).

To conduct the interviews, the GSS program has been using random digit dialing (RDD) and computer-assisted telephone interviewing (CATI) methods. However, due to changes in communication technology (i.e., availability of caller display features, increases in mobile phone use), there has been a decline in response rates over time. After 2010, GSS started to use a database that combines landline and mobile phone numbers from the Census and various administrative sources with Statistics Canada's dwelling frame. For the interviews, only the CATI method has been used (Statistics Canada, 2020b).

Study sample

Most recent GSS cycles focused on themes related to caregiving, families, time use, social identity, volunteering, and victimization. The GSS that is used in this chapter is GSS Cycle 30 that has specific focus on Canadian families at work and home to understand their views on work, home, leisure time activities, and how these relate with their health and well-being. This cycle is conducted in 2016 with specific focus on participation in sports and outdoor activities, involvement in cultural activities, use of technology, labor market, and society and community (Statistics Canada, 2020a). While the cycle includes 19,609 respondents from ten provinces, it was divided into two almost equal blocks with each covering questions on participation in sports or cultural activities. As a result, the study sample for this chapter includes 9,765 respondents who responded questions on sports participation block.

Methods and variables

In order to estimate the determinants of participation in sports activities, I use the regression model below.

$$S_{ij} = \beta_0 + \beta_1 X_{ij} + \beta_2 H_{ij} + \theta P_j + \varepsilon_{ij}$$

where S_{ij} stands for sports participation of individual i who lives in province j. The matrix X_{ij} includes a wide range of socioeconomic and demographic factors. It is also likely that individuals' health behaviors influence their choices in participation in sports activities. To capture these factors, individuals' behavior measuring their dietary habits, smoking, and alcohol consumption is included in the regression. These are denoted with the matrix H_{ij} in the model above. P_j and ε_{ij} show the provincial fixed effects and error terms. Given that the outcome variable is a binary indicator for sports participation, this model will be estimated using a probit specification.

With an appropriate variable measuring sports participation, it is quite straightforward to estimate the regression model above. However, many survey data sets including various health surveys in Canada do not provide an appropriate measure for this variable. The GSS Cycle 30 is an exception with its rich content on sports participation. This cycle has a series of questions on participation in sports activities including the reasons for not participating in sports activities, and additional details for participation of spouse/common-law partners in sports activities. In this study, the variable measuring the participation in sports activities is created using the specific question asking the respondents to report their regular participation in any sports during the past 12 months (Statistics Canada, 2020c). As indicated to the respondents, sport is

> defined as activities involving training and competition with some level of physical intensity or organization, and regular participation means at least 2 or 3 times a month in season or for a certain period of the year. Non-competitive aerobics, aquafit, bicycling for recreation or transportation only, body building, car racing, dancing, fishing, fitness classes,

hiking, jogging, lifting weights (non-competitive), motorcycling, snowmobiling, and non-competitive walking are excluded.

(Statistics Canada, 2016: 310)

In addition to several variables measuring individuals' health behavior, there is demographic and socioeconomic information reported (except income data) for each respondents. Family income data were not reported but obtained by linking tax data for respondents who provided permission for this linkage. This was achieved for more than 89% of the respondents. Missing information for all other respondents was imputed (Statistics Canada, 2020a). All variables used to estimate the model above are listed in Appendix Table A.1 with their definitions.

Results

This section below presents descriptive and regression results regarding participation in sports activities, the reasons for (non-)participation, and its socioeconomic and demographic determinants.

Participation and reasons for non-participation in sports

As widely acknowledged, individuals participate in sports and social activities with various expectations. While most of the participants engage in sports activities for physical health and fitness, there are other reasons for participating in these activities. A wide range of studies reported that the most important benefits of sports participation are health and fitness, entertainment, relaxation, sense of achievement, socialization, and skill development (Bloom et al., 2005; European Commission, 2004; Garcia Ferrando, 2006). A similar issue was integrated into the GSS, and the survey participants were asked to report the importance of each of the five benefits of sports participation. Table 17.1 below shows the percentage of participants reporting the importance of the corresponding benefits on a scale of 1 (very important) to 4 (not at all important).

As indicated in the table, a significant majority of the survey participants report that participation in sports provides them with each benefit to be very or somewhat important. However, among these five benefits, physical fitness and health, and fun, recreation, and relaxation stand out as very important benefits that sports participation provides to the participants. Among all survey participants, while less than half of the participants reported that other three benefits are very important for them, for these two benefits, more than 69% of them reported that they are very important in their decision to participate in sports.

Table 17.2 below shows a list of reasons that the participants in the survey reported that they did not participate in sports activities. As seen in the table, about a quarter of the survey participants reported that they did not

Table 17.1 Reported Benefits from Participation in Sports Activities (percentage)

	Very important	Somewhat important	Not very important	Not at all important
Physical health and fitness	68.35	26.60	3.63	1.42
Family activity	44.28	29.98	14.52	11.22
New friends and acquaintances	34.35	43.12	16.78	5.75
Fun, recreation, and relaxation	70.79	26.15	2.26	0.80
Achievement and skill development	45.37	41.30	10.58	2.74

Note: This information is generated using the following survey question: How important is sport in providing you with physical health and fitness/family activity/new friends and acquaintances/fun, recreation, and relaxation/achievement and skill development?

Table 17.2 Reasons for Not Participating Regularly in Sports (percentage)

	Yes	No
No particular reason	27.77	72.23
Have no time	23.88	76.12
Injury or health concerns	20.11	79.89
Age	15.62	84.38
Disability	6.51	93.49
No programs available	2.78	97.22
Too expensive	5.73	94.27
No religious accommodation	0.12	99.88
Other physical activity	21.89	78.11
Other	8.93	91.07

Note: This information is generated using the following survey question: *Are there any particular reasons why you did not regularly participate in sports?*

participate in sports activities due to having not enough time, having an injury or health concerns, or having involved in other physical activities. These results are similar to the previous literature focusing on physical activities (Brownson et al., 2001).

Determinants of participation in sports

This subsection presents the results for the determinants of participation in sports. Table 17.3 shows the reported health behavior (diet, alcohol consumption, and smoking) by sports participation. The upper panel of the second (third) column presents the percentage of sports participants (non-participants) with healthy dietary habits ranked from poor/fair to very good/excellent. The lower panel shows the percentage of those who are either daily or weekly

Table 17.3 Reported Health Behavior by Participation in Sports (percentage)

	Participant (A)	Non-participant (B)	Difference between groups (A-B)*
Healthy dietary habit			
Poor/fair	12.0	16.5	−4.5
Good	37.7	42.1	−4.4
Very good/excellent	50.4	41.4	9.0
Alcohol consumption			
Daily	16.1	11.9	4.1
Weekly	40.1	27.4	12.7
Smoker	10.6	16.4	−5.8

Note: *These percentage-point differences between two groups are statistically significant in all cases with p-values < 0.001.

drinkers, and smokers. The last column shows the differences in reported health behavior between two groups.

As shown in the table, sports participants are more likely to report that their dietary habit is very good to excellent, and they are less likely to be a smoker and more likely to be a daily or weekly drinker. The last column of the table presents the percentage difference in corresponding health behavior between sports participants and non-participants. As shown in the table, sports participants are 9% points more likely to report good/excellent dietary habits as opposed to non-participants. They are also on average 5.8% points less likely to be a smoker. In terms of alcohol consumption, the sports participants are more likely to be daily (around 4% points) or weekly (about 13% points) drinkers.

To get a better sense about the association between sports participation and other health behaviors, I present the regression results in Tables 17.4 and 17.5. In these regressions, we include a set of socioeconomic and demographic determinants of sports participation. Additional determinants capturing individuals' other health behaviors are also included. In these tables, marginal effects of each of the factors that are computed from the probit regressions are presented. The appendix tables show the results from both probit and ordinary least squares (OLS). As can be seen from the tables below, the OLS results are qualitatively similar to the effects reported in Tables 17.4 and 17.5. These marginal effects are computed for the entire sample, and for a subsample of survey participants who are married (or have common-law partners). Table 17.4 shows the marginal effects for socioeconomic and demographic characteristics, while Table 17.5 presents the same effects for variables measuring individuals' health behaviors.

The results in Table 17.4 show that individuals with higher education and income are more likely to participate in sports activities. Compared to individuals with less-than-high-school education, individuals with high school

336 Nazmi Sari

Table 17.4 Marginal Effects from Probit Regressions: Socioeconomic and Demographic Characteristics

	Entire sample		Married subsample	
	Marginal effect	t-value	Marginal effect	t-value
Age-groups (reference: 65 and above)				
15–24	0.397	11.71	0.273	2.95
25–44	0.167	7.84	0.164	5.63
45–64	0.072	4.45	0.074	3.48
Education (reference: < high school)				
High school	0.035	2.06	0.118	3.73
Above high school	0.041	2.44	0.104	3.64
University and above	0.117	6.11	0.186	5.93
Family income (reference: <25,000)				
25,000–49,999	0.081	4.02	0.013	0.24
50,000–74,999	0.104	4.83	0.057	1.07
75,000–99,999	0.122	5.20	0.058	1.08
100,000–124,999	0.123	4.78	0.068	1.23
125,000 and above	0.134	5.79	0.084	1.60
Social class (reference: lower class)				
Upper	0.098	1.95	0.117	1.60
Upper middle	0.097	5.20	0.082	2.91
Middle	0.046	3.60	0.043	2.09
Other socioeconomic/demographics				
Dwelling owned	0.006	0.49	0.001	0.03
Male	0.130	14.38	0.146	11.41
Married	−0.022	−1.95	N/A	N/A
Household size	−0.005	−0.77	−0.017	−1.69
# of children	0.008	0.99	0.003	0.20
Visible minority	−0.004	−0.28	0.016	0.61
Immigrant	−0.053	−4.18	−0.070	−3.84
CMA	0.036	3.20	0.044	2.82
Employment status (reference: all others★)				
Employed	0.029	1.96	0.068	3.07
Unemployed	0.007	0.18	0.089	1.29
Retired	0.044	2.15	0.102	3.31
Sample size	9358		4841	

Note: Both models include provincial fixed effects. Marginal effects are computed using the probit regression models presented in Appendix Tables A.2, and A.3. For definition of each variable, see Appendix Table A.1. ★The reference group for employment status includes those in school, caring for children, doing household work, people with long-term illness, people with parental leave, and those doing unpaid volunteering work.

education, above-high-school education, and university degrees are 3.5, 4.1, and 11.7% points more likely to participate in sports activities, respectively. In the married subsample, these effects are much larger, ranging from 10.4 to 18.6% points. The impact of family income is positive and significant for the entire sample, but the level of significance decreases in the married subsample. In general, as income increases, the likelihood of participation in sports increases as well. Compared to low-income respondents, participation in sports is about 8–13% points higher for high-income groups.

Consistent with earlier literature, age, sex, being married, living in larger urban centers, and being immigrant are all significant determinants of participation in sports. Males' participation is about 13% points higher than females' participation. This effect is similar in the married subsample. As opposed to older people (aged 65 and older), participation in sports among younger people is significantly higher. The difference in participation between the corresponding age-group and people aged 65 and older is about 40, 17, and 7% points for those aged 15–24, 25–44, and 45–64, respectively. While being immigrant and being married (or having a common-law partner) are negatively associated with participation in sports, the effect is relatively low (about 5 and 2% points, respectively). As also indicated in earlier literature, individuals living in larger urban centers participate in sports activities more (about 3.4% points in the entire sample and 4.4% points in the married subsample) than others living outside of these urban centers. Employment status is also a significant determinant of sports participation. In both samples, employed and retired people, compared to others, are more likely to participate in sports activities. The association reaches about a 10% point difference for retirees and a 6.8% point difference for employed people in the married subsample.

For both samples, the results are shown for variables measuring health behavior in Table 17.5. Individuals with good-to-very good/excellent dietary habits participate more in sports activities. This difference is about 3–9% points. As expected (Pate et al., 1996), smokers, compared to non-smokers, participate less (6.3% points for the entire sample and 3.6% points for married people) in sports activities. Alcohol consumption (daily or weekly) is positively associated with participation in sports. Compared to infrequent drinkers or non-drinkers, daily or weekly drinkers' participation in sports is about 7% points higher in both subsamples.

Table 17.5 Marginal Effects from Probit Regressions: Individuals' Health Behaviors

	Entire sample		Married subsample	
	Marginal effect	t-value	Marginal effect	t-value
Dietary habit (good)	0.031	2.24	0.036	1.63
Dietary habit (very good/ excellent)	0.092	6.48	0.088	4.02
Daily alcohol	0.062	4.15	0.076	3.69
Weekly alcohol	0.070	6.63	0.073	4.95
Smoker	−0.063	−5.65	−0.036	−1.94
Spouse participates in sports			0.117	8.30
Sample size	9358		4841	

Note: Both models include provincial fixed effects. Marginal effects are computed using the probit regression models presented in Appendix Tables A.2, and A.3. For definition of each variable, see Appendix Table A.1.

In order to assess the impact of spousal participation in sports, an additional variable is included in regression for the married subsample. As expected, individuals' sports participation is positively associated with their spouses' (or common-law partners') participation in sports. This effect is almost 12% points higher for those with spouses participating in sports as opposed to others. As shown here, and mentioned earlier, potential behavioral influences (i.e., consumption complementarities as indicated in Bernheim, 1994) are stronger within the family and friend circle.

Conclusion

In this chapter, a set of determinants of sports participation has been examined, starting with a rich set of socioeconomics and demographic characteristics and individuals' health behavior. Using a cycle of the GSS data from Canada, this chapter estimates the association between these determinants and participation in sports. This is done using a clearly defined variable that measures sports participation based on information derived from survey participants' response to the question about their regular participation in any sports. With this unique feature of GSS data set, this chapter complements the existing literature focusing on determinants of leisure time physical activities.

The results show that several socioeconomic and demographic factors play a significant role in individuals' sports participation. As income, education, being male, being employed or retired, and higher social status increase the likelihood of participating in sports, other factors such as age, being immigrant, being married, and smoking decrease the participation. These effects are qualitatively similar in the entire sample and the married subsample. As expected, the results also show that people with good-to-excellent dietary habits are more likely to be sports participants. Spousal participation in sports is also another factor that increases the likelihood of sports participation.

While individual-level characteristics are important determinants of sports participation, there are other factors influencing the participation decision. Especially for organized sports activities, availability of favorable physical environment (i.e., facilities and green space) and institutional structure (i.e., sport teams, professional and/or amateur leagues) are additional factors determining the participation in sports activities. Due to the lack of information on these details, this chapter only focused on individual-level determinants. These additional factors and their impacts on participation need to be studied in future studies. These future studies have the potential to enhance our understanding and would guide public policies focusing on creating more favorable environment for participation in sports and physical activity.

Appendix

Table 17.A.1 List of Variables and Their Definitions

Variable name	Variable definition
Participation in sports	Whether the individual involved in sports training and competition with some level of physical intensity or organization, and regular participation (at least two or three times a month in a season or for a certain period of the year)
Spouse participates in sports	Whether spouse or common-law partner participated in sports
15–24	Individual aged between 15 and 24
25–44	Individual aged between 15 and 24
45–64	Individual aged between 15 and 24
High school	Individuals with high school education
Above high school	Individuals with above-high-school education but no BA degree
University and above	Individuals with BA degree and above
$25,000–49,999	Individuals' family income between $25,000 and 49,999
50,000–74,999	Individuals' family income between $50,000 and 74,999
75,000–99,999	Individuals' family income between $75,000 and 99,999
100,000–124,999	Individuals' family income between $100,000 and 124,999
125,000 and above	Individuals' family income $125,000 and above
Upper	Individuals' reported social class = upper class
Upper middle	Individuals' reported social class = upper middle class
Middle	Individuals' reported social class = middle class
Dwelling owned	Individual owns the dwelling
Male	Sex of the individual
Married	Marital status: married or has a common-law partner
Household size	Number of people living in the same dwelling
# of children	Number of children in the family
Visible minority	Whether the individual is a member of a visible minority
Immigrant	Whether the individual is an immigrant
CMA	Whether the individual lives in larger urban population centers
Employed	Employment status during the last 12 months: employed
Unemployed	Employment status during the last 12 months: unemployed
Retired	Employment status during the last 12 months: retired
Dietary habit (good)	Individual has good dietary habits
Dietary habit (very good/excellent)	Individual has very good-to-excellent dietary habits
Daily alcohol	Individual is a daily consumer of alcohol
Weekly alcohol	Individual is a weekly consumer of alcohol
Smoker	Daily or occasional smoker

Table 17A.2 Regression Results for Sports Participation

	OLS		Probit	
	Coefficient	t-statistics	Coefficient	t-statistics
Age-groups (reference: 65 and above)				
15–24	0.305	12.50	1.109	12.45
25–44	0.140	8.12	0.544	8.39
45–64	0.056	3.96	0.249	4.55
Education (reference: < high school)				
High school	0.016	1.13	0.121	2.11
Above high school	0.020	1.45	0.142	2.48
University and above	0.094	6.17	0.388	6.44
Family income (reference: <$25,000)				
$25,000–$49,999	0.049	3.26	0.271	4.24
$50,000–$74,999	0.066	4.06	0.342	5.17
$75,000–$99,999	0.082	4.64	0.391	5.64
$100,000–$124,999	0.084	4.34	0.390	5.22
$125,000 and above	0.104	5.71	0.438	6.20
Social class (reference: lower class)				
Upper	0.093	2.27	0.310	2.15
Upper middle	0.086	5.59	0.319	5.57
Middle	0.035	2.98	0.165	3.52
Other socioeconomic/demographics				
Dwelling owned	0.004	0.38	0.020	0.49
Male	0.124	14.53	0.456	14.44
Married	−0.026	−2.41	−0.080	−1.96
Household size	−0.004	−0.69	−0.016	−0.77
# of children	0.008	0.98	0.029	0.99
Visible minority	−0.006	−0.41	−0.015	−0.27
Immigrant	−0.056	−4.10	−0.200	−3.92
CMA	0.033	2.94	0.134	3.09
Employment status (all others*)				
Employed	0.024	1.75	0.103	1.96
Unemployed	0.001	0.02	0.024	0.18
Retired	0.033	1.93	0.152	2.20
Health behavior				
Dietary habit (good)	0.026	2.08	0.110	2.25
Dietary habit (very good/ excellent)	0.082	6.42	0.321	6.56
Daily alcohol	0.054	4.06	0.209	4.38
Weekly alcohol	0.067	6.90	0.240	6.84
Smoker	−0.065	−5.45	−0.243	−5.20
Constant term	−0.113	−3.86	−2.313	−19.09
Sample size	9358		9358	

Note: Both models include provincial fixed effects. *The reference group for employment status includes those in school, caring for children, and doing household work, people with long-term illness, people parental leaves, or those doing unpaid volunteering work.

Table 17A.3 Regression Results for Sports Participation (Married Subsample)

	OLS Coefficient	OLS t-statistics	Probit Coefficient	Probit t-statistics
Spouse participates in sports	0.112	8.72	0.385	8.61
Age-groups (reference: 65 and above)				
15–24	0.183	2.7	0.762	3.27
25–44	0.145	5.94	0.523	5.94
45–64	0.063	3.25	0.252	3.53
Education (reference: < high school)				
High school	0.065	2.88	0.375	3.96
Above high school	0.057	2.63	0.343	3.74
University and above	0.135	5.78	0.594	6.22
Family income (reference: <$25,000)				
$25,000–$49,999	0.009	0.22	0.043	0.24
$50,000–$74,999	0.036	0.88	0.188	1.12
$75,000–$99,999	0.035	0.85	0.191	1.13
$100,000–$124,999	0.046	1.09	0.222	1.30
$125,000 and above	0.064	1.54	0.277	1.65
Social class (reference: lower class)				
Upper	0.114	1.89	0.356	1.76
Upper middle	0.069	2.99	0.265	3.06
Middle	0.029	1.56	0.152	2.05
Other socioeconomic/demographics				
Dwelling owned	0.001	0.03	0.002	0.03
Male	0.140	11.43	0.501	11.29
Household size	−0.014	−1.50	−0.057	−1.69
# of children	−0.001	−0.06	0.009	0.20
Visible minority	0.011	0.46	0.053	0.62
Immigrant	−0.074	−3.70	−0.258	−3.55
CMA	0.039	2.47	0.158	2.71
Employment status (reference: all others*)				
Employed	0.053	2.64	0.237	3.02
Unemployed	0.063	1.16	0.278	1.40
Retired	0.077	3.14	0.334	3.45
Health behavior				
Dietary habit (good)	0.026	1.35	0.123	1.65
Dietary habit (very good/excellent)	0.073	3.68	0.300	4.02
Daily alcohol	0.068	3.78	0.244	3.89
Weekly alcohol	0.069	5.10	0.244	5.07
Smoker	−0.037	−1.99	−0.129	−1.86
Constant term	−0.184	−3.12	−2.604	−10.73
Sample size	4841		4841	

Note: Both models include provincial fixed effects. *The reference group for employment status includes those in school, caring for children, and doing household work, people with long-term illness, people parental leaves, or those doing unpaid volunteering work.

References

Babey, S.H., Hastert, T.A., Yu, H., and Brown, E.R., 2008. Physical activity among adolescents: when do parks matter? *American Journal of Preventive Medicine*, 34(4): 345–348.

Barron, J.M., Ewing, B.T., and Waddell, G.R., 2000. The effects of high school athletic participation on education and labor market outcomes. *Review of Economics and Statistics*, 82: 409–421.

Bernheim, B.D., 1994. A theory of conformity. *Journal of Political Economy*, 102(5): 841–877.

Brownson, R.C., Baker, E.A., Housemann, R.A., Brennan, L.K., and Bacak, S.J., 2001. Environmental and policy determinants of physical activity in the United States. *American Journal of Public Health*, 91(12): 1995–2003.

Cerin, E., and Leslie, E., 2008. How socio-economic status contributes to participation in leisure-time physical activity. *Social Science & Medicine*, 66(12): 2596–2609.

Cohen, D.A., McKenzie, T.L., Sehgal, A., Williamson, S., Golinelli, D., and Lurie, N., 2007. Contribution of public parks to physical activity. *American Journal of Public Health*, 97(3): 509–514.

Craig, C.L., Brownson, R.C., Cragg, S.E., and Dunn, A.L., 2002. Exploring the effect of the environment on physical activity: a study examining walking to work. *American Journal of Preventive Medicine*, 23(2): 36–43.

Dishman, R.K., Sallis, J.F., and Orenstein, D.R., 1985. The determinants of physical activity and exercise. *Public Health Reports*, 100(2): 158–171.

Downward, P., Lera-Lopez, F., and Rasciute, S., 2014. The correlates of sports participation in Europe. *European Journal of Sport Science*, 14(6): 592–602.

Grossman, M., 1972. On the concept of health capital and the demand for health. *Journal of Political Economy*, 80(2): 223–255.

Humpel, N., Owen, N., and Leslie, E., 2002. Environmental factors associated with adults' participation in physical activity: a review. *American Journal of Preventive Medicine*, 22(3): 188–199.

Humphreys, B.R., and Ruseski, J.E., 2007. Participation in physical activity and government spending on parks and recreation. *Contemporary Economic Policy*, 25: 538–552.

Humphreys, B.R., and Ruseski, J.E., 2011. An economic analysis of participation and time spent in physical activity. *The BE Journal of Economic Analysis & Policy*, 11(1), DOI: 10.2202/1935-1682.2522.

Humphreys, B.R., McLeod, L., and Ruseski, J.E., 2014. Physical activity and health outcomes: evidence from Canada. *Health Economics*, 23(1): 33–54.

Huston, S.L., Evenson, K.R., Bors, P., and Gizlice, Z., 2003. Neighborhood environment, access to places for activity, and leisure-time physical activity in a diverse North Carolina population. *American Journal of Health Promotion*, 18(1): 58–69.

Kaczynski, A.T., and Henderson, K.A., 2008. Parks and recreation settings and active living: a review of associations with physical activity function and intensity. *Journal of Physical Activity & Health*, 5(4): 619–632.

Kaczynski, A.T., Potwarka, L.R., and Saelens, B.E., 2008. Association of park size, distance, and features with physical activity in neighborhood parks. *American Journal of Public Health*, 98(8): 1451–1456.

Kaplan, M.S., Newsom, J.T., McFarland, B.H., and Lu, L., 2001. Demographic and psychosocial correlates of physical activity in late life. *American Journal of Preventive Medicine*, 21(4): 306–312.

Kohl, H.W., and Hobbs, K.E., 1998. Development of physical activity behaviors among children and adolescents. *Pediatrics*, *101*(Supplement 2): 549–554.

Kokolakakis, T., Lera-López, F., and Panagouleas, T., 2011. Analysis of the determinants of sports participation in Spain and England. *Applied Economics*, *44*(21): 2785–2798.

Lechner, M., 2009. Long-run labour market and health effects of individual sports activities. *The Journal of Health Economics*, 28, 839–854.

Lechner, M., 2015. Sports, exercise, and labor market outcomes: increasing participation in sports and exercise can boost productivity and earnings. *IZA World of Labor*, doi: 10.15185/izawol.126, http://wol.iza.org/sports-exercise-and-labor-market-outcomes.

Lechner, M., and Sari, N., 2015. Labor market effects of sports and exercise: evidence from Canadian panel data. *Labour Economics*, *35*: 1–19.

Limstrand, T., 2008. Environmental characteristics relevant to young people's use of sports facilities: a review, *Scandinavian Journal of Medicine & Science in Sports*, *18*(3): 275–287.

Owen, N.H., Leslie, E., Bauman, A., and Sallis, J.F., 2004. Understanding environmental influences on walking: review and research agenda. *American Journal of Preventive Medicine*, *27*(1): 67–76.

Pate, R.R., Heath, G.W., Dowda, M., and Trost, S.G., 1996. Associations between physical activity and other health behaviors in a representative sample of US adolescents. *American Journal of Public Health*, *86*(11): 1577–1581.

Rodriguez, D.A., Khattak, A.J., and Evenson, K.R., 2006. Can new urbanism encourage physical activity?: Comparing a new Urbanist neighborhood with conventional suburbs. *Journal of the American Planning Association*, *72*(1): 43–54.

Saelens, B.E., and Handy, S.L., 2008. Built environment correlates of walking: a review. *Medicine and Science in Sports and Exercise*, *40*(7 Suppl): S550–S566.

Saelens, B.E., Sallis, J.F., and Frank, L.D., 2003. Environmental correlates of walking and cycling: findings from the transportation, urban design, and planning literatures. *Annals of Behavioral Medicine*, *25*(2): 80–91.

Sallis, J.F., Hovell, M.F., and Hofstetter, C.R., 1992. Predictors of adoption and maintenance of vigorous physical activity in men and women. *Preventive Medicine*, *21*(2): 237–251.

Sallis, J.F., Hovell, M.F., Hofstetter, C.R., Elder, J.P., Hackley, M., Caspersen, C.J., and Powell, K.E., 1990. Distance between homes and exercise facilities related to frequency of exercise among San Diego residents. *Public Health Reports*, *105*(2): 179–185.

Sallis, J.F., Cerin, E., Conway, T.L., Adams, M.A., Frank, L.D., Pratt, M., Salvo, D., Schipperijn, J., Smith, G., Cain, K.L., and Davey, R., 2016. Physical activity in relation to urban environments in 14 cities worldwide: a cross-sectional study. *The Lancet*, *387*(10034): 2207–2217.

Sallis, J.F., Prochaska, J.J., Taylor, W.C., Hill, J.O., and Geraci, J.C., 1999. Correlates of physical activity in a national sample of girls and boys in grades 4 through 12. *Health Psychology*, *18*(4): 410–415.

Sari, N., 2009. Physical inactivity and its impact on healthcare utilization. *Health Economics*, *18*(8): 885–901.

Sari, N., 2010. A short walk a day shortens the hospital stay: physical activity and the demand for hospital services for older adults. *Canadian Journal of Public Health*, *101*(5): 385–389.

Sari, N., 2011a. Exercise, physical activity and healthcare utilization: a review of literature for older adults. *Maturitas*, 70(3): 285–289.

Sari, N., 2011b. Does physical exercise affect demand for hospital services? Evidence from Canadian panel data. In: P.R. Guerrero, S. Kesenne, and B.R. Humphreys (eds.) *The Economics of Sport, Health and Happiness: The Promotion of Well-being through Sporting Activities*, Northampton: Edward Elgar, 81–100.

Sari, N., 2014. Sports, exercise and length of stay in hospitals: is there a differential effect for chronically ill people? *Contemporary Economic Policy*, 32(2): 247–260.

Sari, N., and Lechner, M., 2015. Long-run health effects of sports and exercise in Canada. CCHE/CCES Working Paper No. 150018. Toronto, ON: Canadian Centre for Health Economics.

Statistics Canada, 2020a. General Social Survey: Canadian at Work and Home. GSS Cycle 30. https://www23.statcan.gc.ca/imdb/p2SV.pl?Function=getSurvey&SDDS=5221&wbdisable=true Retrieved November 2, 2020.

Statistics Canada, 2020b. The General Social Survey: An Overview. www150.statcan.gc.ca/n1/pub/89f0115x/89f0115x2013001-eng.htm Retrieved September 30, 2020.

Statistics Canada, 2020c. General Social Survey, Cycle 30, 2016 [Canada]: Canadians at Work and Home. Study Documentation. Social and Aboriginal Statistics Division, Statistics Canada.

Statistics Canada, 2016. General Social Survey, Cycle 30, 2016 [Canada]: Canadians at Work and Home. Documentation of the Questionnaire. Social and Aboriginal Statistics Division, Statistics Canada.

Trost, S.G., Owen, N., Bauman, A.E., Sallis, J.F., and Brown, W., 2002. Correlates of adults' participation in physical activity: review and update. *Medicine and Science in Sports and Exercise*, 34(12): 1996–2001.

Trost, S.G., Pate, R.R., Dowda, M., Saunders, R., Ward, D.S., and Felton, G., 1996. Gender differences in physical activity and determinants of physical activity in rural fifth grade children. *Journal of School Health*, 66(4): 145–150.

Trost, S.G., Pate, R.R., Saunders, R., Ward, D.S., Dowda, M., and Felton, G., 1997. A prospective study of the determinants of physical activity in rural fifth-grade children. *Preventive Medicine*, 26(2): 257–263.

U.S. Department of Health and Human Resources, 1996. *Physical Activity and Health: A Report of the Surgeon General*. U.S. Department of Health and Human Resources, Centers for Disease Control and Prevention, National Center for Chronic Disease Prevention and Health Promotion, Atlanta: 81–172.

Warburton, D., Nicol, C.W., and Bredin, S.S.D., 2006. Health benefits of physical activity: the evidence. *Canadian Medical Association Journal*, 174(6), 801–809.

Index

Note: **Bold** page numbers refer to tables, *Italic* page numbers refer to figures and page number followed by "n" refer to end notes.

Acland, D. 319
action bias 26–27
adrenalin stimulant, esports 19
aerodynamic recumbent bicycle 90
aggression 14, 120, 121
Ajzen, I. 291
Akerlof, G.A. 2, 214
Alavy, K. 253
alcohol consumption 179, 314, 332, 335, 337
Allen, E.J. 176
Almudi, I. 85
AlphaGo 38–41
alternative behavioural explanations 149–151, **152**
Altman, H. 1, 2, 4, 52, 201, 222
Altman, M. 1, 2, 4, 52, 201, 222
American Basketball League (ABL) 133, 135n9
American football 52, 64, 70, 82, 279n25
Amez, S. 160
Anders, C. 250, 255
Andersen, A. 174
Andreff, W. 3, 73n4, 99
Ansari, P. 264, 276n1, 277n6, 277n9
anthropometric characteristics 211, 212
anticipatory emotions 36
anti-doping; inefficiency 107; law 101; policy 100, 102, 104; rules 110, 115, 116; tools 102, 103
Apesteguia, J. 166, 167, 169n4, 174, 181n5
Arkes, H.R. 24
Arrondel, L. 166, 167
artificial intelligence (AI) 38, 55, 41; and eSport 42–43; poker 41–42

asymmetric effect 16
asymmetric information 2–4, 53, 201, 208, 215, 227
Athens Olympics 106–107
athletes 34, 100, 102; beautiful 201, 204, 212–213; behaviour 3; reference point behavior of 173–176; satisfaction 177; sexy 212–213
athletics, engineering in 89
attention 33–34
auctions; clearance rates 145; data 144–146; details 145, **145**; foal 140, 142, 145; procedures 144–146; thoroughbred 151; winning bidder at 143
Australian Bureau of Statistics 130
Australian Cricket Board (ACB) 133
Australian Football League (AFL) 25, 272, 280n29
Australian Rules Football (ARF) 248, 276
Australian Rules Football League (AFLW) 133
average returns 147–149
Azarenka, V. 128
Azar, O.H. 159

Baert, S. 160
Baggio, R. 17
Ballantyne, A. 188
Barajas, A. 273
Bar-Eli, M. 27, 159
Barra, A. 233
Bartling, B. 175
Barty, A. 4, 190, **191,** 193–196, 196n6
baseball 26, 52, 80, 82, 91, 123, 228, 235, 257, 264

346   *Index*

basic normalization (BN) 254
basketball 12, 18, 31, 32, 36, 52, 82, 126, 133, 173, 179
Bauman, A. E. 310, 321n3
Baumeister, R.F. 16, 161
Bayesian analysis; data for two winners of 2019 French Open singles 186–196; service points, outcomes of 188–190
Bayesian "updating factor" 188, 193–195, 196n3
Bayes, T. 186
Bayes' theorem 4, 186, 188, 195
Beane, B. 26
beauty 4, 12; as bad heuristic 209–212; as fast and frugal heuristic 201–204; premium 204–206, 212–215
Becker, G.S. 101, 102, 213, 291, 309
Becker's coefficient of discrimination 202, 205, 214, 216
Beckman, E.M. 253
behavioural economics 228; biases 23–34; cooperation 35–36; disruptions 15; economic incentives 318–320; emotions 36–37; esports 19–20; goal setting 21; group risk 22–23; habit formation 316–318; institutional factors 13–14; interdependent preferences 21–22; methodological pluralism 1–2; mismatched incentives 23; modelling realism 1–2; pressure 15–19; Prospect Theory 20–21; rule changes 12–13; social capital 37–38; sports participation and physical activity 303–316; strategic interactions 22; time inconsistency 318–320; in women's sport 119–135
Beijing Olympics 88
Bell Labs 38
benevolent sexism 121, 122, 124
Benz, M.-A. 248, 255, 257, 266
BerberVillar, R. 248
Berger, J. 173, 174
Bernheim, B.D. 330
betting markets 147, 177, 182n14, 244, 250–256, 258, 259
Bhagat, R.S. 15
biases 60; action 26–27; attention or hyper attention 33–34; confirmation 68, 71; expert and judge's 28–31; hot hand fallacy and momentum effect 31–33; outcome 27–28; projection 308–309; status quo 210; sunk cost fallacy or escalation effects 24–26

biathletes 17, 161
bidding, pairwise correlations of 149, **150**
Big Data 15, 19
Billings, D. 41
Billy Beane 222, 231
Bird, E.J. 110, 116n5
Bizzozero, P. 178
Black women 202, 205
Blumer, C. 24
Boardman, C. 90, 91
boardsailing 85, 87
Bobby, R. 23
Böheim, R. 161, 166
Bonferroni correction technique 149
Borland, J. 248
Borooah, V. 4
Boston Red Sox 26
bounded rationality 33, 55, 58, 203, 204, 209, 223, 236
Brandes, L. 175
Brazil 17, 126
breakaways 35, 36
Breivik, G. 108
broadcast 40, 64, 80, 101, 122–125, 132–134, 256, 279n25
Brouwer, T. 35, 36
Brown, E. 188
Brown, K.M. 251
Bryson, A. 30
Budzinski, O. 182n15
Buechel, B. 110
Bundesliga, away team characteristics 269–272
buoyancy 88
Buraimo, B. 178, 253, 254, 256, 257, 265
Burns, B.D. 31, 32
Butler, B. 3
Butler, D. 143, 255
Butler, J.L. 16, 161
Butler, R. 143
buyers 140, 142, 151, 154n4

caffeine 100
Camerer, C.F. 25, 43
Campenaerts, V. 91
Canada, socioeconomic and demographic correlates of sports participation in 328–338
Canadian General Social Survey (GSS) 6, 331–338
Cao, Z. 18
Cardazzi, A.J. 179
Card, D. 179, 245

career incentives; for men 132, **132**; for women 131, **131**
career pathways 125–127
Carrera, M. 319, 321n4
Carron, A.V. 169n6
Caruso, R. 14, 255, 257
causal analysis 289, 296, 298
censored regression model 248, 252
Center for Adaptive Behavior and Cognition (ABC) 202–203
Centers for Disease Control and Prevention (CDC) 302
ceteris paribus 52, 62, 66, 69, 207, 208, 225
Champions Cups 14
championship uncertainty 249
Chan, H.F. 12
Charness, G. 318
Chase, W.G. 39
chess 38–41
The Chess Machine: An Example of Dealing with Complex Task by Adaptation (Newell, A.) 39
Choi, J. 310, 321n3
choking 16–18, 161
chronic diseases 304
CHZ model 250, 253, 255, 258
Clarke, S. 188
coaches, reference point behavior of 173–177
Coates, D. 25, 178, 182n14, 244–246, 250, 253
Coates, J. 32
cocaine 100
Coffey, B. 143
cognitive psychology 36, 58, 59, 203
Cohen-Zada, D. 18, 159, 160, 165, 174
Collins, C. 5
collusive behaviour 13, 14
colour effect 34
competitive pressure 14, 18
competitive sports 14, 100, 102–105, 108, 109
computational machines 228, 236
computer-assisted telephone interviewing (CATI) 331
computer-/software-assisted statistical analysis 229
confirmation bias 68, 71
Conley, C.A. 31
context-dependent factors 67
conventional economics 54, 55, 61, 65, 203, 206, 223, 224
Cooke, A. 256

Cook, P.J. 127, 128
cooperation 35–36
cooperative competition 38
Cooper, I. 234
coopetition 38
correlational analysis 294–296
corruption 13, 14, 30, 100, 110
corticoids 108
cortisol stimulant, esports 18, 19
counterfactual emotions 36
counterfactual thinking 176–177
County Championship and National League 256
Courneya, K.S. 169n6
court judge behavior 180
COVID-19 pandemic 30, 277n8, 299, 304, 321
Cox, A. 254
Coyne, C. 83
crime 3, 102–104, 108, 178–180, 186, 330
cue–behavior association 308
Cup Winners' Cup 160, 162
cycling 89–91, 116n4
Cyert, R.M. 67
Czarnitzki, D. 252

Dagan, Y. 162
Dahl, G.B. 179, 245
Dantas, L.F. 268
data analytics 228–231
Dawson, A. 1
decision-makers 53, 55–61, 204, 223, 227
decision-making 2, 3, 11, 13, 142, 203; computers, impact of 229; errors in 53, 57–58, 60, 71; heuristics 208, 222–238; *Moneyball* significance for 235–236; optimal 231, *232*; smart 60; in sport teams 223; technical change in 230, *230*
Deep Blue (IBM) 38
Deepmind 41, 44n10
DeGennaro, R.P. 144
Dejonghe, T. 1
DellaVigna, S. 318
Demmert, H.G. 264
demographic/biological domain 311, **311**, 312
difference-in-difference models (Diff in Diff) 299
discrimination 214; gender 119, 121; media and sponsorship 122–125; wage 129–132

disequilibriums, market 129–132
disincentives 119, 125–127
disorganisation 132–134
disruptions 15
diving 28, 29, 87, 123
Djokovic, N. 128
Dobelli, R. 23
Dobson, S. 266
Dodds, F. 90
Dohmen, T.J. 16, 17, 30, 161, 166, 169n4
Dolan, P. 291
doping behaviour 99; from cheating behaviour to economic crime 100–104; compulsory doping diary 111; current combat against 104–108; doping-negative tests 111; doping-positive tests 111; inefficiency 104–108; not unveiling diary and doping test refusal 111–112; outcome of requested doping tests and potential sanction 112–116; restriction, policy recommendations for 103; unveiling diary on request 111; wrong incentives 104–108
Down Patrick 141
Down Royal 141
Downward, P. 1
Drake, J. 85
Driver, B.L. 291
Duggan, M. 13
Duhautois, R. 166

Earl, P. 82
Eber, N. 110
ecological models (ECO) 310
ecological rationality 58
economic agents 55–57, 65, 204, 207, 208, 213–215, 224, 228
economic crime 3, 100–104
economic incentives 85, 110, 318–320
economic inefficiency 2, 224–227
editing phase 172
Edmans, A. 178
education 103, 126, 290, 293, 310, 329, 335, 336
effective voice 71
efficiency 3, 52, 67, 71, 102, 116, 209, 215
effort discretion 214
effort provision 173–176
electronics, miniaturization of 38
Elmore, R. 175
Elster, J. 36
Ely, J. 178

emotional cues 177, 179, 180, 245
emotions 36–37
Empire State Games 176, 182n13
endowment effect 20, 209, 246, 319
engineering, in athletics 89
English Football League 252, 254
English Premier League (EPL) 133, 175, 252, 254, 277n3
Epsom Derby 141, 143
Eren, O. 180
erotic capital 205
errors 3, 18, 24, 53, 57–58, 60, 66–72, 152, 165, 209, 210, 224, 232, 233
escalation effect 24–26
eSport 19–20, 78; artificial intelligence and 42–43; emerging trajectory of 91–93
European football, spectator no-show behavior 266–275
evaluation phase 172
evolutionary economics 82, 83
expectations 175–176
ex post analysis 147, **147**
ex post productivity evaluation, of thoroughbred foals 139

Falter, J.-M. 248
family violence 178–179
fans; heterogeneity 246; reference point behavior of 177–180
Faure, F. 90
FC Barcelona 254
Federation International du Ski (FIS) 29
Federation Internationale de Football Association (FIFA) 16, 14, 17, 80
Federation Internationale de Natation Amateur (FINA), and hydrodynamic swimsuit 87–89
female coaches, in female competitions 127, **127**
feminism 121
Fernie, S. 143
Fick, S. 176
FIFA Women's World Cup final (2019) 123
figure skating 28, 29, 217n2
Finkelstein, E.A. 318
First-Person Shooter (FPS) 34, 92
first serve analysis 193–194
fixed-effects models 296, 299
flat racing 141
Fleck, J.L. 268
Flepp, R. 178

Folk theorem 35
football 14, 17, 30, 63, 70, 79, 81, 120, 130, 133, 134, 175, 179, 212, 247, 248
Football Association (FA) 132–133
Forrest, D. 252, 256, 257, 265
Forst, D. 26
Fort, R. 258, 264
France 85, 90, 99
Franck, E. 178
Frankel, A. 178
Frank, R.H. 127, 128
Frauen-Bundesliga women's soccer 248
free-riding 35, 36
free throws 18, 31, 161
French Premiere Division football (soccer) league 248
Frey, B.S. 5, 36–37
Friedman, M. 6n2, 13
Furlong, J. 187

"gain–loss" utility 245–247
Gamrat, F.A. 144, 147, 149, 151, 153
García, D. 178
García, J. 248
Garicano, L. 30
Garnier, A. 105
Gasparetto, T. 273
Gauriot, R. 160, 169n3, 175, 181n8
Genakos, C. 174
gender discrimination 119; unequal access 121; unequal pay for equal work 119
gender disparity 123
Ge, Q. 179, 180
German Bundesliga 16, 26, 28, 166, 175, 252
German Socio-Economic Panel (GSOEP) 5, 292
Germany 85; average life satisfaction of residents 292, 293, **293**; spectator no-show behavior in 269, **270**
Gerrard, B. 235
Gigerenzer, G. 2, 32, 33, 57–58, 202, 203
Gilovich, T. 31, 160, 176
Global Action Plan on Physical Activity (GAPPA) 2018–2030 302, 320
Global Financial Crisis (GFC) 22
Global World Index Trends Report 135n5
Gneezy, U. 318
Go 38–39
GoalDiff 164–166
goalkeepers 27

goal setting 21
Goddard, J.A. 266
Goff, B.L. 23, 82
Goffs 139, 145
Goldman, M. 173, 174
golfers 175
governance 3, 71, 81, 83, 84, 92
Grant, D. 176
Great Britain, thoroughbred industry 139–143
Green, E.A. 174
Groothuis, P.A. 25
de Groot, A. 39, 40
group, risk 22–23
"group think" 22
Grübl, D. 161
Gullo, A. 5
Gus Lobel 222, 236
gymnastics 121, 123, 126, 217n2

habit formation 308–309, 316–319, 321
habitual exercise 308
habitual participation 303, 321n2
habituation 20
Hackinger, J. 26
halter-breaking 140
Hamacher, S. 268
Hamermesh, D.S. 201, 212
Hamilton, J.C. 161
handball 264
happiness and sport 289, 290; causal analysis 296; correlational analysis 294–296; empirical analysis 292–298; sports participation 296–298, **297**; theoretical approach and data 291–292
Harb-Wu, K. 17, 161, 166
Hardy, S. 82
Haugen, K. 110
health belief model (HBM) 310
Heath, C. 177
He, C. 176
Heckman selection model 253
Helliwell, J.F. 292
herding 68, 209
Heuer, A. 175
heuristics 4, 13, 58, 68, 69; anthropometric characteristics as 211; bad and good 208, **209**; decision-making 222–238; fast and frugal 202–204
Hickman, D.C. 18
Highfield, R. 35
Hill, J.R. 25

Hirschman, A.O. 71
Hoang, H. 24, 25
hockey 12, 52, 178, 212, 234, 264
Ho Fai Chan 2, 3
Hohn, U. 89
home advantage 166, 169n6
home teams 30, 161, 166–168, 169n6, 252, 256, 279n22
"home win preference" 245–247, 252, 258
home win probability (HP) 245, 246, 248, 250–255
hooligan violence 30
hot hand fallacy 31–33, 160
'The Hour' 89, 90
Hour Record 91
Huang, H. 291
Hughes, M. 187
Hugland, D. 231–233
human capital 3, 5, 37, 69, 71, 119, 128, 131, 134, 222, 237
Humphreys, B.R. 1, 5, 178, 245, 246, 250, 251, 253, 254, 291
hydrodynamic swimsuit 87–89
hyper attention 33–34

ice hockey 12, 52, 178
Ilie, A. 34
imperfect information 2, 60, 69, 202, 215, 227
incentives 13; economic 318–320; financial 319; mismatched 23; monetary 101; program 319; strategic 174
income 36, 37, 130, 151, 173, 201, 202, 204, 205, 212, 226, 267, 290, 310, 331, 333, 337, 338
incursion sports 79
inefficiency 3, 53, 54, 107, 206, 207
Infosys 188, 196n4
Ingram, B. 188
in-season changes 15
institutions 13–14
interdependent preferences 21–22
International Amateur Athletic Federation (IAAF) 88
International Football Association Board (IFAB) 162
International Human Powered Vehicle Association (IHPVA) 90
International Olympic Committee (IOC) 80
International Skating Union (ISU) 29, 30, 87

internet of things (IoT) devices 19
inverted "U" shape function 16
IOC Medical Commission 101
Ireland, thoroughbred industry 139–143
Irish Racing 146
irrational agents 55
Italy 17

javelin throwing 89
Jennett, N. 247, 249
Jetter, M. 160, 165
Johnsen, H. 256
Johnson, B. 103, 107
Jordan, M. 22
Joustra, S. 181n7

Kahane, L.H. 1
Kahneman, D. 2, 33, 55, 59, 172, 181, 246
Kamenica, E. 178
Kang, D. 310
Karg, A.J. 272, 280n31
Kassis, M. 174
Kausel, E.E. 28
Keefer, Q.A. 25
Kesenne, S. 1
'kit' 80
Klepper, S. 83
Klumpp, T. 168n2
knock-on effect 122, 131, 134
Knowles, G. 252
Kocher, M.G. 166, 167, 174
Koehler, J.J. 31
Kokolakakis, T. 330, 331
Koning, R. 181n7
Konjer, M. 205, 217n1, 217n7
Koszegi, B. 245
Kournikova, A. 204
"Kournikova syndrome" 205
Kreps, D.M. 113
Krumer, A. 4, 16–18, 159, 161, 163, 166, 174, 181n1, 181n7

labor market 264, 332
Lackner, M. 161
Larrick, R.P. 177
Laslier, J.F. 166
league standings 247–250
leasing agreements 142
Lechner, M. 291
Leeds, D.M. 25
Leeds, M.A. 25
Lee, J. 310
Lee, M. 310

Leibenstein, H. 2, 52, 55, 60, 66, 67, 73n1, 207, 218n10, 224, 237
Lemke, R.J. 252
Lenz, M.V. 166, 174
Levitt, S.D. 13
Levy, M.R. 319
Lewis, M. 232
life ban 103, 111, 114, 115
life satisfaction 5, 291–298
Lin, D. 29
Lindo, J. 179
Long-Term Capital Management 22
loss aversion 5, 175, 178, 209, 244, 246, 252
Louisiana Department of Public Safety and Corrections 180
Louisiana State University (LSU) football team 180
lucrative races 143
Lusher, L. 176
Lye, J. 248
LZR Racer suit 88, 89

machine learning 228–231
macroeconomic simulations 304
Madalozzo, R. 248
Madey, S.F. 176
Mago, S.D. 159
Major League Baseball (MLB) 175–176, 252, 277n3
Major League Soccer (MLS) 249
Malaysian Semi-Pro Football 249
Malmendier, U. 318
Maloney, M.T. 143
Malueg, D.A. 159
managerial decisions 173–176
Manning, S. 3
March, J. 55, 56, 59, 67
marginal cost 204, 213
marginal revenue 204, 212–215, 258
Marie, O. 179
market disequilibriums 129–132
market failures 132–134
market inefficiency 224
Markle, A. 177
martial sports 79
material emotions 36
material payoffs 30
Matthews, R. 195
McDonald, H. 272, 280n29, 280n31
McEvoy, C.D. 257
media and sponsorship discrimination 122–125

media scrutiny 14
Medvec, V.H. 176
Meehan, J.W. 257
Meier, H.E. 248
Meier, P. 160
Melzer, M. 264
Men's World Cup 123, 130
mental models 3, 53, 54, 68–70, 209
Merckx, E. 90, 91
Merkel, S. 28
metabolic equivalent of task (MET) 304
Metcalf, D. 143
Metropolitan Criminal Statistics System (MCSS) 179
Metz, N.E. 18
Mexico Olympic Games 103
Miceli, T.J. 246, 251
micro-micro economic theory 66, 67, 71
Miller, J.B. 160, 181n8
Mills, B.M. 257, 258
Misbehaving (Thaler) 33
Mitew, T.E. 92
Mocan, N. 180
Models of My Life (Simon) 39
momentum effect 31–33
monetary incentives 101, 319, 320
monetary rewards 19, 318
Moneyball 4, 26, 61, 62, 69, 206, 222–224, 226; narrative 227, 228, 231–236; significance for decision-making 235–236
Monte Carlo simulation 257
Montevideo 179
Mont Ventoux 99
Moore, C.L. 92
Morgulev, E. 159
Moser, F. 90
Moses, M.M. 5
Moskowitz, T. 169n6
Motomura, A. 25
mountain biking 81, 82
multi-equilibrium framework 60–65
Munyo, I. 179, 180
Murphy, K.M. 309

Nadal, R. 4, 128, 190, **192,** 193–196, 196n6
Nalbantis, G. 182n14, 182n15
NASCAR accidents 34
Nash equilibrium 109
National Basketball Association (NBA) 24, 126, 173, 251
National Football League (NFL) 175, 250

National Hockey League (NHL) 12, 249
National Hunt races 143, 145
National Incident-Based Reporting System (NIBRS) 178
nationalistic bias 28–30
National Rugby League Women's (NRLW) 130
NCDs *see* non-communicable diseases (NCDs)
Neale, W.C. 177, 243, 245
negative list 101, 103, 106–109, 111, 115, 116n1
negative returns 3, 140, 147–149, 151–153, 154n2
neoclassical economics 56, 59, 203
neoclassical rationality 59
net returns 144, 146–148, *149*, 151, 154n4
Newell, A. 39, 40
new sports, origin of 82–85
New York Yankees 26
NFL Monday Night Football games 257
Nguyen, J. 272
Nicholson, M. 122
Noll, R.G. 264
non-communicable diseases (NCDs) 303–305, 320
non-economic aspects, of beauty or sexy premium 212–221
non-linear relationship 144, 272, 279n24, 293
no-over-doping strategy 113, *113*, 114
Norli, O. 178
North, D.C. 2
Nowak, M. 35

Oakland Athletics (A's) 26, 222, 228, 231–233, 235, 237
Obree, G. 90
occupational status 310, 329
O'Donoghue, P. 188
O'Donoghue, T. 309
Office of Juvenile Justice (OJJ) 180
Oguntimein, B. 25
Oh, J. 268
Oliveira, F.L.C. 268
OLS *see* ordinary least squares (OLS)
Olympic combat sports 34
Olympic Games 14, 17, 29, 79, 103, 119, 120, 123, 173, 176
on-base percentage (OBP) 232, 233
one-hour cycling world record 89–91
'open innovation' 84

opium 100
optimality 59, 202, 203, 216, 223, 237
optimality frontier 223, 224
ordinary least squares (OLS) 253, 254, 293, 294, 335
organizational efficiency 53, 55, 60, 62, 63, *63*, 226, **226**
organizational inefficiency 54, 55, 60–65, 226, 238n1
Osborne, A. 122
outcome bias 27–28
outcome uncertainty 247, 256–258
overshooting 81, 82, 84
Owen, N. 310, 321n3, 330
Owen, P.D. 252
ownership 3, 54, 64, 65, 139, 141, 144, 149, 151, 153

Page, L. 32, 160, 169n3, 175, 181n8
Pagliero, M. 174
pairwise correlations of bidding 149, **150**
Palacios-Huerta, I. 30, 166, 167, 169n4, 174, 181n5
Paton, D. 256
Paul, R.J. 249, 257
Pawlowski, T. 4, 181n1, 182n14, 182n15, 250, 255, 259
payoffs 13, 21, 23, 30, 35, 110, 128, 132, 233
pay-per-view buys 251
PED *see* performance-enhancing drug (PED)
Pedace, R. 175
Peel, D. 250, 252, 254
penalty kicks 16–18, 27, 30, 174
penalty shoot-outs, in European cups 159–169; data 162, **162**; descriptive statistics 163, **163**; home effect 166–168; psychological momentum 164–166, **165, 167**; variables 162–164
Pérez Carcedo, L. 251
Pérez, L. 254
performance 173–176
performance-enhancing drug (PED) 100, 101, 103, 106, 107, 111, 115, 116n1, 116n2
Pérignon, C. 248
Pettersson-Lidbom, P. 30
Pfeffer, I. 320
Philadelphia 76ers 31
physical activity 321n2, 328; determinants of 312, **313–315, 317**, 329; environmental determinants of

329–330; habitual 303; health benefits of 303–305; participation in leisure time 329–331
physical exercise 100
physical health 289, 290, 293–296, 298, 333
physical inactivity 302–305, 312, 321, 328
Piatti, M. 34
Pippen, S. 22
Pitt, B. 26
placebo effect 19
"Pluribus" 41
poker 37, 41–42
Polborn, M.K. 168n2
policymakers 328
political economy 207
Pope, D. 173–176
Popp, N. 272
Potters, J. 35, 36
Potts, J. 79, 82, 84
Poulett-Harris, L. 133
Predace, R. 25
premium, beauty or sexiness 204–206, 212–215
Prendergast, C. 30
pre-Olympic events 29
pressure 15–19, 34, 161
pressure drag 88
Priks, M. 30
Principia Mathematica 40
prisoner dilemma game 108, 109, **109**
private purchase 142
probability of winning 4, 13, 16, 34, 38, 66, 108, 109, 114, 159, 160, 163–168, 188, 189, 222
procedural rationality 60, 66–72, 72, 203, 204, 227
process rationality 58, 236, 237
production possibility curves (PPF) 230
productivity 55, 61–62, 65, 67, 139, 145–146, 148, 153, 204–209, 212–214, 216, 229, 238n1
profit maximization 54, 73n1
projection bias 308–309
"prosecutor's fallacy" 186
Prospect Theory 20–21, 172–173, 246
proxy 4, 37, 103, 163, 202, 205, 232, 247, 254–255, 258
psychological momentum 20, 174; defined 159; penalty shoot-outs, in European cups 164–166
Psychology Review (Gigerenzer) 33

Quirk, J. 258

Rabin, M. 245, 309
Racing Post Bloodstock Sales Database 145
RAND Employer Survey 318
random digit dialing (RDD) 331
randomization of referees 12
Rao, J.M. 173, 174
Rapoport, A. 35
Rascher, D.A. 248
Rasskin-Gutman, D. 40
rate of return 62–65, *63*, 208–210, 226, 228
rational agents 55, 66, 67, 225
rational decision-makers 55–61
rationality 55, 56, 58
Ratten, V. 83
Ray, M.A. 144, 152
reality and imagination 19
realized emotions 36
Real Madrid 254
Reams, L. 251
referees; biases 29; randomization of 12
reference-dependent preferences (RDP) 5, 244, 245
reference point behavior 172, 245; of athletes and coaches 173–177; of fans 177–180
regression discontinuity designs (RDD) 25, 299
regression models 234, 248, 251, 252, 254, 255, 332
relative success 67, 68
rent-seeking 81
revenue 62, 73, 91, 102, 122, 135, 154, 204, 205, 208, 212, 213, 216, 217n2, 243
Richardson, T. 181n1
Riedl, D. 175
risk, group 22–23
"risky shift" 22
Rodríguez, P. 1, 248
Rosenboim, M. 18
Rosenqvist, O. 160, 165
Rossi, M.A. 179, 180
Rottenberg, S. 177, 245, 264
round numbers 176, 177
Royer, H. 319
Roy, P. 255
rugby 34, 52, 79, 82, 106, 178, 212, 264
rule changes 12–13, 81

rules-driven sports 79–80
Ruseski, J.E. 5, 291

sabermetrics 223, 230, 233, 235–238
Sacheti, A. 249
sailboard, US patent for 85
St. Leger Stakes 143
Salaga, S. 251
Sallis, J.F. 310, 321n3
Sampaio, C.H. 268
Sanjurjo, A. 160, 181n8
Sari, N. 6
Sarmiento Barbieri, I. 179
satisficing 2, 57, 59, 60, 223–225, 236
Sauermann, J. 30
Sauer, R.D. 144, 147, 149, 151, 153
Savage, D.A. 2, 3, 16
Savulescu, J. 110
Scelles, N. 253
Schaffner, M. 37
Schmidt, S.L. 265, 277n6
Schneider, R. 179
Schneider, S. 291
Schreyer, D. 5, 181n1, 249, 253, 255, 257, 264, 265, 277n7, 277n9, 278n15
Schunk, D. 175
Schweitzer, H. 85
Schweitzer, M.E. 175
"screening fallacy" 187
SCT *see* social cognitive theory (SCT)
season ticket holders (STHs) 265–267, 272, 275
second serve analysis 194–195
sedentary behavior; defined 304; health benefits of 303–305; prevalence of 304
self-control 309, 319, 320
self-defeating strategy 3, 115
self-determination theory (SDT) 306–307, 316–318
self-efficacy 307, 312, 320
Self-Report Habit Index 316
Seltzer, M. 29
sensitivity 188
Serrano, R. 255
serve in winning points in tennis; Bayesian analysis of service point outcomes 188–190; estimates using data for Barty and Nadal from 2019 French Open 190–195, **192, 195**; first serve analysis 193–194; reliability **189**; second serve analysis 194–195
sexiness; as bad heuristic 209–212; as fast and frugal heuristic 201–204; premium 204–206, 212–215

sexism 121, 122, 124
sexy health and fitness 210
shakeouts 82, 83
Shakina, E. 273
Shannon entropy 250
Shapir, O.M. 18, 174
Shapiro, S. 251, 272
Sharapova, M. 128
Sheffrin, H. 71
Sheremeta, R.M. 159
Sherry, E. 122
Shmanske, S. 1
Shtudiner, Z. 159
signals/signalling 24, 32, 69, 104, 120, 126, 152, 211, 274
Sim, B. 249
Siminski, P. 179
Simmons, J. 272
Simmons, R. 143, 252–256, 265
Simon, E. 217n3
Simon, H. 1, 4, 13, 33, 36, 39, 40, 55, 56, 58, 59, 64, 23, 206, 222, 223, 225, 227, 228, 231
Simonsohn, U. 176
Simpson, T. 99
Skans, O.N. 160, 165
skateboarding 81
ski jumping 28, 29
skill gaps 128
Slovic, P. 42
smart behavior 59
Smith, J.K. 25, 175
Smith, R. 163
Smith, V. 57
smoking 308, 314, 315, 329, 332, 334, 338
snowboarding 81
soccer *see* football
social capital 37–38, 205
social cognitive theory (SCT) 307, 312
social emotions 36
social learning theory (SLT) 307
social norms 13, 42, 92, 109, 110, 112, 113, 120, 180
social payoffs 30
social pressure hypothesis 16
social support 16, 315, 316, 320
socioeconomic status (SES) 292, 310, 321n1, 329
Solmes, J.P. 248
Solow, R. 229, 231
Solvoll, M. 256
Sosenka, O. 91
Spanish First Division football 248

Spanish La Liga football (soccer) games 251
specificity 188
spectator no-show behavior 266–275
Speedo 88
sponsors 62, 101, 122, 123, 134
sponsorship 42, 99, 101, 122–125, 128, 133, 134
sport activity 289, 292, 295, 298
sports participation 290, 291; and average life satisfaction 293, **293**; benefits 333, **334**; in Canada, socioeconomic and demographic determinants 328–338; and happiness **295,** 296–298, **297,** 298; health behavior 334, **335**; health benefits of 303–305
sports participation and physical activity (SPPA); behavioral attributes and skills 312–315; behavioral theories for 305–309; habit formation 308–309; health benefits 303–305; physical environment factors 316; projection bias 308–309; psychological, cognitive, and emotional factors 312; self-determination theory 306–307; social and cultural factors 315–316; social cognitive theory 307; theory of planned behavior 306; time-inconsistent preferences 308–309; transtheoretical model 307–308
sports; competitive 14; happiness and 289–299; institutional dynamics in 78–93; new, origin of 82–85; non-participation 333–334, **334**; organization 52, 53, 6; participation, determinants of 334–338; reference point behavior and 172–182; rule changes 12–13; rules-driven 79–80; sentiment 178; statisticians 230, 231, 233, 234; taxonomy of 79–82; technology-driven 80–82; trajectory 83–85
sports data 11, 16, 17, 24, 26, 28, 35, 36, 43, 52, 60, 69, 70, 181, 227, 228, 235, 237
sports demand 177–178
sports economics 5, 11, 12, 22, 243, 244, 279n25, 320
sports inefficiency, and persistence of bad beauty heuristic 206–209
sports information literacy 69
sports teams 52, 53, 73n2, 73n3; community-owned 52–54; decision-making in 223; investor-owned 54; x-inefficient 54

SPPA *see* sports participation and physical activity (SPPA)
stadium attendance demand research 264–281
Stadtmann, G. 252
Stäglin, R. 264
stakeholders 267
standard normalization 254
stanozolol 107
statistical analysis 5, 69, 187, 224, 227–229, 231, 233–235
status quo bias 210, 211, 216
Staw, B.M. 24, 25
steeplechase 141
Stehr, M. 319
steroids 103
STHs *see* season ticket holders (STHs)
Stigler, G.J. 2
stock market, investors' behavior 178
strategic momentum 159
strategic thinking 22
Strauss, B. 175
stress 15–19, 34, 131
Strumbelj, E. 254
strychnine 100
sub-optimal choices 68, 69, 225, 226
sub-optimal decision 34, 56, 71, 202, 231, 233, 236
sub-optimal performance 53, 55, 65, 68, 72, 206, 207, 224–227
Sullivan, S.E. 15
Summer Olympic Games 29
Sumo Wrestling 13
sunk-cost effect 24–26
Sunstein, C.R. 2
survey-based research 259
Sutter, M. 166, 174
Su, X. 268
Sweden 126
Swensen, I.D. 179
swimming 79, 87, 88, 91, 93, 123
swimsuits 87–88, 93
Swiss Super League club 266
Sydnor, J. 319
Szymanski, S. 163, 247

Tainsky, S. 251, 257
Talladega Nights 44n2
Tattersalls 145
team sports 15, 21, 35, 116, 128, 178, 212
'techno-doping' 87, 88
technology-driven sports 80–82
technology-first sports 78

tennis 4, 18, 32, 91, 128, 159, 160, 175, 178, 187, 188, 196, 212
Tennis Grand Slam 128
testosterone 32
Thaler, R.H. 2, 33
Theil index 247, 250, 254, 255
theory of planned behavior (TPB) 306
Thomas, D.A. 250, 252, 254
Thomas, S. 3, 79, 82, 84
thoroughbred horseracing; auctions 139–142, 144–146, 151–154; 'broken in' 142; ex post productivity evaluation 139; high-stakes bidding and returns to ownership 139–154; ownership 139, 141–142
Thought and Choice in Chess (de Groot) 39
1,000 Guineas Stakes 143
Tice, D.M. 161
Tierney, K. 3
time inconsistency 318–320
tipping behavior 180
tit-for-tat 35
Todd, P.M. 58
Tollison, R.D. 23
Toma, M. 18
Torgler, B. 2, 4, 16, 37, 257, 265, 276n1, 276n3
transtheoretical model (TTM) 307–308, 312
Trost, S.G. 310, 321n3
Trouble with the Curve 4, 222, 224, 226, 234, 236
TTM *see* transtheoretical model (TTM)
Tversky, A. 2, 31, 33, 55, 59, 160, 172, 246

UCI '*Absolute Record*' 91
UCI *Hour Record* 91
UEFA Champions League 28, 160, 162
UEFA Euro Cup 16
UEFA Europa League 162
UEFA European Cup 17
uncertainty-of-outcome hypothesis (UOH) 5, 178, 243, 244; fan attendance 247; league standings and past outcomes 247–250; outcome probabilities estimated from betting markets 250–256; outcome uncertainty 247, 256–258; theoretical basis 244–247
Under 20s World Cups 14
Unierzyski, P. 188
Union Cycliste Internationale (UCI) 88, 90
Unreal Tournament 34

UOH *see* uncertainty-of-outcome hypothesis (UOH)
upset wins 177, 179, 180
Urbaczewski, A. 175
Urschel, J.D. 175
'user innovation' 84
U-shaped relationship 217n9, 248
utility function 58, 59, 203, 214, 245, 246
utility maximization 54

Vallone, R. 31, 160
Van Ours, J.C. 15
van Tuijl, M.A. 15
violence 14, 120, 178, 179
viscous drag 88
vote trading 29, 30

WADA *see* World Anti-Doping Agency (WADA)
wage discrepancy 130, 132
Wagner, G. 110, 116n5
Walker, J.K. 160, 165
walking 40, 304, 330, 333
Warburton, D.E. 304
Watanabe, N. 272
Weatherston, C.R. 252
Weber, R.A. 25, 43
Weinbach, A.P. 249, 257
Weingarten, E. 177
Wertheimer, M. 181n3
Wertheim, L.J. 169n6
whistle-blowing 110, 112, 113
Whites 202
Whyte, S. 4
Wilson, P. 249
Wimbledon 128, 132, 178, 188
windsurfing 81, 93, 94; consolidation of sector 85–86; decline of sector 86–87; emergence of sector 85; trajectory of 85–91
Winfree, J. 257
winner effect 32
winner-takes-all markets 127–129
winning bids 140–141, 146, 148, 153
within-biathlete variation 17
Women's Basketball League (WBL) 133
Women's Big Bash League (WBBL) 133
Women's Cricket Australia (WCA) 133
Women's National Basketball Association (WNBA) 126, 133
Women's Super League (WSL) 133
Women's Tennis Association (WTA) 132
Women's World Cup 123, 135n5

World Anti-Doping Agency (WADA) 103–107
World Athletics 80
World Health Assembly (WHA) 302
World Health Organization (WHO) 302, 304, 321n1
Wright, A. 83
Wu, G. 177

x-efficiency 55, 60–63, 207; determinants of 71, 72; measuring 65–66; procedural rationality and 66–72

x-inefficiency 2, 52, 60–65, 224, 225

Yates, A.J. 159
yearling markets 140
Youth Services 180

Zammuto, R. 83
Zeelenberg, M. 26
Zhou, L. 178, 245, 253
Zhuang, J. 175
Zitzewitz, E. 28–30

Printed in the United States
by Baker & Taylor Publisher Services